Kubernetes Autoscaling

Build efficient, cost-optimized clusters with KEDA and Karpenter

Christian Melendez

‹packt›

Kubernetes Autoscaling

Portfolio Director: Kartikey Pandey
Relationship Lead: Deepak Kumar
Project Manager: Sonam Pandey
Content Engineer: Apramit Bhattacharya
Technical Editor: Simran Ali
Copy Editor: Safis Editing
Indexer: Hemangini Bari
Proofreader: Apramit Bhattacharya
Production Designer: Salma Patel
Growth Lead: Shreyans Singh

First published: December 2025

Production reference: 01071125

Published by Packt Publishing Ltd.
Grosvenor House
11 St Paul's Square
Birmingham
B3 1RB, UK.
ISBN 978-1-83664-383-8
www.packtpub.com

Forewords

Christian has been at the forefront of tackling some of AWS's biggest customers' biggest problems. He has 10+ years of cloud infrastructure experience and a deep knowledge of Kubernetes born out of that experience. I saw Christian use his knowledge of clusters, autoscaling, Karpenter, and KEDA to solve customer's autoscaling problems firsthand while working with him at AWS.

Autoscaling Kubernetes isn't just an advanced enterprise customer concept. It's a core component of a Kubernetes cluster, as fundamental as networking interfaces and storage controllers. If you are running Kubernetes in the cloud, there's no reason you shouldn't be running it with an autoscaler, and Karpenter and KEDA have made that experience as easy as ever.

That's not to say that these components are without their own messiness and quirks. Autoscaling isn't always easy. The failure domains, cost increases, and odd behaviors can be rampant without a strong understanding of the fundamentals. Reading through this book will give you the knowledge that you need to run these autoscalers seamlessly on your clusters in production. It will give you a deep, broad understanding of how these components work, as well as how they should be configured. *Kubernetes Autoscaling* makes sure you are exposed to the fundamentals and can safely take that knowledge forward into your infrastructure.

Jonathan Innis

Senior Software Engineer, Figma

Karpenter maintainer

I met Christian when I was working on the Karpenter project at AWS. We were both knee-deep in the realities of autoscaling: balancing cost, availability, and user experience. Christian's deep knowledge of autoscaling and experience helping many companies with autoscaling issues and cost optimization shine through in this book.

Scaling computers has always been a hard problem. Twenty years ago, we were still filing tickets to rack servers. Kubernetes gives us APIs, controllers, and an ecosystem of tools that make scaling almost magical. But abstractions only go so far. Anyone who has watched a cluster thrash because of a misconfigured HPA or application downtime due to a VM not coming up knows that autoscaling is powerful but tricky.

That's why this book matters. *Kubernetes Autoscaling* doesn't just catalog tools such as KEDA or Karpenter; it shows you how to think about scaling, how these parts work together, and how to apply them in the messy real world.

If you've ever wrestled with scaling applications or clusters, you'll find clarity here. Christian has distilled years of experience into practical guidance, and you'll come away not just knowing what buttons to push, but why.

Brandon Wagner

Senior Software Engineer, AWS
Karpenter maintainer

Cloud software, especially Kubernetes, is designed with elasticity in mind. But does that mean automatic scaling is a solved problem? Not quite. There's a wealth of tools that enable different autoscaling strategies, yet it's still practitioners who tune the dials, set the guardrails, and make sure services stay responsive no matter how big the next traffic spike is, and they must do it with an eye on cost. At the forefront of today's autoscaling capabilities are two open source projects: Karpenter and KEDA. This book introduces powerful features of both and shows how to use them together to get the best results.

I've only known Christian since 2024, but we quickly found common ground: cloud-native technologies and engaging with open source communities, both online and at conferences. And, yes, enjoying a good beer. We also share a passion for helping teams reduce their cloud spend, which may be one of the reasons you picked up this book.

My favorite story about why Christian is the right author for this topic comes from ContainerDays 2025 in Hamburg. After our co-presented talk, "Double the Efficiency: Kubernetes Autoscaling with Karpenter and KEDA," the Q&A turned to using KEDA alongside Argo Rollouts – caveats, gotchas, the works. We usually split questions: he takes Karpenter (given close collaboration with the Karpenter team), I take KEDA (I'm a member of the KEDA maintainers team). This time, I was drawing a blank. Christian jumped in with a level of insight that spanned not only KEDA internals but also a comprehensive knowledge of Argo Rollouts. That breadth, exposure across projects, hands-on experience, and a deep feel for the cloud-native ecosystem are all what make him such a strong guide for this book. Whether you're chasing performance, reliability, or a saner cloud bill, you're in good hands. Turn the page.

Jan Wozniak
KEDA maintainer

Contributors

About the author

Christian Melendez is Principal Specialist Solutions Architect and EMEA Lead for Compute at AWS, with a strong background in Kubernetes platform engineering, and over 19 years of experience in the tech industry. He has been working with Kubernetes since 2017, helping large enterprises across different industries to optimize their workloads in the cloud. Christian is the creator of Karpenter Blueprints and an active contributor to autoscaling solutions in the cloud-native space. He frequently delivers talks and workshops around the world on Karpenter, KEDA, performance, and Kubernetes optimization strategies.

To my lovely wife and kids for their continuous support and inspiration, my mom for raising me and always believing in me, my sister for her genuine interest, and my father-in-law for all the good vibes. To my CloudMas friends, especially to Juancho and Oscar. To my AWS friends for all their help, especially to Carlos, Rob, Mike, Arpit, Jurgen, Edu, Borja, Steve, Fede, Guille, German, Nati, Flamur, Liz, and Jens. I can't name everyone, but if I've gifted you this book or signed your copy, you've helped me in one way or another.

About the reviewer

Farhan Ahmed is a Software Engineer experienced in building cloud-native applications using Java, Spring Boot, AWS, and Kubernetes. He is passionate about learning and sharing knowledge within the developer community. Farhan contributes to K8GB, a CNCF open source project, and creates technical content to help others understand cloud and Kubernetes concepts. He holds the AWS Solutions Architect Associate and Terraform Associate industry certifications and enjoys exploring new technologies in the cloud-native ecosystem.

I would like to thank God for His blessings and my parents for their constant support and encouragement throughout this journey. I am grateful to the Packt Publishing team for giving me this opportunity to contribute as a technical reviewer. Special thanks to the author for their hard work in creating this valuable resource for the Kubernetes community.

Table of Contents

Chapter 3: Workload Autoscaling with HPA and VPA 45

Chapter 6: Workload Autoscaling Operations   127

Part III: Node Autoscaling and Karpenter   147

Chapter 7: Data Plane Autoscaling Overview   149

Chapter 8: Node Autoscaling with Karpenter — Part 1   171

Preface

If you've been running Kubernetes workloads for a while, you've probably had that moment where you're staring at your cloud bill, wondering how you can optimize the dozens of nodes you end up needing at some point. Or worse, you've been paged at midnight because your cluster couldn't handle a traffic spike, and users are getting errors. Autoscaling is supposed to solve both problems, but to be honest, between HPA, VPA, and Karpenter configurations, things can get complicated very fast.

Throughout this book, you'll explore practical autoscaling strategies that go beyond the basics of scaling based on CPU or memory utilization. You'll learn how to scale based on what influences the performance of your applications, and what your users really care about. This is becoming even more relevant with the growth of AI/ML workloads running in Kubernetes. Usually, it's not about CPU or memory utilization, and with KEDA, you can go beyond these two metrics. Moreover, you'll dive into Karpenter's approach to efficient node provisioning, node optimizations, and disruption management. More importantly, you'll learn how KEDA and Karpenter work together to create an autoscaling strategy that saves money and reduces waste.

Kubernetes autoscaling isn't just about handling traffic spikes. Efficient autoscaling means your infrastructure matches actual demand, scaling to zero when possible and provisioning exactly what you need when load increases. In a way, we'll be contributing to saving the planet one pod at a time.

The examples and patterns in this book come from real production scenarios. I'll cover the edge cases, the things that break, and the monitoring you need to trust your autoscaling setup. You'll find practical guidance for making your clusters more responsive and your cloud bills more reasonable.

Who this book is for

I wrote this book because autoscaling in Kubernetes has evolved significantly beyond the basics, but most of us are still relying on the same patterns we learned years ago. I want you to feel prepared and confident to build efficient Kubernetes clusters with an effective autoscaling strategy. KEDA and Karpenter represent a fundamental shift in how we think about scaling, not just reacting to CPU or memory metrics, but responding to the events that matter for your workloads, and provisioning infrastructure in seconds rather than minutes.

There are many amazing books already covering different topics about Kubernetes, but this book focuses on the efficiency and cost-optimization aspect of a cluster. Thus, I'll assume you already have basic knowledge of Kubernetes and feel comfortable using a terminal to interact with a cluster. While you can simply read the book during your commute, the real value of your learning journey is going to be in doing the hands-on labs in this book. I've found that I learn more by doing than just reading. In fact, if you've gone through any Kubernetes certification, you know that it's more important to have hands-on experience than to know only theory.

What this book covers

Chapter 1, Introduction to Kubernetes Autoscaling, covers the basics you need to know about autoscaling in general, and how all these concepts apply to the Kubernetes ecosystem. You'll learn about the components, concepts, and theory that will be essential when exploring the other chapters. Moreover, your first hands-on lab will be about setting up your Kubernetes cluster.

Chapter 2, Workload Autoscaling Overview, starts by addressing the fundamentals of how to approach autoscaling your workloads in Kubernetes, and the importance of configuring pod resource requests. You'll explore by practicing why monitoring your workload utilization is important to properly right-size your pods to improve your cluster's efficiency and cost. Finally, you'll start learning about the different tools and projects that will help you autoscale your workloads horizontally.

Chapter 3, Workload Autoscaling with HPA and VPA, covers the simplest way of autoscaling your workloads horizontally using HPA, and how to prepare your cluster to use HPA. You'll learn how to configure scaling rules, with CPU and memory, as this will serve as the foundation to later dive deeper into KEDA. Moreover, you'll understand how to use custom metrics to scale and why KEDA becomes even more relevant. Finally, you'll learn about VPA and when to use it, especially as a tool for rightsizing.

Chapter 4, Kubernetes Event-Driven Autoscaling – Part 1, starts to configure workload autoscaling beyond the basics. You'll learn about the inner workings of KEDA and why many teams are using it to scale their workloads smarter. The hands-on labs will help to get started configuring scaling rules using latency instead of CPU utilization. Moreover, you'll learn about KEDA's famous features, such as scaling to (and from) zero, controlling autoscaling speed, and how to scale Kubernetes jobs.

Chapter 5, Kubernetes Event-Driven Autoscaling – Part 2, dives into more advanced (and not so famous) features of KEDA. For instance, you'll learn about how to configure scaling rules based on schedule, scaling HTTP-based workloads from (and to) zero, scaling modifiers for complex scaling rules, and how to use KEDA with cloud providers.

Chapter 6, Workload Autoscaling Operations, focuses on all the operational work of using HPA, VPA, and KEDA in your cluster. You'll learn how to troubleshoot your autoscaling rules, along with some recommendations about how to solve common problems. Finally, you'll learn how to monitor KEDA's autoscaling rules by using Grafana, and why some metrics are crucial for understanding why KEDA might not be scaling your workloads in the way you intended.

Chapter 7, Data Plane Autoscaling Overview, changes gears to start exploring how to autoscale the nodes in your cluster. You'll understand why you need different projects, such as Cluster Autoscaler and Karpenter, and what specific problem they're addressing in the ecosystem. As the following chapters will focus on Karpenter, during this chapter, you'll dive deep into Cluster Autoscaler setup and best practices (especially around AWS). Finally, you'll explore complementary projects such as Descheduler and Cluster Proportional Autoscaler, and learn why the book will only briefly mention them.

Chapter 8, Node Autoscaling with Karpenter – Part 1, covers Karpenter in more depth, including its history and how it works. Unlike traditional guides and tutorials you can currently find on the internet, this chapter will dive deep into how and when Karpenter launches new nodes, and the considerations it takes when doing so. You'll learn how to deploy Karpenter through infrastructure as code using Terraform, and see Karpenter in action for the first time. Finally, you'll learn how to influence Karpenter to launch nodes using pods' constraints such as node selectors, affinities, anti-affinities, tolerations, and recommendations based on your workload needs.

Chapter 9, Node Autoscaling with Karpenter – Part 2, continues exploring Karpenter, but from the perspective of removing nodes. You'll learn how Karpenter removes nodes and all the considerations it takes to make this process as controlled and clean as possible. Moreover, you'll explore the different types of disruptions Karpenter handles either through consolidation to optimize the cluster further, or because the node's configuration drifted. You'll also learn about the Node-Pool disruption budgets to limit voluntary disruptions. Finally, I'll share a set of practical best practices for Karpenter.

Chapter 10, Karpenter Management Operations, covers the management operation side of having Karpenter running in the cluster. You'll learn about the tools, commands, and techniques you can use to troubleshoot and understand why Karpenter might not be scaling your nodes the way you intended. Moreover, the chapter focuses on common challenges you might face and how to properly address them. You'll learn how to properly upgrade Karpenter with very specific guidance. Finally, you'll learn how to monitor Karpenter with Grafana, and why certain metrics exposed by the controller are crucial to monitor.

Chapter 11, Practical Use Cases for Autoscaling in Kubernetes, focuses on the practical integration with KEDA and Karpenter, with common use cases such as web applications, batch jobs, and GPU workloads, and how to cost-optimize your cluster when using these two projects. For each use case, you'll learn the best practices; the purpose is to guide you on how to implement these recommendations in your environment.

Chapter 12, Patterns and Recommendations, teaches you about two very common use cases when combining KEDA and Karpenter. The first one is about how to properly turn off non-production environments when you're not using them. Then, you'll learn about the set of recommendations you need to implement to work with fault-tolerant workloads. And if your workloads are not there yet, the purpose is that you understand what's required to get there, and why this is relevant in the autoscaling ecosystem. As a final chapter, you'll reflect on what to consider when configuring autoscaling rules and the future trends in the ecosystem, especially around KEDA and Karpenter.

To get the most out of this book

All the labs from *Chapter 1* to *Chapter 6* can be completed on your local computer with a local Kubernetes cluster. However, from *Chapter 7* onward, you will need to use an Amazon EKS cluster to complete the labs. In future editions, I might extend support for other clouds, but all the hands-on labs have been tested in Amazon EKS. Therefore, you'll need to have access to an AWS account.

The estimated cost for running the Amazon EKS cluster is ~$0.34/hour (a monthly estimate of 730 hours is ~$248/month). If you decide to do the GPUs lab, consider an estimate of a +155% increase while running it. Because of this, I'd recommend that you only launch the cluster when you're planning to dedicate time to doing the hands-on labs and delete the cluster when you're done for the day. Every hands-on lab assumes you'll be doing that, so you don't need to worry about saving your progress.

You can use your own computer (I used macOS) or any external server; in either case, you need to install the following software on it:

Software/hardware covered in the book	Operating system requirements
Kubernetes >= 1.34	Windows, macOS, or Linux
Kubectl >= 1.34	Windows, macOS, or Linux
Terraform > 1.13	Windows, macOS, or Linux

I've added specific instructions in *Chapter 1* on how to install and configure all the tools you'll need to complete the labs.

There's a trend of teams moving away from Terraform to OpenTofu, but the provided templates should work with OpenTofu without any issues. However, all hands-on labs have been tested with Terraform.

Download the example code files

The code bundle for the book is hosted on GitHub at `https://github.com/PacktPublishing/Kubernetes-Autoscaling`. We also have other code bundles from our rich catalog of books and videos available at `https://github.com/PacktPublishing`. Check them out!

Conventions used

There are a number of text conventions used throughout this book.

`CodeInText`: Indicates code words in text, database table names, folder names, filenames, file extensions, pathnames, dummy URLs, user input, and X/Twitter handles. For example: "As of the time of writing, you can install Kind with `go install`."

A block of code is set as follows:

```
apiVersion: v1
kind: LimitRange
metadata:
  name: cpu-defaults
spec:
  limits:
  - default:
      cpu: 1200m
    defaultRequest:
      cpu: 900m
    type: Container
```

When we wish to draw your attention to a particular part of a code block, the relevant lines or items are set in bold:

```
...
spec:
  containers:
  - image: christianhxc/montecarlo-pi:latest
    imagePullPolicy: Always
    name: montecarlo-pi
    resources:
      requests:
        cpu: 900m
        memory: 512Mi
...
```

Any command-line input or output is written as follows:

```
$ brew install kind
```

Bold: Indicates a new term, an important word, or words that you see on the screen. For instance, words in menus or dialog boxes appear in the text like this. For example: "**Autoscaling** is at the heart of an efficient and cost-effective **Kubernetes cluster**."

Warnings or important notes appear like this.

Get in touch

Feedback from our readers is always welcome.

General feedback: If you have questions about any aspect of this book or have any general feedback, please email us at customercare@packt.com and mention the book's title in the subject of your message.

Errata: Although we have taken every care to ensure the accuracy of our content, mistakes do happen. If you have found a mistake in this book, we would be grateful if you reported this to us. Please visit http://www.packt.com/submit-errata, click **Submit Errata**, and fill in the form.

Piracy: If you come across any illegal copies of our works in any form on the internet, we would be grateful if you would provide us with the location address or website name. Please contact us at copyright@packt.com with a link to the material.

If you are interested in becoming an author: If there is a topic that you have expertise in and you are interested in either writing or contributing to a book, please visit http://authors.packt.com/.

Share your thoughts

Once you've read *Kubernetes Autoscaling*, we'd love to hear your thoughts! Scan the QR code below to go straight to the Amazon review page for this book and share your feedback.

https://packt.link/r/1836643837

Your review is important to us and the tech community and will help us make sure we're delivering excellent quality content.

Free Benefits with Your Book

This book comes with free benefits to support your learning. Activate them now for instant access (see the "*How to Unlock*" section for instructions).

Here's a quick overview of what you can instantly unlock with your purchase:

PDF and ePub Copies   Next-Gen Web-Based Reader

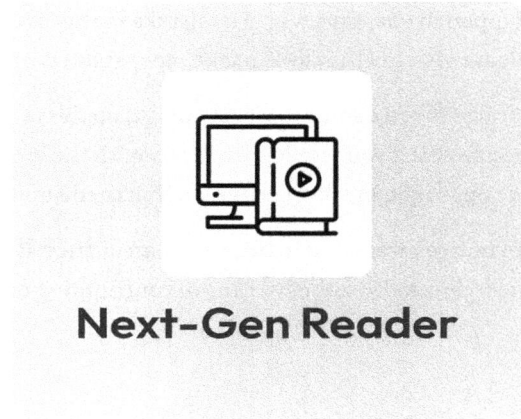

Free PDF and ePub versions   Next-Gen Reader

Access a DRM-free PDF copy of this book to read anywhere, on any device.

Use a DRM-free ePub version with your favorite e-reader.

Multi-device progress sync: Pick up where you left off, on any device.

Highlighting and notetaking: Capture ideas and turn reading into lasting knowledge.

Bookmarking: Save and revisit key sections whenever you need them.

Dark mode: Reduce eye strain by switching to dark or sepia themes.

How to Unlock

UNLOCK NOW

Scan the QR code (or go to packtpub.com/unlock).
Search for this book by name, confirm the edition,
and then follow the steps on the page.

Note: *Keep your invoice handy. Purchases made directly
from Packt don't require one.*

Part 1

Getting started with Kubernetes Autoscaling

Before diving into advanced tools such as KEDA and Karpenter, I need you to have a solid foundation. Kubernetes ships with built-in autoscaling capabilities that many teams either overlook or misconfigure, and understanding how these work is essential for everything that comes later.

This part covers the fundamentals – not just the theory, but the practical aspects of getting autoscaling to actually work in your cluster. You'll start by exploring the core concepts and components that make autoscaling possible, then move on to workload autoscaling using the **Horizontal Pod Autoscaler (HPA)** and **Vertical Pod Autoscaler (VPA)**. You'll learn why pod resource requests matter more than you might think, and how monitoring and rightsizing your workloads directly impacts both cluster efficiency and your ability to scale effectively.

The goal here isn't to make you an expert on the HPA or VPA. Most production environments eventually outgrow these tools. The goal is to understand how Kubernetes thinks about scaling, what metrics matter, and where the native autoscalers fall short. This context is what makes the jump to KEDA and Karpenter make sense, because you'll see exactly what problems they solve and why they exist in the first place.

By the end of this part, you'll have a working cluster, hands-on experience with the HPA and VPA, and a clear picture of when native autoscaling is enough and when you need something more sophisticated.

This part has the following chapters:

- *Chapter 1, Introduction to Kubernetes Autoscaling*
- *Chapter 2, Workload Autoscaling Overview*
- *Chapter 3, Workload Autoscaling with HPA and VPA*

1

Introduction to Kubernetes Autoscaling

Autoscaling is at the heart of an efficient and cost-effective **Kubernetes cluster**. Yet, many organizations struggle with resource management, often leading to significant financial waste or system failures. Understanding and implementing proper **scaling** can be the difference between a thriving, responsive system and one that's constantly on the brink of collapse.

In this chapter, I'll introduce you to the concepts, strategies, and technologies surrounding autoscaling in Kubernetes, exploring its mechanisms, benefits, and challenges. You'll understand why scaling needs to evolve from a manual to an automatic process and how it has become an integral part of modern cloud-native architectures. I've worked with organizations that have achieved between 50% and 70% cost reduction in their compute expenses by making their Kubernetes clusters more efficient. This book aims to guide you on how you can achieve similar optimizations.

In this chapter, I will cover key aspects of Kubernetes autoscaling, including why autoscaling is needed and how it functions within a Kubernetes environment. We'll explore the various types of autoscaling approaches available, examine the challenges that autoscaling helps address, and discuss the new complexities it may introduce. We will be covering the following main topics:

- Scalability foundations
- Kubernetes architecture
- Efficient Kubernetes data planes
- Kubernetes autoscaling categories
- Hands-on lab: Creating a Kubernetes cluster

By the end of this chapter, you'll understand how autoscaling works in Kubernetes and what strategies you need to implement to have efficient and cost-optimized clusters. You'll finish by setting up a Kubernetes cluster, which you'll use to practice what you'll learn in this book. In the following chapters, I'll go into much more depth about how to implement all of the concepts covered here.

Technical requirements

To practice what you'll be learning throughout this book, you need to have access to a Kubernetes cluster. In this chapter, I'm offering two options for cluster creation: a local setup and a cloud-based solution in **Amazon Web Services (AWS)**. If you're just starting out or you want to focus solely on workload scaling in the upcoming chapters, the local option using **Kind** (which stands for **Kubernetes in Docker**) is a good choice. Alternatively, you could use Docker Desktop and turn on Kubernetes or use a Kubernetes playground such as Killercoda or Play with Kubernetes.

However, if you're eager to dive into the full cloud experience from the start, I'll also provide instructions for setting up an Amazon EKS cluster using Terraform. This option will give you a more realistic environment, closely mimicking production scenarios. Just remember, if you choose this route, to delete all resources after your study sessions to avoid unnecessary charges.

To make the process as smooth as possible, all the files I'll use to provision the cluster are available in this GitHub repository: `https://github.com/PacktPublishing/Kubernetes-Autoscaling`. This repository will be regularly updated, ensuring you always have access to the most current configurations.

You need to meet the following prerequisites to complete the hands-on labs:

- Git
- Helm 3.16.1+
- kubectl (latest version)
- Go 1.16+ or Docker, Podman, or nerdctl
- A **command-line interface (CLI)** to run all the commands
- Terraform 1.9.5+ (AWS only)
- AWS CLI 2.17.43+ (AWS only)
- Access to an AWS account to create an Amazon EKS cluster (AWS only)

Free Benefits with Your Book

Your purchase includes a free PDF copy of this book along with other exclusive benefits. Check the *Free Benefits with Your Book* section in the Preface to unlock them instantly and maximize your learning experience.

Scalability foundations

There have been a few times in the past when I was woken up in the middle of the night because the system I oversaw was down. Other times, I worked with the rest of the team pre-provisioning the resources needed because we expected a huge wave of traffic coming at us. To be honest, that wasn't the right approach, as the real load was a bit unpredictable. I wish I had known back then how to proactively avoid these situations and get better nights' sleep. Since we can't travel through time yet, I decided to embark on a journey to help present and future Kubernetes enthusiasts build efficient and cost-optimized clusters using **Kubernetes Event-driven Autoscaling (KEDA)** and Karpenter.

Whether you're here because you want to optimize performance, cut down on cloud costs, or build resilient systems that adapt seamlessly, we need to start with the basics – such as the foundations of scaling. So, before we dive deep into Kubernetes-specific autoscaling tools and techniques, let's explore what scaling really means in computing and why automation is the game-changer.

Scaling is the ability of a system to handle increasing amounts of work by adding resources to manage the load efficiently. It's a fundamental concept in computing that has become increasingly crucial in the era of cloud-native applications and microservices architectures. The true power of scaling lies in its **automation** – the ability to adjust resources dynamically without human intervention, which is essential for managing the rapid and unpredictable demand.

The following diagram illustrates the pitfalls of static resource allocation:

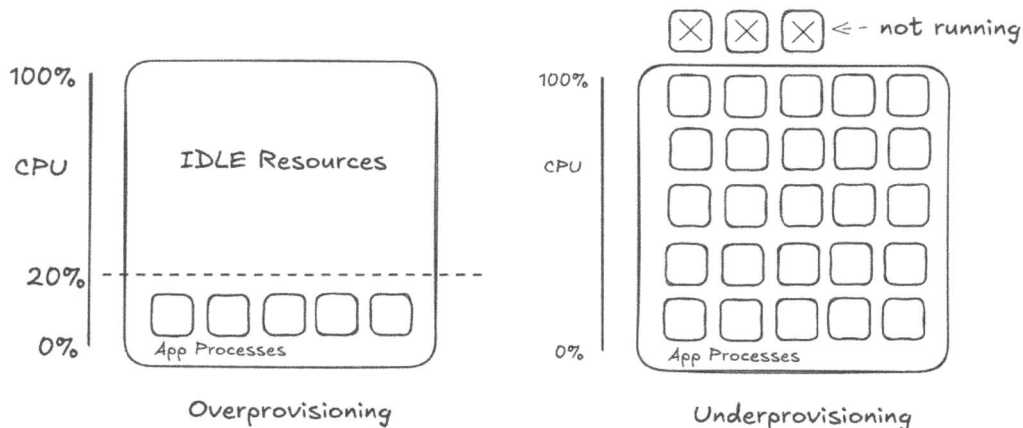

Figure 1.1 – Challenges with static and manual infrastructure

As you can see in *Figure 1.1*, **Overprovisioning** wastes resources and increases costs, while **Under-provisioning** risks poor performance and potential system failures. Autoscaling offers a solution to both these problems. Consider an online retailer during a flash sale: with autoscaling, their system automatically detects increased load and rapidly provisions additional resources to handle the traffic spike. As the sale ends and traffic subsides, it scales back down, releasing unnecessary resources. This dynamic approach ensures optimal performance during peak times, while also minimizing costs during periods of lower demand. By automatically adjusting resources in real time, autoscaling can help you maintain a balance between performance and efficiency, adapting to unpredictable demand patterns without manual intervention.

A bit of history

The concept of autoscaling took a significant leap forward in 2009 when AWS introduced Auto Scaling (known now as **Amazon EC2 Auto Scaling**). This feature allows you to automatically adjust the compute capacity to meet your application demands at the lowest possible cost. This shift toward automation not only improved efficiency but also allowed organizations to be more responsive to fluctuating demands, rather than getting bogged down in system administration and operational burdens if done manually.

After 2009, numerous organizations began implementing and refining autoscaling strategies. Netflix, for instance, documented their approach of aggressive scaling up and down to meet variable consumer demands. Other companies, such as Dropbox, Spotify, and Airbnb, also shared their experiences and best practices for autoscaling in cloud environments. The way I like to see this is that this collective knowledge and experience from various industry leaders contributed to the evolution of autoscaling technologies and practices. As cloud-native architectures became more prevalent, the need for more sophisticated, application-aware autoscaling mechanisms grew.

Kubernetes, with its origins in Google's experience running large-scale production workloads, embodies many of these autoscaling best practices. From its beginnings, Kubernetes was designed with the principles of efficient resource allocation and automatic scaling in mind.

By building autoscaling into its core functionality, Kubernetes took the lessons learned from years of cloud scaling experiences and made them accessible to a wider range of applications and organizations. This native support for autoscaling has been a key factor in Kubernetes' widespread adoption, as it allows teams to focus on building and improving their applications rather than managing the underlying infrastructure scaling.

Horizontal and vertical scaling

Now that you understand the importance of scaling and its automated nature, let's explore the two primary approaches to scaling: vertical and horizontal. These methods offer different ways to increase a system's capacity to handle load, each with its own advantages and challenges.

Vertical scaling

Vertical scaling, often referred to as "scaling up," involves boosting the capabilities of an existing machine or instance. This method typically focuses on enhancing a single node's processing power, memory capacity, or storage. Picture a scenario where your application server is struggling with its current workload. A vertical scaling solution might involve upgrading a **node** from two vCPUs with 4 GiB of RAM to a node of eight vCPUs with 16 GiB of RAM, as shown in *Figure 1.2*:

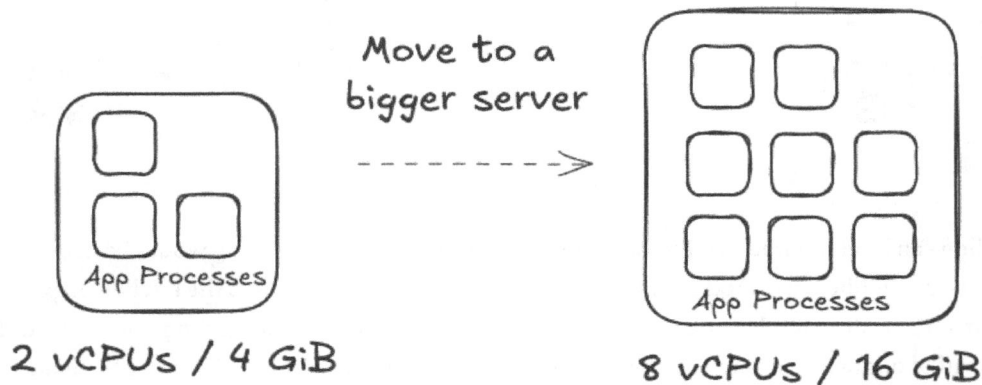

Figure 1.2 – Vertical scaling example

Figure 1.2 show that this approach is simple, particularly for applications not designed with distributed architecture in mind. It's often the go-to solution for improving the performance of monolithic applications or certain types of databases that prefer running on a single, powerful machine.

However, vertical scaling isn't without its drawbacks:

- **Costs**: The cost of high-end hardware can escalate rapidly
- **Physical limitations**: There is an upper bound to how much you can enhance a node
- **Potential interruptions**: Hardware upgrades cause system downtime
- **Reliability**: Having one (or few) node(s) creates a potential single point of failure

While vertical scaling can offer quick performance boosts, it may not provide the adaptability and robustness required for your workload, especially if it's very dynamic.

Horizontal scaling

Horizontal scaling, often called "scaling out," takes a different approach to handling increased load. Instead of boosting a single node, horizontal scaling involves adding more nodes to your system. The following diagram illustrates an example of this:

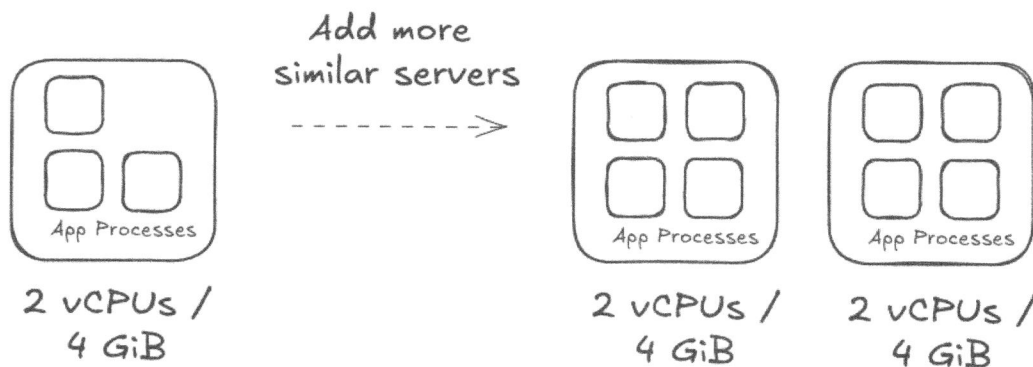

Figure 1.3 – Horizontal scaling example

Scaling can be compared to what happens in a restaurant: vertical scaling would be like hiring a super-chef, while horizontal scaling would be like adding more cooks to the kitchen. In practice, horizontal scaling might look like this: if your web application is struggling with high traffic, instead of upgrading a single server, you'd add more similar servers to distribute the load. This approach aligns well with modern, distributed architectures and cloud-native applications.

Horizontal scaling offers several advantages that make it particularly useful for dynamic and distributed systems. For starters, the theoretically unlimited scalability it provides: as demand grows, you can continually add more machines to your system to meet these increasing needs. This approach also enhances fault tolerance significantly; if one node experiences problems or fails entirely, the other nodes in the system can compensate, ensuring continued operation and minimizing downtime. Furthermore, with horizontal scaling, you can closely match your system's capacity to current demands, effectively avoiding the costly pitfall of over-provisioning resources. Horizontal scaling is particularly well suited for stateless applications, microservices architectures, and distributed systems.

However, horizontal scaling could also pose some challenges:

- **Complexity**: Applications need to be designed to work across multiple nodes
- **Consistency**: Ensuring data remains consistent across all nodes can be tricky
- **Network overhead**: Communication between nodes can introduce latency
- **License costs**: Some software licenses may charge per node

In the context of Kubernetes, which we'll explore in depth later, horizontal scaling is a fundamental concept. Kubernetes' ability to automatically scale the number of pods running an application is a prime example of horizontal scaling in action. However, you'll see when vertical scaling might make more sense or can even help you right-size your workloads.

Kubernetes architecture

Before I dive into the specifics about autoscaling in Kubernetes, let's have a quick overview of the Kubernetes architecture and its components, especially those involved in the autoscaling aspect of Kubernetes.

Assuming you're already familiar with Kubernetes, you know that each cluster is composed of several nodes where one or more components run (e.g., `kube-apiserver`, `kube-scheduler`, or `kubelet`). A node is essentially a server, machine, or instance. Depending on where you're hosting your Kubernetes cluster, you'll encounter different terminology. In this book, I'll stick with *node*.

As shown in *Figure 1.4*, a very simplified version of the Kubernetes architecture, Kubernetes cluster nodes are grouped into two: the **control plane** and the **data plane**.

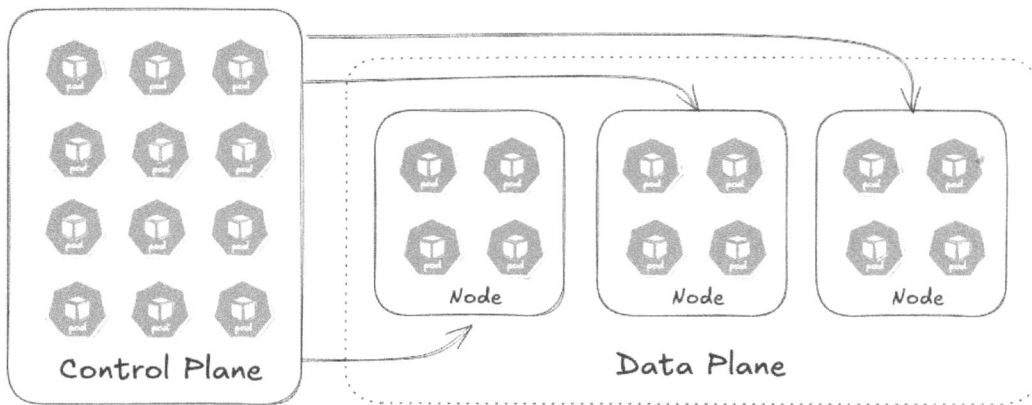

Figure 1.4 – A very simple Kubernetes architecture overview

In *Figure 1.4*, you can see the control plane nodes on the left side. The control plane nodes contain all the components that manage the overall state of the cluster, as per the Kubernetes documentation. If you set up your cluster on your own using tools such as kubeadm, kops, or kubespray, you need to manage the scaling of the nodes yourself. On the other hand, if you set up your cluster using managed services such as **Amazon Elastic Kubernetes Service (Amazon EKS)**, **Google Kubernetes Engine (GKE)**, or **Azure Kubernetes Service (AKS)**, the companies offering these services handle the scaling of the nodes for you. Whichever setup you have, this book won't cover the autoscaling aspect for the control plane, focusing instead on the **data plane**.

In *Figure 1.4*, you can see the data plane nodes on the right side. These nodes are where your workloads run. The more workloads you deploy to the cluster, the more nodes you'll end up having. This is because each node should host a limited set of pods, mainly for two reasons: you don't want to have all your pods on a single large node for high availability reasons, and a node can't host more than 110 pods per node (as per the current official Kubernetes documentation).

The big question now is: how many nodes does your workload need? How can you ensure you're not wasting resources while also not constraining the cluster? In other words, how do you build an efficient Kubernetes cluster? It's tricky, so let's talk about what makes a data plane efficient, at least from a compute perspective.

> **Note**
>
> Even though there are other aspects besides compute, such as storage and networking, that have an impact on how you define the number of nodes, this book will only focus on the compute aspect. However, as we'll see in the upcoming chapters, aspects such as networking have an impact on how you scale your nodes. We'll dive deep into that later.

Efficient Kubernetes data planes

Understanding how to optimize your Kubernetes data plane is crucial for building cost-effective, high-performing clusters that can adapt to changing workloads. To do so, we'll explore what efficiency means in the context of Kubernetes, why it's important, and the key factors that contribute to an efficient data plane. Then, I'll cover the challenges of achieving and maintaining efficiency, as well as strategies for optimizing resource utilization.

What do I mean by efficiency?

To answer this question, let's first talk about what efficiency means in a broader sense. Efficiency, in general terms, is the ability to accomplish a task with minimal waste of time and effort. It's about achieving the desired outcome while using the least number of resources possible – in other words, no wasting of resources. In a formula, as shown in *Figure 1.5*, it looks like this:

$$Efficiency = Allocated / Usage$$

Figure 1.5 – Efficiency formula for compute resources

Now, let's apply this concept to Kubernetes, specifically to the data plane nodes. In this context, efficiency means optimizing the utilization of compute resources to achieve the best performance at the lowest cost. It's not just about using all available resources; it's about using them wisely and effectively.

As the focus of this book is on compute, this means that efficiency is about maximizing the use of available CPU and memory while minimizing waste. In traditional on-premises environments, efficiency might have been less of a concern as hardware costs were often treated as a sunk cost. However, in the cloud, where you typically pay for what you use (also known as *pay as you go*), efficiency has a direct impact on your monthly bill. This makes resource optimization not just a best practice but a financial imperative.

So, as this book will focus on the cloud, an efficient Kubernetes data plane in the cloud context involves several key aspects:

- **Right-sizing your resources**: Ensuring your pods have enough resources to run effectively, but not so much that they're wasting capacity
- **Maximizing node utilization**: Filling your nodes with an optimal number of pods to avoid running unnecessary nodes
- **Scaling appropriately**: Increasing or decreasing resources in response to actual demand, rather than over-provisioning for peak loads
- **Avoiding idle resources**: Identifying and eliminating unused or underutilized resources that you're still paying for
- **Choosing appropriate instance types**: Selecting the most cost-effective node types for your workloads

By focusing on these aspects of efficiency, you can significantly reduce your cloud costs. For instance, an inefficient cluster might have nodes running at 30% capacity, meaning you're essentially paying for 70% of unused resources. An efficient cluster, on the other hand, might consistently run at 70-80% capacity, dramatically reducing waste and, consequently, costs. Of course, these numbers can vary depending on the type of workloads you have and the technical debt they might carry.

Achieving this level of efficiency isn't straightforward. In the following chapters, I'll dive into the details of how you can address the key aspects I mentioned before. The goal is to help you build and maintain an efficient data plane, striking the right balance between performance, reliability, and cost-effectiveness. However, before doing that, it's important to understand the challenges and considerations to achieve efficiency in Kubernetes (actually, for compute in general).

Challenges and considerations

Several factors across the entire application stack influence performance and efficiency. The design of your application components, including layers, dependencies, and how they interact, have an impact on efficiency. The underlying infrastructure, from the physical hardware to the operating system, plays an important role in overall performance. How Kubernetes schedules pods and scales resources directly affects resource utilization. Moreover, network performance factors such as latency, throughput, and the configuration of load balancers can impact the efficiency of your cluster.

Achieving efficiency is challenging due to several factors. Workloads often have diverse resource requirements; some may be CPU-bound while others are memory-bound, leading to uneven resource utilization across nodes. Kubernetes typically scales at the pod or node level, which can be too coarse for optimal efficiency, and make it complicated. And let's not forget that there's a delay between when additional resources are needed and when they become available. Workloads with dependencies often require resource buffers while waiting on these dependencies, leading to periods of underutilization, which might not be much but still are things you need to consider.

Non-technical factors can also lead to inefficiency. Overprovisioning out of an abundance of caution is common, especially for critical workloads. This is a very typical scenario for peak seasons when it's better to keep business continuity than an ideal efficiency number.

While striving for an efficient Kubernetes data plane is important for cost optimization, it's a complex challenge that requires a holistic approach. It involves not just infrastructure management but also application design, careful capacity planning, and, sometimes, a willingness to accept calculated risks. As you proceed through this book, you'll explore strategies and tools that can help you navigate these challenges and achieve a more efficient Kubernetes cluster.

Now that you understand the complexities and challenges of achieving efficiency in Kubernetes environments, let's explore the autoscaling mechanisms that Kubernetes provides to address these challenges.

Kubernetes autoscaling categories

When working with Kubernetes, there are two primary categories of scaling that require attention, as alluded to earlier. The first category pertains to the **application workloads**, represented by pods, while the second category involves the underlying infrastructure of the **data plane**, specifically the nodes. This distinction is crucial because each category requires different approaches and tools for effective autoscaling.

Application workloads

The first step in your Kubernetes efficiency journey focuses on application workloads, specifically the pods that run your applications. This is a critical starting point because it directly impacts how efficiently your cluster utilizes resources and responds to changing demands. Central to this optimization is setting appropriate resource requests for your pods. This is crucial because kube-scheduler uses these requests to make decisions about pod placement. If requests are set too high, you may waste resources and limit the number of pods that can be scheduled. Conversely, if set too low, your applications may underperform or face resource contention.

The recommended approach for scaling application workloads is horizontal scaling – adding or removing pod replicas as demand fluctuates. This is typically achieved using the **HorizontalPo-dAutoscaler (HPA)**. While I'll dive deeper into HPA in the next chapter, it's worth noting that this tool automatically adjusts the number of pod replicas based on observed metrics such as CPU or memory utilization, or custom metrics that you define. There are other tools in the same vein, such as KEDA, which in essence does a similar job to HPA, but the options to scale are broader. I'll dive into much more details about this in the next chapters.

Let's consider an example: imagine you have a web application that experiences varying levels of traffic throughout the day. During peak hours, the CPU utilization of your pods might spike to 80% or higher, similar to what you see in *Figure 1.6*:

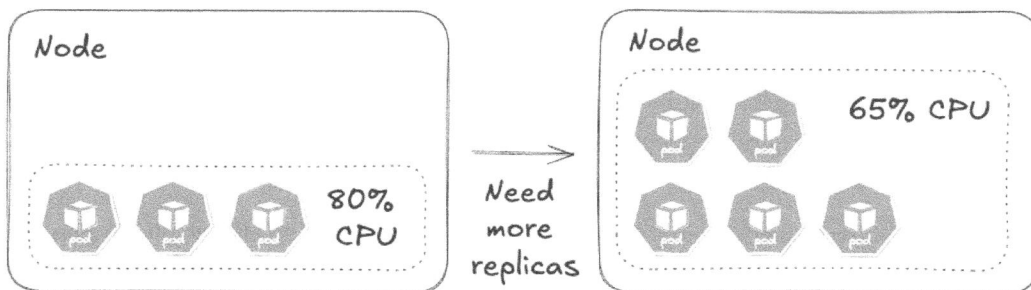

Figure 1.6 – Pods scaling out due to resource utilization

The preceding figure illustrates that when pods from a deployment are using 80% of their CPU capacity, it's time to add more replicas to prevent the workload from underperforming. In this scenario, the HPA could automatically increase the number of pod replicas to distribute the load. As traffic subsides and CPU utilization drops, the HPA would then reduce the number of replicas, conserving resources.

Let's consider an example: imagine you have a web application that experiences varying levels of traffic throughout the day. During peak hours, the CPU utilization of your pods might spike to 80% or higher. As you can see in *Figure 1.7*, the HPA automatically increases the number of pod replicas to distribute the load. As traffic subsides and CPU utilization drops, the HPA would then reduce the number of replicas, conserving resources.

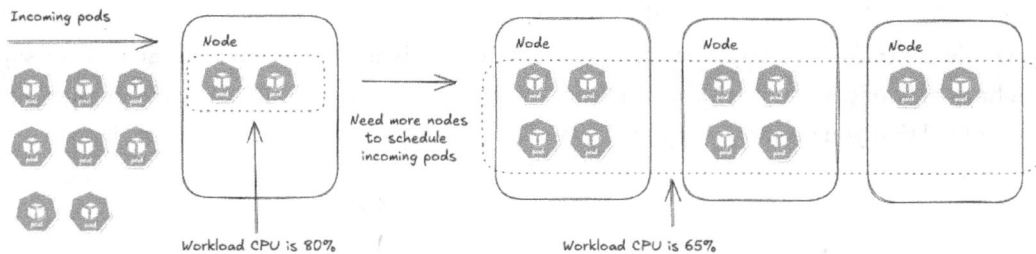

Figure 1.7 – Web application scaling out using an HPA rule

While horizontal scaling is the recommended best practice, there are situations where adjusting the resources of individual pods might be necessary. The **VerticalPodAutoscaler (VPA)** is a tool that can help with this, automatically adjusting CPU and memory requests based on historical resource usage. However, it's important to note that vertical scaling is generally less flexible and can lead to pod restarts, which may cause brief service interruptions. We'll dive deeper into this later in *Chapter 3* as well.

In general, I advocate for horizontal autoscaling over vertical autoscaling for the following reasons:

- **Better fault tolerance**: If one pod fails, others can continue serving requests
- **Improved resource utilization**: It's often easier to fit many small pods across your nodes than a few large ones
- **Easier rolling updates**: With multiple replicas, you can update your application without downtime

Data plane nodes

Scaling the data plane nodes becomes necessary when the cluster's capacity to run pods reaches its limit, especially when nodes are added only as needed. What I didn't say before is that when you scale out your workloads by adding more pods (following the recommendation for horizontal scaling), you may eventually reach a point where the cluster lacks the capacity to run these additional pods. This results in unscheduled pods, which serve as a trigger for the second category of Kubernetes autoscaling: scaling the data plane nodes. Tools such as **Cluster Autoscaler (CAS)** and Karpenter are designed to address this challenge. These projects react to the presence of unscheduled pods in the cluster by adding more capacity. Both have built-in logic to interact with the underlying infrastructure and provision additional nodes as needed. I'll dive deep into these tools in the following chapters.

Let's continue with our web application example. As the load increases and more pods are added to handle the traffic, you might reach a point where all existing nodes are at capacity. Let's say you have only one node capable of running 4 pods, and your HPA or KEDA scaling policy has determined that you need now 10 pods to handle the current load; see the following figure:

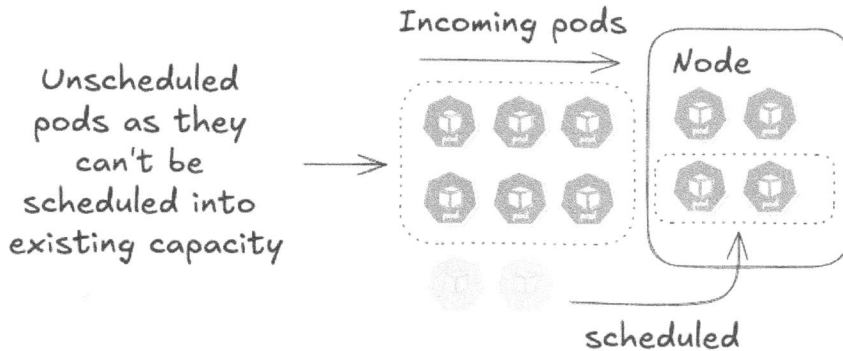

Figure 1.8 – Unscheduled pods as there are not enough nodes to support the scaling event

As shown in *Figure 1.8*, only two additional pods could fit into the existing node. This leaves six pods unscheduled.

At this point, Karpenter or CAS would spring into action. They would detect the unscheduled pods and initiate the process of adding a new node to the cluster. In a cloud environment, these tools already know which APIs to call to provision a new node and automatically register it to the cluster, eliminating the need for manual intervention. See the following figure for an example of this process:

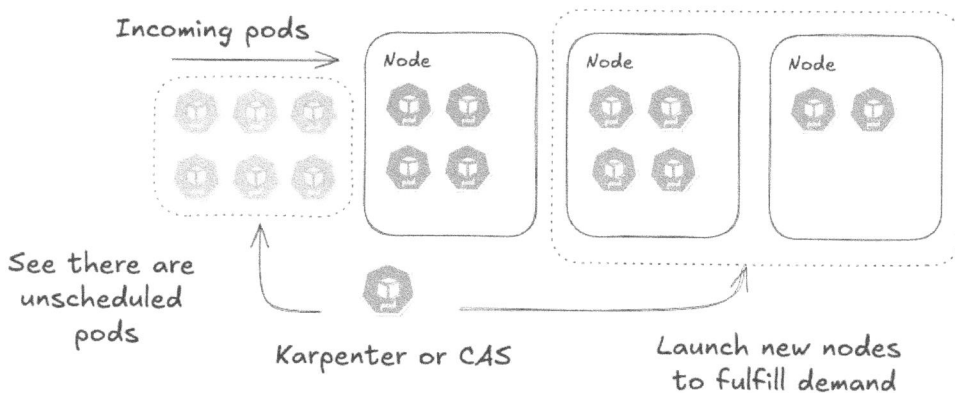

Figure 1.9 – Karpenter or CAS adding more nodes when it's needed

In *Figure 1.9*, you can sese that once the new node is ready, `kube-scheduler` will place the un-scheduled pods on this newly available capacity. This process happens automatically, ensuring that your application can scale to meet demand without manual intervention or overprovisioning.

Conversely, when demand decreases and fewer pods are needed (thanks to HPA or KEDA), these same tools ensure that any extra nodes added during the peak are removed, maintaining the cluster's efficiency, as shown:

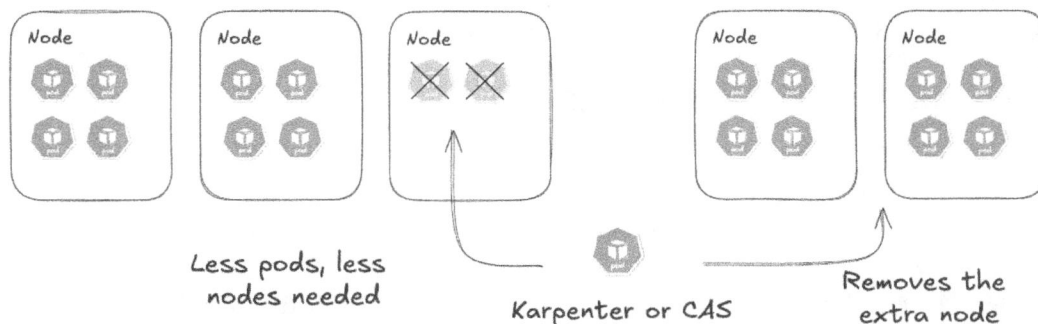

Figure 1.10 – Karpenter or CAS removing nodes when they're not needed anymore

For instance, as you can see in *Figure 1.10*, if traffic drops and you only need 90 pods, CAS or Karpenter might remove two nodes from the cluster, returning to the original 10-node configuration

It's important to note that we're advocating for horizontal scaling at this level as well – adding or removing entire nodes rather than trying to resize existing ones. Unlike with pods, there are no established projects for the vertical autoscaling of nodes, as this approach introduces unnecessary complexity and potential instability to the cluster.

By leveraging these node autoscaling capabilities in conjunction with pod-level autoscaling, you can create a highly responsive and efficient Kubernetes cluster. This setup allows your cluster to dynamically adapt to changing workloads, ensuring optimal resource utilization and cost-effectiveness. Hold tight, I'll tell you how to implement all of this in the following chapters.

Now that I've covered the theoretical foundations of Kubernetes autoscaling, it's time to set up your practice environment for this book.

Hands-on lab: Creating a Kubernetes cluster

Enough theory – it's time to get our hands dirty! Grab your computer, open your terminal, and prepare to dive into the practical side of Kubernetes autoscaling. In this section, I'll guide you through creating your very own Kubernetes cluster, providing you with a sandbox environment to experiment with the concepts we've discussed.

If you already have a Kubernetes cluster that you could use for the workload autoscaling chapters, skip this section and go to the summary of the chapter.

Local Kubernetes cluster with Kind

Kind is a tool that enables you to create and manage local Kubernetes clusters by leveraging Docker containers as simulated nodes. It was primarily created for testing Kubernetes itself, but has become popular among developers for local development and **continuous integration (CI)** pipelines. Kind allows you to quickly spin up a multi-node Kubernetes cluster on your local machine, making it ideal for testing, learning, and developing Kubernetes-native applications without the need for a cloud provider or physical servers.

Installing Kind

Please visit the official site for the most recent installation methods: `https://kind.sigs.k8s.io/docs/user/quick-start/`. As of the time of writing, you can install Kind with `go install`, from the source, using release binaries, or with community-managed packages such as `brew` (Mac) or `choco` (Windows). If you're using Docker Desktop, you need to turn off Kubernetes.

For instance, if you have a Mac, simply run this command to install Kind:

```
$ brew install kind
```

To confirm it's working, you can see which version you installed with this command:

```
$ kind version
```

Creating a Kind cluster

To create a Kubernetes cluster, simply run this command:

```
$ kind create cluster --name kubernetes-autoscaling
```

Next, run this command to configure access to the cluster:

```
$ kubectl cluster-info --context kind-kubernetes-autoscaling
```

Confirm that you can use the cluster by getting the list of Kubernetes nodes:

```
$ kubectl get nodes
```

You should see an output similar to this that shows the Kubernetes nodes:

```
NAME                                    STATUS   ROLES          AGE
VERSION
kubernetes-autoscaling-control-plane    Ready    control-plane  15m
v1.31.0
```

You're now ready to use a local Kubernetes cluster without incurring any cloud costs. However, if you're able and willing to practice with an environment similar to what you'll interact with in *Chapter 7* and beyond, proceed to the following section.

Cloud Kubernetes cluster in AWS

Let's create an Amazon EKS cluster using Terraform, an infrastructure-as-code tool that allows you to define your desired cluster state as code. You'll be using a custom Terraform template that leverages the Amazon EKS Blueprints for Terraform project. This template will set up a complete Amazon EKS cluster, including a VPC, a Kubernetes control plane, and the necessary IAM roles and service accounts. It will also configure a managed node group for essential system components.

If you're not familiar with Terraform or HCL syntax, reviewing Terraform's documentation can be helpful (https://developer.hashicorp.com/terraform/docs).

> **Note**
>
> Terraform uses AWS credentials that must be configured in your environment. The recommended and more secure approach is to authenticate using: **named AWS CLI profiles** (via aws configure --profile your-profile), **IAM roles via instance metadata** (for EC2 or CloudShell environments), or **AWS SSO or IAM Identity Center**. Avoid hardcoding AWS_ACCESS_KEY_ID and AWS_SECRET_ACCESS_KEY unless absolutely necessary, as this approach is less secure and harder to manage.

Creating an Amazon EKS cluster

Start by cloning this repository to your computer using Git:

```
$ git clone https://github.com/PacktPublishing/Kubernetes-Autoscaling.git
```

Change directory to the chapter01 folder using this command:

```
$ cd Kubernetes-Autoscaling/chapter01/terraform
```

Before you start, make sure your AWS credentials are properly configured in the terminal you'll be using. Then, you need to create an environment variable for the AWS Region you'll be using. For example, if you're using the Ireland Region (eu-west-1), you need to run a command like this:

```
$ export AWS_REGION=eu-west-1
```

To begin the process of creating the cluster, run this command:

```
$ sh bootstrap.sh
```

This script includes several Terraform commands that must run in a specific order and will take around 20 minutes to complete. Once finished, configure access to the new cluster:

```
$ aws eks --region $AWS_REGION update-kubeconfig --name kubernetes-
autoscaling
```

This command updates your ~/.kube/config file, allowing kubectl to connect to your new cluster.

Confirm that you can use the cluster by getting the list of Kubernetes nodes:

```
$ kubectl get nodes
```

You should see an output similar to this that shows the Kubernetes nodes:

```
NAME              STATUS   ROLES    AGE     VERSION
ip-10-0-107-82... Ready    <none>   4m18s   v1.34.1
ip-10-0-57-88...  Ready    <none>   4m18s   v1.34.1
```

The output has been shortened, but essentially what you should see is the list of nodes registered to the EKS cluster. These nodes will serve as a base for you to practice what you'll learn in the upcoming chapters.

Removing the Amazon EKS cluster

To keep cloud costs at a minimum while you study, make sure you turn down the resources created by Terraform so you don't pay while not using the cluster. The next time you come back to study, you'll need to create the cluster again by following the steps from the previous section.

To remove all of the resources created by Terraform, run the following command:

```
$ sh cleanup.sh
```

This script includes several other commands that need to run in a specific order.

Summary

In this chapter, you've explored the fundamental concepts of Kubernetes autoscaling, understanding its critical role in achieving efficient and cost-effective Kubernetes clusters. You've learned about the complexities of scaling both application workloads and infrastructure nodes, examining the challenges and considerations that come with each. You've learned about the importance of proper resource allocation, the benefits of horizontal scaling, and the tools Kubernetes provides to automate these processes.

By implementing the autoscaling mechanisms exposed here, you're not just optimizing for performance and cost – you're also contributing to a more sustainable approach to cloud computing. Efficient resource utilization means less wasted energy and reduced carbon footprint. As we move forward, remember that every optimization you implement, every unnecessary pod you eliminate, and every node you right size is a step toward more sustainable practices. In the world of Kubernetes, we're truly saving the planet, one pod at a time.

In the next chapter, we'll dive deeper into workload autoscaling, exploring how HPA, VPA, and KEDA work together to make your Kubernetes applications truly adaptive and efficient.

Get This Book's PDF Version and Exclusive Extras

UNLOCK NOW

Scan the QR code (or go to packtpub.com/unlock).
Search for this book by name, confirm the edition,
and then follow the steps on the page.

*Note: Keep your invoice handy. Purchases made
directly from Packt don't require one.*

2

Workload Autoscaling Overview

In the previous chapter, I covered the importance of autoscaling in general, the concept of efficiency in compute, and how to implement autoscaling in Kubernetes. But I also introduced the two main categories of autoscaling in Kubernetes: infrastructure and workload. Building on that foundation, this chapter focuses on the latter – workload autoscaling.

Efficiently scaling workloads in a Kubernetes cluster is crucial for maintaining optimal performance and resource utilization. Building efficient workloads will have an impact on how many nodes you'll end up needing in a Kubernetes data plane.

This chapter goes deeper into workload autoscaling, discovering the challenges, strategies, and tools available to help you get started with building efficient workloads.

Additionally, I'll explore the key components that contribute to effective workload autoscaling, along with its challenges. Most importantly, this chapter will focus on understanding how the Kubernetes scheduler works, the importance of observability, and why workload **rightsizing** is so crucial. With this groundwork laid, I'll then cover the different workload autoscaling mechanisms, such as HPA, VPA, and KEDA. I briefly introduced them in the previous chapter, and now we'll learn their basics. After this, you'll gain hands-on experience by diving deeper into these concepts in the next chapters.

By the end of this chapter, you'll have a solid knowledge base of how to implement workload autoscaling in Kubernetes, to then go deeper into each of the workload autoscaling mechanisms I mentioned before.

In this chapter, we'll cover the following topics:

- Challenges of workload autoscaling
- How does the Kubernetes scheduler work?
- Workload rightsizing
- Workload autoscalers

Technical requirements

For this chapter, you'll continue using the Kubernetes cluster you created in *Chapter 1*. You can continue working with the local Kubernetes cluster; there's no need yet to work with a cluster in AWS. If you turned down the cluster, make sure you bring it up for every hands-on lab in this chapter. You don't need to install any additional tools as most of the commands are going to be run using kubectl.

You can find the YAML manifests for all resources you're going to create in this chapter in the chapter02 folder in the book's GitHub repository (https://github.com/PacktPublishing/ Kubernetes-Autoscaling). In this chapter, you're going to use a sample application that I built and pushed to the Docker registry. If you want to explore the source or build and push the image to a different registry, you can find all the source code in the chapter02/src/ folder.

Challenges of autoscaling workloads

Before I dive into any solutions or recommendations on Kubernetes, it's important to recognize that while the concept of workload autoscaling may seem straightforward, its implementation can be quite complex. Let me explain why by describing some of the key challenges that arise when attempting to scale workloads efficiently.

For starters, it's important to understand the interconnected nature of workload and infrastructure scaling. While workloads are typically scaled based on resource utilization, nodes should be scaled according to resource reservation. These two aspects are intrinsically linked, and their interaction can lead to unexpected outcomes. For instance, if workload replicas are increased without proper rightsizing, you may find yourself needing more nodes to accommodate all the necessary workload replicas, potentially leading to inefficient resource usage.

The diversity of application behaviors presents another significant challenge. Consider a simple application, such as a backend API, shopping portal, or a Pi calculation using the Monte Carlo simulation, where CPU utilization directly correlates with the number of requests per second. This is illustrated in the following figure:

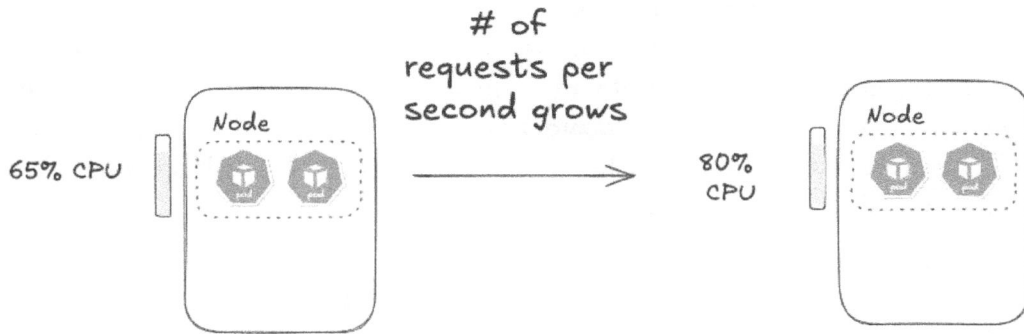

Figure 2.1 – CPU utilization might correlate to the number of requests per second

In *Figure 2.1*, you can see that as the number of requests grows, the CPU utilization grows as well. In such cases, setting scaling policies based on CPU utilization thresholds might be very effective. However, not all applications behave in this predictable manner, nor do they have the same requirements. This variability in application behavior is a major challenge, and it's important to note that this issue isn't unique to containers or Kubernetes but is relevant across various computing environments.

Some applications may be memory-intensive or may even reserve a specific amount of memory at startup, employing their own mechanisms for memory management, such as garbage collection or defragmentation. In these cases, memory utilization alone may not be an adequate metric for scaling decisions.

Moreover, there are scenarios where traditional resource metrics such as CPU and memory utilization may appear normal, but the application still experiences issues. For example, as shown in *Figure 2.2*, some requests might fail due to increased latency or intermittent network problems when interacting with external dependencies, especially if proper retry mechanisms are not in place.

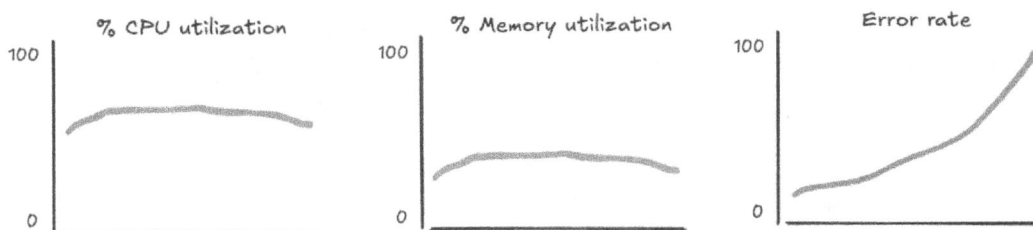

Figure 2.2 – Applications might still fail even if CPU and memory utilization looks good

The key takeaway is that while CPU and memory metrics might be suitable scaling indicators for some applications, more complex applications may require consideration of other factors, such as latency, number of requests, queued messages, or even business **key performance indicators (KPIs)**. Therefore, it's crucial to invest time in understanding how your application behaves under various load conditions to determine the most appropriate metrics for scaling. This knowledge will inform your autoscaling strategy and help you avoid potential pitfalls.

As we move forward, you'll explore how to make use of these different metrics I mentioned to configure your scaling policies, what factors to consider, and how Kubernetes schedules pods. The following sections will focus on these aspects, primarily from a Kubernetes perspective, with the aim of highlighting why it's vital to understand what impacts your application's performance and scaling needs.

Let's begin by examining how kube-scheduler works, as this forms the foundation for efficient workload autoscaling in Kubernetes.

How does the Kubernetes scheduler work?

This important job of scheduling pods is done by kube-scheduler, Kubernetes' default scheduler, which is responsible for assigning pods to nodes based on various factors, including, but not limited to, nodeSelectors, affinities, tolerations, and, most importantly, resource requests. For now, we'll focus primarily on resource constraints.

Essentially, kube-scheduler operates in three main steps:

1. **Filtering**: It identifies all nodes that can accommodate the pod based on available resources, mainly memory and CPU. If there are none, the pod is deemed unschedulable.
2. **Scoring**: It ranks the filtered nodes to determine the most suitable one.
3. **Binding**: It assigns the pod to the node with highest score, choosing randomly if multiple nodes are equally suitable.

While the operation of kube-scheduler involves many intricate details and variables, our focus will be on one crucial aspect: the pod's resource requirements. Understanding these requirements is essential because they directly influence the scheduler's decision-making process.

In Kubernetes, you can specify these resource needs through the pod specification using requests and limits. Through requests, you specify the minimum CPU and memory your container is guaranteed, and this is what the scheduler uses to match a pod with an appropriate node. Through limits, you define the maximum amount of CPU and memory a container can use, and this is enforced at runtime by the kubelet.

These specifications, typically expressed in terms of CPU and memory, play a very important role in how kube-scheduler filters and scores nodes for pod placement.

> **Note**
>
> Starting with Kubernetes v1.32, you can now define default resource requests and limits directly at the pod level using the new resources field in podSpec, rather than only under each container. At the time of writing, this feature is in alpha, which means the API and behavior may change in future releases. Always check the latest Kubernetes documentation for the most relevant information about this ability.

Configuring requests

When you define resource requests for containers within a pod, you're basically telling kube-scheduler how much resources the node needs to guarantee. This information helps the scheduler make informed decisions about where to place your pod in the cluster, ensuring it lands on a node with sufficient resources to meet its needs. The following figure illustrates how kube-scheduler places a pod on a node where it fits based on its resource requests:

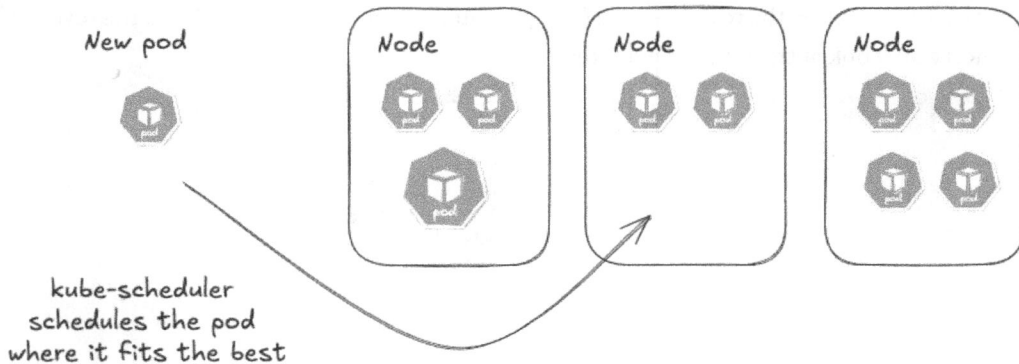

Figure 2.3 – kube-scheduler scheduling a pod to the node with the best ranking score

In *Figure 2.3*, you can see that kube-scheduler decided to schedule the pod on the node that has the best ranking score. The second node is the one that has the resources available for the new pod coming to the cluster, while the other two were already at their capacity.

While this scheduling mechanism ensures that pods have access to their requested resources, it doesn't always lead to optimal resource utilization. In practice, pods may not use all the resources they've requested. This can result in low node efficiency, as there's often a discrepancy between requested and actually utilized resources. Consequently, this mismatch can lead to the underutilization of cluster capacity, highlighting the importance of rightsizing pod resource requests.

For an effective autoscaling configuration, *you should always configure requests* carefully. Moreover, this practice ensures predictable and deterministic results when kube-scheduler assigns pods to nodes and is crucial for setting up effective scaling policies. Without proper resource specifications, you may encounter unexpected behavior, inefficient resource utilization, and potential performance issues as your application scales.

Configuring limits

Resource management in Kubernetes extends beyond scheduling. While resource requests are used for pod placement, you can also configure resource limits. These limits are enforced during runtime by the kubelet on each node. The kubelet ensures that containers don't consume resources beyond their specified limits, even if the node has additional capacity available. If a container attempts to exceed its limit, the kubelet will restrict its resource usage or terminate the process, depending on the resource type (compressible or non-compressible) and the severity of the violation. Look at the following figure:

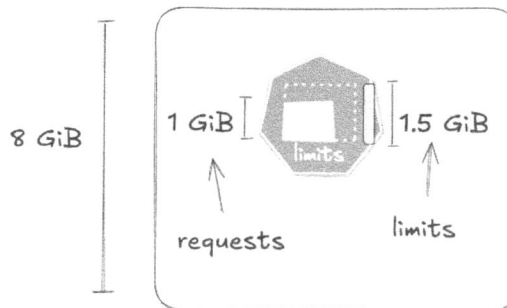

Figure 2.4 – A pod requesting 1 GiB, but limiting to 1.5 GiB in a node with 8 GiB of capacity

In *Figure 2.4*, you can see that the pod is requesting **1 GiB** of memory as the minimum guaranteed allocation. However, it's setting a limit of **1.5 GiB** to cap its maximum resource consumption. The bar at the side of the pod represents how much of the allocated resources the pod is currently using.

What if you don't specify resource requests or limits?

pods are scheduled as a best-effort, but will be the first ones to be evicted/throttled when the node experiences memory or CPU pressure. If no limits are configured, the pod can consume as much resources as it needs. As a safety mechanism, you could configure a **LimitRange** for a given namespace. A LimitRange is a Kubernetes policy object that defines resource constraints within a namespace. It will apply default values if you don't set resources in your pod, ensuring efficient resource allocation. Alternatively, you can configure a webhook to set default values before pods are scheduled; tools such as **Kyverno** can simplify this task.

Pod configuration example

In Kubernetes, you configure the resource units like this:

- **CPU**: It is measured in units, meaning one CPU unit is one physical or virtual core. These units can be fractional, such as 0.5 (half of a CPU) or 0.2 (200 millicpu or 200 m). You'd typically see the "m" format.
- **Memory**: It is measured in bytes. It can be configured as a number only, or accompanied with a suffix such as M or Mi for megabytes. There are other suffixes, but let's keep it short and simple for now. You'd typically see the "Mi" suffix.

Here's an example configuration of a pod with resources and limits configured:

```
apiVersion: v1
kind: pod
metadata:
  name: montecarlo-pi
spec:
  containers:
  - name: montecarlo-pi
    image: christianhxc/montecarlo-pi
    resources:
      requests:
        memory: "512Mi"
        cpu: "900m"
      limits:
        memory: "512Mi"
```

Notice how limits are higher than resources. kube-scheduler will guarantee that the node selected has at least 512Mi of memory available.

What if the pod exceeds the resource limits?

CPU is a compressible resource; when the CPU utilization limit is met, the container is throttled (no more CPU time for it) but it can continue running. With memory, it is different. If the memory utilization of a container is met, the process that is trying to use more memory is stopped. Typically, this causes Kubernetes to restart the container.

Recommendations for configuring resources and limits

Use your judgment after testing how your application behaves. You could run a set of tests, or monitor live traffic. But generally speaking, you could consider the following recommendations:

- **For CPU, consider setting requests slightly higher**: You could set your requests value close to your 95th percentile usage. Moreover, avoid setting CPU limits unless you need to control noisy neighbors in a multi-tenant environment or there's a limitation for licensing. Leaving CPU limits unset lets your workloads burst beyond their requests when spare CPU is available, adapting to varying demand (especially if it's spiky) without being unnecessarily throttled. Also, remember that kube-scheduler only considers requests when placing pods; CPU limits are enforced at runtime by the kubelet and can cause throttling even if the node has idle capacity.

- **For memory, consider setting requests equal to limits**: This gives a predictable behavior for your containers, and kube-scheduler provides the highest priority and stability for your workloads. If you still want to have different values, be cautious about setting limits significantly higher than requests. This can lead to node overcommitment, as the kube-scheduler may place more pods on a node than it can actually handle under peak conditions, potentially causing workload interruptions or out-of-memory events.

By now, you have a better understanding of how the kube-scheduler schedules pods, and why it's very important to configure resource requests to your workloads. Next, let's talk about ways of configuring these request units properly, as it's going to become the most important process to have an efficient Kubernetes data plane.

Workload rightsizing

What does rightsizing mean in the context of Kubernetes? Rightsizing refers to the process of accurately configuring resource requests and limits so that pods only ask for the resources they actually need. This practice aligns with the efficiency and cost optimization goals you're aiming to achieve within your clusters. This section introduces a simple approach to configuring proper resource requests for your pods.

Unfortunately, rightsizing is often left until the end, when organizations notice that their cluster costs are escalating due to the overprovisioning of resources. Our aim is to guide you on the right path from the very beginning. After all, if you need to configure resource requests, why not do it correctly from day one?

To start this process effectively, it's important to have visibility into the resource utilization of workloads running in your cluster. Let's begin by guiding you through the steps to configure your cluster for monitoring resource usage. This visibility will form the foundation for making informed decisions about rightsizing your pods, ensuring that they request only the resources they truly need for optimal performance.

Monitoring

First, you need to set up the tool to monitor how much resources your pods are actually using. This information is crucial for making proper decisions based on data, rather than speculation or previous configurations on virtual machines or previous environment setup. It's important to have monitoring in place as rightsizing is a continuous process, not something you do just once. Applications are constantly changing, either adding or removing functionality, which affects their resource needs.

Note that the ecosystem of tools and platforms to help you monitor and rightsize your applications is growing. Some of these options are paid, but as your Kubernetes cluster keeps expanding, paid options might give you time to focus on solving customer problems rather than trying to reinvent the wheel. In this book, we'll rely on open source tools such as **Prometheus** and **Grafana** to help you gain hands-on experience without having to analyze which tool is best for your specific use case. However, keep in mind that in the long run, you might derive more value from using a third-party tool tailored to your needs.

Prometheus and Grafana

Prometheus is an open source solution that digs into your cluster, pulling metrics from all over – the API server, your nodes, and even individual pods. It doesn't just gather data; it transforms your cluster into a data-rich environment, enabling you to query data and alert based on certain rules you specify. Grafana, complementing Prometheus, helps you visualize this data through interactive dashboards. When combined, these tools provide an excellent starting point for observability. Prometheus collects and stores metrics of your cluster's performance, while Grafana transforms this data into visual dashboards, allowing you to easily identify trends, anomalies, and potential issues. This combination helps you not only observe but also understand and optimize your Kubernetes resource request configurations for pods, which is something you'd want to do regularly.

Hands-on lab: Setting up Prometheus and Grafana

Head over to your terminal and make sure you have your cluster up and running. If you need to bring it up again, go back to *Chapter 1* to do it, and then come back to this.

To install Prometheus and Grafana using **Helm**, you first need to add the Helm Chart repository from Prometheus, update the Helm repos, and install the Prometheus stack. To do so, run these commands:

```
$ helm repo add prometheus-community https://prometheus-community.github.
io/helm-charts
$ helm repo update
$ helm install prometheus prometheus-community/kube-prometheus-stack
--namespace monitoring --create-namespace
```

When the installation is done, you should be able to open Grafana. To do so, you first need to get the administrator username and password to log in.

To get the Grafana admin user, run this command:

```
$ kubectl get secret prometheus-grafana -n monitoring -o jsonpath="{.data.
admin-user}" | base64 --decode ; echo
```

To get the Grafana admin password, run this command:

```
$ kubectl get secret prometheus-grafana -n monitoring -o jsonpath="{.data.
admin-password}" | base64 --decode ; echo
```

Finally, to access Grafana, run this command:

```
$ kubectl port-forward service/prometheus-grafana 3000:80 -n monitoring
```

Open a web browser and enter http://localhost:3000/. You should see the Grafana login page, as shown in the following figure. Enter the username and password and click on **Log in**:

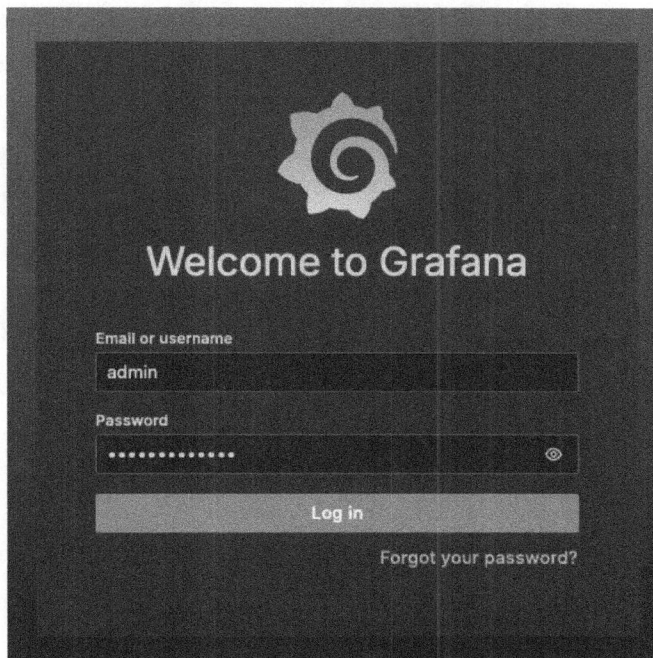

Figure 2.5 – Grafana UI login page

For now, that's it. You'll come back to Grafana in a moment.

Hands-on lab: Determining the right size of an application

Now that you have access to Grafana and Prometheus, let's deploy an application to the cluster, make some calls, and analyze the resource utilization. To get started, run the following command to deploy an application to run Pi simulations using the Monte Carlo method (it involves running multiple simulations with random sampling to obtain numerical results):

```
$ kubectl create deployment montecarlo-pi --image=christianhxc/montecarlo-
pi:latest
```

This command creates a Kubernetes deployment using default values. You can explore the pod definition, but you won't see a resources section. Nonetheless, notice that the pod has been scheduled despite not having configured resource requests.

Now, expose the deployment through a service by running this command:

```
$ kubectl expose deployment montecarlo-pi --port=80 --target-port=8080
```

Similar to before, this command creates a Kubernetes service using the default values.

Let's generate some traffic to the application by making a call every 10 milliseconds:

```
$ kubectl run -i --tty load-generator --rm --image=busybox:1.28
--restart=Never -- /bin/sh -c "while sleep 0.01; do wget -q -O- http://
montecarlo-pi/monte-carlo-pi?iterations=10000000; done"
```

This command creates a pod that will terminate once you stop the command. This pod is using a **BusyBox image** to call the service endpoint using the wget command.

As a result, you'll see the output you get after every call to the application. As long as you don't see any type of error, leave that running for about three to five minutes. Then, go back to Grafana and open the **Dashboards** page located at the following URL: http://localhost:3000/dashboards. The Grafana stack you've deployed comes with a default set of dashboards. Let's open the one named **Kubernetes | Compute Resources | Workload**, and change the time range to see the data from the last five minutes.

> **Note**
>
> If the **Kubernetes | Compute Resources | Workload** dashboard is not available in Grafana by default, we have the JSON model in the GitHub repository under /chapter02/grafana/kubernetes_resource_workload.json. To import it, you need to create a new dashboard and import it using a JSON model.

You should see something similar to the following:

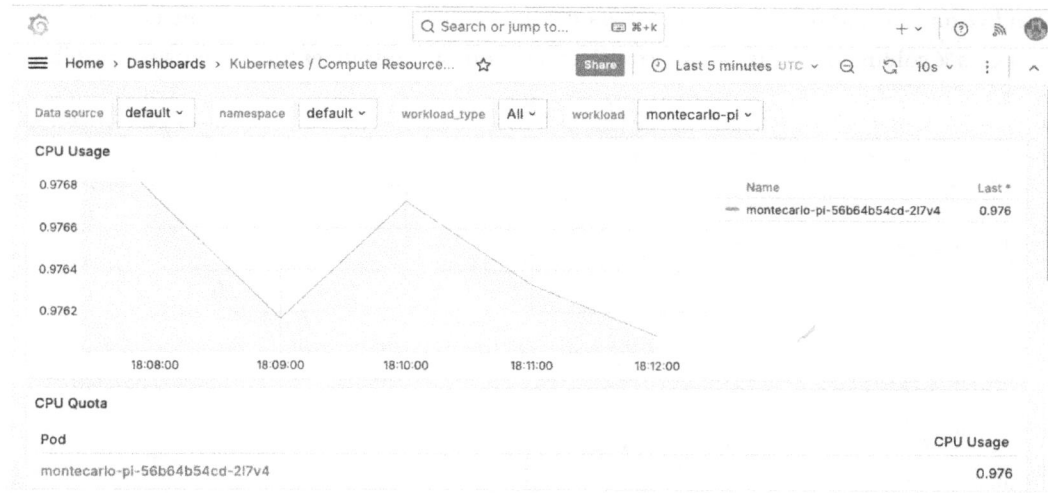

Figure 2.6 – Kubernetes | Compute Resources | Workload dashboard showing the CPU usage

For now, let's focus only on CPU usage. In *Figure 2.6*, you can see that the application is using 976 m of CPU on average. Stop the command (*Ctrl + C*) you had run to generate traffic to the application. You'll see how the CPU usage starts to go down. Now that you have data to support how much CPU your application is using, let's configure proper CPU requests by adding an extra 20% by requesting 1,200 m of CPU. As this might be the maximum usage the pod could have, you're giving some threshold in case there's a traffic spike. Run the following command to adjust the resource requests:

```
$ kubectl patch deployment montecarlo-pi --patch '{"spec": {"template":
{"spec": {"containers": [{"name": "montecarlo-pi", "resources":
{"requests": {"cpu": "1200m"}}}]}}}}'
```

Let's send some traffic again for another three to five minutes:

```
$ kubectl run -i --tty load-generator --rm --image=busybox:1.28
--restart=Never -- /bin/sh -c "while sleep 0.01; do wget -q -O- http://
montecarlo-pi/monte-carlo-pi?iterations=10000000; done"
```

After five minutes, stop the command (*Ctrl + C*), and go back to Grafana. You should now see a **CPU Requests %** column that tells you how much of the requested resources the pod is using, as follows:

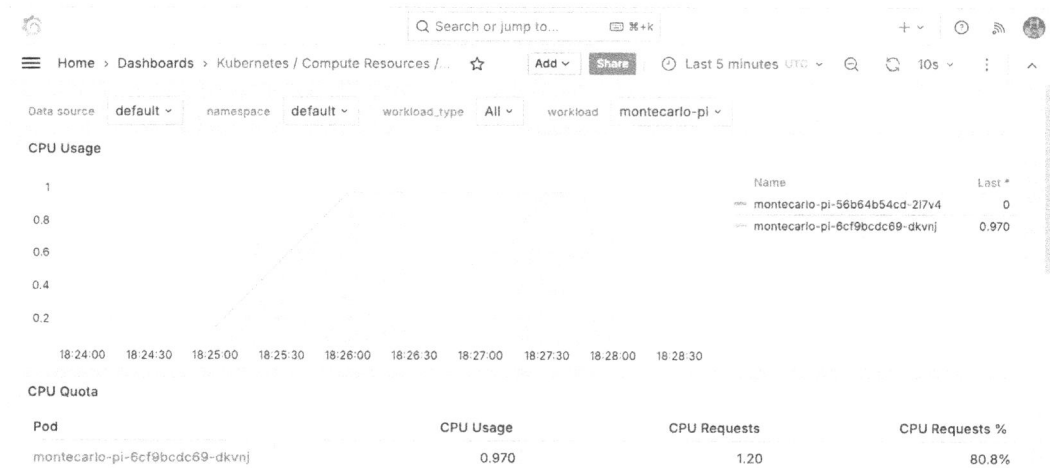

Figure 2.7 – Dashboard showing the CPU used and requested

In this case, we could say that the pod has 80.8% efficiency, which is not a bad number. You could tune in to the requests to achieve a higher or lower percentage, but you need to make sure that by changing these values, you don't affect the application's performance. We'll use this data to later configure effective autoscaling policies.

> **Note**
>
> The previous lab showed you how to manually rightsize a workload, but you might want to explore the Robusta **Kubernetes Resource Recommender (KRR)** project to automate this process a bit more. KRR is an open source command-line tool that analyzes historical resource usage data collected by Prometheus to provide precise recommendations for CPU and memory requests and limits for your pods. Through a visual dashboard, KRR suggest resource values that reflect actual usage patterns. The tool operates externally as a CLI without requiring any additional agents inside your cluster, so you can run it locally or integrate KRR into your CI processes. For more details, you can visit the project's repository on GitHub at `https://github.com/robusta-dev/krr`.

Establishing defaults

As you've seen by now, proper monitoring is crucial for setting up appropriate resource requests and limits configurations to pods. However, for some organizations, this process of rightsizing might take some time to implement properly. Now that you understand the importance of right-sizing, you may want to at least enforce defaults when pods are deployed to Kubernetes without specified request values.

In Kubernetes, you can establish default value configurations for memory and CPU at the name-space level without any third-party tools. Alternatively, if you need more granular control or different mechanisms, you can configure mutating admission webhooks to modify a pod before it reaches the Kubernetes API server and enforce default request values. Tools such as Kyverno, **Open Policy Agent (OPA)**, or Gatekeeper are candidates to consider for this purpose.

Establishing default requests and limits

Kubernetes provides a **LimitRange** object to set default values for requests and/or limits for CPU and memory if a container doesn't specify them. You can also configure minimum and/or maximum values that a container or pod must meet; otherwise, the pod won't be created in that namespace. LimitRange rules apply only to new pods; they don't modify the ones that are already running in the cluster. This also applies if you modify a LimitRange.

Note that even though you configure these values at the namespace level, the constraints or configurations apply to individual pods. If you want to limit the total resources that all pods (aggregated) within a namespace can use, you should use the **ResourceQuota** object instead. A ResourceQuota is an object that sets aggregate resource consumption limits for a namespace, controlling the total amount of CPU, memory, and other resources that can be used by all pods within that namespace.

> **Note**
>
> LimitRange can be configured to enforce storage requests and/or limits values for `PersistentVolumeClaim` as well, but we won't cover that in this book.

Here's an example of a LimitRange policy to set default requests and limits values:

```
apiVersion: v1
kind: LimitRange
metadata:
  name: cpu-defaults
spec:
  limits:
  - default:
      cpu: 1200m
    defaultRequest:
      cpu: 900m
    type: Container
```

With this rule, you're telling Kubernetes that every container in a new pod within this namespace will have default request and limit values if not explicitly specified. If you want to apply this configuration to the pod as a whole rather than individual containers, type should be set to pod. Following what you did in the monitoring section, if you determine that a container is using a maximum of 900m of CPU, you might configure a defaultRequest (requests) value of 900m and a default (limits) value of 1200m.

LimitRange is a good protection mechanism when teams are not yet into the habit of specifying resource requests for every container. However, I'd still recommend setting request values for each container based on measured or expected usage. When you rely only on broad, default values, this can result in overprovisioned nodes and wasted resources. It's not efficient, and it will be costly. Also, consider that if you use LimitRange rules at the pod level, you may lose the ability to fine-tune resource guarantees for individual containers when there are multiple container in a pod.

Let's get hands-on again to learn how to set up default requests for memory and CPU at the namespace level in Kubernetes.

Hands-on lab: Setting up default requests for CPU and memory

Go back to the command line, and let's remove the previous deployment:

```
$ kubectl delete deployment montecarlo-pi
```

Let's create a dedicated namespace to configure default requests for future pods:

```
$ kubectl create namespace montecarlo-pi
```

Next, create a LimitRange rule to configure default requests for CPU and memory:

```
$ cat <<EOF | kubectl apply -f -
apiVersion: v1
kind: LimitRange
metadata:
  name: cpu-memory-requests
  namespace: montecarlo-pi
spec:
  limits:
    - defaultRequest:
        cpu: 900m
        memory: 512Mi
      type: Container
EOF
```

Deploy the same application as in the previous section, the Monte Carlo simulation:

```
$ kubectl create deployment montecarlo-pi --image=christianhxc/montecarlo-pi:latest -n montecarlo-pi
```

You didn't configure any resource requests, but the LimitRange rule should have modified the pods. Inspect the pod created using this command:

```
$ kubectl get pod -n montecarlo-pi -o yaml
```

You should see the pod specification in YAML format, but pay close attention to the `resources` section from the container:

```
...
spec:
  containers:
  - image: christianhxc/montecarlo-pi:latest
    imagePullPolicy: Always
    name: montecarlo-pi
    resources:
      requests:
        cpu: 900m
        memory: 512Mi
...
```

As you can see, the safety mechanism to set up default configuration values has worked effectively. With this in place, you're now ready to configure autoscaling policies for your workloads in a consistent and deterministic manner.

Let's explore a few options you have for scaling your applications.

Workload autoscalers

The reason I've been discussing how kube-scheduler works and emphasizing the importance of configuring proper request values is to lay the groundwork for setting up scaling policies based on accurate data. This approach will help your workloads become more efficient, reducing waste without compromising application performance.

As mentioned earlier, this book will focus on three key workload autoscalers: HPA, VPA, and KEDA. I'll introduce each by explaining their purpose, the problems they solve, and how they might be used in combination. In the following chapters, we'll dive deeper into the details of how to implement and optimize these autoscalers, ensuring you can leverage their full potential.

HorizontalpodAutoscaler (HPA)

HPA is often the starting point, and sometimes the only option people use for autoscaling their workloads. It's simple and a native resource of Kubernetes. HPA has been an integral part of the ecosystem since its introduction in Kubernetes 1.1. Developed by the Kubernetes community, HPA addresses the challenge of managing fluctuating workloads running in Kubernetes. It automatically adjusts the number of pod replicas (horizontal scaling) for compatible Kubernetes objects such as **Deployments**, **ReplicaSets**, and **StatefulSets**.

HPA's primary purpose is to solve the problem of efficiently scaling applications in response to varying demand. It does this by monitoring specified metrics and adjusting the number of replicas accordingly. While CPU utilization is the default metric, HPA can also work with memory usage, custom metrics, and even external metrics. These metrics are sourced from various components within the Kubernetes ecosystem. **Metrics Server** provides CPU and memory data, while systems such as Prometheus can supply custom metrics. For more complex scenarios, external monitoring systems can feed metrics into HPA.

To illustrate HPA's functionality, consider a web application such as the Monte Carlo simulation we've been using, experiencing varying traffic throughout the day. HPA can be configured to maintain an average CPU utilization of 70% across all pods. As shown in *Figure 2.5*, as traffic increases and CPU usage rises above this threshold, HPA will automatically increase the number of pod replicas.

Conversely, during periods of low traffic, it will scale down the number of replicas, optimizing resource usage and potentially reducing costs.

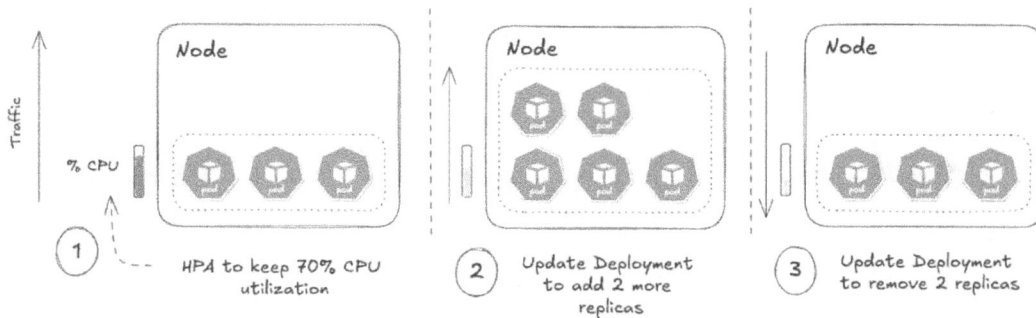

Figure 2.8 – HPA scaling out based on CPU utilization

HPA efficiently manages the number of pod replicas but doesn't adjust resources for individual pods nor containers. When it comes to adjusting resources allocated to individual pods, HPA isn't the solution. For this type of scaling, we have VPA.

VerticalpodAutoscaler (VPA)

VPA is designed to automatically adjust the CPU and memory resources allocated to containers in pods. Unlike its horizontal counterpart HPA, VPA focuses on optimizing the resource requests and limits of individual containers, rather than scaling the number of pod replicas. VPA was introduced by Google in 2018 as part of their efforts to enhance Kubernetes' autoscaling capabilities. While it's not a native Kubernetes resource like HPA, VPA has become part of many Kubernetes deployments due to its ability to fine-tune resource allocation.

VPA can be applied to various Kubernetes objects, including `Deployments`, `ReplicaSets`, `StatefulSets`, `DaemonSets`, and even individual pods. VPA addresses the common problem of over- or under-provisioning resources, which can lead to either wasted cluster capacity or performance issues. To make its scaling decisions, VPA relies on historical and current resource usage metrics. It primarily focuses on CPU and memory utilization, gathering this data from Metrics Server.

Consider a scenario with a large, legacy monolithic application or a complex database system that's challenging to scale horizontally due to intricate internal dependencies or stateful components. In *Figure 2.6*, as the data grows, its resource needs increase. VPA would continuously monitor this application's resource usage to recommend or adjust its requests accordingly.

Conversively, if it determines that the system is consistently using less resources, it can recommend or automatically apply lower resource requests.

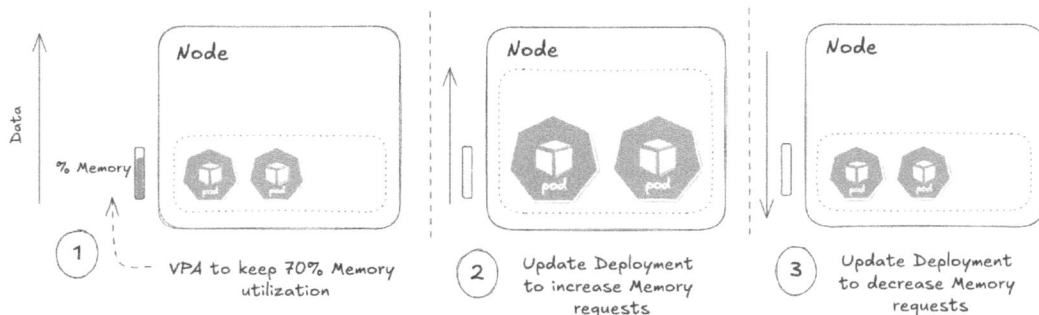

Figure 2.9 – VPA scaling up based on CPU utilization

When VPA needs to adjust the resources for a pod, it typically does so by deleting the existing pod and creating a new one with the updated resource specifications. This process can lead to a brief period of downtime for that specific pod. Additionally, even though VPA can work alongside HPA, they should be used carefully when combined, as their actions can potentially conflict. We'll address these concerns in the next chapter.

Kubernetes Event-driven Autoscaling (KEDA)

HPA provides a solid foundation for autoscaling in Kubernetes, but relying solely on CPU and memory metrics may not capture the full picture of how an application performs under varying loads. Certainly, HPA can use custom metrics, but this might increase complexity when configuring scaling policies. This is where KEDA comes into play, offering a flexible but simple approach to scaling.

KEDA is an open source project that was initially developed by Microsoft and Red Hat in 2019. Although it's not a native Kubernetes resource, KEDA has gained significant traction in the community due to its versatility and power. It extends Kubernetes' autoscaling capabilities beyond traditional resource metrics, allowing for scaling based on event sources and custom metrics.

Similarly to the other autoscalers, KEDA can be applied to various Kubernetes objects, including `Deployments`, `StatefulSets`, and `custom resources`. Its primary purpose is to scale applications based on events and application-specific metrics, rather than just system-level resource utilization. This makes KEDA particularly useful for event-driven architectures, microservices, and applications with unpredictable or bursty workloads.

One of KEDA's key differantiators is its ability to use a wide range of metrics for scaling decisions. Unlike HPA, which primarily focuses on CPU and memory, KEDA can scale based on metrics from various sources, such as message queues, databases, streaming platforms, and other external systems. This allows for more nuanced and application-aware scaling decisions.

For example, as per *Figure 2.10*, consider a microservice that processes orders from a message queue:

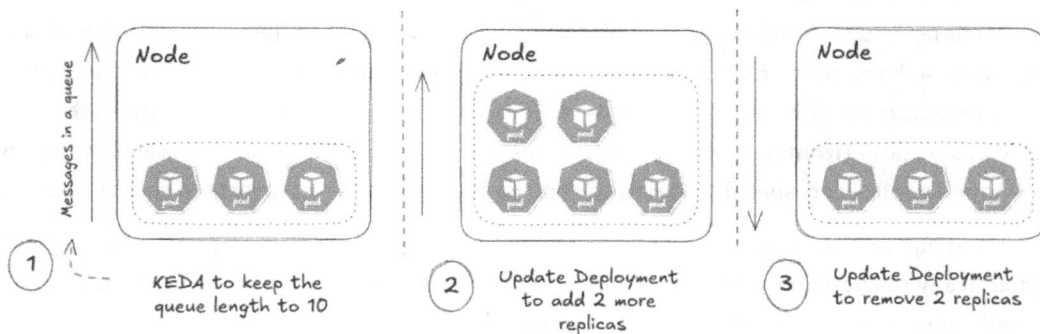

Figure 2.10 – KEDA scaling out based on latency

As evident in the figure, with KEDA, you could scale this service based on the number of messages in the queue. As the queue length grows, KEDA would automatically scale up the number of pods to process orders more quickly. When the queue empties, it would scale back down, optimizing resource usage.

KEDA is not without its limitations. You might find that a specific connector you need isn't available, or conversely, you might feel overwhelmed by the sheer number of connectors to choose from. It's worth noting, though, that the KEDA maintainers team is addressing quality concerns by requiring any new connector to implement automated test suites, ensuring reliability and consistency across the growing ecosystem of scalers

That's all for the basics of Kubernetes workload autoscalers. Each has its strengths, and knowing when to use HPA, VPA, or KEDA can make a big difference in how your workloads perform. We will dive deeper into these tools in the following chapters, and you will see how you can use them to automatically scale your workloads to begin having an efficient Kubernetes cluster.

Summary

In this chapter, we've explored the fundamental concepts of workload autoscaling in Kubernetes, emphasizing the importance of efficient resource management and the challenges that come with it. We've seen how proper monitoring and rightsizing are crucial for optimizing your cluster's performance and cost-efficiency.

We introduced three key autoscaling mechanisms: HPA, VPA, and KEDA. Each of these tools addresses different aspects of the autoscaling challenge. HPA focuses on adjusting the number of pod replicas based primarily on CPU and memory metrics. VPA complements this by fine-tuning the resource allocation within individual pods, which is particularly useful for applications that are difficult to scale horizontally. KEDA extends these capabilities further by enabling scaling based on events and application-specific metrics, offering more granular control over your scaling policies.

By leveraging the right combination of these tools, you can ensure that your applications respond dynamically to changing workloads while optimizing resource utilization. In the next chapter, we will delve deeper into implementing HPA and VPA.

Get This Book's PDF Version and Exclusive Extras

UNLOCK NOW

Scan the QR code (or go to packtpub.com/unlock).
Search for this book by name, confirm the edition, and then follow the steps on the page.

Note: *Keep your invoice handy. Purchases made directly from Packt don't require one.*

3

Workload Autoscaling with HPA and VPA

After exploring the workload autoscaling fundamentals in Kubernetes, it's time to turn our attention to two of the primary autoscaling mechanisms: the **Horizontal Pod Autoscaler (HPA)** and the **Vertical Pod Autoscaler (VPA)**. This chapter will provide an in-depth look at HPA and VPA, expanding on the foundational concepts we've already discussed. We'll start by diving deep into HPA, examining its basic functionality and its integration with the Kubernetes Metrics Server.

Through hands-on exercises, you'll learn how to implement scaling using both basic and custom metrics with HPA. We'll cover best practices for configuring autoscaling policies with HPA. Next, we'll shift the focus to VPA. We'll break down how it works and the different ways you can use it. You'll gain practical experience in implementing automatic vertical scaling and leveraging VPA's recommender mode for rightsizing your applications.

As we progress, we'll see how HPA and VPA can work together to keep your workloads running smoothly and efficiently, demonstrating how these tools can be combined to achieve continuous workload efficiency.

By the end of this chapter, you'll have a thorough understanding of HPA and VPA, their configuration options, and best practices for implementation. This deep dive into these two critical autoscaling tools will set the stage for KEDA in the subsequent chapter, further expanding your workload autoscaling capabilities in Kubernetes.

In this chapter, we'll cover the following topics:

- The Kubernetes Metrics Server
- HPA basics
- HPA custom metrics
- VPA basics
- How to work with HPA and VPA together

Technical requirements

For this chapter, you'll continue using the Kubernetes cluster you created in *Chapter 1*. You can continue working with the local Kubernetes cluster. If you turned down the cluster, make sure you bring it up for every hands-on lab in this chapter. You don't need to install any additional tools, as most of the commands are going to be run using kubectl and helm. You can find the YAML manifests for all resources you're going to create in this chapter in the chapter03 folder from the book's GitHub repository you already cloned in *Chapter 1*.

The Kubernetes Metrics Server

Before diving into the details of how to use HPA, let me cover a crucial component: the Kubernetes Metrics Server. In the previous chapter, I explored the use of Prometheus and Grafana for rightsizing pods based on historical usage patterns. However, HPA, by default, utilizes a different source of metrics to determine when to scale pod replicas.

The Metrics Server plays a crucial role in this process, providing real-time resource utilization data that HPA relies on for making scaling decisions. It serves as the primary source of container resource metrics for Kubernetes' autoscaling mechanisms.

In the following sections, I'll cover the *what* and *why* of the Metrics Server in detail, discussing its purpose, importance, and implementation within a Kubernetes cluster.

The Metrics Server: The what and the why

The Kubernetes Metrics Server is a cluster-wide aggregator of resource usage data. While not a built-in component of Kubernetes, it's a crucial add-on that collects and aggregates essential metrics about the resource consumption of nodes and pods in a cluster. The Metrics Server is designed to support Kubernetes' built-in autoscaling mechanisms. It focuses solely on gathering CPU and memory usage for nodes and pods, making it a lean and purpose-built tool.

As shown in *Figure 3.1*, the Metrics Server operates by collecting resource metrics from the kubelet on each node. It aggregates this data and makes it available through the Kubernetes Metrics API. The process begins with the kubelet collecting resource usage statistics via its **cAdvisor** integration. The Metrics Server then queries each node's kubelet for this data every 15 seconds by default. After aggregating the data, it exposes it through the Metrics API, allowing Kubernetes components such as HPA to query for up-to-date metrics.

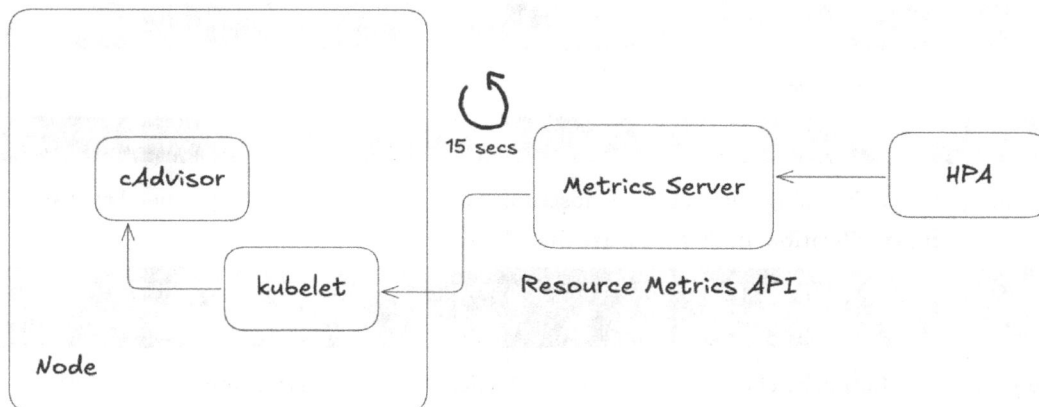

Figure 3.1 – How HPA collects metrics for CPU and memory from the applications

As you've seen, the Metrics Server only provides the current state of resource usage, not historical data. Its focus is solely on CPU and memory metrics, and the data is stored in memory rather than persisted to disk. The Metrics Server is solely used for autoscaling your workloads. For monitoring needs, solutions such as Prometheus, or any other paid solution, will serve you better. You can even use Prometheus as a source for scaling using custom metrics. I'll cover this later in this chapter.

Now that you have a better understanding of the Metrics Server and why it's important, let's set it up in a Kubernetes cluster.

Hands-on lab: Setting up the Metrics Server

> **Note**
>
> If you're using the Kubernetes cluster in AWS created using the Terraform templates in *Chapter 1*, you can skip this section, as the Metrics Server comes pre-installed in the Terraform blueprint I've provided for the book.

To install the Metrics Server using Helm, follow these steps.

Add the official Metrics Server Helm repository:

```
$ helm repo add metrics-server https://kubernetes-sigs.github.io/metrics-
server/
```

Update your Helm repository cache:

```
$ helm repo update
```

Install the Metrics Server:

```
$ helm install metrics-server metrics-server/metrics-server
```

Optionally, if you're using a local or self-hosted Kubernetes cluster, you might need to disable TLS certificate verification. In this case, use the following command instead:

```
$ helm install metrics-server metrics-server/metrics-server --set args="{-
-kubelet-insecure-tls}"
```

Verify the installation by checking whether the Metrics Server pod is running:

```
$ kubectl get pods -n kube-system | grep metrics-server
```

Once these steps are completed, your Metrics Server should be up and running. You can verify that this pod is properly configured with CPU (100m) and memory (200Mi) requests. While you can adjust this configuration if needed, these default settings should provide good performance for most clusters with up to 100 nodes.

Hands-on lab: Using the Metrics Server

Once you have this add-on installed, HPA and VPA will use it behind the scenes. It will also expose some of the data it collects through the kubectl top command. This command allows you to see how many resources either nodes or pods are consuming.

For instance, let's view the resource usage of all the nodes in your cluster with the following:

```
$ kubectl top nodes
```

You should see an output similar to this (depending on how many nodes):

```
NAME          CPU(cores)   CPU%   MEMORY(bytes)   MEMORY%
ip-10-0-...   1676m        42%    1691Mi          11%
ip-10-0-...   2402m        61%    3209Mi          21%
```

As you can see, it's a much simpler version of the top command in Linux, typically used for monitoring purposes. It only shows you the CPU millicores and memory bytes each node has, and what percentage of those resources are being used at the moment you ran the command.

You can also see the resource usage for all the pods in a given namespace:

```
$ kubectl top pods -n default
```

You should see an output similar to this (depending on which pods you have running):

```
NAME                              CPU(cores)   MEMORY(bytes)
montecarlo-pi-5d9d967b77-hh87b    14m          36Mi
```

Notice that for pods, it only shows you the usage numbers, not the percentage. But that's sufficient for HPA and VPA. Remember, this command and the Metrics Server shouldn't be used as a monitoring tool. However, for a quick status overview, it's adequate.

If you want to learn more about other options, such as sorting or filtering resources, you can add the --help flag to each command.

Now that you have the Metrics Server working, let's get into the details of how to configure autoscaling policies with HPA and VPA.

HPA basics

I introduced you to HPA in the previous chapter. The main job of HPA is to handle dynamic workloads by *automatically adjusting the number of pod replicas based on demand to a Deployment, a StatefulSet, or any resource that implements the scale subresource.* HPA typically looks at CPU or memory usage to make its decisions, but it's not limited to just those metrics. It can also work with custom metrics or external data, but I'll cover this later in this chapter. So, how does HPA make the decision to either add or remove pods, or simply not act? Let's see.

How HPA scales resources

HPA operates on a feedback loop, using a simple calculation to determine the number of replicas needed. Let's say you have a Deployment targeting 70% CPU utilization across all its pods. The process begins with HPA querying the Metrics Server (typically every 15 seconds) to get the current CPU utilization for all pods in the target Deployment. It then calculates the average CPU utilization across these pods.

HPA uses the following formula to determine the desired number of replicas:

```
desiredReplicas = ceil[currentReplicas * (currentMetricValue /
desiredMetricValue)]
```

Following the 70% CPU target example, if the current average CPU utilization (currentMetricValue) is 80% and we have 5 replicas, HPA would scale out to 6 replicas:

```
desiredReplicas = ceil[5 * (80 / 70)] = 6
```

If the current utilization then drops to 60%, HPA would go back to 5 replicas:

```
desiredReplicas = ceil[5 * (60 / 70)] = 5
```

When you're using multiple metrics, the desiredReplicas calculation is done for each metric, and the largest number is chosen. Keep this in mind, as this will become an important aspect in *Chapter 5*. It's important to note that HPA has a tolerance (default 0.1 or 10%) to prevent unnecessary scaling for minor fluctuations. If the ratio of currentMetricValue to desiredMetricValue is between 0.9 and 1.1, HPA won't initiate any scaling action.

After determining the desiredReplicas value, HPA updates the replica count on the Deployment object. Kubernetes then creates or removes pods to match this new desired state. This feedback loop continues indefinitely, allowing your application to automatically adjust to changing load conditions. However, to prevent rapid fluctuations, HPA typically observes a cooldown period (default is 5 minutes) after each scaling action before performing another.

Defining HPA scaling policies

To define an autoscaling policy with HPA, you need to create a Kubernetes object of the HorizontalPodAutoscaler kind. The current API version for this resource is autoscaling/v2. The following is an example of the simplified YAML manifest for an HPA object, which we'll break down and explain in detail:

```
apiVersion: autoscaling/v2
kind: HorizontalPodAutoscaler
metadata:
  name: cpu-usage-70
spec:
  scaleTargetRef:
    apiVersion: apps/v1
    kind: Deployment
    name: montecarlo-pi
```

```
    minReplicas: 1
    maxReplicas: 10
    metrics:
    - type: Resource
      resource:
        name: cpu
        target:
          type: Utilization
          averageUtilization: 70
    behavior:
      scaleDown:
        ...
      scaleUp:
        ...
```

Let's break down the key fields:

- `scaleTargetRef`: Specifies the target resource to scale, such as a Deployment
- `minReplicas`: Defines the lower bound for the number of replicas
- `maxReplicas`: Defines the upper bound for the number of replicas
- `metrics`: Specifies the metric(s) to use for scaling, such as CPU utilization
- `behavior`: Defines policies for scaling up and down to prevent rapid fluctuations

While using YAML manifests is recommended for **Infrastructure as Code (IaC)** practices, you can also create an HPA rule using kubectl. Here's an example command:

```
$ kubectl autoscale deployment montecarlo-pi --cpu-percent=70 --min=1
--max=10
```

This command creates an HPA rule for the `montecarlo-pi` deployment, targeting 70% CPU utilization, with a minimum of 1 replica and a maximum of 10. It's exactly the same as the YAML manifest you reviewed before.

Hands-on lab: Scaling using basic metrics with HPA

Let's put into practice what we've learned so far. Grab your computer and open the CLI.

We're going to use **ApacheBench (ab)**, a benchmarking tool from Apache, to send load to the application. You don't need to install this tool locally as we're going to run it within the Kubernetes cluster.

To have an almost real-time visibility of what's happening while you see HPA in action, we're going to use the watch command. This comes natively on Linux, but if you're using macOS or Windows, you need to install watch. In macOS, you simply need to run brew install watch. In Windows, use the **Windows Subsystem for Linux (WSL)** or install it using choco install watch.

Go to the book's GitHub repository folder that you've already cloned, and change to the chapter03 directory. In case you haven't done it, run these commands:

```
$ git clone https://github.com/PacktPublishing/Kubernetes-Autoscaling.git
$ cd Kubernetes-Autoscaling/chapter03
```

Deploy the sample application

Run the following command to deploy the sample application we're going to use:

```
$ kubectl apply -f hpa-basic/montecarlopi.yaml
```

It's the same application as before, but this time it comes with the CPU and memory requests configured, as you learned already how important it is. Make sure the application is working by running the following command:

```
$ kubectl port-forward svc/montecarlo-pi 8080:80
```

Open the following URL in a browser:

```
http://localhost:8080/monte-carlo-pi?iterations=100000
```

You should see an estimated value of Pi, meaning that the application is working. You can close the port-forward command as it's not needed anymore. We're going to use ab to send load to the application.

Create the HPA autoscaling policy

Now that the application is running, before you send some load to see autoscaling in action, let's create the autoscaling policy. Run this command:

```
$ kubectl apply -f hpa-basic/hpa.yaml
```

I'm not including the YAML manifest definition here as it's the same we explored before, but please open it and confirm that it's an HPA rule for the montecarlo-pi deployment, targeting 70% CPU utilization, with a range of 1 to 10 replicas. It doesn't have a scaling behavior configured yet, so it's relying on defaults for that section.

Confirm that the HPA rule is there with this command:

```
$ kubectl get hpa
```

You should see an output similar to this:

```
NAME      REFERENCE   TARGETS      MINPODS  MAXPODS  REPLICAS  AGE
mont...   Deploy...   cpu: 0%/70%  1        10       1         41s
```

Look at the TARGETS column; it's using 0% of CPU initially. It might take 15 seconds until you see a number, so you might need to run the command again to see it.

Run load tests

By now, you have everything you need to scale your application automatically. So, let's send some load to see HPA in action. To do so, you have two options. The first one is to expose the application or use port-forward, then run ab locally. But a simpler option is to run ab within Kubernetes. Let's go with that option.

In the chapter03 folder, there's already a YAML manifest to create a Kubernetes Job that uses a container image with ab preinstalled, and it's configured to send load to the montecarlo-pi Service. Explore the YAML file, and you'll see that it's running this command:

```
ab -n 10000 -c 10 -t 150 http://montecarlo-pi/monte-carlo-
pi?iterations=100000
```

This command means that ab is going to send 10,000 requests with 10 concurrent calls, and it will run for a maximum of 150 seconds. When ab finishes, you'll get a report of how it went; we'll explore that later.

So, run the following command to deploy the ab loadtest:

```
$ kubectl apply -f ab-k8s/loadtest.yaml
```

Watch autoscaling working

Open four additional terminals with the following commands. In the first one, you're going to watch the CPU usage of all the pods by running this command:

```
$ watch kubectl top pods
```

In the second one, you're going to watch all the pods running in the cluster:

```
$ watch kubectl get pods
```

In the third one, you're going to watch ab logs:

```
$ kubectl logs job/montecarlo-pi-load-test -f
```

In the fourth one, you're going to watch the HPA scaling rule:

```
$ kubectl get hpa
```

Pay close attention to what's happening in these three new terminals. Little by little, you'll see that the CPU usage of the application is going up (around 3000 m), and HPA is going to start changing the Deployment replicas to maintain a target CPU usage of 70%.

Notice what HPA is saying initially on the TARGETS column. As ab is sending the load all at once, the CPU of the single replica is going to have a minimum of 3000 m usage, and HPA is going to say that it's 324% usage, way more than the 70% target.

However, you might see that HPA is taking a while to scale up. Why? Remember that HPA relies on the Metrics Server, which collects data every 15–30 seconds, and HPA also has its own check interval of 15 seconds by default. HPA's scaling algorithm is designed to prevent rapid fluctuations, potentially waiting to confirm persistent load increases before initiating scaling actions.

If you want to speed up the scaling-up process, you can change its behavior to this:

```
apiVersion: autoscaling/v2beta2
kind: HorizontalPodAutoscaler
metadata:
  name: montecarlo-pi-hpa
spec:
  # ... other fields ...
  behavior:
    scaleUp:
      stabilizationWindowSeconds: 0
      policies:
      - type: Percent
        value: 100
        periodSeconds: 15
```

This configuration removes the stabilization window for scaling up and allows a 100% increase every 15 seconds.

To scale down the replicas, HPA takes way more time. Why? HPA uses a 5-minute window (by default) to calculate the desired number of replicas for scaling down. Scaling down too quickly could lead to service disruptions if traffic suddenly increases again.

If you want to speed up the scaling down process, you can change its behavior to this:

```
apiVersion: autoscaling/v2beta1
kind: HorizontalPodAutoscaler
metadata:
  name: montecarlo-pi-hpa
spec:
  # ... other fields ...
  behavior:
    scaleDown:
      stabilizationWindowSeconds: 60  # 1m instead of 5m
      policies:
      - type: Percent
        value: 100
        periodSeconds: 15
```

Similar to the scale-up configuration, this configuration allows a 100% decrease every 15 seconds, but the stabilization window for scaling down is 60 seconds instead of 5 minutes.

Let's repeat the testing with the preceding HPA configuration changes to see the application scaling up much faster and scaling down moderately faster. Remove the ab job first:

```
$ kubectl delete -f ab-k8s
```

Then, deploy the new HPA version. You'll find the YAML manifest in the hpa.fast.yaml file, which is essentially the same as you had before, but with the behavior section. Please explore it, and then run the following command to update it:

```
$ kubectl apply -f hpa-basic/hpa.fast.yaml
```

Run the ab job to start over with the load tests:

```
$ kubectl apply -f ab-k8s/loadtest.yaml
```

Now, watch the four terminals you opened earlier to monitor the pods and HPA. You should see that pods are scaling up and down much faster than before, and the CPU usage is reaching its target much quicker, too. It's important to run these types of tests to adjust the scaling speed to your specific needs.

To clean up the environment after this hands-on lab, run these commands:

```
$ kubectl delete -f ab-k8s
$ kubectl delete -f hpa-basic
```

Now that you've seen how HPA works with CPU-based scaling, let's go a step further. CPU and memory are useful, but they don't always tell the whole story. What if your app needs to scale based on how many requests it's receiving, how long a queue is, or even business-specific metrics such as active sessions?

In the next section, we'll explore how to extend HPA to use custom metrics for a more tailored scaling decision.

HPA and custom metrics

You now know the basics of using HPA with CPU and memory metrics. But these two metrics may not always capture the full picture of your application's scaling needs. For some applications, scaling behavior might be better determined by other metrics such as latency, number of requests, or queue length.

But how can HPA scale using other metrics? By either using customer or external metrics. Kubernetes offers the Metrics API, and it provides access to HPA to use different types of metrics through APIs, such as the following:

- **Resource Metrics API**: This is the core API that provides CPU and memory usage for pods and nodes, and it's primarily used by HPA, as you've seen before in *Figure 3.1*.

- **Custom Metrics API**: This allows for the exposure of application-specific metrics. It's extensible, enabling you to define and use metrics that are tailored to your specific applications. We're going to see this in action later in this chapter.

- **External Metrics API**: This provides access to metrics from sources outside the cluster, such as cloud provider metrics. This API is not covered in this book.

The Metrics API acts as an abstraction layer, providing a standardized way for Kubernetes components to request and receive metric data, regardless of the underlying metrics collection system, as you explored already with HPA using the metrics provided by the Metrics Server. This abstraction is what allows Kubernetes to work with various monitoring solutions, including Prometheus, without needing to understand the specifics of each system.

We've explored how to use the Resources Metrics API already and feed it with the Metrics Server component. Now, we'll explore how to make HPA use the Custom Metrics API. In this book, we'll cover how HPA can use the External Metrics API using the **Kubernetes Event-Driven Autoscaling (KEDA)** project in *Chapter 4*.

How does HPA work with custom metrics?

For HPA to use custom metrics, you need two key components:

- A way to collect and store these metrics
- An adapter that can expose these metrics through the Custom Metrics API

You might be able to achieve this with your existing monitoring system. As shown in *Figure 3.2*, a common approach involves integrating Prometheus with the **Prometheus Adapter**. In this setup, Prometheus serves as the metrics collector and storage solution. The Prometheus Adapter then acts as a bridge, implementing the Custom Metrics API and exposing the data collected by Prometheus through this standardized interface. This combination allows HPA to make scaling decisions based on a custom set of metrics different from CPU and memory, such as latency or number of requests.

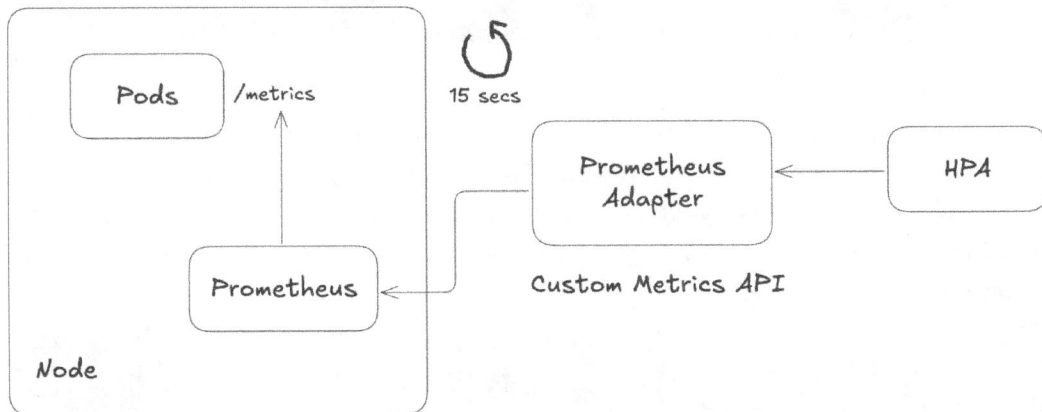

Figure 3.2 – How HPA collects custom from Prometheus

Let's get into the details of what you saw in *Figure 3.2* flow. The Prometheus Adapter registers itself with the Kubernetes API server as an API Service. This registration informs Kubernetes that the adapter can handle requests for custom metrics. The adapter is then configured with rules that define how to translate Prometheus metrics into Kubernetes custom metrics, specifying which Prometheus metrics to expose and how to name them in the Kubernetes API.

When HPA requests a metric, the API server forwards this request to the Prometheus Adapter. The adapter translates this into a Prometheus query, executes it against the Prometheus server, and then translates the results back into the format expected by Kubernetes.

The adapter exposes these metrics at an API endpoint that follows the Kubernetes Custom Metrics API format. For example, a metric might be accessible at a path such as `/apis/custom.metrics.k8s.io/v1beta1/namespaces/default/pods/*/monte_carlo_latency_seconds`. HPA can then be configured to use these custom metrics in its scaling decisions. Let's see that in action.

Hands-on lab: Scaling using custom metrics with HPA

Before you get started, make sure to have the Prometheus stack running. You already did this in the previous chapter, but just in case you need to install the stack again, here's the command to do it:

```
$ helm upgrade --install prometheus prometheus-community/kube-prometheus-stack \
  --namespace monitoring \
  --create-namespace
```

Confirm that all the pods are running using this command:

```
$ kubectl get pods -n monitoring
```

Deploy the Prometheus Adapter

As you can see, this stack doesn't come with the Prometheus Adapter; you need to install it separately. Go to the `chapter03` folder from the book's GitHub repository. Here, you can find the `prometheus-adapter/values.yaml` file with the configuration you need to use the Prometheus service to collect metrics, and the query to expose the custom metrics from the application. Now, simply run the following command:

```
$ helm install prometheus-adapter prometheus-community/prometheus-adapter \
  --namespace monitoring \
  -f prometheus-adapter/values.yaml
```

Explore the configuration from the `values.yaml` file. It instructs the Prometheus Adapter to look for histogram metrics named `monte_carlo_latency_seconds_bucket` with a non-empty namespace and pod labels. It then transforms these metrics into a custom Kubernetes metric named `monte_carlo_latency_seconds`, calculating the 95th percentile of the latency over a 2-minute window using the `histogram_quantile` function. This allows HPA to use this derived latency metric for scaling decisions, based on the recent performance of your Monte Carlo simulation pods.

Explore the application source code at chapter02/src/main.go, where it's using the Prometheus client library to expose the monte_carlo_latency_seconds metric using a histogram to track the latency using monteCarloLatency.Observe(duration.Seconds()). This approach is chosen because Prometheus scrapes these metrics every 15 seconds, and you don't want to lose data points since the last time Prometheus scraped.

> **Note**
>
> We're adding this additional code so that you can see how to instrument an application to expose metrics. However, if you look closely at the /metrics endpoint, you'll find the http_request_duration_seconds_bucket metric that serves a similar purpose to the one we added. This is because the promhttp library already exposes a common set of metrics.

Deploy the sample application

Go back to the chapter03 folder, and redeploy the Monte Carlo application:

```
$ kubectl apply -f hpa-custom/montecarlopi.yaml
```

Make sure the application is working by running the following command:

```
$ kubectl port-forward svc/montecarlo-pi 8080:80
```

Open the following URL in a browser:

```
http://localhost:8080/monte-carlo-pi?iterations=100000
```

Then, try the /metrics endpoint:

```
http://localhost:8080/metrics
```

You'll see an output similar to this one:

```
# TYPE monte_carlo_latency_seconds histogram
monte_carlo_latency_seconds_bucket{le="0.001"} 0
monte_carlo_latency_seconds_bucket{le="0.005"} 1
monte_carlo_latency_seconds_bucket{le="0.01"} 1
...
monte_carlo_latency_seconds_count 11
```

Deploy the Service monitor

You now need a way to tell Prometheus to scrape the metrics from the application. To do so, you need to create ServiceMonitor, a custom resource definition where you configure which Service endpoint to scrape. The manifest definition is like this:

```
apiVersion: monitoring.coreos.com/v1
kind: ServiceMonitor
metadata:
  name: montecarlo-pi
  labels:
    app: montecarlo-pi
    release: prometheus
spec:
  selector:
    matchLabels:
      app: montecarlo-pi
  endpoints:
  - port: http
```

Deploy the Service monitor using the following command:

```
$ kubectl apply -f hpa-custom/monitor.yaml
```

Wait around 30 seconds to confirm you can see the new custom metric:

```
$ kubectl get --raw "/apis/custom.metrics.k8s.io/v1beta1/namespaces/
default/pods/*/monte_carlo_latency_seconds"
```

You should see an output similar to this one:

```
{
  "kind": "MetricValueList",
  "apiVersion": "custom.metrics.k8s.io/v1beta1",
  "metadata": {},
  "items": [
    {
      "describedObject": {
        "kind": "pod",
        "namespace": "default",
        "name": "montecarlo-pi-574cc7ff9f-h77wp",
```

```
      "apiVersion": "/v1"
    },
    "metricName": "monte_carlo_latency_seconds",
    "timestamp": "2024-10-08T20:57:08Z",
    "value": "0",
    "selector": null
  }
]
}
```

You might not see any value yet, but that's fine; you'll generate some load later.

Create the HPA autoscaling policy

You're going to deploy the following HPA rule to use the application custom metric:

```yaml
apiVersion: autoscaling/v2
kind: HorizontalPodAutoscaler
metadata:
  name: montecarlo-pi-latency-hpa
spec:
  scaleTargetRef:
    apiVersion: apps/v1
    kind: Deployment
    name: montecarlo-pi
  minReplicas: 1
  maxReplicas: 10
  metrics:
  - type: Pods
    pods:
      metric:
        name: monte_carlo_latency_seconds
      target:
        type: AverageValue
        averageValue: 500m
```

This HPA rule is configured to automatically scale the application based on the `monte_carlo_latency_seconds` custom metric. It aims to maintain an average latency of 500 milliseconds (`500m`) across all pods, scaling between 1 and 10 replicas as needed. The rule uses the `Pods` metric type and the `AverageValue` target type, indicating it's working with a per-pod metric and trying to keep the average value across all pods at or below the specified threshold.

Run load tests and see HPA in action

Run the following command to send some load to the application for a few minutes:

```
$ kubectl apply -f ab-k8s/loadtest.yaml
```

Open three additional terminals with the following commands. In the first one, you're going to watch the CPU usage of all the pods by running this command:

```
$ watch kubectl top pods
```

In the second one, you're going to watch all the pods running in the cluster:

```
$ watch kubectl get pods
```

In the third one, you're going to watch the HPA scaling rule:

```
$ kubectl get hpa
```

Little by little, you'll see that the CPU usage of the application is going up, but not more than `1200m`, contrary to what you saw in the previous hands-on lab. This is because the new version of the Deployment has limits configured, like this:

```
resources:
  requests:
    cpu: 900m
    memory: 512Mi
  limits:
    cpu: 1200m
    memory: 512Mi
```

This means that Kubernetes won't let the pods consume more than `1200m`; instead, Kubernetes will start throttling the container. Therefore, the latency will go up, and that's the reason why you see HPA changing the Deployment replicas to maintain a target latency of `500m`. As before, when the latency goes back to `0m`, HPA will start removing replicas. You can speed up this process in the same way you did in the previous lab.

To clean up the environment after this hands-on lab, run these commands:

```
$ kubectl delete -f ab-k8s
$ kubectl delete -f hpa-custom
```

So far, you've explored how HPA can scale your application horizontally by adding more replicas based on resource usage or even custom metrics such as latency. But what if scaling out isn't the best option? Some workloads might benefit more from having bigger pods rather than more pods, even if it's temporary, while you make your workload scale horizontally.

In the next section, we'll dive into VPA, a tool that helps you rightsize your pods by adjusting CPU and memory requests and limits. Unlike HPA, it focuses on optimizing the size of each pod instead of increasing the number of replicas. Let's take a closer look at how it works and when you should consider using it.

VPA basics

I introduced you to VPA in the previous chapter. Its primary function is to analyze and adjust (or provide recommendations for) the CPU and memory requirements of containers running in a pod. VPA doesn't add more replicas; it simply adjusts (or recommends) the size of a pod. VPA can be applied to vertically scale various Kubernetes objects, including *Deployments*, *ReplicaSets*, *StatefulSets*, and even individual pods. So, how does VPA make the decision to adjust the size of containers in a pod? Let's see.

How VPA scales resources

VPA works with three different controllers that you deploy in the cluster:

- **Recommender**: This controller continuously monitors the resource usage of pods and containers, analyzing historical data to generate optimal resource recommendations. Then, it calculates the ideal CPU and memory requests for each container, taking into account factors such as usage patterns, application behavior, and defined constraints.

- **Updater**: This controller is responsible for applying the recommendations generated by the Recommender. It decides when and how to update the resource requests of running pods. Depending on the VPA mode (`Auto`, `Recreate`, or `Initial`), the Updater may evict pods to apply new resource settings or wait for pods to be naturally recreated during deployments or restarts.

- **Admission Controller**: This controller intercepts pod creation requests. When a new pod is about to be created, it checks whether there's a VPA policy applicable to that pod. If so, it modifies the pod's resource requests according to the latest recommendations before the pod is actually created. This ensures that even newly created pods start with optimized resource settings.

As shown in *Figure 3.3*, VPA starts by gathering CPU and memory usage data from pods in the cluster from the Metrics Server. It's an ongoing process, so it allows VPA to understand the application's resource needs over time. Then, VPA generates recommendations for optimal CPU and memory allocations for each container within a pod. These recommendations aim to strike a balance between ensuring the application has enough resources to perform well and avoiding over-provisioning, which could lead to wasted resources.

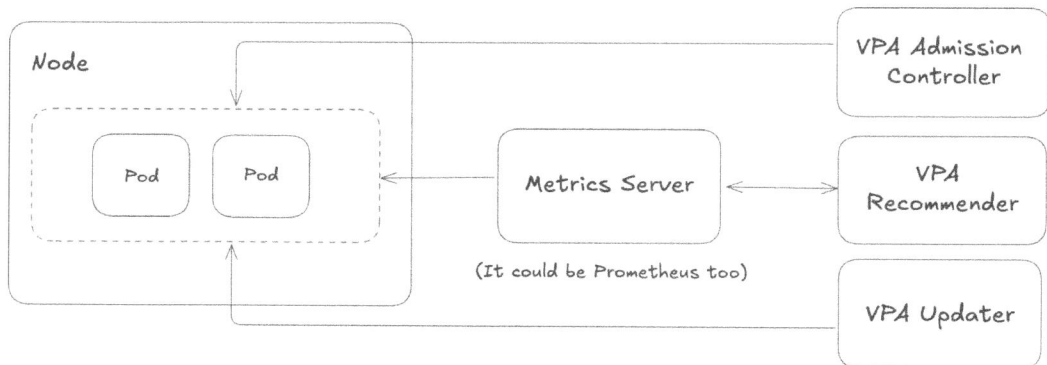

Figure 3.3 – How VPA scales workloads

Then, VPA can automatically apply these usage recommendations by updating the pod specifications by terminating the pod first. Then, through an Admission Controller, it modifies the pod spec before it has persisted. Alternatively, it simply provides the recommendations without taking action. VPA respects configured resource policies, such as minimum and maximum limits. It also considers factors such as **out-of-memory (OOM)** events and CPU throttling when making recommendations.

Lastly, keep in mind that using VPA alongside HPA for CPU and memory scaling can lead to conflicts, as both tools attempt to solve the same problem in different ways. However, VPA can work well with HPA when the latter is scaling based on custom or external metrics.

Defining VPA scaling policies

Now, let's look at how to define a VPA scaling policy. As VPA is not a native Kubernetes feature, you define autoscaling policies through a **custom resource definition (CRD)** called VerticalPodAutoscaler.

Here's a simple VPA rule:

```
apiVersion: autoscaling.k8s.io/v1
kind: VerticalPodAutoscaler
metadata:
  name: montecarlo-pi-vpa
spec:
  targetRef:
    apiVersion: "apps/v1"
    kind: Deployment
    name: montecarlo-pi
  updatePolicy:
    updateMode: "Auto"
  resourcePolicy:
    containerPolicies:
    - containerName: '*'
      minAllowed:
        cpu: 100m
        memory: 512Mi
      maxAllowed:
        cpu: 1200m
        memory: 512Mi
      controlledResources: ["cpu", "memory"]
```

In this example, VPA will automatically adjust CPU and memory for all containers in the montecarlo-pi Deployment.

Let's break down each section:

- targetRef indicates which Kubernetes object this VPA should manage. In this case, it's a Deployment named montecarlo-pi.

- The updatePolicy section defines how VPA should apply changes, and there are four modes you can configure:

  - Auto: applies recommendations by updating resource requests on new pods at creation time and by evicting pods to update existing ones. If the InPlacePodVerticalScaling feature gate is enabled (it's enabled by default since Kubernetes 1.33), VPA can perform in-place scaling. In other words, it will modify the container CPU/memory without eviction, avoiding pod restarts and disruption. We'll get back to this at *Chapter 8* and discuss what could be impact at the time of writing this book with Karpenter.

  - Recreate: Apply recommendations at creation time, or recreate existing pods. For now, it's the same as Auto, as in-place update is not GA yet. However, it will be recommended to use only if you really need to recreate the pods when applying recommendations.

  - Initial: Apply recommendations only when pods are created.

  - Off: Recommendations can only be seen by inspecting the VPA object.

- The resourcePolicy section is used to define rules, such as limits that VPA needs to respect:

  - containerPolicies allows you to set policies for specific or all containers

  - minAllowed and maxAllowed set the resource boundaries to respect

  - controlledResources is to specify which resources VPA should manage

This basic policy provides a good starting point, but remember that you can refine these settings based on your application's specific needs and your cluster's resources. You might set different limits for different containers, or create **pod disruption budgets** (**PDBs**) to be less aggressive if you're dealing with a critical application.

If you don't want to apply recommendations automatically, you can use the Initial mode to still get the benefits of VPA, but apply them the next time a deployment or upgrade happens, as this will create new pods. Alternatively, you can simply use the Off mode to get recommendations from VPA, but you'll own the decision of applying them or not. You can also exclude containers that don't need to scale by using Off under the containerPolicies section.

It's worth mentioning that VPA will update resources only if there is more than one replica. You can change this behavior either for all VPA rules within the VPA Updater component using the min-replicas parameter, or by adding a minReplicas value to the corresponding VPA rule, like this:

```
...
updatePolicy:
    updateMode: 'Auto'
...
```

The recommendation is to configure this value at the VPA rule level, as there might be workloads for which you'd prefer VPA not to perform any action to avoid causing downtime.

Now that you understand how to configure VPA policies and what each field does, it's time to see it in action. In the next section, you'll use VPA in the Auto mode to dynamically adjust resource allocations based on real usage.

Hands-on lab: Automatic vertical scaling with VPA

To watch VPA in action, we're going to start using VPA in the Auto mode to adjust the resources of pods (vertical scaling) without any human intervention.

Deploy VPA components

You first need to deploy the VPA components. To do so, run the following commands in a new terminal outside of this book's repository:

```
$ git clone https://github.com/kubernetes/autoscaler.git
$ cd autoscaler/vertical-pod-autoscaler
$ ./pkg/admission-controller/gencerts.sh
$ ./hack/vpa-up.sh
```

Confirm that the VPA pods are up and running:

```
$ kubectl get pods -n kube-system | grep vpa
```

Wait until you see the recommender, the updater, and the admission pods running. Then, close this terminal and go back to the one you're using for the book's repository.

Deploy the sample application

Make sure you're in the chapter03 folder from the book's GitHub repository, and run the following command to create the VPA rule:

```
$ kubectl apply -f vpa/vpa.auto.yaml
```

Explore the VPA rule; you'll see that it's using the Monte Carlo deployment that you're about to deploy, and it's defining minimum and maximum values for CPU and memory. This is recommended so that you define boundaries for VPA to act, and you don't let the application scale infinitely. Don't worry about setting these numbers right at the beginning, especially if you have no idea how many resources the application needs. You can tune them up later when you know more about your application.

Let's continue using the Monte Carlo application; deploy it using this command:

```
$ kubectl apply -f vpa/montecarlopi.yaml
```

Notice the montecarlo-pi deployment doesn't have any resource requests or limits configured. This is so you can see how VPA will do that job for you based on the data about CPU and memory that is collected from the Metrics Server, or initially, the default configuration that VPA might have.

Open a new terminal to monitor how the VPA rule acts:

```
$ watch kubectl get vpa
```

Wait around one minute, and you should see something like this:

```
NAME              MODE    CPU    MEM       PROVIDED    AGE
montecarlo...     Auto    100m   262144k   True        60s
```

Describe the VPA rule to learn what recommendations it is giving you; run this command:

```
$ kubectl describe vpa montecarlo-pi-vpa-auto
```

You'll see something similar to this output:

```
...
  Recommendation:
    Container Recommendations:
      Container Name:  montecarlo-pi
      Lower Bound:
        Cpu:     100m
        Memory:  262144k
      Target:
        Cpu:     100m
        Memory:  262144k
      Uncapped Target:
        Cpu:     25m
```

```
        Memory:   262144k
    Upper Bound:
        Cpu:      100m
        Memory:   262144k
...
```

Notice that it has four groups of recommendations:

- `Lower Bound` is the minimum resource value to apply
- `Target` is the values it will assign to the container when the pod is created
- `Uncapped Target` is the value to use if there are no `minAllowed` or `maxAllowed` constraints within the VPA rule
- `Upper Bound` is the maximum resource value to apply

Open a new terminal to watch the pods created to see the changes VPA will make:

```
$ watch kubectl get pods
```

After two minutes have passed, you'll see that pods will start being recreated. If you describe the new pod, you should see that it now has requests assigned:

```
...
    resources:
      requests:
        cpu: 100m
        memory: 262144k
...
```

The pod now has `100m` for CPU, as that's the minimum allowed as configured by the VPA rule. However, for the memory request, the pod has `262144k` (256Mi). But the VPA has a minimum of 50Mi, right? Well, VPA assigned the default minimum from the VPA recommender pod of 256Mi. The default minimum from the recommender takes precedence if it's higher than what the VPA rule has configured. You can change this configuration with the `pod-recommendation-min-memory-mb` parameter from the VPA recommender deployment.

Run load tests and see VPA in action

Now, run the following command to send load to the application for a few minutes:

```
$ kubectl apply -f ab-k8s/loadtest.yaml
```

You should see that the VPA shows a different CPU value now, something like this:

```
NAME            MODE    CPU     MEM         PROVIDED    AGE
montecarlo...    Auto   1554m   262144k     True        6m
```

However, this time, you won't see pods being recreated automatically, and if you check the VPA recommender logs, you'll see something like not updating a short-lived pod. This is because, by default, VPA will wait for at least 12 hours to evict pods. You can configure this with the in-recommendation-bounds-eviction-lifetime-threshold parameter at the VPA updater deployment.

You might not want to wait too long to see that in action, so let's force a rollout:

```
$ kubectl rollout restart deployment montecarlo-pi
```

Describe one of the new pods. You should see that it has requests assigned, like this:

```
...
    resources:
      requests:
        cpu: 1554m
        memory: 262144k
...
```

You might see that a pod replica is still pending. Check the pod events by describing the pod, and you'll see Kubernetes reporting that it couldn't find a node available to run the pod. This can be addressed by scaling the data plane with projects such as Cluster Autoscaler and Karpenter, but we'll cover that in *Chapter 7*.

To clean up the environment after this hands-on lab, run these commands:

```
$ kubectl delete -f ab-k8s
$ kubectl delete -f vpa
```

You've now seen VPA in action, making recommendations and adjusting resource requests based on actual usage. A common question I hear is *Can you use both HPA and VPA together?* The answer is yes, with some important caveats.

In the next section, we'll explore how HPA and VPA can complement each other, what limitations you need to be aware of, and how to configure them to avoid conflicts.

How to work with HPA and VPA together

In the previous hands-on lab, you might have noticed that when you forced a new rollout to rec-reate the pods, VPA assigned CPU and memory resources based on what it knew at that moment. However, if you wait until the load test finishes and the application pods are no longer receiving traffic, the CPU usage drops to just a few millicores. You can confirm this with the kubectl top command.

VPA takes a more conservative approach compared to HPA. This is because applications that need to scale vertically usually don't have very spiky behavior, and their load tends to be more predictable. Moreover, when VPA recreates a pod, it could potentially cause downtime for your application, especially if you're only working with one replica.

Another important aspect is that VPA and HPA perform different actions on your application, and if you use the same metric (e.g., CPU) to define autoscaling rules, you might end up with a race condition scenario. In this case, if CPU utilization goes beyond 70%, HPA will add more replicas, but by the time new pods are created, VPA might have decided to recommend higher CPU requests. Consequently, your level of efficiency could be very low, and you might end up with constant fluctuations within your application.

Before you conclude that these two can't work together, let me share a few setups I've observed from different organizations that are using HPA and VPA in conjunction:

- Use HPA to scale workloads horizontally, and only use VPA rules in the Off mode to get resource request recommendations for CPU and memory. Then, use these recommenda-tions to manually adjust the workloads and let HPA scale automatically.
- Use only HPA to scale workloads horizontally. To rightsize the applications, use a moni-toring stack such as Prometheus + Grafana, Kubecost, or any other third-party tool that companies are already using. There are also some paid third-party tools that can perform rightsizing either automatically or with a one-click operation.
- Use only VPA for applications that can't scale horizontally, either because they're legacy applications or adding a new replica is complex, costly, and time-consuming (e.g., due to data replication). In pre-production environments, VPA is usually configured in the Auto mode, and for production environments, in the Off mode (to plan updates accordingly).

I've seen these options I just described being used for different types of workloads within the same company or project. There's no right or wrong answer; it's a matter of which setup works best for your application. As long as you make informed decisions based on data and try to automate as much as possible, you'll be taking advantage of HPA and VPA features. In the next two chapters, you'll learn about a project that takes a different approach to application workload autoscaling: KEDA.

Summary

In this chapter, we've explored two Kubernetes autoscaling tools: HPA and VPA. We've seen how HPA dynamically adjusts the number of pod replicas based on observed metrics, primarily CPU and memory usage, but also custom and external metrics when properly configured. We've also delved into VPA's capabilities for automatically adjusting resource requests and limits for containers, optimizing resource allocation within pods.

We've walked through practical examples of implementing both HPA and VPA, discussing their configuration options, best practices, and potential pitfalls. We've seen how these tools can significantly improve resource utilization and application performance when properly implemented.

Throughout our exploration, we've emphasized the importance of making data-driven decisions when configuring autoscaling policies. We've discussed various approaches to combining HPA and VPA, or using them separately, depending on the specific needs and constraints of different applications and environments. The key takeaway is that there's no one-size-fits-all solution; the best autoscaling strategy depends on your specific use case and workload characteristics.

As we conclude this chapter, it's clear that while HPA and VPA are powerful tools, they may not cover all autoscaling scenarios in complex, modern applications. This brings us to our next chapter, where we'll explore KEDA. In the upcoming chapters, we'll dive deep into KEDA's concepts, its integration with Kubernetes, and how it can complement or even replace traditional autoscaling methods in certain scenarios.

Get This Book's PDF Version and Exclusive Extras

UNLOCK NOW

Scan the QR code (or go to packtpub.com/unlock).
Search for this book by name, confirm the edition,
and then follow the steps on the page.

*Note: Keep your invoice handy. Purchases made
directly from Packt don't require one.*

Part 2

Workload Autoscaling and KEDA

By now, you've seen what the HPA and VPA can do, and you've probably noticed their limitations. Scaling based on CPU or memory works fine for some workloads, but what about when your application needs to scale based on queue depth? Or, when you want to scale to zero during off-hours to save costs? When is latency a better indicator of load than CPU utilization? This is where KEDA comes in.

KEDA extends the built-in HPA without replacing it. Instead of being limited to CPU and memory metrics, KEDA lets you scale based on pretty much any event source you can think of – for example, message queues, databases, HTTP traffic, scheduled times, cloud provider metrics, and more. It works alongside the HPA, giving you the flexibility that your workloads actually need.

This part covers KEDA in depth, starting with the basics of how it works and why so many teams have adopted it. You'll learn how to configure scaling rules based on real application signals, such as latency, instead of generic resource metrics. You'll explore KEDA's most useful features, including scaling to (and from) zero, controlling how fast your workloads scale up or down (reusing HPA constructs), and handling batch workloads with Kubernetes jobs.

Then, we'll move on to the more advanced stuff, with schedule-based scaling for predictable traffic patterns, HTTP autoscaling that can bring pods back from zero in seconds, scaling modifiers for complex rules, and how to integrate with cloud provider services. Finally, we'll cover the operational side of how to troubleshoot when things don't work as expected, monitoring your scaling rules with Grafana, and understanding the metrics that tell you why KEDA is (or isn't) scaling your workloads the way you want.

By the end of this part, you'll understand not just how to configure KEDA, but how to operate it reliably in production.

This part has the following chapters:

- *Chapter 4, Kubernetes Event-Driven Autoscaling — Part 1*
- *Chapter 5, Kubernetes Event-Driven Autoscaling — Part 2*
- *Chapter 6, Workload Autoscaling Operations*

4

Kubernetes Event-Driven Autoscaling — Part 1

In the previous chapter, we dived into autoscaling workloads using HPA and VPA. These solutions provide a very good starting point if your scaling needs are simply about CPU and memory, but it gets complicated if you need other types of metrics, especially for event-driven architectures. This is where **Kubernetes Event-Driven Autoscaling (KEDA)** comes into play.

This chapter will start to dive deep into KEDA. We'll begin by understanding the need for KEDA and how it simplifies working with HPA. Then, we'll delve into KEDA's architecture and components, providing you with a good understanding of how it works. Then, we'll cover KEDA's **Custom Resource Definitions (CRDs)** and practice using them.

Moreover, we'll explore the wide array of event sources and scalers supported by KEDA, demonstrating its versatility in handling various workloads. You'll learn how to scale different Kubernetes resources, including Deployments, Jobs, and StatefulSets, with hands-on examples using metrics such as latency and message queue length.

We'll also introduce you to KEDA's HTTP add-on, a feature for scaling HTTP-based applications. By the end of this chapter, you'll have a good understanding of KEDA, including how it works, its capabilities, its limitations, and how to leverage it to build more responsive and efficient Kubernetes applications.

In this chapter, we'll cover the following topics:

- KEDA: What it is and why you need it
- KEDA's architecture
- KEDA scalers
- KEDA CRDs
- Scaling Deployments
- Scaling jobs

Let's dive in and explore KEDA!

Technical requirements

For this chapter, you'll continue using the Kubernetes cluster you created in *Chapter 1*. You can continue working with the local Kubernetes cluster; there's no need yet to work with a cluster in AWS. If you turned down the cluster, make sure you bring it up for every hands-on lab in this chapter. You don't need to install any additional tools as most of the commands are going to be run using `kubectl` and `helm`. You can find the YAML manifests for all resources you're going to create in this chapter in the `chapter04` folder from the Book's GitHub repository: `https://github.com/PacktPublishing/Kubernetes-Autoscaling`.

KEDA: What it is and why you need it

Modern, complex, and distributed applications are not affected solely by CPU and memory utilization. These two metrics might only tell part of the story of what's impacting your application's performance, which ultimately determines why you might need more (or fewer) replicas for your applications to work as expected. But didn't we learn about using metrics other than CPU and memory in the previous chapter? It's possible to use custom or external metrics with HPA, and you even practiced it, right? So, what exactly is KEDA, and why do we need it?

KEDA is an event-driven autoscaler for Kubernetes workloads. It was initiated as a joint collaboration between Microsoft and Red Hat in 2019. In 2020, KEDA was donated to the **Cloud Native Computing Foundation** (**CNCF**), making it vendor-neutral. In August 2023, KEDA graduated as a CNCF project, which can tell you about its importance in the Kubernetes ecosystem.

The primary purpose of KEDA is to simplify the process of working with custom and external metrics for scaling your applications. As you saw in the previous chapter, for HPA to work with custom metrics, you need an adapter component to *translate* those metrics so that Kubernetes can understand them.

While you might not have issues working with this added complexity, it's important to remember that each component or layer between your metrics source and HPA rules can introduce latency, potentially causing your autoscaling rules to react slower than desired.

KEDA's advantage lies in its ability to interact directly with the metrics source and expose those metrics to the External Metrics API. It works in tandem with HPA by creating and managing HPA objects automatically, acting as an abstraction layer to help you simplify the setup for using external metrics, without even requiring you to rewrite your application. In other words, when you create a `ScaledObject` in KEDA, it automatically creates and manages the associated HPA object under the hood. This direct interaction can lead to faster and more efficient scaling decisions. However, it's recommended to not combine KEDA and HPA to scale the same workload, as they would compete with each other and could cause conflicting scaling actions leading to race conditions.

Moreover, KEDA is significantly more extensive and flexible than HPA alone. It supports a wide range of metric sources (or scalers), allowing you to scale your applications based on various event sources such as message queues, databases, and monitoring systems such as Prometheus. More importantly, KEDA has the ability to scale from/to zero for most of the scalers, helping you to have a cost-effective resource utilization for applications with intermittent workloads.

> **Note**
>
> It's worth mentioning that since Kubernetes 1.16, you can enable the alpha feature gate called `HPAScaleToZero` to enable HPA to scale to zero for object and external metrics only. This feature has remained in alpha status across multiple Kubernetes versions, which means it may not be stable or widely adopted yet. Therefore, cloud providers might not enable it by default. It's important to note that this feature has remained in alpha status for several versions, indicating that it may not be stable or widely adopted yet.

KEDA's architecture

Before you learn how to use KEDA, it's important to understand KEDA's architecture and components. At its core, KEDA consists of three main components: **KEDA Operator**, **KEDA Metrics Server**, and an **Admission Webhook controller**. The purpose of these three components is to provide you event-driven autoscaling for your workloads.

The following figure illustrates the high-level architecture of KEDA and its interaction with your workloads:

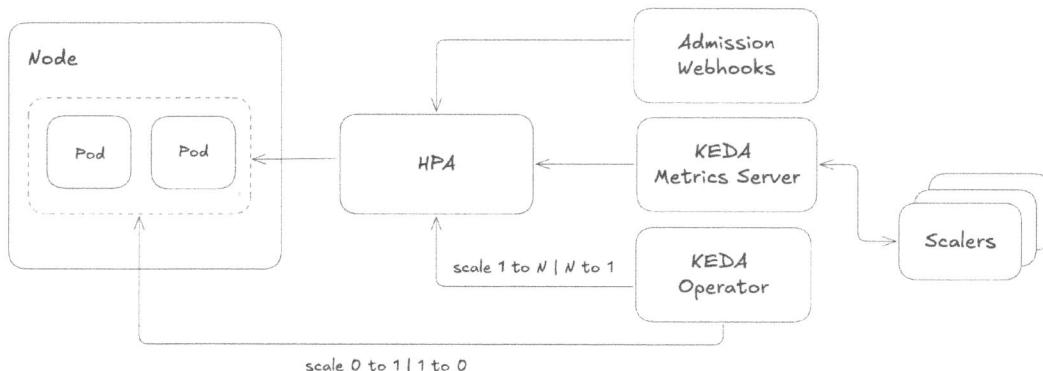

Figure 4.1 – KEDA's architecture components

Let me explain further what you see in *Figure 4.1*. When you need to configure an autoscaling rule using KEDA for a workload, you first need to create a rule using either a `ScaledObject` or `ScaledJob` CRD (which I'll cover in the *KEDA CRDs* section of this chapter). Based on this, KEDA automatically creates an HPA resource and uses KEDA Metrics Server to expose external metrics to it. HPA then continuously monitors the defined event sources and calculates how many replicas your workload needs. KEDA is responsible for scaling the target object from zero to one replica, and from one to zero replicas when scale-to-zero is enabled. When more than one replica is required, KEDA first scales the workload to one replica to activate the trigger, then delegates scaling from one to N replicas to HPA. In other words, KEDA handles the activation phase (from zero to one, and from one to zero), and HPA handles the scaling phase (from one to N, and N to one replica). Throughout this autoscaling process, the Admission Webhooks control creation and update requests for KEDA resources, enforcing best practices and preventing conflicts such as multiple `ScaledObjects` managing the same workload.

Let's further explore each component and its role in the KEDA ecosystem.

KEDA Operator

KEDA Operator monitors your cluster for KEDA-specific CRDs such as `ScaledObjects` and `ScaledJobs`. When it detects these custom resources, it starts to work by creating and managing the necessary HPA objects based on the scaling rules defined in those CRDs. Moreover, KEDA Operator interacts directly with external event sources, such as message queues, databases, or custom metric endpoints by querying them to determine current scaling needs.

As I said before, this direct interaction eliminates the need for intermediate adapters, reducing latency and improving the responsiveness of your autoscaling setup.

KEDA Metrics Server

KEDA Metrics Server complements KEDA Operator by exposing metrics collected from event sources to Kubernetes via the External Metrics API. This makes the metrics accessible to the HPA objects, allowing Kubernetes' native autoscaling mechanisms to consume the event-driven metrics. This enables Metrics Server to use KEDA's event-driven scaling without having to modify your Kubernetes setup or your applications.

Admission Webhooks

KEDA's Admission Webhooks act as an admission controller that intercepts resource creation and update requests to the Kubernetes API server, validating these changes to prevent misconfigurations and enforce best practices. A key function of these webhooks is to prevent multiple ScaledObjects from targeting the same scale target, ensuring the integrity and predictability of your autoscaling setup. Admission Webhooks are enabled by default when you install KEDA, providing an additional layer of safety and consistency in your Kubernetes cluster(s).

What Kubernetes objects can KEDA scale?

KEDA can scale the following resource types:

- **Deployments:** This is the most common use case, ideal for stateless applications
- **StatefulSets:** It is ideal for applications that require stable, unique network identifiers or persistent storage such as databases
- **Custom resources:** KEDA can scale custom resources defined by Operator, opening up possibilities for scaling complex, application-specific workloads, such as ArgoCD objects

Let's dive deeper into the specific CRDs that KEDA introduces and how you can leverage them to define sophisticated scaling behaviors for your applications.

KEDA scalers

One of the most important features that makes KEDA shine as a Kubernetes workload autoscaler is its event sources and scalers. These components are essentially the reason why KEDA is able to respond to a wide variety of external events, including basic ones such as CPU and memory utilization, meaning that you won't need to use HPA and KEDA; you can transition to use only KEDA.

For instance, a CPU trigger in KEDA will look like this:

```
triggers:
- type: cpu
  metricType: Utilization # Or 'AverageValue'
  metadata:
    value: "70"
```

For a memory scaler, simply change the type parameter to memory. Pretty similar to HPA, right? But KEDA goes far beyond these two metrics, allowing your applications to scale dynamically based on a diverse range of events and metrics, often working in conjunction with one another.

Remember that KEDA continuously monitor sources. When you create a KEDA scaling rule, it does monitor sources for specific triggers that indicate a need for scaling.

Note

A the time of writing, KEDA supports 70+ scalers, and keeps growing thanks to the community behind the project, covering a vast landscape of technologies, platforms, and cloud providers.

You can configure multiple triggers in the same KEDA rule. With this, KEDA will start scaling as soon as one of the triggers specified meets the criteria. Then, it calculates the desired number of replicas for each trigger, and it will use the highest number.

These scalers range from simple CPU and memory metrics to complex, application-specific indicators. For instance, you can scale based on the length of a message queue, the number of unprocessed items in a database, or even custom metrics exposed by your application. Each scaler is responsible for querying its associated event source at regular intervals. When the scaler detects that a predefined condition has been met, such as a queue length exceeding a certain threshold, it communicates this information back to KEDA Operator, which then uses this data to adjust the scaling of your application, either by creating new pods or removing unnecessary ones.

For scenarios where you need even more flexibility or have stringent security requirements, KEDA offers the concept of **external scalers**. These are standalone services that implement KEDA's External Scaler API, allowing you to keep sensitive scaling logic or credentials outside of your Kubernetes cluster. External scalers can be particularly useful when dealing with proprietary systems or when you need to implement complex scaling logic that doesn't fit well within the constraints of a built-in scaler. We'll dive deeper into external scalers in *Chapter 5*.

Let's now explore how to use KEDA with its CRDs.

KEDA CRDs

KEDA CRDs allow you to define and manage scaling behaviors in a Kubernetes-native way, extending the cluster's API to include KEDA-specific resources. Let's explore each of these CRDs and how they contribute to KEDA's scaling capabilities.

ScaledObject

ScaledObjects define how a Deployment, StatefulSet, or custom resource should scale using triggers. Based on the event type configured for the trigger, KEDA will use that scaler to monitor its events or metrics, and expose it so that HPA can use it to scale out or scale in.

One of the key features of ScaledObject is the ability to pause autoscaling, which can be particularly useful during maintenance windows or when you need to temporarily override KEDA's scaling decisions. We'll dive deep into more advanced features in *Chapter 5*.

Here's an example of a ScaledObject that scales a Deployment based on the length of a Rabbit-MQ queue:

```
apiVersion: keda.sh/v1alpha1
kind: ScaledObject
metadata:
  name: consumer-app-scaler
spec:
  scaleTargetRef:
    name: consumer-app
  pollingInterval: 30
  cooldownPeriod:  300
  minReplicaCount: 0
  maxReplicaCount: 30
  triggers:
  - type: rabbitmq
    metadata:
      queueName: orders
      mode: QueueLength
      value: "20"
    authenticationRef:
      name: consumer-app-trigger
```

This `ScaledObject` will scale the `consumer-app` Deployment based on the length of the `orders` queue in RabbitMQ. It checks the queue every 30 seconds (`pollingInterval`). The application then consumes multiple events from the queue, and KEDA can scale the deployment up to 30 replicas (`maxReplicaCount`). When there are no messages, KEDA will scale down the deployment to zero replicas (`minReplicaCount`).

Now, let's break down the parameters from the previous `ScaledObject` example:

- `scaleTargetRef` is the resource KEDA will scale. If the target is a Deployment, you simply specify the name. But if the target is a StatefulSet or a custom resource, you need to specify the API version and its kind.
- `pollingInterval` is the interval that KEDA uses to check the trigger source. By default, the interval is 30 seconds.
- `cooldownPeriod` is the period that KEDA waits after the last trigger was reported active before scaling the resource back to zero. By default, the period is 300 seconds.
- `minReplicaCount` is the minimum number of replicas KEDA will set the resource when scaling down. By default, the minimum number is zero.
- `maxReplicaCount` is the maximum number of replicas KEDA will set the resource when scaling up. By default, the maximum number is 100.
- `triggers` is where you define the properties of the scalers to use.

The `ScaledObject` CRD has many more parameters and properties that we'll continue exploring throughout this chapter and the next one. For now, you have at least an idea of what a basic configuration looks like. As we progress, you'll learn how to leverage these additional features to create more sophisticated and tailored scaling solutions for different use cases.

ScaledJob

`ScaledJobs` are designed for batch jobs or tasks that need to run to completion. They create Kubernetes jobs based on scaling rules. Instead of processing multiple events within a Deployment, KEDA will create one Job per event, and process it. When the Job finishes processing the event, or fails because there was an error, the Job will be terminated. It's up to the process, or application in this case, how many events will pull down, and based on this, you need to configure the scaling rule.

Here's an example of a `ScaledJob` to process messages from a RabbitMQ queue:

```
apiVersion: keda.sh/v1alpha1
kind: ScaledJob
metadata:
```

```
    name: rabbitmq-consumer
spec:
  jobTargetRef:
    template:
      spec:
        containers:
        - name: rabbitmq-client
          image: rabbitmq-client:v1.0.1
          command: ["receive",  "amqp://user:PASSWORD@rabbitmq.default.
svc.cluster.local:5672"]
          envFrom:
          - secretRef:
              name: rabbitmq-consumer-secrets
        restartPolicy: Never
  pollingInterval: 10
  minReplicaCount: 0
  maxReplicaCount: 30
  triggers:
  - type: rabbitmq
    metadata:
      queueName: orders
      mode: QueueLength
      value: "20"
      authenticationRef:
        name: consumer-app-trigger
```

This `ScaledJob` will create jobs to process messages from the `orders` queue, when there are at least 20 messages in the queue (`value`). It will create up to 30 Job replicas (`maxReplicaCount`). By default, it will keep a history of 100 successful and 100 failed jobs, but these can be configured using the `successfulJobsHistoryLimit` and `failedJobsHistoryLimit` parameters.

Now, let's break down the parameters from the previous `ScaledJob` example:

- `jobTargetRef` is the spec you configure for the Job KEDA will create, and the `template` field is required for that same reason.
- `pollingInterval` is the interval that KEDA uses to check the trigger source. By default, the interval is 30 seconds.

- `minReplicaCount` is the minimum number of replicas KEDA creates. By default, the minimum is zero. If it's different from zero, KEDA will keep a minimum of jobs running, which is useful in case you don't want to wait for new jobs to be ready.

- `maxReplicaCount` is the maximum number of replicas KEDA will create every poll interval. If there are jobs running, KEDA will deduct those running jobs from the calculation. By default, the maximum number is 100.

- `triggers` is where you define the properties of the scalers to use.

The `ScaledJob` CRD has many more parameters and properties that we'll continue exploring throughout this chapter and the next one. For now, you have at least an idea of what a basic configuration looks like.

TriggerAuthentication and ClusterTriggerAuthentication

There might be some KEDA scalers that will require authentication. To cover this need, the `TriggerAuthentication` and `ClusterTriggerAuthentication` CRDs provide a way to securely manage authentication parameters. The difference between these two is that `TriggerAuthentication` is namespace-scoped, while `ClusterTriggerAuthentication` is cluster-wide.

Continuing with the RabbitMQ example, here's a `TriggerAuthentication` example that uses a Kubernetes secret to authenticate with the RabbitMQ server:

```
apiVersion: keda.sh/v1alpha1
kind: TriggerAuthentication
metadata:
  name: consumer-app-trigger
spec:
  secretTargetRef:
  - parameter: host
    name: rabbitmq-consumer-secret
    key: RabbitMqHost
```

With `TriggerAuthentication`, you decouple the authentication part from the scaling part, and you can reuse authentication within multiple `ScaledObject` instances. I showed you a very simple example of the CRD manifest. You can check the official documentation to see what else you can configure, and in the next chapter, we'll explore a few other parameters. For example, you can configure a Pod Identity when using a cloud provider, use vault secrets from Hashi Corp, or work with secrets management solutions from cloud providers such as AWS Secrets Manager, Azure Key Vault, or GCP Secrets Manager.

Hands-on lab: Installing KEDA

Let's start with your first hands-on lab for this chapter. Go to your terminal, spin up your Kubernetes cluster again (go back to *Chapter 1* to follow the lab to set up your environment), and run the following commands to install KEDA:

```
$ helm repo add kedacore https://kedacore.github.io/charts
$ helm repo update
$ helm install keda kedacore/keda --namespace keda --create-namespace
```

When the installation finishes, you should be able to see the KEDA controllers:

```
$ kubectl get pods -n keda
```

You should see an output like this:

```
NAME                         READY   STATUS     RESTARTS  AGE
keda-admission-webhooks-...  1/1     Running    1         3m
keda-operator-...            1/1     Running    1         3m
keda-operator-metrics-...    1/1     Running    1         3m
```

Alright, you're now ready to use KEDA to scale your workloads. Let's do that next.

Scaling Deployments

As you can tell by now, KEDA offers a more flexible approach compared to traditional HPA methods. For instance, the ability to scale to zero, which isn't possible with standard HPA as the minimum number of replicas is always one. I'd say that this is one of the most attractive features of KEDA. However, scaling to zero might not be suitable for certain applications, such as web services where you don't want to miss any incoming requests. We'll explore this concept in more depth later in *Chapter 5* when we discuss KEDA's HTTP add-on.

Similarly to HPA, KEDA also provides fine-grained control over scaling behavior. In addition to setting minimum and maximum replica counts, you can define cooldown periods to prevent rapid scaling oscillations and even implement advanced scaling policies. It's worth noting that while KEDA creates and manages HPAs behind the scenes, it abstracts away much of the complexity involved in setting up custom metrics adapters. This abstraction makes it significantly easier to implement advanced scaling scenarios that would be challenging with standard Kubernetes resources alone. You'll understand better what I mean after a few hands-on labs.

In the following hands-on sections, we'll explore practical examples of using KEDA to scale Deployments. First, we'll be translating a custom metrics example from *Chapter 3* into a KEDA-based solution, showcasing how KEDA simplifies the process. Then, we'll delve into a common scenario for scaling a queue consumer. Let's get into it.

Hands-on lab: Scaling using latency

You've already practiced scaling your workloads using CPU utilization with HPA in the previous chapter. So instead of that, let's see how you'll scale your application using a custom metric. You already did this with HPA, but this time, I want you to see the main difference in KEDA where you don't need the Prometheus Adapter, because KEDA will go directly to the source (Prometheus) to calculate the replicas the workload needs. This has additional advantages, such as being able to use multiple Prometheus instances, and no need to configure an adapter through a `ConfigMap` (which has a limitation of 1 MB size anyway).

So, let's open a terminal, and change directory to the book's GitHub repository in the `chapter04` folder. Then, run the following command to deploy the Monte Carlo application:

```
$ kubectl apply -f api/montecarlopi.yaml
```

Notice that similarly to before, the application is intentional on how much CPU and memory is requesting, and it's limiting them as well to influence the response time when the load increase so that we can scale out horizontally:

```
resources:
  requests:
    cpu: 900m
    memory: 512Mi
  limits:
    cpu: 1200m
    memory: 512Mi
```

Before you continue, let's confirm you have all the Prometheus pods running, as well as the Prometheus service by running this command:

```
$ kubectl get pods -n monitoring
```

> **Note**
>
> If you don't have the Prometheus stack installed, go back to *Chapter 2* to install it.

The application is exposing custom latency metrics at the /metrics endpoint, and in order to push those metrics to Prometheus, you need to add a ServiceMonitor. There's a YAML definition for this in the repository as well; if you explore the chapter04/api/monitor.yaml file, you'll see that it simply targets the application:

```
spec:
  selector:
    matchLabels:
      app: montecarlo-pi
  endpoints:
  - port: http
```

Deploy the service monitor by running this command:

```
$ kubectl apply -f api/monitor.yaml
```

Wait around five minutes for Prometheus to consider this new monitor to start scrapping metrics from the application's /metrics endpoint. After this time has passed, deploy KEDA's ScaledObject to define an autoscaling rule for the application using the monte_carlo_latency_seconds_bucket metric. You should be using the following trigger:

```
triggers:
  - type: prometheus
    metadata:
      serverAddress: >
        http://prometheus-kube-prometheus-prometheus.monitoring.svc:9090
      metricName: monte_carlo_latency_seconds
      threshold: "0.5" # You can't specify 500m, it needs to be
translated to seconds
      query: >
        sum(histogram_quantile(0.95,
        rate(monte_carlo_latency_seconds_bucket{namespace="default",
        pod=~"montecarlo-pi-.*"}[2m])))
```

Notice that it's pointing directly to the Prometheus service at the serverAddress parameter, and it's also defining a latency target of 0.5 seconds at the threshold parameter. Additionally, look at the query parameter. It has a very similar query to the one you used in *Chapter 3* when using the Prometheus adapter.

Deploy the preceding scaled object by running this command:

```
$ kubectl apply -f api/latency.yaml
```

Confirm that the HPA rule has been created by running this command:

```
$ kubectl get hpa keda-hpa-montecarlo-pi-latency
```

Let's see autoscaling in action by sending some load test; run this command:

```
$ kubectl apply -f ab-k8s/loadtest.yaml
```

Now, monitor what happens by running this command:

```
$ watch kubectl get scaledobject,hpa,pods
```

You should see that the latency starts to increase by looking at the TARGET column of the HPA rule, and the number of replicas starts to increase very rapidly to try to keep the latency number at its target of 0.5 seconds (or 500 ms). Even if the latency doesn't meet its target with 10 replicas, for this lab, it's fine as we only wanted to see how KEDA's autoscaling rule reacts to a metric exposed by the application. You can play around by adjusting the maxReplicaCount parameter from the ScaledObject to see whether with a maximum of 15 replicas the latency meets its target.

Wait around 10 extra minutes to see how the number of replicas go back to 1 after the TARGET column from HPA goes back to 0.

To clean up this lab, run the following commands:

```
$ kubectl delete -f api
```

Controlling autoscaling speed

In the previous chapter, when we dived deep into HPA speed of scaling, you learned you can control HPA's speed by configuring advance settings such as scaleUp and scaleDown behaviors. For instance, you can make KEDA react faster when scaling up, and react more conservative (or faster than the default behavior) when scaling down. As KEDA is using HPA under the hood, you can customize the scaling speed through the advanced parameter in a ScaledObject, like this:

```
...
advanced:
  behavior:
    scaleUp:
      stabilizationWindowSeconds: 0
      policies:
```

```
    - type: Percent
      value: 100
      periodSeconds: 15
  scaleDown:
    stabilizationWindowSeconds: 60
    policies:
    - type: Percent
      value: 100
      periodSeconds: 15
  ...
```

Notice that we continue using the same configuration from the previous chapter. Feel free to give it a try to confirm that you were able to replicate the same autoscaling rule you had in HPA. But effectively, the previous configuration won't wait to scale up as `stabilizationWindowSeconds` is 0, and will wait 60 seconds to starts scaling down. Both behaviors are using the `Percent` type, and the same policy configuration, which means that it can increase or decrease 100% of the current pods every 15 seconds (`periodSeconds`).

Scaling to zero

One of the most attractive features of KEDA is the ability to scale down to zero replicas. You can reduce waste/costs when your application isn't needed. KEDA can bring your deployment to zero replicas when needed, and then scale it back up when activity resumes.

Scaling to zero works well in certain scenarios. For example, if you're scaling based on the number of messages in a queue, KEDA can scale to zero when the queue is empty. However, scaling to zero isn't suitable for all types of applications or scalers. Take REST APIs as an example. If you're scaling based on latency or number of requests, scaling to zero can cause problems. When there are no replicas running, the application won't be able to handle any requests at all, leading to errors or timeouts. This can result in a poor user experience. Because of this limitation, scaling to zero is best suited for event-driven workloads where you can afford to have periods of inactivity without impacting service availability. Although, it's worth noticing that scaling to zero even with HTTP-based applications is doable if using the `CronJob` scaler combined with other scalers or using KEDA's HTTP add-on. We'll dive deep into scaling to zero HTTP-based applications in the next chapter.

It's important to consider your application's nature and requirements before deciding to implement scaling to zero. For always-on services or APIs, maintaining at least one replica might be a better approach to ensure continuous availability.

Let's see scaling from and to zero in action by scaling a queue-based workload.

Hands-on lab: Scaling from/to zero

A queue-based workload is a scenario where scaling to zero makes perfect sense. If there are messages in the queue, KEDA activates the Deployment and adds the necessary replicas to process messages in the queue. As messages are consumed, less replicas are needed. When there are no messages in the queue, KEDA pauses the Deployment in order to have zero replicas running.

A simple way to demonstrate this scenario is to use a RabbitMQ queue. Think of a video or image encoder; you might have a producer that sends messages to the queue, and a consumer that processes messages from the queue. We've provided a simple app that does something similar. We'll get into the details of how it was built, and why we're configuring KEDA in such a way.

Deploying a RabbitMQ queue

Let's start by deploying a RabbitMQ queue to your cluster by running these commands:

```
$ ../common/rabbitmq.sh install
```

Wait around two minutes and the RabbitMQ pod should be running.

> **Note**
>
> If you're using kind, you need to add the `--set volumePermissions.enabled=true` parameter to the `helm install` command.

It would be nice if you can keep an eye open to the messages that arrive to the queue. To do so, let's make use of RabbitMQ's UI. Run this command to expose the service locally:

```
$ kubectl port-forward svc/rabbitmq 15672:15672
```

Open the following URL in the browser: `http://localhost:15672/#/queues`. You should see a screen similar to the following one:

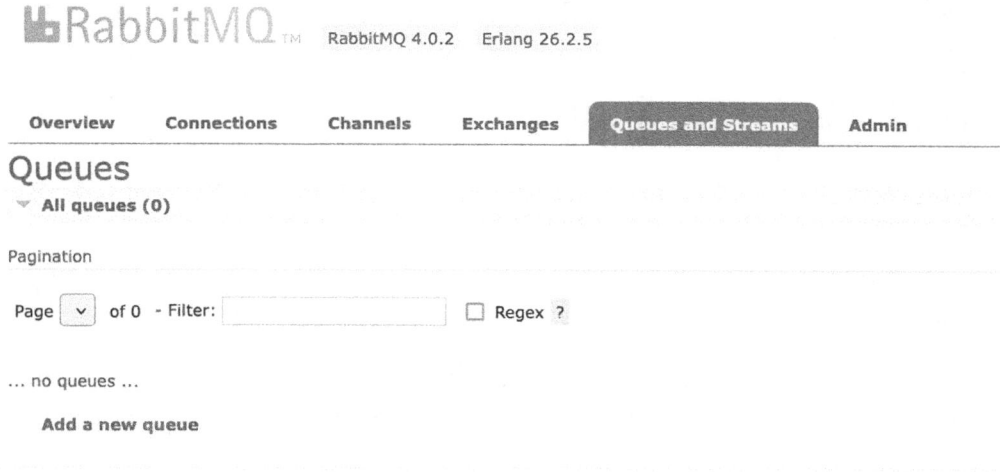

Figure 4.2 – RabbitMQ UI showing the Queues tab

You'll come back to this screen later.

Deploying the sample application

The application you'll deploy next is a queue consumer that processes messages one at a time (but you can configure it to process more). To simulate it's doing something, it waits 3 to 5 seconds (randomly), then it acknowledges to the queue that the message has been processed. The app keeps processing messages from the queue, and it stops once there's a "silence" period of time (30 seconds by default) with no messages. As you can tell, it's a simple application that consumes messages in batch from a queue. Feel free to explore it and learn more about reading the source code at `chapter04/src/consumer/main.go` from the GitHub repository.

The important aspect I want you to notice is that *it processes one message at a time, and it does it continuously as long as there are messages to consume.* When you do it this way, it's easier to know how many resources the pod needs to request per unit of processing, which then translates into making an efficient use of the resources available in the cluster. Moreover, this setup makes it easier to configure KEDA's autoscaling policies, which we'll explore in a moment.

So, let's deploy the app together with the KEDA's `ScaledObject`. Run this command:

```
$ kubectl apply -f queue-deployment/consumer.yaml
```

The important bits to highlight are the deployment's configuration:

```
...
            env:
              - name: RABBITMQ_URL
                value: >
                    "amqp://user:autoscaling@
                    rabbitmq.default.svc.cluster.local:5672"
              - name: QUEUE_NAME
                value: "autoscaling"
              - name: BATCH_SIZE
                value: "1"
            resources:
              requests:
                cpu: 300m
                memory: 128Mi
              limits:
                cpu: 500m
                memory: 128Mi
  ...
```

Notice that it's configured to process one message at a time with the `BATCH_SIZE` environment variable, and it's being intentional about how many resources it needs. The rest of the configuration is very standard. Now, look at the `ScaledObject` configuration:

```
apiVersion: keda.sh/v1alpha1
kind: ScaledObject
metadata:
  name: queue-consumer
spec:
  scaleTargetRef:
    name: queue-consumer
  pollingInterval: 5
  cooldownPeriod:  90
  maxReplicaCount: 15
  triggers:
    - type: rabbitmq
      metadata:
        queueName: autoscaling
```

```
     mode: QueueLength
     value: "5"
  authenticationRef:
     name: rabbitmq-auth
```

Let's see in detail a few of its parameters:

- `pollingInterval`: With this setting, you'd be checking every 5 seconds to see whether there are new messages in the queue. Consider this value based on how much time it takes a message to be processed, and the max number of replicas you can launch.

- `cooldownPeriod`: This one is important; it's the time it waits to start removing replicas when there are no more messages in the queue. Think about the last message a pod will process, and consider how much time, as a maximum, it will take to finish processing. Otherwise, you'll end up interrupting the process because of the scaling down event. If it's too big, you'll end up having the pod in the IDLE state for more time, and if it's too low, you'll end up affecting the app's performance. You need to test to decide on a number that works for you.

- `maxReplicaCount`: As the sky isn't the limit, you need to specify a limit on how many pods can be created. In this case, at a peak point, 15 pods will take care of processing all the messages from the queue. If you want messages to be processed quicker, one way is to need to increase this value. Just be mindful about the cluster's capacity; at this point, you haven't configured node autoscaling yet. It's also worth mentioning that there's no `minReplicaCount` configuration, meaning that the default value of zero is used.

- `value`: This is basically the number of messages in the queue (as `mode` is `QueueLength`) that will trigger this rule. As it's processing one message at a time, you could configure it to be 1, but I used 5 so you can see that you can delay the scaling operation for a bit and launch initially more than one pod to start.

Deploying a message producer

We have also prepared a producer application that will send messages, all at once, to the RabbitMQ queue. You can configure the number of messages to generate using the MESSAGE_COUNT environment variable. For this lab, we'll be sending 150 messages all at once. You can run the producer as many times as you'd like to test this lab. So, to start sending messages to the queue, run this command:

```
$ kubectl apply -f queue-deployment/producer.yaml
```

You won't see much other than a new Kubernetes job being launched.

Watching KEDA in action

Go back to RabbitMQ's UI; to watch the autoscaling queue, you can go directly to this URL: http://localhost:15672/#/queues/%2F/autoscaling.

You'll see that the messages have arrived to the queue, and some of them have been processed already. Look at the following screenshot for reference:

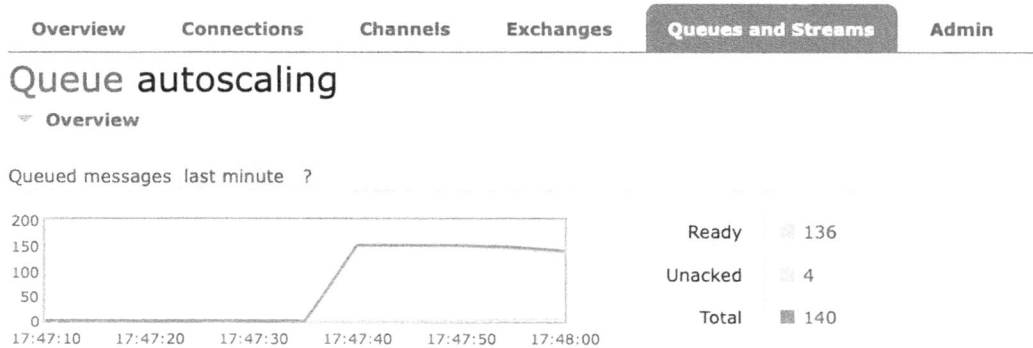

Figure 4.3 – RabbitMQ UI showing the messages from the autoscaling queue

Then, in a new tab, run this command to watch how pods are being created:

```
$ watch kubectl get scaledobject,hpa,pods
```

Notice how KEDA started creating four to five pods to start processing messages. Then, it continues to create new pods as there are still messages in the queue. Finally, when all messages are processed, around three minutes after you launched the producer, you'll see how quickly pods were removed, keeping the number of replicas to zero. You might want to increase the cooldownPeriod value to see how pods are kept after the process has finished. Even though this is great for cluster's efficiency, it might not be good for your application's performance, especially if you have a long-running process. In the next section, we'll explore an alternative for this. Feel free to run this test again by deploying the producer application again.

Cleanup

To remove all resources created for this lab, run the following command:

```
$ kubectl delete -f queue-deployment
```

Scaling Jobs

In the previous lab, you saw how KEDA can scale from zero to a maximum number of replicas as long as there are messages in the queue to process, and it can go back to zero when there aren't messages to process. However, you might have noticed that KEDA is scaling down too quickly, and pods might have not finished processing a message.

As suggested before, you can play around with the `cooldownPeriod` parameter by making it longer. You'll see how pods are kept there, and if you look at the logs, you'll see that they'll print a message saying the application is exiting as there are no messages to process. Then, Kubernetes will mark the pod as `Completed`, but then pods will be restarted to start over again.

Alternatively, you could handle the `SIGTERM` signal from within the application to delay the pod termination. We're not going to do that now, but you'll see it in action later in this book, in *Chapter 12*.

So, instead of trying to figure out what the proper `cooldownPeriod` you need to configure is, let's use KEDA's `ScaledJob` instead of scaling a Deployment. To do so, you need to create a Kubernetes job for each message (or batch if you set `BATCH_SIZE`), and let each job complete when its work is done.

`ScaledJob` instances are useful for long-running jobs where the cost of terminating a pod simply because there are no more messages in the queue is too costly.

Let's see that in action.

Hands-on lab: Scaling jobs

During this hands-on lab, you're going to practice deploying the same application as the previous lab, but as a set of Kubernetes jobs. Even though the sample application is not a representative of a long-running job, it's still serving the purpose of using KEDA to scale a job-based workload, let the job finished when it needs, and avoid trying to guess a proper configuration to avoid disruption when KEDA scales down. This process will make even more sense when we need to protect jobs when underutilized nodes are being deleted by projects such as Karpenter.

Exploring the ScaledJob rule

Before you start playing around, take a look at the new `ScaledJob` rule definition:

```
apiVersion: keda.sh/v1alpha1
kind: ScaledJob
metadata:
  name: queue-job-consumer
  namespace: default
```

Notice that the first section is very similar; the only difference is the kind value. The main difference relies in the spec section where you define the job template:

```
spec:
  jobTargetRef:
    template:
      spec:
        containers:
        ... # Same spec definition as the Deployment one
  pollingInterval: 5
  maxReplicaCount: 15
  successfulJobsHistoryLimit: 1
  failedJobsHistoryLimit: 2
```

I've removed the container's spec as it's the same as the Deployment one, but notice that we have included two new parameters: successfulJobsHistoryLimit to keep one job that finished successfully so that you can check the logs to confirm there was no error when KEDA scales down, and failedJobsHistoryLimit to keep to two failed jobs so that you can debug why the job failed. These two parameters are optional, and I added them simply for troubleshooting purposes. Failed and completed jobs are not reserving resources in the cluster.

Deploying the sample application

After exploring the ScaledJob rule, let's deploy it by running this command:

```
$ kubectl apply -f queue-job/consumer.yaml
```

At this point, there aren't any messages in the queue, so no jobs should be launched, but everything is ready now to consume messages when they arrive to the queue.

Deploying a message producer

Same as the previous lab, I've prepared a producer application that will send messages, all at once, to the RabbitMQ queue. Deploy the job using this command:

```
$ kubectl apply -f queue-job/producer.yaml
```

A new pod is created, and it will be removed after sending all the messages.

Watching KEDA in action

Let's launch the RabbitMQ's UI by running this command to expose the service locally:

```
$ kubectl port-forward svc/rabbitmq 15672:15672
```

Then, open `http://localhost:15672/#/queues/%2F/autoscaling` in the browser to monitor the messages in the `autoscaling` queue. You'll see that the messages have arrived to the queue, and they've started being processed by the multiple jobs launched by KEDA.

In a new **Terminal** tab, run this command to watch how jobs are being created:

```
$ kubectl get scaledjob,jobs
```

Notice how KEDA created up 15 jobs at once to start processing messages. Let's look at the logs of the last completed job to confirm that it has completed without any errors. To do so, run the following command (replace 4cgp2 with the corresponding value):

```
$ kubectl logs job.batch/queue-job-consumer-4cgp2
```

You should get all the execution logs, but pay close attention to the last line:

```
... No new messages for 30s. Processed 21 messages. Exiting.
```

This means that the application finished without any problems, and more importantly, it wasn't interrupted when KEDA started to remove unnecessary jobs as there were no additional messages to process.

Cleanup

To remove all resources created for this lab, run the following command:

```
$ kubectl delete -f queue-job
$ helm uninstall rabbitmq
```

So that's it for now. You now have seen KEDA in action first by scaling the same application you used in the previous chapter when practicing with HPA. KEDA simplified the setup, and helped you scale faster as it was going directly to the metrics source instead of relying on the feedback loop from Prometheus metrics adapter.

But that's not really where KEDA shines. Therefore, I wanted you to practice the event-driven feature where KEDA shines, and it's basically the one that allows you to scale from/to zero replicas for certain type of workloads such as processing jobs. We only used the RabbitMQ scaler in this chapter, but the philosophy for the rest of scalers is pretty similar. Lastly, I showed you a more effective way to scale long-running jobs where the cost of interruption during the scaling down operation is too costly.

Summary

As you can tell by now, KEDA takes Kubernetes scaling to the next level, giving you more options to control how your application scales up and down. Besides the diverse set of scalers KEDA has to offer, one of the coolest things we looked at in this chapter was the ability for scaling from/to zero. This feature can really help cut down on resource waste and costs, especially for applications that don't need to run all the time. But we also saw that it's not a one-size-fits-all solution. For some apps, such as REST APIs, scaling to zero can cause more problems than it solves.

We explored KEDA CRDs, and particularly how to use `ScaledObjects` to manage scaling deployments by extending HPA capabilities. KEDA is still giving you a lot of control over things such as cooldown periods and how many replicas you want running. Moreover, you saw `ScaledJobs` in action for those batch jobs or tasks that need to run until they're done, without getting cut off mid-process.

Keep in mind that while KEDA gives you a better way for scaling workloads, you still need to think carefully about how to properly configure scaling rules based on what your application needs. It's all about finding the right balance for each specific app and situation. Head over to the next chapter to learn more about some advanced KEDA features.

5

Kubernetes Event-Driven Autoscaling — Part 2

In the previous chapter, I covered the basics of KEDA and why it has become so popular, and you were able to play around with its basic functionality. Now, I'll go a little bit deeper into some of KEDA's advanced features, accompanied by hands-on labs.

To be more precise, in this chapter, I'll continue exploring a few other KEDA scalers, introducing additional patterns and use cases that showcase KEDA's versatility by showing you very useful implementations I've seen among different companies. For instance, we'll explore how to implement time-based scaling to turn down replicas outside of your working hours to reduce waste by not having idle resources when you're not using them.

Moreover, we'll also spend some time exploring KEDA's HTTP add-on. For situations where a specific scaler isn't available, we'll discuss fallback strategies, including pausing autoscaling and caching metrics. As we progress, we'll dive into advanced autoscaling techniques, such as utilizing complex triggers with scaling modifiers and extending KEDA's capabilities through external scalers. We'll then shift our focus to KEDA's implementation on cloud providers such as AWS, Azure, and Google Cloud. Moreover, you'll learn about the best practices for configuring KEDA in a secure manner.

By the end of this chapter, you'll have a much better understanding of KEDA's advanced features and be prepared to implement more sophisticated autoscaling strategies in your Kubernetes environments. Learning these techniques will help you optimize resource usage, improve application responsiveness, and maintain a more cost-effective, resilient infrastructure. Remember, our ultimate goal is to maintain an efficient Kubernetes cluster as much as possible.

We will be covering the following main topics:

- Autoscaling in KEDA continued
- Scaling based on schedule
- KEDA's HTTP add-on
- What if a KEDA scaler is not available?
- Advanced autoscaling features
- KEDA with cloud providers

Technical requirements

For this chapter, you'll continue using the Kubernetes cluster you created in *Chapter 1*. You can continue working with the local Kubernetes cluster for the first half of the chapter. If you turned down the cluster, make sure you bring it up for every hands-on lab in this chapter. You don't need to install any additional tools, as most of the commands are going to be run using kubectl and helm. You can find the YAML manifests for all resources you're going to create in this chapter in the chapter05 folder from the book's GitHub repository you already cloned in *Chapter 1*.

The second part of this chapter is going to be hands-on with EKS, so you'll need to create an EKS cluster. The hands-on lab will tell you when you need to use it, but it's basically for the ones where we use the AWS scalers. You'll need to go back to *Chapter 1* for the instructions on how to create an EKS cluster using Terraform. You'll simply need to reuse the template I created for the book and run one single command. So, make sure you have access to an AWS account you could use to practice before you proceed.

Autoscaling in KEDA continued

In the previous chapter, we began to see KEDA in action by using the ScaledObject and ScaledJob CRDs. You also learned that there are multiple scalers available, and we could dedicate considerable time to discussing each of them. However, the purpose of this book is to help you build a solid knowledge base and enable you to explore and adapt KEDA's features to your various application needs. That's why, in this chapter, I want to start by exploring a few other common scenarios where KEDA can help you be more efficient with your infrastructure resources, which, in turn, will help you reduce some infrastructure costs.

By now, you might have an idea of KEDA's capabilities, but there are many other features we didn't have time to discuss in the previous chapter. Because I believe these features are important and I don't want you to miss them, I've decided to dedicate some pages to more advanced features, patterns, practices, and integrations that you might need in the near future.

So, let's dive in and start learning how to save money by deactivating workloads at certain times of the day.

Scaling based on schedule

You have already learned that KEDA can scale your workloads down to zero replicas. A frequent question I get from customers is, "How do I turn down the dev environment while the team is not using it?" This becomes very important when your applications are running in the cloud, where you pay for what you use.

KEDA has the cron scaler, which you can use to define a start and end time to set a certain number of replicas to the target object. It's possible to define a time zone (the IANA Time Zone Database) and configure the schedule using the Linux format cron. In case you don't know or don't remember this format, it's basically like this:

```
* * * * *
| | | | |
| | | | +-- Day of the Week (0 - 6) (Sunday = 0)
| | | +---- Month (1 - 12)
| | +------ Day of the Month (1 - 31)
| +-------- Hour (0 - 23)
+---------- Minute (0 - 59)
```

In this bit of code, essentially, each field can contain the following:

- An asterisk (*) representing "every" unit (e.g., every minute, every hour)
- A number to specify an exact value
- A range (two numbers separated by a hyphen (-)) to specify a range of values
- A list (comma-separated values) to specify multiple values

For instance, you can use 0 8 * * * to say 8 AM or 0 18 * * * to say 6 PM.

To use the cron scaler, you'd define the following trigger:

```
triggers:
  - type: cron
    metadata:
      timezone: US/Pacific
      start: 0 8 * * 1-5     # Start at 8:00 AM from Mon/Fri
      end: 0 18 * * 1-5      # End at 6:00 PM from Mon/Fri
      desiredReplicas: "1"
```

Effectively, this means that KEDA will scale the target to one replica from 8 AM to 6 PM from Monday to Friday using the Pacific time zone of the United States. Outside of this schedule, KEDA will scale the target to the `minReplicaCount` value (0 by default). However, it's worth mentioning that a limitation of this scaler is that it doesn't behave like traditional cron jobs with recurring executions, but rather defines time windows for scaling. You'll learn in the next hands-on lab how to use this cron trigger in combination with another scaler to scale based on demand.

Note

There's a GitHub issue (#3566) discussing the possibilities of adding a new time-window trigger to improve scaling using time windows, as the Cron scaler could cause confusion in some scenarios where users expect it to behave like traditional cron jobs. At the time of writing, no decision has been made, but if you need to deactivate workloads during non-working hours, using the cron scaler is the only way to go, at least for now.

Hands-on lab: Scaling to zero during non-working hours

A very common scenario to optimize costs is to turn down environments during non-working hours; this, of course, applies to any pre-production environment. So, imagine that your workload is being used only from 8:00 AM to 6:00 PM from Monday to Friday. Additionally, within that schedule, you might want to continue using a CPU utilization trigger to spin up replicas for when to keep a CPU threshold. To do so, you need to do the following.

You have to use both the `cron` and the `cpu` trigger within the `ScaledJob` rule; it should look like this:

```
...
spec:
  scaleTargetRef:
    name: montecarlo-pi
  minReplicaCount: 0
  maxReplicaCount: 10
  triggers:
  - type: cron
    metadata:
      timezone: US/Pacific
      start: 0 8 * * 1-5
      end: 0 18 * * 1-5
```

```
        desiredReplicas: "1"
  - type: cpu
    metricType: Utilization
    metadata:
      value: "70"
```

Notice that the previous `ScaledObject` is defining a `minReplicaCount` of zero. This means that outside of the schedule configured in the `cron` trigger, KEDA will set the target to zero replicas, which is what we wanted to achieve in the first place.

To see this in action, let's deploy the Monte Carlo application and the `ScaledObject` rule. Go to the `chapter05` folder from the GitHub repository, and run the following commands:

```
$ kubectl apply -f montecarlopi.yaml
$ kubectl apply -f cron
```

If you're running this lab during the schedule configuration, you should see one pod for the application running.

> **Note**
>
> You might need to adjust the schedule configuration to see it working, depending on when you're running this lab.

To confirm that the other trigger is working, let's send, for a very short period of time, some load to the application to make it use more CPU by running the following command:

```
$ kubectl apply -f ab-k8s
```

Then, to watch how pods are being created and how the triggers are making KEDA scale the workload to use more replicas, run the following command:

```
$ watch kubectl get scaledobject,hpa,pods
```

Notice that the `cpu` trigger started to work together with the `cron` trigger, and the replicas might grow to something around three replicas. When the load test finishes and the stabilization window from HPA has passed, KEDA will bring the replicas to 1 as per the schedule from the `cron` trigger.

If you'd like to see how KEDA sets the replicas to zero, change the `timezone` configuration from `ScaledObject` to a different one, such as `Europe/London`. The idea is that you force KEDA to apply the configuration you might have outside of the schedule configured. The trigger should look like this:

```
- type: cron
  metadata:
    timezone: Europe/London
```

Apply the changes by running this command:

```
$ kubectl apply -f cron
```

Wait for the cooldown period to finish, which by default is 300 seconds, and you'll see that KEDA removes the HPA rule.

To clean up all the resources for this lab, run this command:

```
$ kubectl delete -f cron, montecarlopi.yaml, ab-k8s
```

In this lab, you learned how to combine a cron-based trigger with a CPU utilization trigger to create a cost-efficient autoscaling pattern as it optimizes costs by scaling to zero during non-working hours, while still being responsive to real-time CPU load during active periods.

Next, let's explore a different approach to autoscaling based on incoming HTTP traffic using KEDA.

KEDA's HTTP add-on

Previously in the book, I mentioned that KEDA's **HTTP add-on** is used to let your HTTP-based workloads scale to/from zero replicas. KEDA's HTTP add-on is an extension that provides a way to scale HTTP workloads based on incoming traffic, including the ability to scale to zero when there's no demand.

The HTTP add-on introduces a custom resource called `HTTPScaledObject`, where you can specify the application details, and the add-on takes care of creating the necessary Kubernetes resources to scale the application. With `HTTPScaledObject`, you basically tell KEDA how to interact with an HTTP-based application and scale it based on how much traffic it should be able to handle. For instance, you can configure how to scale based on the request rate or concurrency. You can also set up hostname-based routing to manage multiple applications within the same cluster, each responding to its own domain name.

Note

While alternatives such as **Knative** and **OpenFaaS** exist, KEDA's HTTP add-on focuses solely on HTTP autoscaling within the Kubernetes ecosystem. It integrates with the KEDA core and HPA. However, it's important to note that KEDA's HTTP add-on is currently in beta status. This means that it may still undergo changes and improvements. Therefore, we've decided not to explore this add-on in depth for now, but we think it's an important add-on that might shape KEDA's future. Notice that **Kedify**, a commercial offering for KEDA, offers a production-ready version of the HTTP add-on.

In this section, you learned how KEDA's HTTP add-on provides native support for autoscaling HTTP workloads based on traffic, and how it can help reduce resource usage by scaling to zero during idle times. This is particularly valuable for workloads that receive sporadic traffic or are based on a schedule such as a development environment.

Now, let's shift focus to explore what to do when KEDA can't scale your workloads, either because a scaler is unavailable, misconfigured, or needs to be paused for operational reasons.

What if a KEDA scaler is not available?

There might be times when KEDA is not scaling applications because either there's an error with the scaler configuration, the scaler is not available, or maybe you need to momentarily pause any scaling action because you're in a maintenance window (e.g., performing an important deployment or upgrading the Kubernetes cluster). KEDA offers solutions for each of these cases.

Let's explore each of them in more detail.

Caching metrics

The KEDA Metrics Server receives requests from HPA, which by default queries every 15 seconds. When useCachedMetrics is disabled (the default), each HPA request results in a query to the external service. KEDA also polls scalers during the polling interval (default 30 seconds) for activation decisions. When you have multiple ScaledObjects making queries every 15 seconds to the same scaler, the scaler might get throttled or be unresponsive due to the high demand. For this reason, KEDA has a property called useCachedMetrics, within a trigger section, to enable or disable (default) a cache for metric values from the scaler during the polling interval. This means that you could reduce to 50% (in the default scenario) the number of calls you make to the scaler, or even more if you extend the polling interval configuration.

When you enable the metrics cache, a request to the KEDA Metrics Server reads the value from the cache every time instead of making a direct query to the external service.

Let's continue using one example from previous labs and enable the cache for the RabbitMQ trigger. The configuration will now look like this:

```
triggers:
  - type: rabbitmq
    useCachedMetrics: true
    metadata:
      queueName: autoscaling
      queueLength: "5"
    authenticationRef:
      name: rabbitmq-auth
```

Consider enabling the cache for commonly used scalers for applications that can wait for some time to get a fresh value from the scaler. However, if your application needs to scale as soon as possible, caching the metric value might not be suitable. In this case, it's better not to use caching to ensure that KEDA retrieves the most up-to-date metrics directly from the source.

> **Note**
>
> You can't cache metrics for `cpu`, `memory`, the `cron` scaler, or cron scalers. The `useCachedMetrics` feature is also not supported for `ScaledJobs`.

Pausing autoscaling

Imagine that a KEDA scaler is not available, is not working properly, or you simply need to run a maintenance operation where any scaling action might actually cause a problem. KEDA has the ability to pause autoscaling, so instead of removing any `ScaledObject` resource, modifying its scaling behavior, or even making a change within the application, you simply need to add (or change) a special set of annotations in the `ScaledObject` resource.

To pause a `ScaledObject`, you can add the following annotation(s):

```
metadata:
  annotations:
    autoscaling.keda.sh/paused-replicas: "0"
    autoscaling.keda.sh/paused: "true"
```

You don't need to specify both annotations; with either one or the other, you can pause autoscaling. However, in some scenarios, using both annotations together can be beneficial. This combination is useful during maintenance windows or operational tasks where you need to guarantee a stable replica count and prevent any scaling changes.

Let me explain what each of these annotations does so that you can choose properly:

- `autoscaling.keda.sh/paused-replicas` will set the desired number of replicas to the configured value in this annotation and will pause autoscaling. Use this annotation if you need to override the existing number of replicas for your workload. The existing number of replicas might be too low or too high, and you'd like to set the number of replicas that can offer service continuity for your application.

- `autoscaling.keda.sh/paused` will pause autoscaling, but it will keep the existing number of replicas for your workload. This approach is simpler, and it might be the option that works most of the time, especially if the pausing period is short or scaling up or down is too costly (and not worth it).

To resume autoscaling, you need to remove the paused annotations from the `ScaledObject`. Note that simply changing `autoscaling.keda.sh/paused` to `false` will not work. The annotation must be complete.

Fallback scaling actions

Imagine that you might have no idea that a scaler is not working, or something goes wrong with the scaler during non-working hours. You might have your monitoring systems configured to let you know about it, but as a safety mechanism, you might want to configure a `ScaledObject` to fall back to a certain number of replicas if KEDA fails to collect metrics from a target a certain number of times.

To configure fallback, you need to use the following section:

```
fallback:
  failureThreshold: 3
  replicas: 6
```

In this code, `failureThreshold` is the number of consecutive times KEDA fails to get metrics from the source, and `replicas` is the desired number of replicas you want to have if the failure threshold is met.

> **Note**
>
> You can't configure fallback for ScaledJob objects, for cpu and memory scalers, or any scaler whose metric type is AverageValue rather than a target value.

So far, you've learned how to handle scenarios when KEDA can't scale using tools such as pausing and fallback configuration. These mechanisms ensure that your applications remain stable and available even if they can't scale.

Now, let's dive deeper and look at how KEDA can support **complex autoscaling logic** with advanced features such as **scaling modifiers** and **external scalers**, which let you set up auto scaling rules to use very specific scaling requirements.

Advanced autoscaling features

After all the KEDA features we've explored so far, along with the vast number of scalers available, you might find yourself in a scenario where something is still missing to meet your scaling configuration needs. To try to cover complex autoscaling rules, KEDA offers advanced features that you might find useful, such as scaling modifiers or using external scalers. Let's explore each of these options in more detail.

> **Note**
>
> We have tried to cover the most common and stable KEDA features in this book, but KEDA might have added additional features that we didn't cover, or we didn't include them for different reasons. So, before you decide to use any of the upcoming advanced features, make sure you're not adding unnecessary complexity and understand very well what your autoscaling needs are.

Scaling modifiers

There might be times when, even with the ability to configure multiple triggers for complex autoscaling rules for your workloads, you might need to configure custom conditions to scale. Why? Consider that when you have multiple triggers, HPA calculates how many replicas are needed for each metric and uses the maximum one. If you have three cron triggers, the maximum desired number of replicas will be used. But maybe you'd like to sum all of them, particularly in scenarios where each trigger represents an independent source of expected load. Summing them can ensure that your application scales appropriately to handle combined demand across all those dimensions.

Let me give you another example. Let's say you have an application that processes messages from a RabbitMQ queue and then persists some aggregated data into a MySQL database. Scaling only based on the number of messages in the queue might, at some point, cause problems for the database. You might have no problems processing tons of messages, but you might need to be careful not to bring the database down. Therefore, you need to consider metrics such as write latency or replica lag time to decide whether you want to scale based on the RabbitMQ trigger or stop adding replicas until the database is stable.

To solve this problem, KEDA offers a feature called **scalingModifiers** (which went GA in KEDA 2.15) that can help you take autoscaling to the next level. When you opt in for this option, KEDA will use this configuration to decide how to scale. You define a formula where you can reference metrics obtained from scalers and use mathematical and/or conditional statements. This formula returns a value, a composed metric, that joins all the metrics from the scalers that support scalingModifiers (i.e., CPU and memory are ignored) into only one, and the calculated value will be the one used to scale. In other words, *the new composed metric takes precedence over what each scaler would have scaled independently*.

Let's continue using the previous example to help you understand how it works and how to use it. If the database write latency is below 100 ms, it means the database is working fine. Therefore, you can continue using the number of messages in the queue to decide how to scale. If not, you need to pause autoscaling by matching the formula value to the target value. It's like saying to KEDA, "Hey, we're good, no need to scale up or down."

Here's what the configuration will look like:

```
...
advanced:
  scalingModifiers:
    target: "5"
    activationTarget: "1"
    metricType: "AverageValue"
    formula: "db_write_latency < 100 ? queue : 5"
...
```

Let's break down each of these parameters:

- target is the new value you define to scale; it's the target the autoscaling rule needs to maintain. It will add or remove replicas to keep the target.

- `formula` is where you manipulate the new metric that needs to be a single value (not *boolean*). You can use metrics from other scalers (in this example, the `db_write_latency` and queue scalers), use mathematical operations, and use conditional statements. KEDA uses the **Expr** expression language. You can learn more about what expressions you can use at `expr-lang.org` or `github.com/expr-lang/expr`. If `fallback` is configured, `formula` won't modify any metric.

- `activationTarget` is optional, and it's the target value you define to activate scaling – in other words, to go from the 0 to 1 replica. By default, it is 0.

- `metricType` is optional, and it's the metric type to use for the composed metric from `formula`. By default, it is `AverageValue`, but it can be `Value` too.

> **Note**
>
> You can't configure `scalingModifiers` for `ScaledJob` objects or for `cpu` and `memory` scalers. Additionally, when using `scalingModifiers`, only the composite metric from the formula is sent to HPA. All other triggers that aren't included in the formula will be ignored.

Important considerations with scalingModifiers

Before we finish exploring this KEDA feature, let me guide you through a few considerations that you might want to keep in mind:

- First, each trigger used in your formula must have a unique name field defined, as the formula references triggers by their names rather than their types. This is different from regular `ScaledObjects` where naming triggers is optional.

- Another critical aspect to understand is that when scaling modifiers are enabled, KEDA creates a composite metric that completely replaces all individual trigger metrics. This means only the result of your formula is sent to HPA, and any triggers not referenced in the formula are effectively ignored for scaling decisions. This behavior can be surprising if you expect other triggers to continue working independently alongside your scaling modifiers.

- The Expr language itself is designed to be memory-safe and deterministic, making it suitable for production scaling decisions. However, complex formulas may impact the performance of your scaling decisions, so it's recommended to keep expressions as simple as possible while still meeting your requirements. Remember, this formula gets evaluated every time KEDA needs to make a scaling decision.

- Debugging scaling behavior becomes more complex when using scaling modifiers since you're working with a single composite metric instead of multiple individual metrics. Consider implementing logging or monitoring for the individual metric values and formula results to help with troubleshooting when things don't scale as expected.

Let's see scaling modifiers in action with the following hands-on lab.

Hands-on lab: Pausing autoscaling when resources are constrained

In *Chapter 4*, you already practiced scaling a Kubernetes deployment using a RabbitMQ trigger. I'm going to continue using that lab with the additional complexity I've been discussing to help you explore scaling modifiers. Imagine the application is persisting some processed data to a MySQL database. You want to avoid bringing down the database if too many messages end up arriving in the queue, and you need to scale up accordingly. To prevent that, we'll use an external metrics API to get the database write latency in milliseconds. If the write latency is 100 ms or higher, you need to pause autoscaling and resume it when the database is stable.

Start by creating a RabbitMQ queue by running this command:

```
$ helm install rabbitmq --set auth.username=user --set auth.
password=autoscaling bitnami/rabbitmq —wait
```

Next, deploy the consumer application that processes one message from the queue at a time. We won't explore the YAML manifest as it's the same as in the previous chapter. Run this command to deploy the consumer:

```
$ kubectl apply -f formula/consumer.yaml
```

For now, the consumer will have only one replica consuming messages.

To make this lab easier to configure, I've created a dummy API that returns a static number representing the database write latency. It returns JSON like this:

```
{
  "database": {
    "metrics": {
      "write_latency": 150
    }
  }
}
```

Deploy the dummy API by running this command:

```
$ kubectl apply -f formula/dummyapi.yaml
```

Confirm that the API is working by running this command:

```
$ kubectl port-forward svc/dummyapi 8080:80
```

Then, open `http://localhost:8080/` in a new browser window. Notice that the write latency is 150, which means the database is not stable, and the consumer shouldn't scale up with new messages in the queue.

To configure that autoscaling rule, let's deploy a `ScaledObject` with two triggers – one for the RabbitMQ queue and one to query the dummy API – like this:

```
...
  triggers:
    - type: rabbitmq
      name: queue
      metadata:
        queueName: autoscaling
        mode: QueueLength
        value: "5"
      authenticationRef:
        name: rabbitmq-auth
    - type: metrics-api
      name: db_write_latency
      metadata:
        targetValue: "100"
        url: "http://dummyapi.default.svc.cluster.local/"
        valueLocation: 'database.metrics.write_latency'
...
```

Notice that each trigger now has a `name` setup, which is required when using `scalingModifiers` as you need a way to reference them. Also, we're using the `metrics-api` scaler, which is used to scale based on a metric provided by an API you might own, like in this lab.

Then, notice how these two triggers are used in the `formula` field to configure the autoscaling rule we saw previously. It should look like this:

```
...
  advanced:
    scalingModifiers:
      target: "5"
      formula: "db_write_latency < 100 ? queue : 5"
...
```

Remember, the formula is saying that when the database write latency is 100 ms or higher, pause autoscaling to avoid creating new replicas. You don't need to write this autoscaling rule from scratch; to deploy it, simply run the following command:

```
$ kubectl apply -f formula/scalingmodifiers.yaml
```

Before you start testing this scenario, let's run a command to see that no new replicas are being created when you send messages to the queue, as the database isn't stable for now. Run this command in a new terminal:

```
$ watch kubectl get pods,scaledobject,hpa
```

Ignore any `CrashLoopBackOff` error you might have; the pod will be restarted, and it will work again as we discussed in *Chapter 4*. Notice that HPA only has one target and not two because even if you have two triggers, KEDA created the HPA object using the one you provided in the `formula` field. The output should look similar to this:

```
NAME  REFERENCE       TARGETS    MINPODS MAXPODS REPLICAS AGE
...   queue-consumer  5/5 (avg)  1       15      1        2m
```

Let's send a few messages to the queue by running the following command:

```
$ kubectl apply -f formula/producer.yaml
```

You might want to see how many messages you have in the queue, so run the following command to expose the RabbitMQ UI:

```
$ kubectl port-forward svc/rabbitmq 15672:15672
```

Then open `http://localhost:15672/#/queues/%2F/autoscaling` in a new browser window. When prompted for login, type `user` as the user, and type `autoscaling` for the password. You should see that messages are being consumed slowly, as you only have one replica running. If the consumer pod is in `CrashLoopBackOff`, simply delete it and let Kubernetes recreate it.

Let's simulate that the database is stable now by changing the static value configuration from the dummy API deployment. You need to change the following environment variable:

```
env:
  - name: DUMMY_VALUE
    value: "150"
```

To make this change, run the following command:

```
$ kubectl set env deployment/dummyapi DUMMY_VALUE=85
```

This is when scaling modifiers shine. Notice that as soon as HPA is able to get the new value from the dummy API, new pods will be created, as the database is stable now. Messages from the queue will be consumed very rapidly now.

To clean up the resources created by this lab, run these commands:

```
$ kubectl delete -f formula
$ helm uninstall rabbitmq
```

In this hands-on lab, you learned how to use scaling modifiers to build conditional autoscaling logic in KEDA. By combining multiple triggers, one for message queue length and another for database write latency, you were able to pause scaling when a backend system was under pressure and resume it once the system stabilized. This is useful when building context-aware autoscaling strategies that respond not only to application demand, but also to the health of dependent systems.

Now let's look at how to go beyond those limits. In the next section, we'll explore **external scalers**, which allow you to extend KEDA's functionality when built-in scalers aren't enough.

Extending KEDA with external scalers

Another way to extend KEDA's capabilities is by using external scalers. KEDA offers several built-in scalers, which I'd recommend you explore before creating an external scaler. However, if the scaler you need doesn't exist yet, or your organization needs to own the code because you need to interact with private APIs, then you might consider creating an external scaler. Another reason might be that the scaler's complexity requires a separate controller to create additional resources, similar to what the HTTP add-on does when creating a resource to hold incoming requests when scaling from 0 to 1. This book won't cover how to create an external scaler, as that would involve going into coding one in depth and would require its own chapter; instead, we'll simply cover at a high level what you'd need to do to create one and how to use it.

KEDA's built-in scalers run within the KEDA operator, while external scalers run outside of KEDA, and you'd need to communicate with them through a remote procedure call (or **gRPC**, an open source framework for communication between services originally developed by Google). To build an external scaler, the endpoint needs to implement KEDA's built-in scaler interface so KEDA knows when the scaler is active or not, and can query metrics used to define how many replicas are needed.

To use an external scaler, you have either the external or external-push scaler types. The main difference is that the external-push scaler is able to connect to an endpoint that can stream KEDA requests to receive updates from the scaler. The following is how you'd use an external scaler:

```
triggers:
  - type: external
    metadata:
      scalerAddress: your-internal-scaler-endpoint:8080
      organization: eCommerce
      business_unit: Payment
```

The scalerAddress is the endpoint of the scaler API that implements the scaler interface, and the other two fields are custom fields used to pass parameters to the scaler. KEDA sends the entire metadata object to the external scaler endpoint. There are other fields, such as caCert, tlsClientCert, tlsClientKey, and unsafeSsl, that are used to configure TLS authentication to the scaler endpoint.

When considering external scalers, you should understand that they introduce additional operational complexity to your KEDA setup. Unlike built-in scalers that run within the KEDA operator pods, external scalers require you to deploy and maintain separate services that implement the gRPC interface. This means you need to ensure these services are highly available, properly monitored, and maintained with security patches.

So, before deciding to build an external scaler, explore the existing built-in scalers and consider whether your use case could be addressed by combining multiple triggers with scaling modifiers.

KEDA with cloud providers

Another very common use case of KEDA is the integration with scalers from different cloud providers. Instead of having to build all the machinery to use metrics provided by the vast number of services from a cloud provider, you can simply make use of the scalers already available in KEDA. Without these scalers, you might need to use other tools such as Prometheus to scrape metrics from cloud providers' services. This would not only make autoscaling for your applications complex, but it would also slow it down as you'd be adding too many components in the middle before making these metrics available to HPA (assuming you wouldn't go and build your own autoscaler).

In the following sections, we'll briefly explore how to use KEDA with cloud providers. This integration is what truly makes event-driven autoscaling a reality in Kubernetes. You'll be able to see this in action in *Chapter 11* and *Chapter 12*, where we'll be using Amazon EKS. However, in this chapter, we'll cover, at a glance, how KEDA can be used in Microsoft Azure and Google Cloud Platform. *The most important aspect is the authentication.* To use KEDA in a cloud provider, you need to consider which permissions are needed – in terms of security, the fewer privileges it has, the better. As each cloud provider has its own set of services, identity configurations, and best practices, we won't go into much depth about it, as it might require a separate chapter for each one of them. However, we'll focus on the most important aspect: security.

KEDA on Amazon EKS

To use KEDA on Amazon EKS, the recommendation is that you first give KEDA's controller the capability to assume other IAM roles, as you don't want to give too many permissions to KEDA's controller for the following reasons:

- For security purposes
- You might not want to restart KEDA's controller every time you need to modify its permissions

So, when you install KEDA, you need to configure which IAM role, which is tied to a Kubernetes service account, the controller will use. Regardless of the identity model you're using on EKS, **IAM Roles for Service Accounts (IRSA)**, or EKS Pod Identity, a Kubernetes service account is tied to an IAM role. We'll skip these configuration steps and how they work for now, as we'll cover them in *Chapter 11*.

Let's say that the Kubernetes service account you'll use for KEDA's controller will be named keda-operator. Therefore, if you're installing KEDA through Helm, you need to make sure the service account is properly configured. By default, it is like this:

```
serviceAccount:
  operator:
    create: true
    name: keda-operator
    automountServiceAccountToken: true
    annotations: {}
```

This service account will be tied to an IAM role called keda-operator as well, and how you do it depends on whether you use IRSA or EKS Pod Identity. If you're using EKS Pod Identity, the IAM policy should look like this:

```
{
  "Version": "2012-10-17",
  "Statement": [
    {
      "Effect": "Allow",
      "Principal": {
        "Service": "pods.eks.amazonaws.com"
      },
      "Action": [
        "sts:AssumeRole",
        "sts:TagSession"
      ],
      "Condition": {
        "StringEquals": {
          "aws:SourceAccount": "ACCOUNT_NUMBER"
        },
        "ArnEquals": {
          "aws:SourceArn": "EKS_CLUSTER_ARN"
        }
      }
    }
  ]
}
```

This IAM policy would be the one that allows KEDA to assume other IAM roles, which in this case will be the ones assigned for workloads (pods) that you want to scale using KEDA. *We're recommending this approach as the workload you want to scale is already interacting with an AWS service.* Therefore, it already has the permissions to interact with the AWS API. For instance, if the workload is consuming messages from an AWS SQS queue, it should have permissions to at least read messages, delete messages, and describe the queue to get its queue length, something like this:

```
{
  "Version": "2012-10-17",
  "Statement": [
    {
      "Sid": "ConsumeSQSQueue",
      "Effect": "Allow",
      "Action": [
        "sqs:DeleteMessage",
        "sqs:ReceiveMessage",
        "sqs:SendMessage",
        "sqs:GetQueueAttributes",
        "sqs:GetQueueUrl"
      ],
      "Resource": "arn:aws:sqs:${AWS_REGION}:${ACCOUNT_ID}:${QUEUE_NAME}"
    }
  ]
}
```

Once KEDA's controller is able to assume other IAM roles, and the workloads are able to interact with the AWS APIs, the next step you need to consider is the authentication configuration for the ScaledObject.

We recommend that you use the authenticationRef property to delegate this configuration to the TriggerAuthentication object, which should have the following manifest:

```
apiVersion: keda.sh/v1alpha1
kind: TriggerAuthentication
metadata:
  name: aws-credentials
spec:
```

```
podIdentity:
  provider: aws
  identityOwner: workload
```

Notice that you're saying it should use AWS as the provider and that it should take the identity (identityOwner) from the workload. KEDA's controller will assume the IAM role that the workload is using to collect the metrics for the AWS scaler configured in the triggers section from the ScaledObject, like this:

```
...
  triggers:
    - type: aws-sqs-queue
      authenticationRef:
        name: aws-credentials
      metadata:
        queueURL: autoscaling
        queueLength: "5"
        awsRegion: "eu-west-1"
```

The advantage of using TriggerAuthentication to configure the AWS credentials is that you can reuse it within other ScaledObjects. Moreover, because we're recommending that you configure authentication using the workload's service account, it will simplify permissions management for you, as KEDA will assume the workload's IAM role, allowing you to configure only the permissions a scaler will need instead of giving KEDA's controller superpowers.

> **Note**
>
> At the time of writing this book, KEDA has five built-in scalers for AWS: AWS Cloud-Watch, AWS DynamoDB, AWS DynamoDB Streams, AWS Kinesis Data Stream, and AWS Simple Queue Service. For authentication, KEDA supports AWS IRSA and AWS Secret Manager. EKS Pod Identity (Wax) is an alternative approach, which we'll explore in *Chapter 11*.

KEDA on Azure Kubernetes Service

To use KEDA on **Azure Kubernetes Service** (**AKS**), you can simply enable the KEDA add-on that installs all the KEDA components integrated with AKS. You can enable it through an **Azure Resource Manager** (**ARM**) template by adding the following section:

```
"workloadAutoScalerProfile": {
    "keda": {
        "enabled": true
    }
}
```

Or, you can also use the Azure CLI and run the following command:

```
$ az aks update --resource-group RESOURCE_GROUP_NAME --name AKS_CLUSTER_
NAME --enable-keda
```

Notice that you basically add the --enable-keda parameter.

> **Note**
>
> While the AKS KEDA add-on installs all built-in scalers, external scalers (such as the one for Azure Cosmos DB) must still be installed separately.

Once KEDA is enabled, you first need to enable the AKS cluster to interact with the Azure APIs that your workloads will need to scale. For this book, we go into depth about the commands you need to run. We'll only cover at a glance what the process looks like.

To continue with KEDA's configuration, the next step is to create an Azure Identity for the workloads and the KEDA operator. Then, to avoid having to specify secrets, you need to create a federated credential between the Azure Identity and the Kubernetes service account that the workload you'll scale is going to use. You also need to create a second federated credential to give permissions to KEDA's controller.

Then, depending on the Azure scaler you'll use, you need to provide the corresponding permissions to the Azure Identity you created. For instance, if you're using the Azure Service Bus scaler, you need to give permissions to this API to the Azure Identity.

Now you need to create a `TriggerAuthentication` object to allow scalers to use the Azure APIs. The manifest should look like this:

```
apiVersion: keda.sh/v1alpha1
kind: TriggerAuthentication
metadata:
  name: azure-credentials
spec:
  podIdentity:
    provider:  azure-workload
    identityId: $MI_CLIENT_ID
```

Notice that the provider is an Azure workload, and that `identityId` is the Azure Identity ID you created before. With this configuration, KEDA will be able to use the workload identity to collect metrics from the scaler configured to scale the workload.

> **Note**
>
> At the time of writing this book, KEDA has nine built-in scalers for Azure: Azure Monitor, Azure Pipelines, Azure Event Hubs, Azure Queue Storage, Azure Application Insights, Azure Data Explorer, Azure Log Analytics, Azure Service Bus, and Azure Blob Storage. Additionally, there are two external scalers: KEDA External Scale for Azure Cosmos DB and Durable Task KEDA External Scaler. Regarding authentication providers, KEDA has support for Azure AD Workload Identity and Azure Key Vault.

KEDA on Google Kubernetes Engine

Using KEDA on **Google Kubernetes Engine** (**GKE**) is pretty similar to what you've seen so far. We won't go into depth on how you'd configure the security aspects of using KEDA on GKE, but we'll explore at a glance what the process looks like.

First, you need to deploy KEDA's components to GKE, and the Kubernetes service account that KEDA's controller will use is going to be tied to a **Google Service Account (GSA)** that will have the proper permissions to use the API of **Google Cloud Platform (GCP)**. Then, depending on the scalers you'll use to scale your workloads, you need to provide the corresponding permissions to the GSA account.

Similarly, as with the other cloud providers, the recommended approach, if your workloads are running in GKE, is to use the TriggerAuthentication object. For GCP, the manifest will look like this:

```
apiVersion: keda.sh/v1alpha1
kind: TriggerAuthentication
metadata:
  name: gcp-credentials
spec:
  podIdentity:
    provider: gcp
```

Notice that here you simply configure GCP as the provider. When your ScaledObject references this authentication object, KEDA's controller will impersonate the IAM service account the workloads you're scaling have.

> **Note**
>
> At the time of writing this book, KEDA has four built-in scalers for GCP: Google Cloud Platform Pub/Sub, Google Cloud Platform Storage, Google Cloud Platform Cloud Tasks, and Google Cloud Operations. And regarding authentication providers, KEDA has support for GCP Secret Manager and GCP Workload Identity.

As you can see, the approach is the same in all three cloud providers, but the difference remains in the service names each provider uses and how they implement such security configurations. The reason we dedicated a section to exploring how KEDA works on cloud providers is to show you how KEDA adapts very well to what each of these cloud providers needs security-wise. Avoid giving extra permissions to KEDA's controller, and instead use the permissions each of the workloads that you're scaling has.

Summary

In this second chapter on KEDA, you were able to explore the benefits and autoscaling capabilities it brings to your applications. While you might have already had an idea from the previous chapter, in this chapter, I wanted to highlight very useful features that not many people know about KEDA. You might have heard that KEDA goes beyond CPU, memory, and external metrics, and that you can use KEDA as an event-driven autoscaler for your workloads. However, in this chapter, I wanted to focus on a few advanced features, along with additional scaling scenarios where KEDA fits very well. Moreover, I wanted to give you an introduction to how KEDA considers security when you need to use scalers from cloud providers such as AWS, Azure, or GCP. I could dedicate one single chapter to go into depth on how to use KEDA for each cloud provider, but as you can see, KEDA works similarly for many of the scalers, and that's the intention of the project.

You explored several features in this chapter, but one I'd like to highlight is scaling modifiers. This feature gives you a lot of flexibility to adapt to almost every autoscaling logic you might need. You can extend KEDA's behavior by pausing or even speeding up scaling based on custom conditions you might have.

Alright, so that's it for now. Head over to the next chapter to close the autoscaling workload section of the book and learn about how you can do troubleshooting with KEDA, and a few other tools to help you optimize your workloads in Kubernetes.

6

Workload Autoscaling Operations

Up until this point, we've been exploring multiple ways to make your workloads more efficient in Kubernetes. In other words, we've discussed how to ensure your workloads are not wasting the resources available in the cluster. You've learned that to have consistent results, you need to be intentional about the number of CPU and memory requests your pods have. By doing so, you can then make use of tools such as HPA, VPA, and KEDA to adjust the number of replicas based on utilization or events that impact the performance of your workloads.

However, how do you know you're doing proper right-sizing for your workloads? How do you keep doing it continuously, as it's not a one-time task? And how do you know why your workloads might not be scaling? Well, you need to learn how to do proper troubleshooting, read logs, interpret metrics, and watch for events in the tools you're using.

In this chapter, we'll focus on the operational aspect of autoscaling your workloads, with a focus on the efficiency aspect. You'll learn how to troubleshoot the different workload autoscaling tools we've explored so far: HPA, VPA, and KEDA. After reading *Chapter 4* and *Chapter 5*, you might have decided to use (or switch to) KEDA for autoscaling your workloads, even if you're not quite there yet on the event-driven aspect. Therefore, we'll show you how to set up a Grafana dashboard to have a quick overview of what could be happening with your KEDA scaling objects. Finally, we'll close this chapter and the whole workload autoscaling section, with some best practices on how to keep your efficiency score in an optimal state.

Learning how to monitor, troubleshoot, and optimize autoscaling using KEDA will help you ensure your applications remain responsive, cost-efficient, and resilient. Especially as your workloads and infrastructure evolve. You'll be building confidence in production environments, where visibility and control are just as important as automation.

We will be covering the following main topics:

- Workload autoscaling operations
- Troubleshooting workload autoscaling
- Monitoring KEDA
- Upgrading KEDA
- Best practices for workload efficiency

Technical requirements

For this chapter, you'll continue using the Kubernetes cluster you created in *Chapter 1*. You can continue working with the local Kubernetes cluster for the first half of the chapter. If you turned down the cluster, make sure you bring it up for every hands-on lab in this chapter. You don't need to install any additional tools, as most of the commands are going to be run using kubectl and helm. You can find the YAML manifests for all resources you're going to create in this chapter in the chapter06 folder from the Book's GitHub repository you already cloned in *Chapter 1*.

Workload autoscaling operations

In an ideal world, systems work as expected all the time. But the reality is that the majority of the systems we interact with need maintenance, and things break all the time. This holds true with all the autoscaling tools and configurations we've explored so far. There might be times when you'll be wondering why HPA, VPA, or KEDA aren't adding or removing replicas to your workloads. As these are Kubernetes components, troubleshooting them is not very unique, and you'll end up reusing most of the tools and techniques you're already using to troubleshoot your workloads.

Additionally, you've learned already, from the constant emphasis in previous chapters, that right-sizing your workloads is a very important task, especially as you configure scaling rules for your workloads, which will become even more crucial when we explore node autoscaling. So far, you've deployed a simple Grafana dashboard in *Chapter 3* to get a first glimpse of how to adjust the resources you request for every workload. But you'll be doing this task continuously as your workloads are going to be in constant change.

Therefore, during this chapter, we'll spend some time exploring how to troubleshoot your workload autoscaling rules. We'll show you a few options (out of many) you have to support with data how efficient your workloads are with the resources available in the Kubernetes cluster. Let's start by looking at how and which logs to read.

Troubleshooting workload autoscaling

In previous chapters, you've practiced how to configure autoscaling rules for your workloads. So far, all of those hands-on labs should have worked without any problems (if not, please open a GitHub issue). These labs have been built to help you learn about the concepts we've been covering so far. However, when you want to apply the concepts learned to your environment, things might not work as expected. So, the following sections are aimed at helping you make the troubleshooting task a bit easier. Moreover, we'll be including typical things to look at for common problems that you might not have experienced while doing the labs from this book. It's worth mentioning that we're assuming you already have a solid understanding of how these tools work, as we'll focus solely on how to do troubleshooting.

Troubleshooting HPA

One of the most common problems in HPA lies in the process of retrieving metrics. You might have some misconfigurations in place, or the metrics provider might not be working. The most basic problem could be one of the following:

- The Metrics Server component is not installed in the cluster or isn't working properly. Therefore, HPA won't be able to get basic metrics such as CPU and memory from the pod(s).

- Custom or external metrics aren't available. For instance, you might have configured a rule to scale using metrics from Prometheus, but there's no adapter translating those metrics, or the query you've configured has an error.

- Networking issues between the cluster and the metric sources.

- **Role-based access control (RBAC)** permissions to interact with the Metrics API.

The solution for all of the problems listed here might be obvious (i.e., deploy the Metrics Server, restart the Metrics Server, fix the scaling rule configuration, give proper RBAC permissions, etc.). But these might not be the only problems you could face. So, instead of giving you an extensive list of problems with their possible solution(s), let's explore a few commands that can help you identify and confirm what could be the problem with HPA scaling rules.

Reviewing HPA conditions and events

Within every HPA, there's a field named `status.conditions` that you could review. Kubernetes updates this field with some details indicating whether or not HPA could scale the target object. For instance, you could get details regarding HPA's ability to collect metrics to determine the number of replicas, whether the rule is active or not, or whether it's possible or not to add/remove replicas. To review the conditions from an HPA object, you need to describe the HPA object by running the following command:

```
$ kubectl describe hpa montecarlo-pi
```

You might get an output like the following:

```
Conditions:
  Type          Status  Reason          Message
  ----          ------  ------          -------
  AbleToScale   False   FailedGetScale  the HPA controller was unable to
  get the target's current scale: deployments/scale.apps "montecarlo-pi"
  not found
```

In this case, the message indicates that the `montecarlo-pi` deployment doesn't exist, therefore HPA is not able to scale. Once you've identified this issue, the next step would be to check whether the deployment name is correct and ensure that the deployment has been created in the correct namespace. If it's missing, you should redeploy the application or update the HPA target reference accordingly. When you look at the `Events` section from the same output after describing the HPA object, you'll see something like this:

```
Events:
  Type      Reason          Age  From                       Message
  ----      ------          ---  ----                       -------
  Warning   FailedGetScale  5s   horizontal-pod-autoscaler
  deployments/scale.apps "montecarlo-pi" not found
```

Similar to the `conditions` field, the `Events` section also provides valuable information about any scaling action that HPA might or might not be taking.

Checking Metrics Server logs

Remember that HPA relies on the Metrics Server component. When HPA can't fetch metrics for resources such as CPU and memory from the target object, then it won't be able to determine the number of replicas needed to meet the target. If you see an error message from the conditions or `Events` section indicating that HPA couldn't fetch metrics for a resource, then you'll need to check the logs from the Metrics Server pod(s).

To check logs from the Metrics Server pod(s), run the following command:

```
$ kubectl logs -n kube-system -l app.kubernetes.io/name=metrics-server
--all-containers=true --tail=20
```

With this command, you're getting logs from all the pods that have the label/value of `app.kubernetes.io/name=metrics-server`, including all containers from the pod(s), and you'll only get the latest 20 log lines. From these logs, you might find the reason why metrics can be fetched from a node, for instance, due to a networking issue. Another common reason is that the Metrics Server pod(s) are failing because they're reaching a memory limit, or any other application error that is causing the pod(s) to fail. If this is happening, you need to check the resource `limits` and `requests` for the `metrics-server` deployment. You may need to increase its memory allocation or investigate and resolve any underlying errors. Also, restarting the `metrics-server` pod can also help in cases where it becomes temporarily unresponsive.

That's pretty much how you can do troubleshooting in HPA. Typically, the information you get from the `conditions` and event fields is enough to have an idea of why scaling is not working as expected. However, there might be times when you simply get an error that says HPA is not able to fetch metrics. If you're getting metrics from Prometheus, make sure that the query doesn't have any errors and that you're getting the value in the format you need.

Troubleshooting VPA

As you already know, VPA doesn't come as a built-in feature in Kubernetes. To use VPA, you need to deploy its three components:

- **VPA updater**
- **VPA recommender**
- **VPA admission controller**

Most of the troubleshooting will be done within the controller and the recommender.

So, what do you need to do if VPA is not doing what you're expecting?

1. Check that the VPA components are up and running.
2. Confirm that the VPA's CRDs were deployed.
3. Validate that the Metrics Server component is up and running.
4. Review the events from the VPA objects.
5. Read the logs from VPA's components to find out what's wrong.
6. Verify why VPA can't apply recommendations.

The first three steps are pretty straightforward, and you already know how to do these after doing the labs from *Chapter 3*. Therefore, let's focus on the rest of the steps, as some need you to understand what to look for and which commands to run.

Reviewing the events and status of the VPA objects

To review the events that Kubernetes emits to the VPA objects, you need to run a command similar to the following to describe the VPA object:

```
$ kubectl describe vpa montecarlo-pi
```

You might not find something in the Events section, but you can have a better understanding of what's happening within the Conditions and Recommendation fields from the Conditions section. For instance, you could get an output like the following:

```
...
Status:
  Conditions:
    Last Transition Time:  2024-11-27T22:03:02Z
    Status:                True
    Type:                  RecommendationProvided
  Recommendation:
    Container Recommendations:
      Container Name:  montecarlo-pi
...
```

From this output, you can see when the last time VPA applied a recommendation was and what the recommended values were. However, if this information is still not relevant or useful, you can then check the VPA components logs.

Reading the logs from VPA components

To check the logs from every component, you can run the following commands:

- VPA recommender logs:

```
$ kubectl logs -n kube-system -l app=vpa-recommender --all-
containers=true --tail=20
```

- VPA updater logs:

```
$ kubectl logs -n kube-system -l app=vpa-updater --all-
containers=true --tail=20
```

- VPA admission controller logs:

```
$ kubectl logs -n kube-system -l app=vpa-admission-controller --all-
containers=true --tail=20
```

Notice that, similar to what you did with HPA, you're getting logs from all the pods from all the containers that have the label/value for the VPA components, and you'll only get the latest 20 log lines. You might find very useful hints about why VPA is not able to apply (or calculate) recommender resources to pods.

Verifying why VPA can't apply recommendations

Let's talk about resources. Imagine your workload has a memory leak or the utilization is growing because it's processing a large payload. However, you might be wondering why VPA is not resizing the pods. This could be because of one of the following:

- You might have VPA maximum allowance or resource limits (at the pod or namespace level) that are not letting VPA apply recommendations.
- The cluster can't allocate bigger pods as there are no resources available.
- The pods you're expecting to be adjusted are not part of a replica controller.
- VPA isn't configured with the Auto or Recreate mode.
- The metrics data history length is too big or too small. By default, VPA checks 8 days back, but it can be adjusted using the history-length parameter. If you're using Prometheus, you might need to check the query to adjust the period length.
- As discussed in *Chapter 3*, the new recommendations will be applied when pods have been running for enough time, which by default is 12 hours (this is to avoid too many pod rotations after applying the first recommendation). You can adjust this configuration using the in-recommendation-bounds-eviction-lifetime-threshold parameter.

These are the most common problems you might encounter with VPA. As long as you keep in mind the role of each component, the vertical autoscaling workflow, and how to find out what's happening by reading logs/events, you might be able to spot problems very quickly.

Troubleshooting KEDA

Similar to VPA, KEDA doesn't come as a built-in feature in Kubernetes. Therefore, when you deploy KEDA to your cluster, you deploy a few pods (components) you'll use to troubleshoot when scaling isn't working. Scaling might not be working mainly because KEDA can't collect metrics from the source, but there might be other reasons we'll explore in a moment.

As a quick reminder, as you learned in *Chapter 4*, there are three KEDA components:

- KEDA's operator
- KEDA's metric server
- KEDA's admission webhook.

You'll likely spend more time reading KEDA's operator logs, as that's like KEDA's brain.

So, what do you need to do if KEDA is not doing what you're expecting?

1. Check that the KEDA components are up and running.
2. Confirm that KEDA's CRDs were deployed.
3. Validate that the Metrics Server is working if using CPU and memory scalers.
4. Validate that you have properly authenticated to the scaler API.
5. Confirm that there aren't any network policies denying traffic to KEDA.
6. Review the events from ScaledObject or ScaledJob objects.
7. Review the events from the HPA objects (if scaling is active).
8. Read the logs from KEDA's components to find out what's wrong.

Let's see how you can check events and review logs from KEDA's components.

Reviewing events from ScaledObject or ScaledJob objects

After confirming KEDA's components are up and running, and CRDs are deployed into the cluster, the next step would be to review the events from the KEDA scaling objects you've created. Suppose that you deploy a ScaledObject object, but not the target workload it's supposed to be scaling.

Deploy a sample ScaledObject object by running the following command:

```
$ kubectl apply -f troubleshooting/scaledobject.yaml
```

To review the events from ScaledObject, run the following command:

```
$ kubectl describe scaledobject queue-consumer
```

You should get an output similar to the following within the Events section:

```
...
    Warning  ScaledObjectCheckFailed  1s (x12 over 11s)  keda-operator
      Target resource doesn't exist
    Warning  ScaledObjectCheckFailed  1s (x12 over 11s)  keda-operator
      ScaledObject doesn't have correct scaleTargetRef specification
```

The event shown was the ScaledObjectCheckFailed event, which appears when the check validation of ScaledObject fails. Notice how KEDA's operator tried to create the HPA object, but the target workload to scale doesn't exist, showing the Target resource doesn't exist error. KEDA emits many different events, but the ones you might need to keep an eye on are the Warning event types. A couple of other examples are KEDAScalerFailed when the scaler fails to create/verify its event source, and KEDAScaleTargetDeactivationFailed when KEDA can't scale to 0 the target. For a full list of events, check KEDA's doc site (https://keda.sh/docs/latest/reference/events/).

> **Note**
>
> If the KEDA link is not working by the time you're reading the book, you can try searching KEDA's doc site for the list of Kubernetes events that KEDA emits.

Reading the logs from KEDA's components

Reviewing events is a good start, but as you can see, they don't give you too many details about what's wrong. Therefore, you need to read KEDA's component logs to get a more precise idea about the error. But before you have a look at that, let me give you the commands you need to keep handy.

To check the logs from every KEDA component, you can run the following commands:

- For KEDA operator logs:

```
$ kubectl logs -n keda -l app=keda-operator --all-containers=true
--tail=20
```

- For KEDA metrics server logs:

```
$ kubectl logs -n keda -l app=keda-operator-metrics-apiserver --all-
containers=true --tail=20
```

- For KEDA admission webhooks logs:

```
$ kubectl logs -n keda -l app=keda-admission-webhooks --all-
containers=true --tail=20
```

If you run the command to read the KEDA operator logs, you should see an error describing in more detail what the problem is (which you already know is because we didn't create the target workload):

```
...ERROR Reconciler error {"controller": "scaledobject",
"controllerGroup": "keda.sh", "controllerKind": "ScaledObject",
"ScaledObject": {"name":"queue-consumer","namespace":"default"},
"namespace": "default", "name": "queue-consumer", "reconcileID":
"ee2eb037-62eb-4386-8322-ae5378400ca0", "error": "deployments.apps
\"queue-consumer\" not found"}
```

Notice how the error logs are more precise, saying that there's no Deployment object called queue-consumer. If you go back to *Chapter 4* and complete the *Hands-On: Scaling from/to Zero* lab, you should see how the error events and logs are gone as you create the missing resources, and KEDA then is able to scale the application without problems.

Centralizing logs and events

Before we move on to the next section, I wanted to make it very clear that the commands you explored before come in handy when you need to have a quick overview of what the problem could be. However, reading events and logs in the command line doesn't scale when you end up having several scaling rules running in the same workload. At some point, there is going to be so much noise that it will be hard to find out what's happening with a specific workload you're struggling to scale.

Therefore, the recommendation would be to use a centralized tool to store and review all the events and logs from the cluster, and have a single pane of glass to troubleshoot easily. Most likely, you already have a solution for this. But if not, tools such as Grafana Loki (in combination with Grafana and Alloy) or Elasticsearch (in combination with Kibana and Logstash) are a few (of many) examples of tools you can use to centralize logs and events from multiple Kubernetes clusters.

So far, you've learned how to identify and resolve common issues in KEDA by inspecting events, checking component logs, and validating deployment configurations. These are very important techniques that will help you troubleshoot and fix problems in a production environment.

Next, let's explore how you can take one step further by looking at how to monitor KEDA itself using Prometheus and Grafana, to give you visibility into the health and behavior of KEDA's internal components.

Monitoring KEDA

Another important aspect for operating KEDA is monitoring. This effectively means observing metrics that define the status or health of a system. So, in this case, we're interested in observing metrics from KEDA's components. In *Chapter 3*, you already used Prometheus and Grafana to monitor the resource utilization of a workload with the purpose of right-sizing the requests of CPU and memory. To monitor KEDA's components, we're going to continue using these tools and take advantage of what KEDA's components already provide.

KEDA's components already expose a certain number of metrics for Prometheus to scrape. As most of the work in KEDA is done in the operator, you'll find that most of the metrics come from this component. However, KEDA also exposes metrics for KEDA's metric server and KEDA's admission webhook. All these metrics can be scraped by Prometheus on port 8080 at the /metrics endpoint.

KEDA will update each ScaledObject or ScaledJob object with the list of metrics that the triggers will be using. If you'd like to get this information, you need to run a command like the following:

```
$ kubectl get scaledobject queue-consumer -o jsonpath={.status.
externalMetricNames}
```

This will return the metrics the scaling object will use, like this:

```
["s0-rabbitmq-autoscaling"]
```

The metrics you get here depend on the scaler you use, and as you continue to deploy more scaling rules using different scalers, you'll start to see a few additional metrics available. For example, the following table shows a few metrics you could use to understand the existing status of your ScaledObject rules:

Name	Description
keda_scaler_active	Indicates whether the scaler is active (1) or inactive (0)
keda_scaled_object_paused	Indicates whether a ScaledObject object is paused (1) or unpaused (0).
keda_scaler_metrics_value	Indicates the current value for each scaler's metric that HPA uses when computing the target (average) number of replicas.

Table 6.1 – Subset of basic metrics emitted by KEDA's operator

This subset of metrics is going to help you understand why KEDA might or might not be scaling your workloads. But if you'd like to understand why KEDA might be having issues scaling your workloads, *Table 6.2* shows a subset of metrics you could use:

Name	Description
`keda_scaler_metrics_latency_seconds`	Latency of retrieving the current metric from each scaler. Useful to know if there are connectivity issues with the scaler.
`keda_scaler_detail_errors_total`	Number of errors for each scaler.
`keda_scaled_object_errors_total`	Number of errors for each `ScaledObject` object.
`keda_scaled_job_errors_total`	Number of errors for each `ScaledJob` object.
`keda_trigger_registered_total`	Number of triggers per trigger (scaler) type.

Table 6.2 – Subset of metrics used for troubleshooting KEDA

Table 6.2 includes a subset of metrics you could use not only to understand how bad or big a problem is, but you can also use these metrics to configure alarms to notify you when something goes outside of a certain threshold. For example, it might not be harmful to get a few errors from time to time. But, if the error rate keeps increasing, you might want to get paged and fix any problems with your KEDA scaling rules as soon as possible. As I said before, these are not the only metrics KEDA emits. The full list of metrics is available on the KEDA docs site (`https://keda.sh/docs/latest/operate/metrics-server/`). Make sure you check the integration with Prometheus to learn more and see other metrics we didn't include in this book, but that might be important for your workload(s).

> **Note**
>
> If the KEDA link is not working by the time you're reading the book, you can try searching KEDA's doc site for the list of metrics that KEDA exposes.

Similar to what I said before about events and logs, you can't operate KEDA with `kubectl` only, even if it provides the information you need. Lucky for us, a while ago, KEDA released a Grafana dashboard to have a single pane of glass to view metrics exposed by KEDA. So, let's go back to the terminal and deploy the Grafana dashboard.

Hands-on lab: Deploying KEDA's Grafana dashboard

Before you deploy the Grafana dashboard, you need to enable KEDA's component to expose the metrics we explored before at the `/metrics` endpoint. By default, Prometheus integration is disabled, and as we've deployed KEDA using Helm, let's update its configuration using Helm as well.

Open a new terminal, and change the directory to the `chapter06` folder from the GitHub repository. You'll find a `monitoring/keda-values.yaml` file with the additional settings you need to enable metrics exposure. The new Helm settings should look similar to this:

```
prometheus:
  operator:
    enabled: true
    serviceMonitor:
      enabled: true
      additionalLabels:
        release: prometheus
... // Same for metricServer and webhooks
```

To update KEDA's Helm release, run the following command:

```
$ helm upgrade keda kedacore/keda --namespace keda -f monitoring/keda-values.yaml
```

KEDA's pods should be recreated with the new settings, and you should also see that a new `ServiceMonitor` has been created to let Prometheus know that it should scrape the `/metrics` endpoint for each KEDA component.

You can confirm this by running the following command:

```
$ kubectl get servicemonitor -n keda
```

You should see three Prometheus service monitors, one for each KEDA component.

Now, let's deploy one of the labs you did in *Chapter 4* to generate some metrics, so that when you deploy KEDA's dashboard, you can see something. In your terminal, don't change directories, and simply run the following command to deploy the application and all its dependencies to configure autoscaling:

```
$ kubectl apply -f ../chapter04/queue-deployment/consumer.yaml
```

Then, run the following command to generate a small load test:

```
$ kubectl apply -f ../chapter04/queue-deployment/producer.yaml
```

While you wait for the load test to finish, let's deploy the Grafana dashboard. To do so, open the Grafana UI by exposing the service locally by running the following command:

```
$ kubectl port-forward service/prometheus-grafana 3000:80 -n monitoring
```

In a browser, open the `http://localhost:3000/` URL.

For the user, type `user`, and for the password, type `prom-operator`. If these credentials don't work, go back to *Chapter 2* to retrieve the username and password from Prometheus stack secrets.

Next, you import the Grafana dashboard, and to do so, follow these steps:

1. Click **Dashboards** from the left menu, or open the `/dashboards` endpoint.

2. Click on the **New** button, and select **Import** in the drop-down menu.

3. Click on the **Upload a dashboard JSON file** section, and pick the file located at `chapter06/monitoring/keda-dashboard.json`.

4. Click on the **Import** button.

The first part is the list of filters for the dashboard. You can filter by **namespace**, **scaledObject**, **scaler**, or **metric**. If you don't see any data, try switching the **datasource** field.

Notice that the first three visualizations show the error rates from the scaler(s) and scaled objects. This is a good source to know when things aren't going well in KEDA. Next, you'll see the current scaler metric values to understand which values KEDA is using to scale. Moreover, you'll see a graph showing the maximum number of replicas and how KEDA has been adding and removing replicas while the load test was running. In this case, I ran the load test twice, which is why you see two changes in *Figure 6.1*:

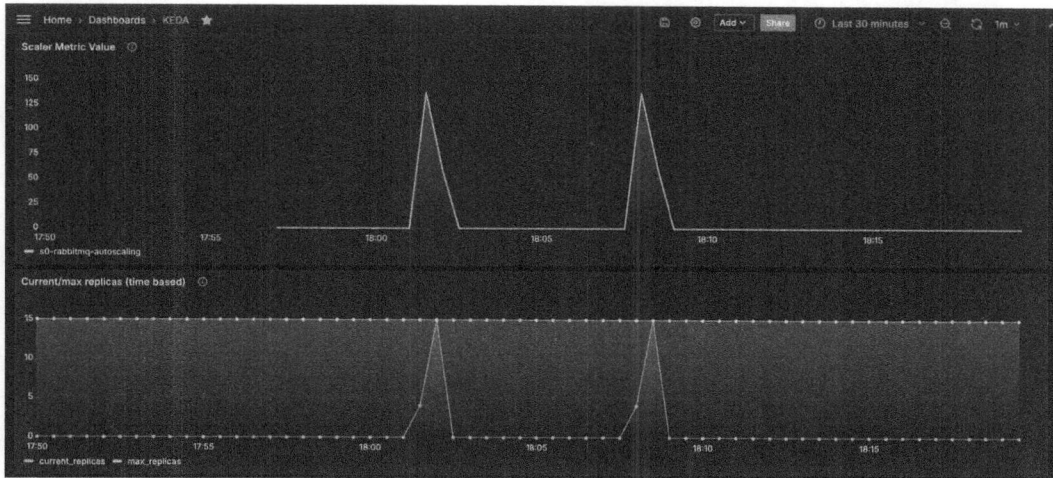

Figure 6.1 – KEDA's dashboard showing the number of replicas in a sample workload

If you continue scrolling down, you will see other visualizations to understand changes in the replica numbers for the workloads you're monitoring. Additionally, you'll see a graph that represents how close you're getting to the maximum number of replicas.

The version of the dashboard we showed in this book might differ from what you get when doing this lab. The reason is simple: KEDA occasionally updates the dashboard, and we may have a different version of the JSON manifest at the time of writing this book. If you'd like to get the latest version of this dashboard, check out KEDA's official repository (`https://github.com/kedacore/keda/blob/main/config/grafana/keda-dashboard.json`).

> **Note**
>
> If the GitHub link for Grafana is not working by the time you're reading this book, you can try searching in KEDA's GitHub repository (`https://github.com/kedacore/keda/`) for the Grafana dashboard or open an issue.

In this lab, you set up KEDA's Grafana dashboard to visualize key metrics and error indicators across scalers and scaling objects. This provides insights into how your workloads are behaving and helps you quickly detect issues when autoscaling isn't working as expected.

Now, let's look at how to keep your installation up to date. In the next section, we'll walk through different strategies for upgrading KEDA.

Upgrading KEDA

Another important topic related to operating KEDA is upgrades. We recommend always using a recent version of KEDA to make the most of it, especially as KEDA will continue adding new features, fixing issues, and adding native scalers. Depending on how you decide to deploy KEDA's components to production, the upgrade process might differ from the one you'll see in this book.

In *Chapter 4*, we used Helm to install KEDA in a very simple way. However, I've seen many organizations switching to a GitOps model using Argo CD and deploying KEDA by using YAML manifests. GitOps and Argo CD allow you to manage your Kubernetes applications using Git. Instead of manually applying changes, you just update a Git repo, and Argo CD makes sure your cluster matches what's in the code. Many companies like using them for apps such as KEDA because it's easier to keep track of changes and fix things if they break.

> **Note**
>
> If you decide to go with the approach described in this section, and you've installed KEDA using Helm, make sure you uninstall KEDA using Helm first, using the following command: `helm uninstall keda -n keda`. Keep in mind that when you uninstall KEDA, all the `ScaledObject` and/or `ScaledJob` objects you have will be removed. Then, install KEDA using the commands discussed later and use `kubectl create` instead of `kubectl replace`.

When you install or upgrade KEDA, it's important that you are specific about the version you want to install. This is so you can control which version to install when upgrading KEDA. It's also important that you read the release notes to understand the impact of using a newer version. CRDs might change, and you'll need to update any existing KEDA objects. Additionally, the release notes are where you'll find recommendations on how to handle any breaking changes. Try to keep KEDA up to date and avoid falling too far behind the latest version. Regular updates help ensure you benefit from the latest features and security improvements while minimizing the complexity of future upgrades.

To upgrade KEDA using only `kubectl`, you can run the following commands:

```
$ export KEDA_VERSION="2.18.0"
$ curl -L -o keda.yaml https://github.com/kedacore/keda/releases/download/
v$KEDA_VERSION/keda-$KEDA_VERSION.yaml
$ kubectl replace -f keda.yaml
```

> **Note**
>
> If you get an error such as `Error from server (NotFound): error` when replacing
> `"keda.yaml": customresourcedefinitions.apiextensions.k8s.io "XXX"`
> `not found`, simply run `kubectl create keda.yaml` and ignore the errors saying
> that an object already exists. When you use tools such as Argo CD, they already have
> internal validations to avoid this problem of using `kubectl replace` or `kubectl`
> `create`, depending on the status of the objects.

Notice that we specified the KEDA version we want to install. Next time you need to upgrade, you'll use the specific version number you want to deploy. Then, it's a good practice to download the release YAML manifest, which includes every component you need. Finally, you simply use `kubectl` to replace existing Kubernetes objects with the most recent ones.

The benefit of downloading the YAML manifest is that you can version it in Git and keep track of the changes you'll apply next. This is key if you're going to use GitOps.

Regardless of the approach you use to upgrade KEDA, make sure that you practice doing it in a pre-production environment, and that you're aware that scaling actions might be paused for a very short period of time.

Upgrading KEDA regularly ensures you benefit from the latest features, improvements, and bug fixes, but more importantly, it allows you to evolve the autoscaling capabilities of your workloads.

Now, let's take a step back and reflect on the broader picture. In the next and final section of this chapter, we'll go over a set of best practices for workload efficiency. These principles will carry forward as we shift focus from application-level scaling to optimizing cluster-wide efficiency in the chapters ahead.

Best practices for workload efficiency

To close this chapter and the whole section about workload autoscaling, let me list the most important practices we've explored so far that will help you achieve a good efficiency score for your workloads. I'm not attempting to summarize everything you've read in only a few lines in this section. The main reason I want to highlight these practices is that they'll be crucial for the following chapters, where we'll explore the efficiency of nodes in a Kubernetes cluster.

First, the most important task is to *understand what influences the performance of your applications*. Throughout the previous chapters, we didn't talk only about CPU or memory utilization. Typically, there are other aspects such as latency, number of requests, error rate, and dozens of other events, such as messages in a queue or custom business metrics (e.g., using scaling modifiers in KEDA). As applications continue to evolve, what affects performance today might not be the same tomorrow. So, it's key that you don't approach this as a one-time task, but as something you need to do continuously. You need to constantly test your applications to understand them better (as we did a few times in the previous chapters).

There's nothing wrong with starting with only CPU or memory utilization as a metric driver for autoscaling your workloads. In fact, these are the first set of attributes kube-scheduler will use to schedule your pods accordingly. So, start by understanding the CPU and memory requirements for your applications.

Once you know how much CPU and memory your applications need, *it's imperative that you configure a proper number of requests for all containers in a pod*. You won't only have a deterministic result when pods are scheduled, but it will also be used as the base to determine how much capacity the cluster needs to have. We'll explore this topic in more depth in the upcoming chapters, and you'll understand why I kept pushing for you to have a proper configuration in this regard.

If you're new to autoscaling, *consider starting with KEDA*. You can begin with CPU and memory, and then use other attributes as we've explored so far. With KEDA, it's possible to scale to zero for almost all the scalers. Moreover, *consider scaling with multiple metrics*. There are times when all the pod replicas don't receive the same amount of traffic, and even if the average CPU utilization looks good, your users might be experiencing high latencies or application errors. Thus, the importance of not treating autoscaling as a one-time process.

Depending on the application needs, there will be times when you need to scale faster or slower. Take advantage of the scaleUp or scaleDown behaviors you can configure in HPA, either to *control the rate (or speed) of replica changes or to prevent replica fluctuation (flapping)*. Some applications can, in fact, have problems if you scale too fast, and you'd like to spin up Kubernetes nodes only when they're really needed.

Always keep these practices in mind as a minimum set of actions you need to take. As you progress in your workload efficiency journey, you might discover another set of practices you'll consider "best." This will be especially true once you finish the next four chapters about autoscaling the nodes you have in the cluster.

Summary

In this chapter, we delved into the operational aspects of workload autoscaling in Kubernetes, focusing on troubleshooting and monitoring techniques for HPA, VPA, and KEDA. We explored common issues that can arise when implementing autoscaling and provided practical approaches to diagnose and resolve these problems.

We began by examining how to troubleshoot HPA, emphasizing the importance of reviewing conditions and events. Similarly, for VPA, we discussed the process of verifying component status, reviewing events, and analyzing logs from all the VPA components. Then we focused on KEDA. We covered how to review events from `ScaledObject` and `ScaledJob` resources and how to interpret logs from KEDA's components. We also stressed the importance of centralizing logs and events for more effective troubleshooting in larger environments.

Beyond troubleshooting, we explored monitoring strategies for KEDA, introducing key metrics that can be used to understand the health and performance of KEDA's components and autoscaling rules. We provided a hands-on guide to deploying a Grafana dashboard for visualizing KEDA metrics, offering a broader view of autoscaling activities when using KEDA.

Another operational aspect we covered was upgrading KEDA. We described some of the best practices and considerations for maintaining an up-to-date KEDA deployment. We discussed different approaches to upgrading, including the use of kubectl and potential integration with GitOps workflows.

Finally, we concluded with a set of best practices for achieving workload efficiency. These practices emphasized the importance of understanding application performance drivers, properly configuring resource requests, and leveraging KEDA's capabilities for advanced autoscaling scenarios. We underscored the need for continuous monitoring and adjustment of autoscaling configurations to ensure optimal performance and resource utilization.

Now, you're ready for the next adventure: the journey to have efficient nodes.

Get This Book's PDF Version and Exclusive Extras

UNLOCK NOW

Scan the QR code (or go to packtpub.com/unlock).
Search for this book by name, confirm the edition,
and then follow the steps on the page.

*Note: Keep your invoice handy. Purchases made
directly from Packt don't require one.*

Part 3

Node Autoscaling and Karpenter

So far, we've focused on scaling workloads by adding and removing pods based on demand. However, you can have KEDA configured to automatically create new pods; it won't matter if there's nowhere for your pods to run. This is where node autoscaling comes in.

Node autoscaling is the other half of the equation. When your workload autoscaling creates new pods that can't be scheduled because your cluster is at capacity, you need a way to add nodes. And when those pods get removed and you're left with underutilized nodes, you need a way to consolidate and remove them to stop wasting resources. This is what tools such as Cluster Autoscaler and Karpenter do: they manage the infrastructure layer so your workload autoscaling can actually work.

We'll start with Cluster Autoscaler, which has been around for years and is still what most teams use. You'll learn how it works, how to set it up properly (especially on AWS), and its limitations. We'll also touch on complementary projects such as Descheduler and Cluster Proportional Autoscaler, though they're not the focus of this book.

Then we'll shift to Karpenter, which is where things get interesting. This part goes beyond the basics. You'll learn how Karpenter decides when and what nodes to launch, how to deploy it to your cluster, and how to influence its decisions using pod constraints such as node selectors and affinities. More importantly, you'll understand how Karpenter removes nodes. This will cover the consolidation process, drift detection, and disruption budgets that control how aggressive it gets with optimization.

The final chapter covers what you need when running Karpenter in production: troubleshooting techniques, upgrade procedures (which can be tricky), common challenges and how to solve them, and monitoring with Grafana. By the end of this part, you'll understand both how to provision capacity automatically and how to manage it operationally without surprises.

This part has the following chapters:

- *Chapter 7, Data Plane Autoscaling Overview*
- *Chapter 8, Node Autoscaling with Karpenter — Part 1*
- *Chapter 9, Node Autoscaling with Karpenter — Part 2*
- *Chapter 10, Karpenter Management Operations*

7

Data Plane Autoscaling Overview

We're halfway through the journey of building automatically efficient Kubernetes clusters for your workloads. In *Chapter 1*, we provided a brief introduction to autoscaling in the Kubernetes ecosystem. In short, autoscaling in Kubernetes is done in two ways: the first is scaling your application pods, and the second is scaling the underlying infrastructure needed to run your application pods. We've spent quite some time diving into the details of how to scale your application pods efficiently. Now, for the next four chapters, we'll focus on how to automatically scale the compute capacity for your Kubernetes clusters.

First, we'll cover what it means to scale the data plane of a Kubernetes cluster. You'll learn why you need to take action and dive into the details to gain a complete view of autoscaling in Kubernetes. Even though the data plane autoscaling concept is basic, you will then learn about the different options you have to autoscale a data plane with projects such as **Cluster Autoscaler** (**CAS**) and **Karpenter**. These are currently the two main projects that take responsibility for adding compute capacity when your application needs it. We'll then briefly explore other relevant scaler projects, such as **Descheduler** and **Proportional Autoscaler**. You'll learn about the problems all of these projects are solving so that you know your options. But after finishing this chapter, we'll focus solely on Karpenter.

This chapter will start by diving deep into CAS, the first project that has been a long-runner in the ecosystem. If you're an existing user of CAS, you might learn new things about how to optimize it for greater efficiency. Moreover, we'll use this section to develop a solid understanding of why Karpenter was created and why its approach differs from CAS. Learning how CAS works is a foundational step toward understanding why Karpenter was created and will help you implement autoscaling best practices for CAS while you decide whether you transition to Karpenter.

In this chapter, we are going to cover the following main headings:

- What is data plane autoscaling?
- Data plane autoscalers
- CAS on AWS
- Relevant autoscalers

Let's get into it and start warming up your console, as you're going to learn by doing.

Technical requirements

For this chapter, you'll continue using the Kubernetes cluster you created in *Chapter 1*. However, from this chapter onward, you won't be able to use the local Kubernetes cluster you've been using (unless you've opted for the cloud option). Also, keep in mind that for this book, we're using Amazon EKS. So, if you haven't created the Amazon EKS cluster yet, go back to *Chapter 1* to learn how to do it. If you've been using this option already, just make sure you bring the cluster up for every hands-on lab in this chapter. You don't need to install any additional tools, as most of the commands are going to be run using kubectl and helm. You can find the YAML manifests for all resources you're going to create in this chapter in the chapter07 folder from the book's GitHub repository you already cloned in *Chapter 1*.

What is data plane autoscaling?

Before we start exploring data plane autoscaling in depth, let's recap how autoscaling works in Kubernetes and what the scaling flow is. As you already know, scaling in Kubernetes is divided into two categories: workload autoscaling and data plane autoscaling. Look at *Figure 7.1*. The first category illustrated is about scaling application workloads. As the demand grows, in this case, the traffic increases five times in the application, and it then needs more pod replicas to fulfill that demand.

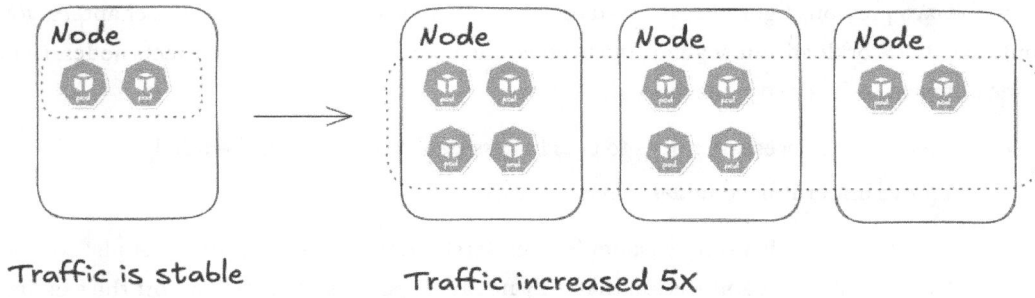

Figure 7.1 – Pod replicas increase based on demand

The second category in *Figure 7.2* is about the Kubernetes worker nodes, better known nowadays as the **data plane**, which works in a proportional manner to the application workload scaling. When more pods are needed and the existing capacity can't host any additional ones, a situation known as unscheduled pods, controllers such as CAS or Karpenter launch new nodes. And, when the application demand shrinks, requiring a smaller number of pods, typically fewer nodes are needed.

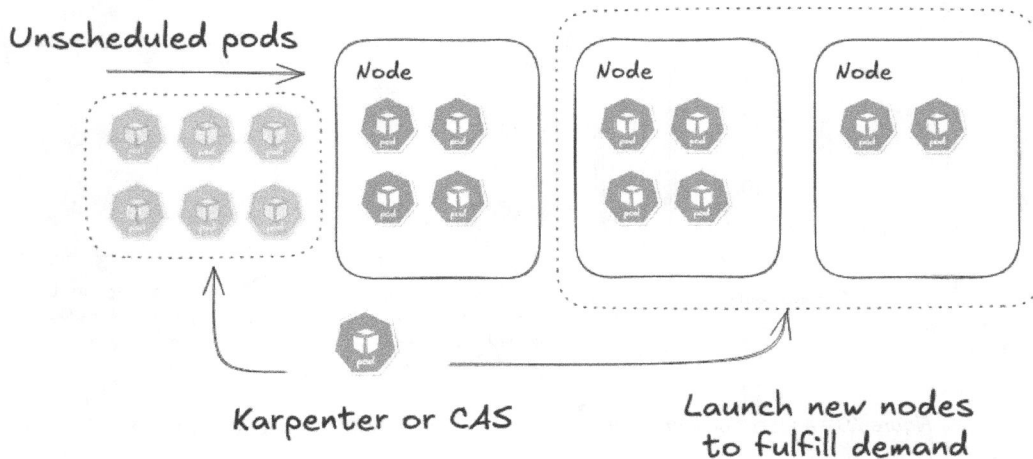

Figure 7.2 – Nodes are launched based on unscheduled pods

From the two previous figures, and based on what you've learned in the previous chapters, you could say that workload autoscaling affects pods, and data plane autoscaling affects nodes. Data plane autoscaling has two goals in mind:

- Provision the necessary nodes to the clusters so all pods can be scheduled
- Remove underutilized nodes to reduce waste.

Let's be more precise with a simple example to understand the implementation details. Look at *Figure 7.3*, representing an application that only needs six pods running to support the existing traffic (**1**). At a certain moment in time, the traffic increases and the existing six pods can't handle the load, causing your application to degrade (**2**). To prevent that degradation from happening, you've configured KEDA to add more pod replicas when the throughput increases. KEDA will update the relevant metrics, and then HPA will update the replica number, let's say to nine replicas. Therefore, you need three extra pods. Kubernetes will try to schedule three more pods in the cluster. But as you can see in *Figure 7.3*, the cluster capacity is very limited (**3**).

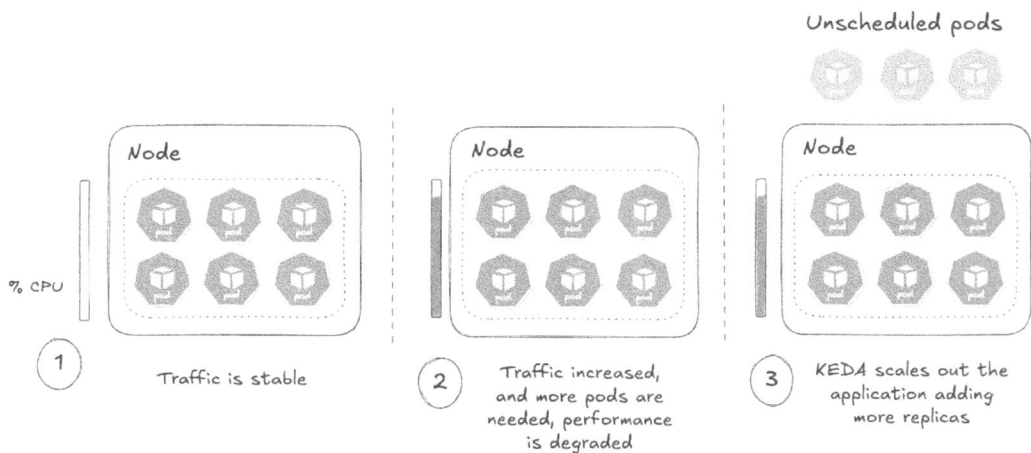

Figure 7.3 – Application workload scaling based on CPU and throughput using KEDA

At this moment, as per *Figure 7.3*, the cluster has no capacity to run three additional pods. Therefore, your application will end up having three unscheduled pods, which will stay in the PENDING state until there's enough capacity in the cluster. KEDA and HPA help you determine how many pod replicas are needed. However, *how many nodes would you need to add?* Data plane autoscalers need to aggregate what unscheduled pods are requesting, and, through bin-packing and scheduling simulations, determine the number of nodes needed. **Bin-packing**, in this context, refers to the efficient allocation of pods to nodes, maximizing resource utilization by fitting as many pods as possible onto each node without overloading it, similar to packing items into containers optimally.

Kubernetes doesn't have a native feature to automatically create new nodes, similar to what HPA does when more pods are needed. Why? Well, there are different tools and providers to create a Kubernetes cluster, and the implementation details of creating nodes vary a lot. For instance, you'll need to use different tools to create a cluster on-premises, AWS, Azure, GCP, or any other infrastructure provider. Each of these providers has its own set of APIs, services, and configuration properties. Moreover, each provider will know better how to use their own APIs.

Therefore, to address this challenge of automatically adding the capacity you need into the cluster, you need to use open source projects such as CAS or Karpenter, which may or may not have support for the infrastructure provider you're using. But that's a different discussion. In the meantime, let's start exploring these two projects. We'll dive a bit into CAS in this chapter, and Karpenter in the following chapters. We're starting with CAS because it will help you understand why Karpenter was introduced and implement autoscaling best practices in CAS to start having efficient clusters right away, in case the transition to Karpenter takes some time.

Data plane autoscalers

Data plane autoscalers operate independently of application-level scaling mechanisms such as HPA or KEDA, focusing solely on cluster-level resource management. This approach helps maintain a balance between having enough capacity for applications to run efficiently and avoiding over-provisioning of resources, regardless of whether the cluster is running in the cloud or on-premises.

Moreover, you might have different applications, with different needs, running on the same node. Scaling nodes based on metrics such as CPU utilization, or even based on other attributes such as latency and throughput, might create conflicts or race conditions with the scaling rules you've configured for the workloads with KEDA or HPA, especially if both are using the same metrics/ events. Therefore, the projects we'll explore next only react when there are unscheduled pods in the cluster. Let me re-emphasize what I just said, as it's very important.

Data plane autoscalers are triggered by unscheduled pods only, not by any other metric or event, such as CPU utilization or the message queue's depth. This is where most newcomers looking to implement Kubernetes autoscaling get confused. Projects such as CAS and Karpenter don't add capacity based on resource utilization; they only add capacity when there are unscheduled pods. Therefore, workload autoscalers and data plane autoscalers complement each other, and you need both to fully implement Kubernetes autoscaling.

Another very common misconception is regarding scheduling. Data plane autoscalers are solely responsible for providing capacity to the cluster, not to schedule pods. `kube-scheduler` is still responsible for scheduling pods. Let's proceed with the next section to examine the approach CAS and Karpenter take to scale nodes.

CAS

CAS was one of the first projects to address the challenge of automatically scaling the data plane of a Kubernetes cluster, and for a long time, it was the only one. The primary function of CAS is to ensure that there are always sufficient nodes available in the cluster to run all pods. When there are pods that cannot be scheduled due to insufficient cluster capacity, CAS will automatically provision new nodes to accommodate these unscheduled pods. Conversely, when nodes are empty, CAS removes these unnecessary nodes for cluster efficiency.

In cloud environments, CAS integrates with cloud provider APIs to manage node groups or auto-scaling groups. For example, in AWS, it can work with EC2 Auto Scaling groups to add or remove instances as needed. In Azure, it works with Virtual Machine Scale Sets, and in GCP with managed instance groups. This integration allows CAS to leverage cloud-native scaling capabilities, making your Kubernetes cluster efficient and cost-effective in cloud deployments.

For on-premises environments, CAS can also be configured to work with various infrastructure provisioning tools. However, the process is often more complex and may require additional setup and integration work. On-premises setups might involve integrating CAS with tools such as OpenStack, VMware vSphere, or bare-metal provisioning systems to manage the lifecycle of physical or virtual machines.

CAS works with various cloud providers and on-premises setups, making it a valuable tool for managing Kubernetes cluster capacity across different environments, though the ease of implementation can vary significantly between cloud and on-premises deployments.

Karpenter

For a very long time, since April 2017, CAS was the only project available for autoscaling the data plane in Kubernetes. However, the landscape changed with the introduction of Karpenter, a Kubernetes cluster autoscaler developed by AWS as an open source project. Karpenter was announced as ready for production in November 2021, and its v1 version was released in August 2024.

Karpenter takes a dynamic and fine-grained approach to node provisioning and manages nodes directly without any abstraction layer, such as Auto Scaling groups in AWS. Like CAS, Karpenter provisions new nodes in response to unschedulable pods, and it attempts to optimize node selection to maximize resource utilization based on pods' resource needs, considering scheduling requirements such as affinities or tolerations. When a node is not needed, Karpenter can remove it or replace it with a smaller one; this process is known as **consolidation**. We'll explore all the details about how this feature works in the next chapter.

Additionally, it's worth mentioning that Karpenter works in tandem with `kube-scheduler`. This means that Karpenter won't schedule pods in the cluster; it will only provision nodes. It's very important that you keep this in mind to make the most of Karpenter. When we look at the implementation details in the next chapter, this will be clearer, and you'll understand why I'm emphasizing this now.

Karpenter uses Kubernetes custom resources for configuration, making it easier to manage and integrate with existing Kubernetes workflows. While initially designed for AWS, Karpenter's design principles aim to make it adaptable to other Kubernetes environments in the future. At the time of writing this book, besides the EKS provider, Microsoft has released the Karpenter provider for **Azure Kubernetes Service (AKS)**. In the next chapter, we'll dive deeper into how the Karpenter project is structured.

In the meantime, let's explore how CAS works in AWS.

CAS on AWS

Note

Before we begin this section, as mentioned earlier, CAS is supported on different platforms and cloud providers. We've decided to focus on AWS in this book for two reasons: first, to maintain consistency across all hands-on labs, and second, to help you better understand why and how Karpenter's implementation differs from CAS. Moreover, if you're not currently using CAS and are planning to start with Karpenter, you may skip this section and move to the *Relevant autoscalers* or *Summary* section in this chapter. However, if you're currently using CAS and not planning to migrate to Karpenter in the near future, this section will help you understand which best practices need to be in place for an efficient data plane.

To use CAS in Amazon EKS, you typically deploy it as a Deployment in the cluster. Once CAS is running, it ensures that the Auto Scaling groups dynamically adjust cluster capacity based on workload demands.

Look at *Figure 7.4*. It's hard to represent how CAS works with a static image, but as we mentioned earlier, when introducing the data plane autoscalers concept, CAS is continuously monitoring the cluster's state, and it reacts when there are unscheduled pods. The purpose of CAS is to ensure that there is enough compute capacity in the cluster to run your workloads. When kube-scheduler notices that there are pods that cannot be allocated due to insufficient resources, CAS initiates the process of expanding the relevant Auto Scaling groups (adding +N to the desired capacity, while avoiding changes to the minimum and maximum values). Conversely, as pods are removed and some nodes remain underutilized for an extended period, CAS orchestrates their removal from the cluster.

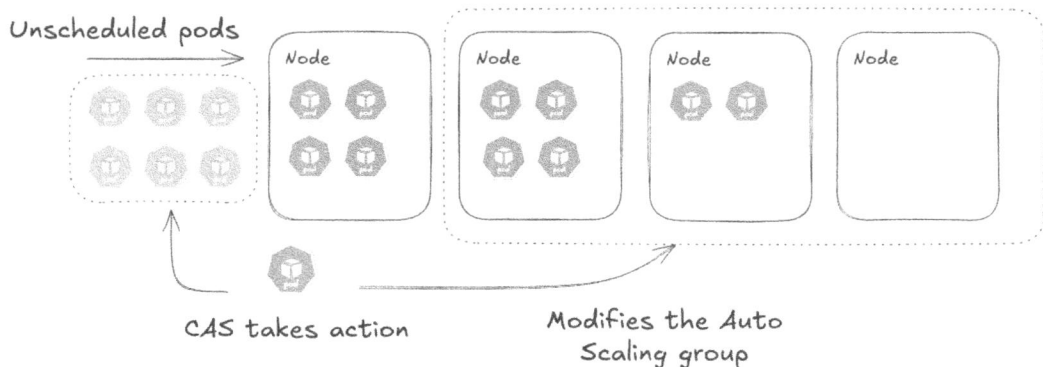

Figure 7.4 – CAS adjusts the compute capacity of relevant Auto Scaling groups

As you're going to deploy CAS as a Deployment within the cluster, you need to ensure that CAS has the necessary IAM permissions to describe and adjust the Auto Scaling groups on your behalf.

In terms of how CAS manages the nodes, there's an **Auto Discovery** mode, which is the preferred method to allow CAS to automatically identify and manage Auto Scaling groups based on predefined tags. This mode also enables CAS to consider Kubernetes scheduling constraints, including node selectors, taints, and tolerations. With all this information from the workloads and nodes, CAS can make informed decisions about scaling, especially when scaling from zero nodes, ensuring that new nodes are compatible with the scheduling requirements of unscheduled pods.

Another important aspect we wanted to cover is how you configure node groups in EKS. Well, there are two ways of doing it:

- **Managed node groups**: With this method, EKS abstracts the complexity of manually provisioning the Auto Scaling group and follows the best practices on how to configure them, along with additional features such as node version upgrades and graceful termination
- **Self-managed node groups**: With this method, you're responsible for provisioning the Auto Scaling group with the proper scripts so nodes register to the cluster when they're created

Both options are an abstraction layer in EKS on top of an Auto Scaling group. However, the recommended approach for node groups is to use managed node groups.

At first glance, that's how CAS works on AWS. There are other implementation details about how CAS works, but they're out of scope for this book. We'll explore a few best practices for CAS simply because they'll become relevant in the next chapter.

So for now, let's see CAS in action.

Hands-on lab: CAS on AWS

> **Note**
>
> This hands-on lab is going to use Terraform to create or update (if you created it already in *Chapter 1*) an EKS cluster. We recommend that you use this method as it will help you get started quickly and focus on learning about how CAS works.

The setup we've been using so far for the Kubernetes cluster has been static. This means that if you deployed too many pods in the cluster, you would see that some pods were unscheduled, as there was no capacity in the cluster. If you've been using the EKS cluster from *Chapter 1*, you've been working with a managed node group of only two nodes. During this lab, you'll deploy around 60 pods to force CAS to react when there are unscheduled pods and see how new nodes are being added automatically.

Step 1: Deploy CAS

Go back to your terminal and make sure you're in the /chapter07 folder from the book's GitHub repository. In here, you'll find a terraform folder that includes the scripts you'll be using to create an EKS cluster with CAS and other add-ons.

If this is the first time you're creating the EKS cluster, you don't need to make any changes to these scripts. However, if you already created the EKS cluster following the instructions from *Chapter 1*, then you'll need to simply remove the # character from the /chapter01/terraform/main.tf file to use Terraform to deploy CAS. This will not only deploy the CAS controller, but it will also take care of configuring it with the proper IAM permissions.

The Terraform template should look like this:

```
...
   enable_cluster_autoscaler = true
...
```

To either create the EKS cluster or apply the changes made to install CAS, run the following commands:

```
$ sh bootstrap.sh
```

If you're creating the EKS cluster, wait around 15 minutes while the control plane is created and ready to register worker nodes, but if you're simply updating it with CAS, wait around 5 minutes. Once the previous command has completed, run the following command to confirm that you have CAS up and running:

```
$ kubectl get pods -n kube-system -l app.kubernetes.io/instance=cluster-autoscaler
```

The CAS pod should have a Running status, and you should be able to proceed. As mentioned before, the EKS cluster already has a static managed node group with only two nodes. We're going to force CAS to add more capacity by deploying a workload with several pods.

Step 2: Remove VPA rules that could resize the sample application

If you didn't create the cluster from scratch in this chapter, you might have some VPA rules configured already from previous hands-on labs. To make sure you keep this lab consistent, let's remove any VPA rule you might have that could resize the sample application. You could remove only the VPA rule that could affect the sample application, but if you want to remove all VPA rules, simply run this command:

```
$ kubectl delete vpa --all
```

Nothing else should be resizing the pods, but we'll confirm it later on anyway.

Step 3: Deploy a sample application to see how CAS adds new nodes

Let's continue using the sample application we've been using in the previous chapters. It doesn't have anything special, but let's note that the requests section looks like this:

```
...
        resources:
          requests:
            cpu: 900m
            memory: 512Mi
...
```

Notice that it follows the recommendation of intentionally requesting a specific number of CPU and memory resources. This is the information CAS will use to decide how many nodes will be added in case there are unscheduled pods, which is something we're going to force in a moment. For now, let's deploy the application:

```
$ kubectl apply -f montecarlopi.yaml
```

You should see only one montecarlo-pi-* pod running. Let's make sure that the pod's requests weren't modified. Run this command to verify it:

```
$ kubectl describe pods | grep -i requests -A 2
```

You should see that the CPU requests remain the same at 900m.

As you were previously adding a few replicas, let's be a bit more aggressive and scale the deployment to 12 replicas. This will require CAS to add a few additional nodes. We're going to keep it simple and scale the application manually. So, run the following command to do so:

```
$ kubectl scale deployment montecarlo-pi --replicas=12
```

As there was enough capacity in the cluster to host most of the pods, some pods should immediately have a Running status, but others will stay with a Pending status. Wait around 30 seconds, and run the following commands to see how many unscheduled pods remain:

```
$ kubectl get pods --field-selector=status.phase=Pending
```

You should see a few unscheduled pods, causing CAS to add new capacity to the cluster by modifying the desired capacity of the Auto Scaling group. Wait around two to three minutes, and you should see all pod replicas running on the new nodes that were added to the cluster. To confirm it, run this command:

```
$ kubectl get nodes
```

The number of nodes you see will depend on how many pods you had running before manually scaling out the sample application. If you didn't have any other applications running, you might see only one extra node.

Step 4: Remove the sample application to see how CAS removes unnecessary nodes

The idea of using CAS is to not only make it easier to add more capacity when it's needed, but also to remove capacity when it's not needed. So, let's remove the sample application by running the following command:

```
$ kubectl delete -f montecarlopi.yaml
```

By default, CAS will wait 10 minutes before a node is removed. So, give it time, and while you wait, you could review the CAS logs to confirm that empty nodes will be removed after 10 minutes. To review CAS logs, run this command:

```
$ kubectl logs -n kube-system -l app.kubernetes.io/instance=cluster-
autoscaler --all-containers=true -f --tail=20
```

Once you see in the logs that the nodes were removed, you could run the previous command you ran to get the list of the nodes to confirm it. Don't proceed to the next step until the extra nodes are removed.

Step 5: Uninstall CAS

In the following chapters, we won't be using CAS anymore, so let's remove it now. If you used the Terraform installation method, simply set the value from line 147 in the /terraform/main. tf file to false, like this:

```
...
    enable_cluster_autoscaler = false
...
```

Then, run the following script again to apply the changes to remove CAS (along with all the other resources Terraform created):

```
$ sh bootstrap.sh
```

Wait around five minutes, and confirm that CAS is no longer installed:

```
$ kubectl get all -n kube-system | grep autoscaler
```

If CAS was uninstalled successfully, the preceding command shouldn't return any results.

You've come to the end of this lab. In this hands-on lab, you learned how to deploy CAS into an existing EKS cluster using Terraform. You simply have to activate a flag, and the Terraform module creates and configures all the resources needed to run CAS in EKS. You then saw CAS in action, adding new nodes when there were unscheduled pods, and then removing the extra nodes 10 minutes after the application was removed.

Now that you have the CAS basics, let's move to the next section to learn about some of the CAS best practices on EKS.

CAS best practices

Even though this book doesn't go in depth about CAS, you might be in a transition phase to Karpenter, and it would be wise to know about the minimum set of configurations and considerations you need to implement when using CAS with EKS and configure efficient Kubernetes clusters. Moreover, it will help you understand why some implementation details in Karpenter are different and why the following recommendations will impact your efficiency score.

Use homogeneous instance types

This practice might be the most important one in terms of compute efficiency. To configure a node group, one of the required parameters is to set an instance type that will be used to launch an EC2 instance. A best practice in AWS, regarding instance types, is to configure not just one type but as many types as possible (the more, the merrier). The reason for this recommendation is to secure the capacity you'll need (although, to truly reserve capacity, you have other mechanisms such as **On-Demand Capacity Reservations (ODCR)**, but that's out of scope for now). When EC2 can't launch instances of a specific instance type (the cloud is not infinite), the Auto Scaling group can launch an EC2 instance of another type, from the multiple ones you've configured that you're flexible to use. This is known as **instance type diversification**.

If your node group is using EC2 Spot instances, then diversification becomes even more important. EC2 Spot instances are spare capacity from On-Demand, and when On-Demand needs that capacity back, you receive a Spot interruption. This means that the EC2 Spot instance will be terminated in two minutes. However, the good news is that the Auto Scaling group can launch an EC2 Spot instance of another type where there's more spare capacity available, and it will pick the cheapest one when there are instance types with similar spare capacity numbers.

But how is all of this previous information relevant to CAS and using homogeneous instance types? Well, when you use multiple instance types, CAS will consider the first type in the list to calculate how many extra nodes are required based on the specs of that first instance type. If the list has types with different specs, and the Auto Scaling group ends up launching instances with different specs than what CAS used to calculate the number of extra nodes to launch, you might end up with the challenge of either wasting capacity (nodes with more specs than the first instance type) or constraining the cluster with smaller nodes (nodes with fewer specs than the first instance type). Of course, at some point, CAS will either remove unnecessary nodes or launch new nodes if there are still unscheduled pods. But while that happens, you'll be paying for resources you don't really need or experience a degradation in your workloads.

Therefore, the recommendation is to use homogeneous instance types, the same CPU, and memory specs. If CAS uses the first instance type to decide how many extra nodes to launch, it won't matter which instance type the Auto Scaling group ends up launching, because it will have the same specs that CAS considered initially.

Limit the number of node groups

While the previous recommendation was to use as many homogeneous instance types as possible in one node group, you need to limit the number of node groups you have in the cluster. The reason is because of how CAS works.

In order to optimize pod scheduling, CAS scans the cluster every 10 seconds (by default), and loads into memory information about the cluster, such as pods, nodes, and EKS node groups, to simulate scheduling and make decisions. For example, if there are multiple node groups, CAS must decide which group to scale out. Therefore, the larger the number of node groups you have, the slower CAS might be in scaling out your cluster.

You might be wondering why someone would need to have multiple node groups in a cluster. In the previous section, you learned that to optimize availability (and efficiency to some extent if using Spot) in a cluster, it's recommended to use homogeneous instance types to mitigate any compute capacity constraints you might face when launching nodes, especially when you are using Spot instances. Another reason could be when organizations use multiple node groups to isolate workloads in a cluster. Instead, if possible, isolate workloads at the Kubernetes namespace level.

Configure a sane scaling speed

While it might be tempting to configure a very small scan interval to achieve faster scaling, this approach can lead to unintended consequences. Although a shorter interval could theoretically make CAS more responsive with spiky workloads or where speed matters very much, it's important to consider that launching new EC2 instances takes time, often several minutes (mostly due to a high number of running agents on bootstrap). Setting an overly aggressive scan interval might result in CAS making unnecessary API calls before the previously requested nodes are even ready.

Moreover, frequent API calls can quickly exhaust rate limits imposed by AWS (and other cloud providers as well), potentially leading to API throttling or even service disruptions. A good practice is to set the scan interval to a value that balances responsiveness with API efficiency. For example, setting the interval to 1 minute instead of the default 10 seconds can significantly reduce API call volume while only marginally increasing the scale-up time. If you do not need to modify the default configuration, just don't do it unless you've run proper testing and understand which values work for your use case.

You can adjust the scan interval using the `--scan-interval` flag. Additionally, you can fine-tune scale-down behavior using flags such as `--scale-down-delay-after-add`, `--scale-down-delay-after-delete`, `--scale-down-unneeded-time`, and `--scale-down-delay-after-failure`. These allow you to control how long CAS waits before considering scale-down operations after various cluster events.

Use a priority expander with multiple nodes

CAS uses **expanders** to decide which node group to scale when multiple options are available. The default expander is random, which, as the name suggests, chooses a node group at random. However, when working with multiple node groups, especially in large and complex environments, you might want more control over the scaling decisions.

This is where the priority expander becomes valuable (not many people know this configuration exists and why it's useful). By using the `--expander=priority` flag, you can define a specific order in which CAS should consider node groups for scaling. For example, this is particularly useful when you have a preferred set of instance types or when using Spot instances.

Let's say you're using Spot instances with different tiers for size because, as you've learned before, it's a good practice to use node groups with homogeneous instance types. Or, maybe you'd like to give priority to instance types from the latest generations. With a priority expander, you can define a priority list of which node types CAS should use, like this:

- A node group with only `large` Spot instances
- A node group with `xlarge` Spot instances
- A node group `2xlarge` Spot instances

CAS will try to scale the first group, and only if it can't (due to capacity constraints or other issues), it will move to the second, and so on. You can define this priority list in a `ConfigMap` like this:

```
apiVersion: v1
kind: ConfigMap
metadata:
  name: spot-priority-expander
  namespace: kube-system
data:
  priorities: |-
    10:
      - .*-spot-large
    20:
```

```
    - .*-spot-xlarge
30:
    - .*-spot-2xlarge
```

While this approach provides fine-grained control, it's important to note that it's a sequential process. If capacity isn't available in the higher-priority groups, it may take longer to eventually scale up using lower-priority options. Even if you configured a short scan interval.

Use a single Availability Zone for persistent volumes

When working with persistent volumes, particularly Amazon EBS volumes, it's crucial to consider **Availability Zone (AZ)** placement. EBS volumes are AZ-specific, meaning a pod using an EBS volume must be scheduled in the same AZ as the volume.

If you're using multi-AZ node groups with persistent volumes, you risk scenarios where pods can't be scheduled because they're assigned to nodes in a different AZ from their volumes. This can lead to data unavailability or, in worst-case scenarios, data loss. This consideration is particularly important for applications that rely on data sharding or replication, such as Elasticsearch. In these cases, improper AZ management could impair the application's ability to maintain data integrity and availability.

To mitigate these risks, consider using single-AZ node groups for workloads that depend on persistent volumes. This ensures that pods are always scheduled in the same AZ as their volumes. Alternatively, if you need multi-AZ resilience, consider using storage solutions that span multiple AZs, such as Amazon EFS or Amazon FSx for Lustre.

An additional benefit of this approach is the reduction of inter-AZ network traffic and latency within the cluster, which can help optimize costs and improve application performance. When data and compute resources are co-located in the same AZ, you avoid the additional latency and potential data transfer costs associated with cross-AZ communication.

> **Note**
>
> Using single-AZ node groups for persistent volumes improves scheduling reliability and performance for certain stateful workloads, but it comes with an availability trade-off. Avoid using single-AZ in scenarios (especially for stateful systems such as Elasticsearch) where you should distribute volumes across multiple AZs. For example, the built-in replication processes of such systems can protect against an AZ outage.

Now that you've seen the key practices to follow when using CAS, it's time to expand your view of the autoscaling landscape. While CAS and Karpenter handle most of the heavy lifting for compute scaling, Kubernetes' ecosystem has additional tools that solve complementary problems, such as balancing workloads more effectively or adjusting control plane components dynamically.

In this next section, we'll take a brief look at some of these tools so that you can better understand your full range of options and when each might be appropriate to use.

Relevant autoscalers

While CAS and Karpenter are the primary tools for managing node-level scaling in Kubernetes clusters, there are other autoscaling projects that address specific needs within the Kubernetes ecosystem. These tools complement the core autoscalers and work in harmony with all the previous projects we've explored so far.

In this section, we'll briefly introduce three such projects: Descheduler, **Cluster Proportional Autoscaler** (**CPA**), and **Cluster Proportional Vertical Autoscaler** (**CPVA**). The aim is to help you get familiar with the autoscaling landscape in Kubernetes and help you identify when and where they might be useful in your own clusters.

Each of these autoscalers serves a unique purpose:

- Descheduler focuses on optimizing pod placement after initial scheduling
- CPA helps scale auxiliary services proportionally to the cluster size
- CPVA aims to vertically scale resources based on cluster metrics

Later, in *Chapters 11* and *12*, we'll see some of these tools in action to help you understand how and when they can be integrated into your autoscaling strategy.

Descheduler

While the initial scheduling of pods is handled by the Kubernetes scheduler, over time, the distribution of workloads can become uneven. This is where the Descheduler comes into play. The Descheduler is an open source project that aims to improve cluster resource utilization by moving pods from over-utilized nodes to under-utilized ones. It runs as a Kubernetes add-on and uses various informers to monitor cluster resources and make decisions based on predefined policies.

Imagine a scenario where some nodes in your cluster are running at 90% capacity while others are barely breaking 30%. The Descheduler can identify this imbalance and evict pods from the highly utilized nodes, allowing them to be rescheduled on the under-utilized nodes. This rebalancing act not only improves overall cluster performance but can also lead to cost savings by optimizing resource usage. To use the Descheduler, you'll need to deploy its controller in your cluster and configure a policy `ConfigMap` with your desired strategies. Common strategies include `LowNodeUtilization` and `RemoveDuplicates`. Once set up, the Descheduler will automatically analyze and rebalance your cluster based on these policies.

When using the Descheduler, it's important to adopt a cautious approach to minimize potential risks. For instance, it's recommended to use **pod disruption budgets** (**PDBs**) to ensure a minimum number of pods remain available during descheduling operations. Moreover, carefully configure the Descheduler's strategies to match your cluster's specific needs, and consider using the simulation mode to test configurations without affecting live workloads. Implement a gradual rollout, starting with a small subset of your cluster and expanding as you gain confidence. Leverage node affinity and anti-affinity rules to guide pod placement and prevent critical workloads from being disrupted. At this point in the book, you should have already guessed that proper resource requests and limits for pods will help the Descheduler make more informed decisions.

CPA

CPA is an open source project that scales workloads based on the size of the cluster itself, and doesn't rely on metrics such as CPU or memory usage. The primary purpose of CPA is to maintain an appropriate number of replicas for cluster-wide services as your cluster grows or shrinks. This makes it particularly useful for managing system components such as `kube-dns` or monitoring services, which typically need to scale in proportion to the overall cluster size. CPA is currently in beta, but I've seen many people using it to scale workloads without problems.

CPA is a controller that continuously monitors the number of schedulable nodes, nodes in the cluster that have available capacity to run new pods, and CPU cores available in your cluster. Based on this information, it adjusts the number of replicas for the target resource using either **linear** or **ladder** scaling methods. To use CPA, you'll need to deploy it as a separate controller in your cluster and configure a `ConfigMap` with your desired scaling parameters. You'll then set up the target workload (such as a Deployment) to be managed by CPA.

It's important to note that CPA may not be the best choice for application-specific workloads that need to scale based on their own unique metrics or usage patterns.

CPVA

While CPA focuses on horizontal scaling, CPVA addresses the vertical scaling needs of cluster-wide services. CPVA's primary function is to automatically adjust resource requests for workloads based on the size of your cluster. This makes it a nice fit for system components or workloads that need to scale vertically as your cluster grows or shrinks. It's worth noticing that CPVA is also in beta.

Similar to CPA, CPVA continuously monitors the number of schedulable nodes and cores in your cluster, using this information to adjust the CPU and memory requests for target workloads. CPVA supports linear scaling and allows you to set configurable minimum and maximum resource limits. To use CPVA in your cluster, you need to deploy the controller and configure a `ConfigMap` with your desired scaling parameters. You then target the workloads you want CPVA to manage, which can include Deployments, DaemonSets, or ReplicaSets.

Before I finish with the *Relevant autoscalers* section, it's important to remember that our aim wasn't to provide an exhaustive deep dive into each tool. Rather, we sought to broaden your awareness of the autoscaling tools related to the Kubernetes data plane. The Descheduler, CPA, and CPVA each offer unique approaches to optimizing cluster resources, and knowing when and how to leverage them can significantly enhance your cluster's efficiency. However, the key takeaway is not about the tools themselves, but about the overarching goal they serve. Regardless of which autoscalers you choose to implement, the ultimate objective remains the same: to create and maintain an efficient Kubernetes cluster that optimally utilizes resources, scales smoothly with demand, and provides a robust platform for your applications.

Summary

In this chapter, you learned about the role of data plane autoscaling in Kubernetes, with a focus on two primary goals: ensuring sufficient nodes are available for all pods to be scheduled and removing underutilized resources to reduce waste, thereby optimizing costs and increasing efficiency.

We began by examining CAS, a tool for managing node-level scaling in Kubernetes clusters. We delved into its operation within Amazon EKS, discussing best practices for implementation and the challenges it addresses. We then introduced Karpenter, another node-level scaling solution, highlighting its differences from CAS and the different approach it brings to the table. We'll dedicate the following three chapters to Karpenter.

It's very important that you don't forget that data plane autoscalers such as CAS and Karpenter are responsible for *cluster-level resource management only*. They work in conjunction with application-level scaling solutions such as HPA, VPA, or KEDA. This complementary relationship ensures that both the infrastructure and the applications running on it can scale efficiently to meet demand. Therefore, this means that *data plane autoscalers are not responsible for scheduling pods*. Their role is to provide or remove the underlying infrastructure resources, while the Kubernetes scheduler remains in charge of placing pods on available nodes.

We finished by exploring other relevant autoscalers, including the Descheduler, CPA, and CPVA. While these tools serve specific purposes and can enhance cluster efficiency in certain scenarios, they are not replacements for core data plane autoscalers.

As we move forward, remember that the ultimate goal is to maintain an efficient Kubernetes cluster. Whether you choose CAS, Karpenter, or a combination of different autoscaling tools, the focus should always be on optimizing resource utilization, reducing costs, and ensuring that your applications have the resources they need to perform optimally. In the next chapter, we'll focus on Karpenter to close the Kubernetes autoscaling loop. So let's get into it.

Get This Book's PDF Version and Exclusive Extras

UNLOCK NOW

Scan the QR code (or go to `packtpub.com/unlock`). Search for this book by name, confirm the edition, and then follow the steps on the page.

Note: Keep your invoice handy. Purchases made directly from Packt don't require one.

8

Node Autoscaling with Karpenter — Part 1

In the previous chapters, you already explored node autoscaling concepts and some of the tooling available to manage node groups. Now, you'll take a closer look at how Karpenter works behind the scenes and why it has become a popular choice to improve resource utilization and reduce operational overhead. Karpenter leverages real-time scheduling simulations and direct integration with cloud provider APIs. This allows it to launch right-sized nodes exactly when they are needed—and remove them just as efficiently when they're not.

Throughout this chapter, you'll be introduced to the foundational components that make Karpenter work. You'll learn how to define a NodeClass, configure NodePools to shape provisioning behavior, and understand the role of NodeClaims in representing and tracking newly launched capacity. You'll also explore Karpenter's bin-packing strategy, scheduling logic, and how it integrates with Kubernetes concepts such as tolerations, affinities, and topology constraints to make intelligent decisions.

In addition to theory and architecture, this chapter includes a hands-on section where you'll deploy Karpenter in an Amazon EKS environment, configure the necessary IAM permissions and networking resources, and see how it responds to a simple scheduling scenario. You'll observe how Karpenter reacts to unscheduled pods, selects from a wide range of instance types, and uses its simulation engine to ensure the efficient placement of workloads.

We will be covering the following main topics in this chapter:

- What is Karpenter?
- History of Karpenter
- Karpenter resources
- Launching nodes
- Deploying Karpenter
- Hands-on lab: Autoscaling with Karpenter
- Workload scheduling constraints

By the end of this chapter, you'll understand not only how Karpenter works but also how to properly configure NodePools and set workload constraints to influence scheduling and provisioning. All of this with only one mission in mind: to help you prepare to build more elastic, cost-effective, and responsive Kubernetes clusters using Karpenter.

Technical requirements

For this chapter, you'll continue using an AWS EKS cluster. To avoid any problems, it's recommended to spin down any previous cluster you've created and instead create a new one from the template you'll find in this chapter. This is going to be the cluster you'll use from now on. You don't need to install any additional tools, since most of the commands are going to run using kubectl and helm. You can find the YAML manifests for all resources you're going to create in this chapter in the chapter08 folder from the book's GitHub repository, which you already cloned in *Chapter 1*.

What is Karpenter?

Even though we started to explore Karpenter in the previous chapter, let's formalize what this project is about. Karpenter is an open source, flexible node provisioning tool for Kubernetes that automatically launches right-sized compute resources (**nodes**) in response to unschedulable pods. When new pods are scheduled, as you can see in *Figure 8.1*, the cluster might not have the capacity to host all the new pods. In this example, the cluster only has the capacity to host two new pods.

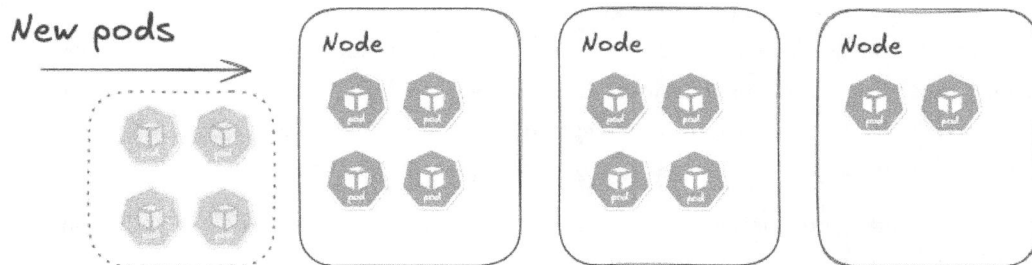

Figure 8.1 – New pods are pending, but there won't be enough capacity to schedule

This is where Karpenter's controller comes in. As illustrated in *Figure 8.2*, Karpenter observes the actual scheduling requirements of pods to decide with more precision which nodes to launch that will fulfill the demand of workloads that the cluster's existing capacity cannot accommodate. If a pod requires specific CPU architecture or memory constraints, or must run in particular Availability Zones, Karpenter considers all these factors in its decision-making process. However, it's worth mentioning that *Karpenter works in tandem with the Kubernetes schedulers; it takes a step ahead, but it doesn't schedule pods.*

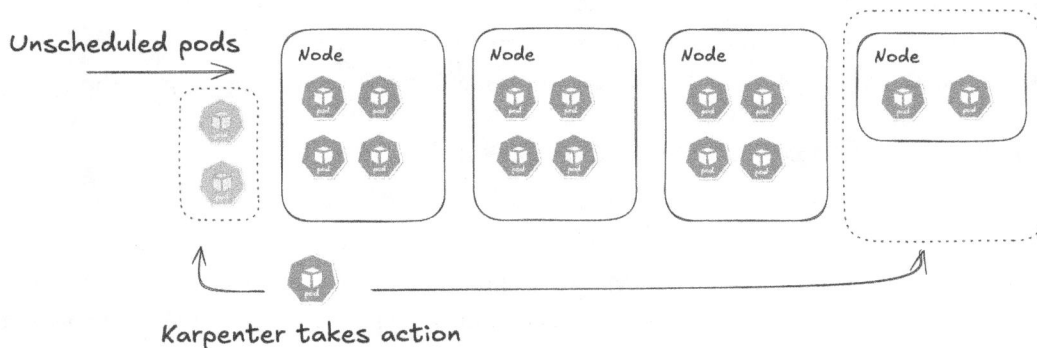

Figure 8.2 – Karpenter takes action and launches a new node

Notice how in *Figure 8.2*, Karpenter launched a smaller node to fit only two pods, and as a result, no resources were wasted. If there were more than two unscheduled pods, Karpenter would have launched a bigger node with the intention that every time a new node is launched, it is as efficient as possible. We'll dive deeper into how Karpenter launches nodes and how you can influence it later in this chapter.

To launch only the capacity that a workload needs, Karpenter implements a **simulation-based approach**. Karpenter runs scheduling simulations to ensure its decisions will lead to optimal pod placement. It doesn't just consider the immediate needs of pending pods but also pod constraints such as affinity rules, **topology spread constraints** (**TSCs**), and node selectors. This forward-thinking approach helps prevent unnecessary node launches and reduces cluster churn.

Karpenter is very good at launching nodes, but as pods come and go, the cluster ends up having fragmentation within node resources. To reduce fragmentation, Karpenter can optimize the cost of nodes you have in the cluster with consolidation capabilities. When it notices that pods could be packed more efficiently, it can intelligently redistribute workloads to reduce costs while maintaining application availability. This consolidation process works hand in hand with its provisioning logic to ensure clusters remain both efficient and stable over time.

Lastly, Karpenter integrates with cloud providers such as AWS, Azure, and GCP (for some, the integration is still in beta). For instance, in AWS, Karpenter can work with hundreds of different instance types, understanding their different characteristics and pricing models, and defers to EC2 to launch the best available type.

So, at a very high level, that's what Karpenter is and how it works. But before we dive deeper into the key concepts of Karpenter and how it helps you build efficient Kubernetes clusters, let's explore how it works in AWS so that you can understand why Karpenter started in the first place.

How does Karpenter work in AWS?

In the previous chapter, we spent some time exploring how CAS works in more depth and what the best practices are for building efficient clusters. You learned that to use CAS in EKS, *you need to define a set of node groups in advance* that your applications will use. Recall that a **node group** is an abstraction of an EC2 Auto Scaling group. Think of it as different t-shirt sizes, types, and textures. Most likely, not all applications in the cluster will benefit from using the exact same node types. Some applications require a lot of resources, others require special storage technology, and some might need to use GPUs. In fact, some applications require so much capacity that diversification becomes critical. All this diversity in your cluster will look like the cluster in *Figure 8.3* with different predefined node groups.

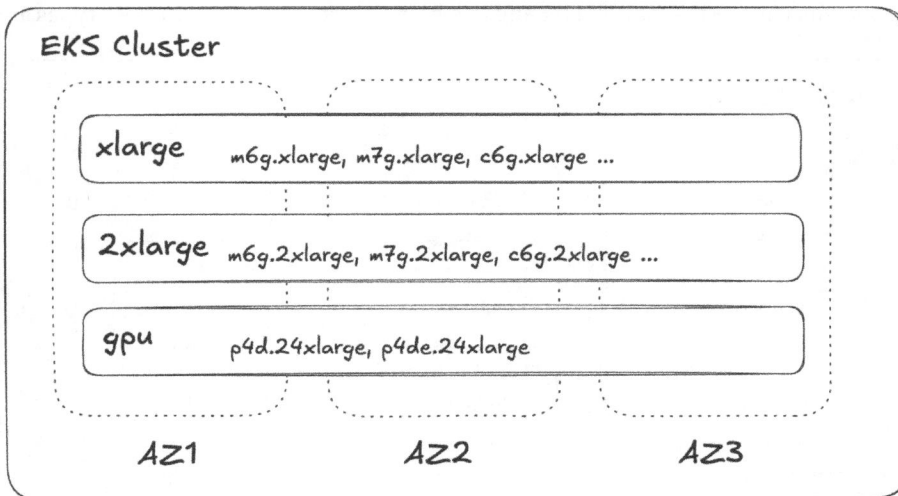

Figure 8.3 – An EKS cluster with different types of node groups

As you can imagine, as your cluster grows, the complexity of managing such clusters will increase as well. Moreover, you need to remember that even though you can reduce the number of nodes by using multiple instance types, these instance types should have similar specifications in terms of CPU and memory. This is because when CAS scales the node group, it only uses the first instance type in the list to simulate how much to increase or decrease the desired capacity by. As a consequence, you could end up wasting resources by launching bigger nodes or constraining applications by launching smaller nodes. In short, CAS lacks granular control over instance type launches.

Karpenter takes a different approach. It doesn't use EC2 Auto Scaling groups, removing the need to create node groups in advance. Instead, Karpenter has direct control over which instance type it launches by using the EC2 Fleet API in instant mode. The instance types it sends aren't necessarily homogeneous, which will result in a cluster with instances of different types and sizes, and that's good in terms of efficiency. This means that it makes a synchronous one-time request to EC2 to launch the capacity it needs, and only what it needs. If the request fails, Karpenter tries with another list of instance types.

In *Figure 8.4*, you can see that the cluster ends up having instances with different types and sizes.

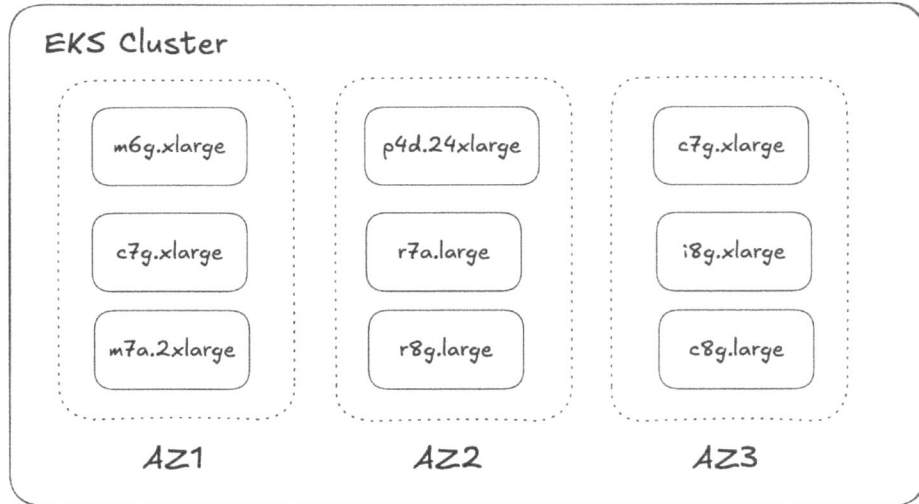

Figure 8.4 – An EKS cluster with instances of different types and sizes

It's important that you keep in mind the instance type diversification you can get with Karpenter as it changes how you manage your cluster and your applications. You could say that *CAS uses an infrastructure-first approach* where you define the types of node groups the cluster will have, and the applications are the ones that adapt to this type of capacity, whereas *Karpenter uses an application-first approach* where the applications specify what type of capacity they need, and you only need to define sane constraints for the instance types that Karpenter could launch. We'll come back to this when diving deeper into how Karpenter launches nodes, but before that, let's explore when Karpenter started and what its current status is.

Migration from CAS

If you're currently using CAS and are considering transitioning to Karpenter, the Karpenter docs site includes a migration guide with step-by-step instructions at https://karpenter.sh/docs/getting-started/migrating-from-cas/.

History of Karpenter

Karpenter was created by AWS in response to the challenges mentioned in the previous section. In 2019, the AWS EKS team approached the Kubernetes Autoscaling **Special Interest Group (SIG)** to discuss how to integrate CAS better with the EC2 API. Then, in 2020, based on the Autoscaling SIG's recommendations to explore these new ideas in a separate project, AWS initiated the Karpenter project on GitHub. In November 2021, AWS announced Karpenter v0.5 as **generally available (GA)**. This is the version where Karpenter introduced the ability to provision right-sized EC2 instances in response to changing application loads, addressing the need for improved application availability and resource utilization in Kubernetes clusters.

Since its initial release, Karpenter has seen substantial growth and evolution. The project quickly gained traction within the Kubernetes community, becoming one of the top 10 most popular AWS open source projects on GitHub with 7.4k+ GitHub stars. It attracted contributions from over 200 developers and fostered discussions among 1,500+ community members on Kubernetes' Slack.

Recognizing the project's potential beyond AWS, in May 2023, AWS contributed the vendor-neutral core of Karpenter to the **Cloud Native Computing Foundation (CNCF)** through the Kubernetes Autoscaling SIG. This move aimed to facilitate additional cloud provider implementations and broaden the project's scope. In October 2023, Karpenter graduated to beta status, reflecting its maturity and stability.

In early 2024, Karpenter v1.0.0 was released, marking its graduation from beta. The beta version introduced APIs such as NodePool and EC2NodeClass, and in v1, these had minor modifications with the aim of committing to maintain backward compatibility in future 1.0 minor releases.

Today, Karpenter has become a Kubernetes-native node life cycle manager. It's been widely adopted by various companies (the AWS provider on GitHub has a list of company names under the ADOPTERS.md file), helping them improve application availability, reduce operational overhead, and increase cost efficiency in their Kubernetes clusters.

Karpenter resources

Before we dive deeper into Karpenter, you need to know the basic elements that you'll be interacting with all the time. Karpenter's functionality is largely defined and controlled through a set of custom resources that extend the Kubernetes API. These **CustomResourceDefinitions (CRDs)** are central to how Karpenter interacts with both the Kubernetes cluster and the underlying cloud infrastructure. In this section, we'll explore the key CRDs that form the backbone of Karpenter's operations: NodeClass, NodePool, and NodeClaims.

NodeClass handles cloud provider-specific configurations such as subnet selections and security group settings, among other settings that we'll explore later. NodePool defines the boundaries of what Karpenter can do, similar to managed node groups in EKS, but with more flexibility. In NodePool, you specify everything from allowed instance types to required labels and taints to maintenance windows. The third element that Karpenter creates to represent a node in the cloud provider is NodeClaims, which is an immutable resource that Karpenter uses to keep track and manage the life cycle of a node. As a user, you'll find it useful to learn more about the status of a node. Let's explore these in more detail.

NodeClass

NodeClass serves as Karpenter's abstraction for cloud provider-specific configurations. This CRD is designed to handle all the infrastructure-specific details that Karpenter needs to understand when launching new nodes in your cloud environment. When Karpenter decides to launch a new node, it references the NodeClass object. While Karpenter works across different cloud providers through its cloud provider interface, each provider implements its own version of NodeClass. For AWS, as seen in *Figure 8.5*, this manifests as EC2NodeClass, which encapsulates all AWS-specific configuration details required for launching EC2 instances.

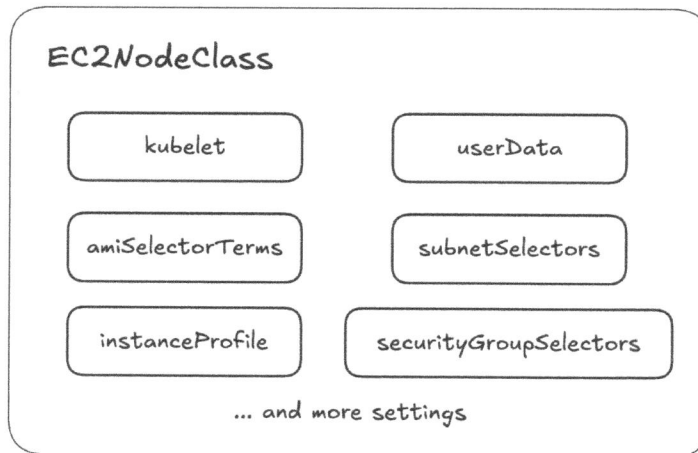

Figure 8.5 – A NodeClass implementation for AWS is called EC2NodeClass

In the context of AWS, EC2NodeClass defines components such as the following:

- Subnet(s), defining Availability Zones where Karpenter can launch nodes
- Security group(s) that will be applied to launched instances

- AMI specifications, defining what image will be used when launching nodes
- Other parameters needed, such as tags or user data

Here's a simple example of an `EC2NodeClass` definition:

```
apiVersion: karpenter.k8s.aws/v1
kind: EC2NodeClass
metadata:
  name: default
spec:
  role: "NodeIAMRoleName"
  amiSelectorTerms:
    - alias: "bottlerocket@1.34.0"
  subnetSelectorTerms:
    - tags:
        karpenter.sh/discovery: "kubernetes-autoscaling"
  securityGroupSelectorTerms:
    - tags:
        karpenter.sh/discovery: "kubernetes-autoscaling"
```

Notice the `selector` paradigm used in the previous `EC2NodeClass`, which is an API construct inspired by the label selectors in Kubernetes. The use of these selectors provides the benefit of aiding in Region expansion. If you follow a similar tagging convention across Regions, `EC2NodeClass` doesn't need to be changed, unlike when using AWS resource IDs.

Let me explain in more detail each of the previous settings:

- `role`: This is where you set the IAM role name that the new EC2 instance will use to interact with AWS, which mainly will be used to connect to the EKS cluster, **IAM roles for service accounts (IRSA)**, and Pod Identity. This configuration is immutable after creation.
- `amiSelectorTerms`: This is where you select which **Amazon Machine Images (AMIs)** your instances can use based on tags, ID, owner, and so on. EC2NodeClasses are multi-arch by default, so you can select multiple AMIs to ensure you can launch instance types across all architectures.
- `subnetSelectorTerms`: Similar to the previous one, this is where you set attributes such as tags or IDs to select which subnets Karpenter can use to launch nodes. This comes in handy when you need to extend the network CIDR by adding more subnets without having to modify the `EC2NodeClass` object.

- securityGroupsSelectorTerms: Similar to the previous one, this is where you set the attributes to select which security groups Karpenter uses to attach to the nodes.

There are other configurations available that we will be exploring as we progress through the book. If you want to know what all the possible configurations are, you can go to the official Karpenter docs site (https://karpenter.sh/docs) to learn more about it. For now, let's continue with the next CRD.

NodePool

NodePool defines the constraints for node provisioning. Without NodePool, Karpenter won't be able to launch nodes. Cloud providers such as AWS offer several compute options (purchase model, capabilities, types, categories, etc.), as per _Figure 8.6_, and you could say that they define the universe for compute. If a cloud provider offers the universe, you can think of NodePool as the definition of a planet with a prescriptive set of options that Karpenter has available from the universe (cloud providers) when making decisions about launching new nodes.

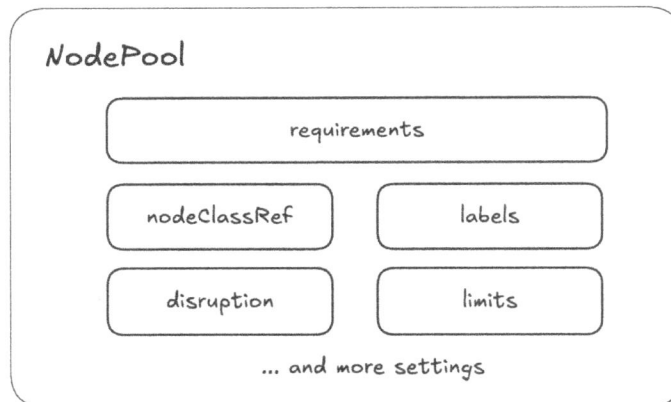

Figure 8.6 – NodePool with most common properties

But it's not just about compute options. In NodePool, you can specify a set of constraints that must be met by any node that Karpenter launches. For instance, you could define constraints such as taints, startup taints, and labels for nodeSelectors or affinities. When there are unschedulable pods, Karpenter will look at the pod's scheduling constraints, such as nodeSelectors, podAffinity, nodeAffinity, tolerations, and resource requests (to choose the proper node size). The aim is for Karpenter to match the pod's constraints with a NodePool, and launch the node(s) that kube-scheduler will use to schedule the pending pods. _If Karpenter can't find a match between pods and NodePools, pods will remain unschedulable._

Unlike CAS, you don't need to have too many NodePools to get instance-type diversification. In fact, the fewer the better as Karpenter will have to scan fewer NodePools to find a match.

NodePools have a field called weight to describe order preferences. This allows Karpenter to use one NodePool before another. For example, if there's a match with multiple NodePools, Karpenter will pick the one with the highest weight. Also, if there are equal weights, then it picks the first NodePool in alphabetical order, but this is not guaranteed since the behavior is non-deterministic. Therefore, the recommendation is to avoid overlapping NodePools with the same weight. Multiple NodePools are recommended when you want to configure soft-tenancy, split ratios, or priority mechanisms, which we'll discuss in more detail in *Chapter 9* and *Chapter 12*.

If you've been working with AWS and have been using node groups, the NodePool concept should feel familiar. However, NodePools offer more flexibility and fine-grained control than managed node groups. Remember, in AWS, Karpenter doesn't use Amazon EC2 Auto Scaling groups but makes a call to the EC2 Fleet API, and this is why you have more control.

In the context of AWS, NodePool defines constraints as follows:

```
apiVersion: karpenter.sh/v1
kind: NodePool
metadata:
  name: default
spec:
  template:
    spec:
      requirements:
        - key: kubernetes.io/arch
          operator: In
          values: ["amd64"]
        - key: kubernetes.io/os
          operator: In
          values: ["linux"]
        - key: karpenter.sh/capacity-type
          operator: In
          values: ["on-demand"]
        - key: karpenter.k8s.aws/instance-category
          operator: In
          values: ["c", "m", "r"]
        - key: karpenter.k8s.aws/instance-generation
```

```
          operator: Gt
          values: ["4"]
      nodeClassRef:
        group: karpenter.k8s.aws
        kind: EC2NodeClass
        name: default
      expireAfter: 720h
      terminationGracePeriod: 24h
  limits:
    cpu: 1000
  disruption:
    consolidationPolicy: WhenEmptyOrUnderutilized
    consolidateAfter: 30s
```

Let me explain each of the settings:

- `requirements`: This setting is perhaps one of the most important ones in `NodePool`. Here, you define the set of constraints for which instance types Karpenter can launch. From the example, you can see that this `NodePool` is going to launch only on-demand Linux nodes with an x86 CPU architecture (or `amd64`), from multiple instance categories (`c`, `m`, or `r`), and from the third generation onward. Most of these requirements are self-explanatory, but we'll dive deeper into this topic in the *NodePool requirements* section.

- `nodeClassRef`: This is where you define which `NodeClass` is associated with this `NodePool`.

- `expireAfter`: This is the duration of time for a node. Once this time expires, the node will be deleted by Karpenter, and the draining process will begin. You might want to set this value to reduce problems with having long-running nodes, such as memory leaks. However, if you want to disable this functionality (i.e., for stateful workloads such as Elasticsearch), you can define a `Never` value instead.

- `terminationGracePeriod`: This is a duration value that you can set to force a node to be terminated once the draining process starts. This setting is useful in cases where you might not want pods to block the drain/termination of your nodes. For instance, pods can still be running due to a restricted **pod disruption budget** (**PDB**) or the `do-not-disrupt` annotation (we'll explore this possibility later in this chapter), but you might want to configure a grace period to force its deletion (after the draining process).

- limits: This is where you define the maximum number of resources a NodePool can manage. As Karpenter could launch a diverse set of nodes, especially in terms of size, instead of specifying a number of nodes, you set a total number of resources, such as CPUs, memory, or even GPUs. The values you can have here depend on the cloud provider. Karpenter will take this value into consideration when choosing instance types. Once the limit has been reached, Karpenter won't launch additional nodes.

- disruption: This is where you define how Karpenter can terminate (or disrupt) a node. We'll dive deeper into this topic later in this chapter. But for now, you can see that in this example, nodes will be removed when they're empty or replaced with smaller ones when Karpenter considers that there's an opportunity to reduce costs.

Similar to EC2NodeClass, in a NodePool, there are other constraints available that are worth exploring. So, let's explore the most important section in NodePool, the requirements section.

NodePool requirements

You already explored the most basic NodePool manifest, and we briefly talked about the requirements section. Remember, here is where you define some of the constraints that Karpenter will consider when launching a node. You could think of this section as *the set of attributes a node will have.*

The set of requirements you define in a NodePool are the ones Karpenter will consider to match them with a pod. If there's an intersection match between the pod and NodePool (as long as there are no negations with the NotIn operator), a node will be launched—in other words, if there's compatibility. For instance, in the previous example, we had this requirement:

```
- key: karpenter.k8s.aws/instance-category
  operator: In
  values: ["c", "m", "r"]
```

If a pod has a nodeSelector with a fixed instance type such as t4.xlarge, Karpenter won't use this NodePool to launch a node since there's no match. As a result, the pod will remain unschedulable until the cluster has capacity available or Karpenter has a NodePool that supports this instance type. Even though this example is specific for the instance category in AWS, you can also use the same match logic for other Kubernetes well-known labels.

These are a set of standardized, predefined labels that provide metadata about nodes, such as their operating system (kubernetes.io/os), architecture (kubernetes.io/arch), or instance type (node.kubernetes.io/instance-type).

In addition to these labels, Karpenter will also use cloud-specific labels such as the following:

- Instance generation (`karpenter.k8s.aws/instance-generation`)

- Instance family (`karpenter.k8s.aws/instance-family`)

- Instance size (`karpenter.k8s.aws/instance-size`)

- Instance CPU (`karpenter.k8s.aws/instance-cpu`)

- Instance memory (`karpenter.k8s.aws/instance-memory`)

Note

To get the full list of well-known Kubernetes labels, make sure you check the Kubernetes official docs at `https://kubernetes.io/docs/reference/labels-annotations-taints/`. For a full list of the labels that Karpenter uses, you can go here: `https://karpenter.sh/docs/concepts/scheduling/#well-known-labels`. It's worth checking the instance type reference doc as well: `https://karpenter.sh/docs/reference/instance-types/`.

Additionally, when you specify any of these requirements, as you've seen, you can use operators such as `In`, `NotIn`, `Exists`, `DoesNotExist`, `Gt` (greater than), and `Lt` (lower than). For instance, you could have a requirement to launch nodes that aren't (`NotIn`) the `small` instance size or that at least have (`Gt`) four vCPUs. The less restrictive you are, the more options you give Karpenter to decide which instance type is best for your workload(s). Keep in mind that the values for each requirement are an array, so even if you're going to need only one value, it needs to be configured as an array of one value.

General recommendations

While you have a lot of flexibility in configuring the set of constraints that `NodePool` can have, you might also feel overwhelmed. But don't worry too much about it. The mindset you need to have when setting `NodePool` constraints is to only constrain the `NodePool` with the requirements you need. Keep in mind that Karpenter will always try to launch the best node possible in terms of cost and efficiency. However, there are certain requirements that Karpenter recommends including and being intentional about.

> **Note**
>
> At the time of writing this book, Karpenter limits the number of requirements to 100 that you can have in a NodePool. This limit includes both the requirements section (including well-known and user-defined labels) and the metadata labels you could use in a NodePool for workload constraint or affinity purposes.

Let's explore deeper the most common and important requirements in a NodePool.

karpenter.k8s.aws/instance-category

Here's where you define the instance categories that NodePool can use. The implementation details vary depending on the cloud provider, but in the case of AWS, this refers to the instance categories. Notice that in the previous example, this constraint has three categories configured: c, m, and r, which are the ones that generally work with most workloads (unless you have a very specific performance need). I want you to pay close attention to this requirement as it's one of the places where Karpenter shines.

Instead of having to specify specific instance types (there are hundreds), you're telling Karpenter that you're flexible to use any of the instance types from those families. Based on the unscheduled pods, Karpenter will decide which instance types are good candidates and will let the cloud provider API decide which instance type to use. We'll dive much deeper into this flow in the next section.

karpenter.k8s.aws/instance-generation

When you use this label, you're telling Karpenter which generations you'd like to use (or not) from the "universe" of instance types a cloud provider has to offer. In the previous example, the NodePool is going to use only the instance types from a generation greater than (Gt) the fourth generation. Most deployments of Karpenter I've seen have constrained generations to some degree.

However, you might want to have a balance between flexibility and performance; therefore, after doing some tests with your application, you might decide to use only the latest three generations. Keep in mind that by being more restrictive, the range of instance types Karpenter and the cloud provider have to choose from will be reduced. So, make sure you do proper testing, and ensure your applications can make the most of the underlying nodes to provide a better price-performance ratio.

karpenter.sh/capacity-type

Along with instance categories and generations you can configure, you also have the ability to constrain the purchase model. For instance, in AWS, you have the option to choose reserved, spot, and/or on-demand. As you configure an array of values, you can specify one, two, or all of them. In the previous NodePool example, Karpenter will only launch on-demand instances of whichever instance type it ends up using. Keep in mind that Karpenter has a strict ordering to capacity types built into its simulation logic.

When you have all types, Karpenter will prioritize reserved, as this is the reserved capacity that you've already paid for (in AWS, this refers to the **On-Demand Capacity Reservations (ODCR)** or **Amazon EC2 Capacity Blocks for ML**). This is followed by spot, which is spare capacity offered with steep discounts, and then on-demand, which you could consider as the listing price.

In AWS, the capacity type value will be sent to the EC2 Fleet API to launch EC2 instances. If the capacity type is reserved or on-demand, Karpenter will specify an allocation strategy to the EC2 Fleet API of lowest-price. EC2 Fleet will try to launch the lowest-priced instance type from the list of instance type options passed by Karpenter. If the capacity type is spot, Karpenter will request to launch instances using the price-capacity-optimized strategy, which will try to find a relatively large capacity pool with lower prices based on the other instance type options passed in the request. Effectively, Karpenter allows the EC2 Fleet API to prioritize the best combination of capacity availability and price in all situations.

kubernetes.io/arch

In this label, you specify the CPU architecture of the nodes that Karpenter can launch. At the time of writing this book, you can configure only two values: amd64 or arm64 (if you're not familiar with the amd64 value, it's also known as x86-64). It's a 64-bit version of the x86 instruction set architecture developed by AMD, but it's now used by Intel as well. Therefore, with this value, you're saying you could use Intel or AMD instances. When you use the arm64 value, Karpenter will launch instances with the ARM-based processors (also known as AArch64, ARMv8-A, etc.), and in the context of AWS, it will launch AWS Graviton instances.

When you have both values, Karpenter will send them both to the cloud provider API. In the case of AWS, the EC2 Fleet API will follow the allocation strategy we mentioned before when exploring the capacity type requirement. If you decide to use both values, you need to make sure that your application can run on both architectures. We'll dive deeper into this topic in *Chapter 11*.

kubernetes.io/os

When you use this label, you specify the operating system that the instances should have. Karpenter supports both linux and windows. For this requirement, it's recommended that you only use one or the other as it will help you to simplify workload configuration too. In this book, we'll focus only on Linux instances.

As we progress through the book, we'll continue exploring other sets of requirements you could use based on the use cases of the workloads running in the cluster. For now, let's leave it there and move on to the next section to dive deep into NodeClaims.

NodeClaim

NodeClaims are immutable objects that Karpenter creates or deletes automatically to keep track of the status and manage the life cycle of a node. You don't need to create or update a NodeClaim (you could but it's not recommended); it's merely a read-only resource that you'll typically use to review the status of a node. A NodeClaim is created after Karpenter has made a scheduling decision, and Karpenter will send a request to the cloud provider to launch a new node. The NodeClaim allows Karpenter to reconcile the result of the scheduling request to launch the CloudProvider request. You'll see here all the requirements and constraints that have been determined through the scheduling simulation process, which we'll dive deeper into in the next section.

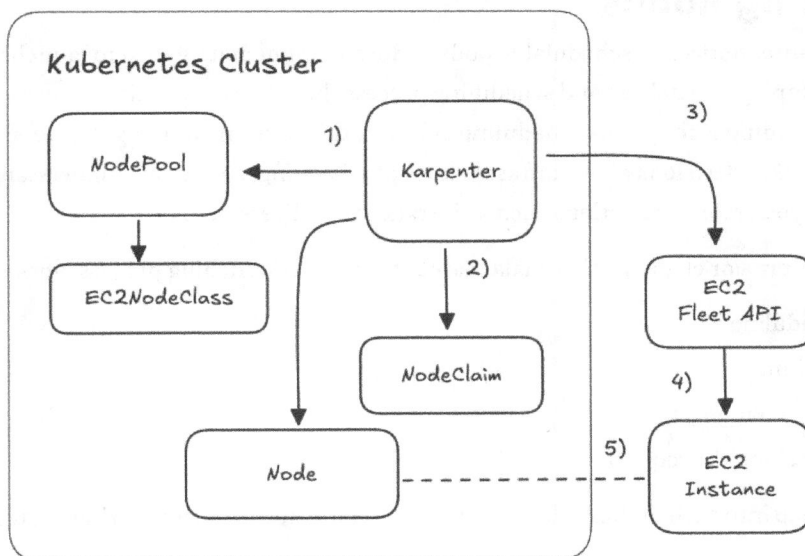

Figure 8.7 – Karpenter interacting with all its components to launch nodes

As you can see in *Figure 8.7*, when pods stay pending because there are no suitable nodes available, Karpenter evaluates these unschedulable pods against the existing NodePools and NodeClasses to find a compatible pairing (**1**). It then calculates the optimal NodeClaim that can fulfill the pod requirements and any other queued workloads (**2**). This NodeClaim is created in the Kubernetes cluster and initiates the life cycle process of the node. Using the NodeClaim specifications, Karpenter talks to the cloud provider (i.e., AWS) to launch an actual EC2 instance (**3**). As the cloud provider provisions the instance (**4**), Karpenter monitors its progress, watching for the instance to register itself with the cluster (**5**). The process continues until the node has successfully initialized.

Even though you won't need to create NodeClaims, it is important that you understand why they exist as you'll see them being referenced several times when inspecting the Karpenter controller logs. For instance, you'll see that a NodeClaim is created right after Karpenter notices that there are unscheduled pods, and if you describe this object, you'll see which instance types were considered to launch a node. Furthermore, you'll be interacting with these objects for troubleshooting purposes to find out why a node hasn't been launched. For example, when you explore the events in these objects, you'll learn more about why nodes couldn't be launched, registered, or initialized.

Now it's time to explore how Karpenter decides which nodes to launch, and what considerations it is making to help you run efficient Kubernetes clusters.

Launching nodes

When Karpenter notices unschedulable pods, it doesn't immediately rush to launch new nodes. Instead, it employs a batching and scheduling process that aims to optimize resource utilization while maintaining Kubernetes scheduling rules. In this section, you're going to explore how Karpenter makes decisions about infrastructure provisioning, so that you understand why I've been giving you recommendations such as instance type diversification.

There are four major elements that make Karpenter's node-launching process work:

1. Scheduling
2. Batching
3. Bin-packing
4. Launching the request

Let's dive deep into each of these elements to understand how Karpenter brings new nodes into your cluster.

1. Scheduling

As you already know, Karpenter works in tandem with `kube-scheduler`; it basically takes one step ahead to reduce the time pods are unscheduled. In other words, while `kube-scheduler` is responsible for allocating existing capacity, Karpenter steps in when that capacity is exhausted. When `kube-scheduler` can't find a suitable node for a pod, it marks it as unschedulable—this is Karpenter's trigger.

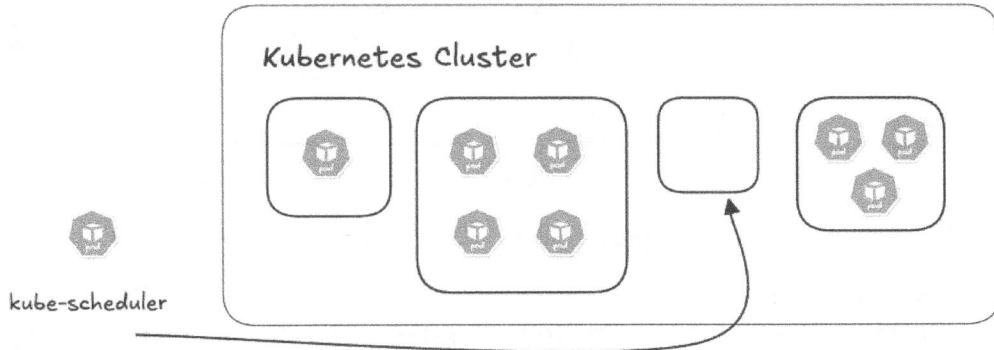

Figure 8.8 – kube-scheduler decides where to schedule the pod

As you can imagine, the Kubernetes scheduling process is complex. Both `kube-scheduler` and Karpenter must consider numerous factors: resource requests, tolerations, node selectors, and TSCs, among others. Karpenter uses these factors to ensure its launch decisions align with your workload's requirements. In *Figure 8.8*, a node was available to schedule the pod to, but how does Karpenter decide which and how many nodes to launch if pods remain unscheduled? To answer this, let's explore the next phase.

2. Batching

Once Karpenter is triggered, its expanding batch window mechanism begins. This means that when pending pods begin arriving, Karpenter watches their timing carefully. It employs an expanding window algorithm that balances between quick launches and efficient bin-packing. As per *Figure 8.9*, the algorithm uses two key time values: a 1-second idle period and a maximum window of 10 seconds. When pods arrive within less than a second of each other, Karpenter keeps expanding the window, up to that 10-second maximum, to optimize node launches. These two settings can be changed through Karpenter's global settings as environment variables: `BATCH_IDLE_DURATION` and `BATCH_MAX_DURATION`. However, I wouldn't recommend that you change them unless you fully understand the implications.

For example, you might want to extend the time Karpenter should wait for more pods to arrive, but it will take more time to launch a node.

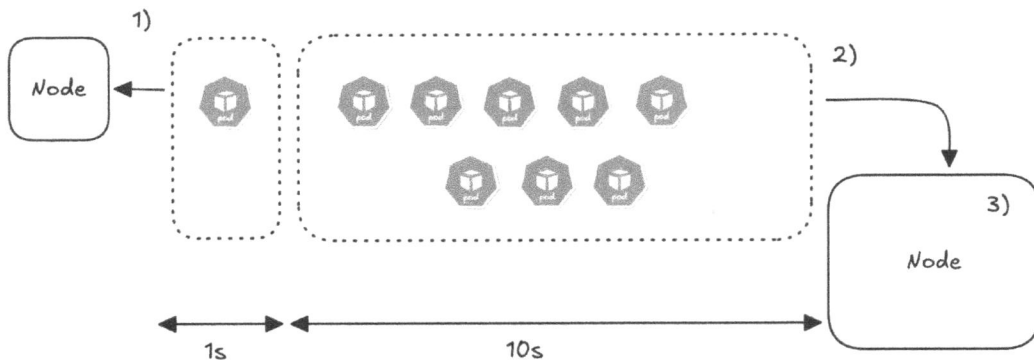

Figure 8.9 – Karpenter launching nodes for batches of pods

Now, consider this scenario, as per *Figure 8.9*: if 8 pods arrive within 10 seconds, Karpenter might launch just 1 node for all of them, maximizing bin-packing and reducing infrastructure costs (**3**). However, if those same eight pods arrive spaced just slightly more than one second apart, you might end up with eight different nodes launched independently, leading to inefficiency.

If new pods keep arriving continuously, Karpenter will keep expanding the batch window, but only up to the maximum batch duration you have configured. It's worth mentioning that pod scale-ups are often correlated, which makes pod batching particularly effective. When this maximum window expires, Karpenter closes the current batch, schedules node provisioning with whatever pods are currently in that batch and then starts a new batching window for any subsequent pods that continue to arrive. This batching strategy enables Karpenter to find a balance between launching capacity quickly and packing the pods efficiently onto fewer nodes, minimizing resource waste and scaling delays.

3. Bin-packing

Karpenter's scheduling process uses the bin-packing algorithm to launch the smallest number of nodes possible. More specifically, it uses the **first-fit-decreasing** (**FFD**) bin-packing algorithm, where items are first sorted in descending order by size, and then each item is placed into the first bin where it fits. Let's explore how Karpenter is implementing this algorithm.

Bin-packing starts with Karpenter getting the entire universe of possible instance types from the cloud provider. These instance types are then sorted by cost, as Karpenter aims to optimize for actual cost. Then, Karpenter sorts pods by their resource requests in descending order, first by

CPU, then by memory. Each pod is assigned to the first compatible instance type that has enough capacity to accommodate it, as per *Figure 8.10*. Karpenter creates virtual nodes (scheduling nodes) during its scheduling simulation. Each of these virtual nodes maintains a full list of compatible instance types that could potentially satisfy its requirements.

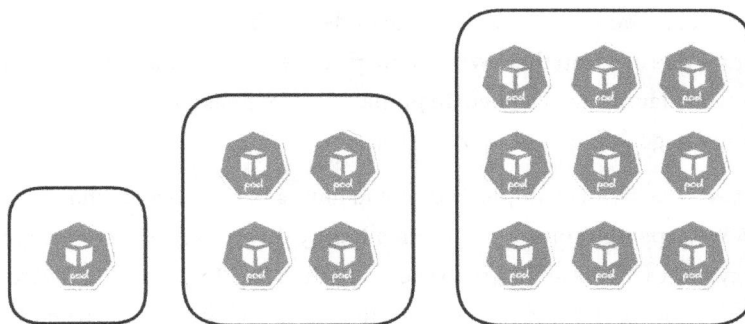

Figure 8.10 – Karpenter's bin-packing process considering pod constraints

As Karpenter adds pods to a virtual node, the constraints change, and the list of compatible instance types may shrink. This is because the bin-packing process intersects all requirements from pods and `NodePool` definitions and considers `DaemonSets` that will need to be scheduled for every new node. For example, if you add a pod that requires ARM architecture, suddenly all x86-only instance types are removed from that virtual node's list of possibilities. Or if the combined CPU and memory requirements grow too large, smaller instance types are filtered out. This dynamic filtering of instance types is what makes the bins "resizable"—they aren't fixed in size like traditional bin-packing problems, but rather adjust based on the accumulating requirements of the pods being packed into them. If Karpenter can launch one node, it generally will, unless pods have constraints such as TSCs causing Karpenter to launch more than one node. Karpenter aims to launch nodes considering cost, but it also needs to consider what `kube-scheduler` will do when the nodes are available in the cluster.

As you can tell by now, the dynamic nature of Kubernetes clusters brings a significant challenge to Karpenter's bin-packing process. The cluster state is in constant flux, with pods being created or deleted, and nodes potentially facing disruptions. This volatility means that by the time Karpenter decides on and launches new nodes, the cluster's needs may have already shifted. To address this, Karpenter makes quick, heuristic-based decisions and acts on them rapidly. While this approach may not yield perfect results in every instance, it allows for continuous optimization. Over time, this strategy ensures that your cluster's efficiency and resource utilization steadily improve, adapting to the dynamic nature of your workloads.

4. Launching the request

Once Karpenter has determined its bin-packing and scheduling simulation decisions, it moves to the actual launch request. This is where Karpenter's cloud provider integration comes into action. Remember that Karpenter might end up making more than one request; it will depend on the pod and NodePool constraints if more than one node is going to be needed. Once the request is fulfilled, Karpenter doesn't stop there with managing the node(s). Karpenter has logic to ensure that nodes that fail to launch are cleaned up properly, and it does some checks before it considers a node fully "ready to go."

Let's be more specific with an example so that you have a better idea of what happens next. For instance, in AWS, Karpenter aims to maintain a highly diverse set of instance types, including larger instance types, to increase variety in the diversified list. This list is passed to the EC2 Fleet API, and it's EC2's allocation strategy that's in charge of which instance type ends up being chosen. Remember, if it's on-demand or reserved, Karpenter will use the lowest-price allocation strategy, which will launch the instance type from the list with the lowest price. And if it's spot, Karpenter will use the price-capacity-optimized allocation strategy, which will launch the instance types with the highest spare capacity available while trying to get the lowest prices. At some point in time, you might end up with a cluster with a variety of different instance types and sizes, as per *Figure 3.11*.

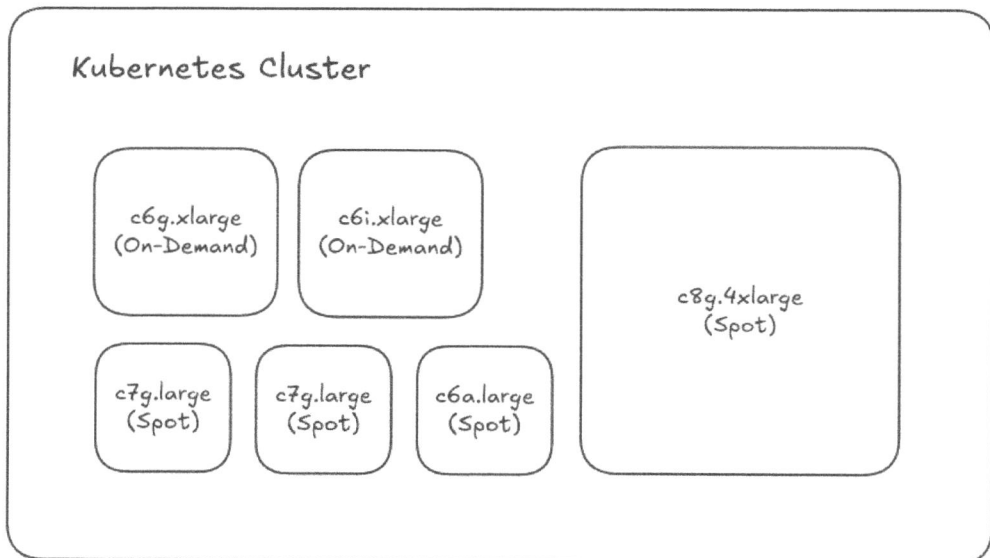

Figure 8.11 – An EKS cluster with different instance types

Now that we've explored in more detail how Karpenter works, let's explore how to get started with Karpenter. We'll start with what's required to deploy Karpenter.

Deploying Karpenter

In a nutshell, to start using Karpenter, you first need to deploy two components:

- The Karpenter controller
- The CRDs we've explored previously

Regardless of where you're hosting your Kubernetes cluster, these are the main components you need, as long as there's a Karpenter provider such as AWS, Azure, or GCP. At the time of writing this book, Karpenter doesn't have an on-premises provider.

In this book, we'll continue using AWS as the cloud provider to run Kubernetes. If you're using any other cloud provider that Karpenter supports, the details on how to deploy each of the Karpenter components will vary and will be specific to that provider. However, there is one aspect that will remain the same: you need a set of nodes to host the Karpenter controller replicas. In essence, the deployment flow will be like this:

1. Create a Kubernetes cluster.
2. Create worker nodes to host the Karpenter controller.
3. Let Karpenter provision worker nodes from now on.

There are two important aspects when you deploy Karpenter:

- Node management
- Permissions for the Karpenter controller pods

First, the nodes that will host the Karpenter controller will need to be managed by someone else rather than Karpenter itself. This means that you need to plan how to scale these nodes (added complexity), or if you want to keep them static, to only run Karpenter in these nodes (simple but manual). Additionally, for high-availability reasons, it's recommended to have two replicas of the Karpenter controller. One replica acts as the leader, using a typical leader-election algorithm. Moreover, you might also decide to use these nodes to host pods from the kube-system namespace.

In AWS, as per *Figure 8.12*, this means that you need to have one managed node group (**1**). Alternatively, to simplify this setup, you have the option to use **AWS Fargate** for EKS (**2**), which is a compute option managed by AWS where you pay only for the resources that your pods need, and AWS takes care of the autoscaling and patching of the underlying nodes. Additionally, AWS offers the EKS Auto Mode option (**3**) to let AWS automatically manage compute, storage, and networking of a Kubernetes cluster. With EKS Auto Mode, you'll have the Karpenter controller running in the control plane and managed by AWS.

However, consider that if you have EKS Auto Mode and self-managed Karpenter, they will fight with each other to launch nodes if you aren't careful.

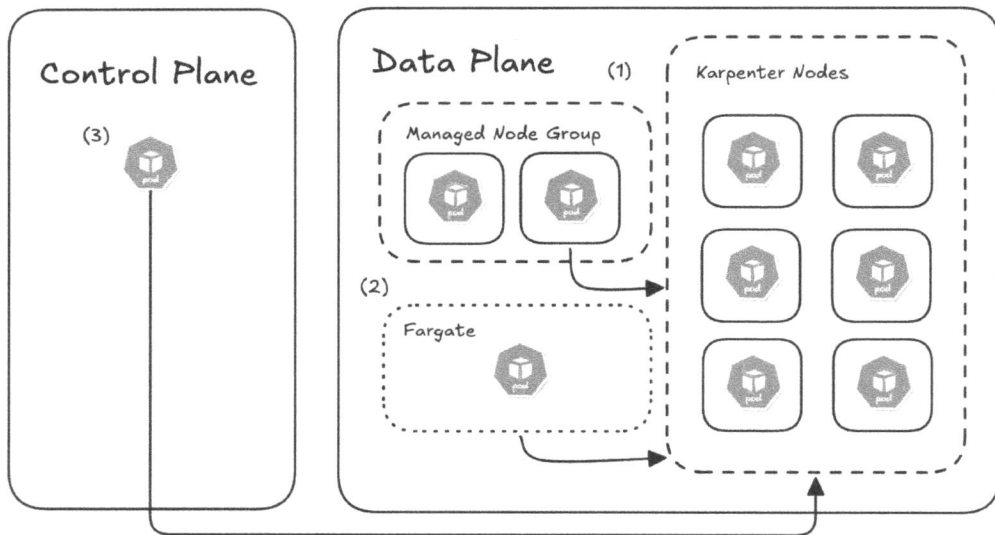

Figure 8.12 – Different ways to deploy the Karpenter controller in AWS

Second, the Karpenter controller pods need to be able to launch and manage nodes with all the resources they need (disks, networking, etc.), register them into the cluster, and interact with other cloud resources.

For instance, in AWS, the Karpenter controller requires a dedicated IAM policy with permissions that allow it to provision and manage EC2 instances. At a minimum, this includes permissions to launch and terminate instances (`ec2:RunInstances` and `ec2:TerminateInstances`), create and manage launch templates and fleets (`ec2:CreateFleet` and `ec2:CreateLaunchTemplate`), and tag resources during provisioning (`ec2:CreateTags`).

We haven't dived very deep into other specific activities that Karpenter performs. But, for instance, the Karpenter controller must also be able to get details about various EC2 resources—for example, subnets, security groups, instance types, access to **AWS Systems Manager (SSM)** parameters and EC2 instance pricing data. Moreover, Karpenter needs the ability to pass a node IAM role to instances (`iam:PassRole`), create and manage instance profiles, and read cluster metadata via `eks:DescribeCluster`. To handle instance life cycle events (e.g., spot interruption warnings), it consumes messages from an Amazon **Simple Queue Service (SQS)** queue that must be populated by **EventBridge** rules. All of these permissions should be scoped to the EKS cluster where Karpenter is running.

Typically, you don't need to worry much about the building blocks for deploying Karpenter along with all the configurations we just explored, as cloud providers such as AWS and Azure already provide resources to help you get started quickly. In the next section, you'll do a hands-lab that helps you get started with Karpenter in AWS.

Hands-on lab: Autoscaling with Karpenter

In the previous chapter, you deployed CAS and 60 pods to see how CAS reacted when there were unscheduled pods. Nodes were added automatically via CAS by modifying the Auto Scaling group to the desired number of nodes. If you didn't do that lab, don't worry; it's not required for this lab. Here, we're going to do something similar to see how Karpenter works.

Creating a fresh EKS cluster

Go back to your terminal and make sure you're in the `/chapter08` folder from the book's GitHub repository. In here, you'll find a `terraform` folder that includes the scripts you'll be using to create an EKS cluster with Karpenter and other addons.

To make this step easier, destroy any previous EKS cluster you've created in this book by running the `cleanup.sh` script. You'll start with a fresh EKS cluster. Once you have no cluster running, start over with the files in this chapter by running the following command:

```
$ sh bootstrap.sh
```

Wait around 15 minutes for the cluster to be up and running. At this stage, Terraform will create an EKS cluster with a managed node group for only the Karpenter controller pods (which we'll deploy later). When the script has finished creating the cluster, update your kubeconfig file to connect to the cluster by running this command (change the eu-west-1 Region if you're using a different one):

```
$ aws eks --region eu-west-1 update-kubeconfig --name kubernetes-
autoscaling
```

You can confirm that you're able to interact with the cluster by running this command:

```
$ kubectl get pods --all-namespaces
```

You should be able to see the list of all pods running in the cluster.

Deploying a sample application

The cluster you've created in the previous step has a managed group with a label to host only critical addons, such as the Karpenter controller pods, like this:

```
labels = {
  "CriticalAddonsOnly" = "true"
}
```

We've done this for two reasons:

- The cluster needs to provide at least two nodes to run the Karpenter pods as they have a required topologySpreadConstraints to make sure that Karpenter can't schedule two pods to the same zone. So, we had to create a node group using multiple Availability Zones.
- We want all other pods to run on nodes created by Karpenter and not in these nodes. We'll use nodeSelectors to make sure this happens.

So now, if we deploy the sample application to the cluster using a nodeSelector with an intent=apps label, what do you think will happen? Let's give it a try. Run the following command to deploy a sample application:

```
$ kubectl apply -f montecarlopi.yaml
```

List the pods running using this command:

```
$ kubectl get pods
```

You'll see that the sample application pod is stuck with a `Pending` status, as the existing nodes can't host this pod. You should see an output similar to this:

```
NAME                READY   STATUS    RESTARTS   AGE
montecarlo-pi-...   0/1     Pending   0          3m50s
```

We're forcing this to happen, but this is the same behavior you'll see when your application is scaling out because HPA is adding more replicas, and there's a point when the cluster doesn't have the capacity to run any additional pods. This is the moment when we need Karpenter to help us add the nodes needed to run the unschedulable pods. Leave the sample application in that state. Let's deploy and configure Karpenter next.

Deploying Karpenter

As you've learned in a previous section, to deploy Karpenter, you need to deploy the CRDs and the Karpenter controller, configure the pod's permissions, and have at least one default `NodePool`. To help you get started quickly, we've created a `karpenter.tf.txt` file in the `chapter08/terraform` folder from the book's GitHub repository, using the Terraform AWS modules. This way, we'll let the module deploy the IAM role with the proper permissions, configure security access, and create any other resources, such as the SQS queue to manage node disruptions.

So, to deploy Karpenter, remove the `.txt` extension from the `karpenter.tf.txt` file and run the bootstrap script again. Here are the commands you need to run:

```
$ cd chapter08/terraform
$ mv karpenter.tf.txt karpenter.tf
$ sh bootstrap.sh
```

Wait around three minutes, and then run the following command to verify that the Karpenter controller pods are up and running:

```
$ kubectl get pods -n karpenter
```

The Karpenter controller pods should have a `Running` status, but if you list the sample application pods, they're still going to have a `Pending` status. This is because to see Karpenter in action, you need to have a `NodePool` deployed to the cluster that matches the pod's constraints. So, let's deploy a default `NodePool` and `EC2NodeClass`.

Deploying a default NodePool and EC2NodeClass

You're going to deploy the same objects that we explored in the previous sections. The only difference is that in EC2NodeClass, we now have to define the name of the IAM role and the tags that Karpenter will use to select the subnets and security groups.

Go back to the root of the chapter08 folder and run the following command:

```
$ kubectl apply -f nodepool.yaml
```

Confirm that the objects have been created by running this command:

```
$ kubectl get nodepool,ec2nodeclass
```

You should see a default NodePool and a default EC2NodeClass listed.

As soon as these objects were created, Karpenter matched the constraints from the unschedulable pods with the default NodePool. You can confirm this by reading the logs from the Karpenter controller. To do so, let's create an alias, since you'll be reading the Karpenter controller logs frequently. Run this command:

```
$ alias kl='kubectl -n karpenter logs -l app.kubernetes.io/name=karpenter
--all-containers=true -f --tail=20'
```

Then, simply run this command to read the most recent logs from Karpenter:

```
$ kl
```

Notice what the logs would say, for instance, found provisionable pod(s), referring to the moment when Karpenter was triggered because there were unscheduled pods. You should also find a message such as computed new nodeclaim(s) to fit pod(s), referring to the moment when Karpenter finished the bin-packing process, and then a message with created nodeclaim referring to the moment when Karpenter created the NodeClaim object. But let me pause here a bit. That log line includes the list of instance types, as well as the total CPU and memory requests that Karpenter used to filter which instance types were good candidates (which will be sent to the EC2 API Fleet API):

```
"requests":{"cpu":"1050m","memory":"512Mi","pods":"4"}
```

But why is it considering 1050m CPU in total if the sample application is requesting only 900m CPU? This is what the sample application has:

```
...
        resources:
          requests:
            cpu: 900m
            memory: 512Mi
          limits:
            memory: 512Mi
...
```

Well, Karpenter also considers the DaemonSets that will be deployed in the new node. In this particular setup, the cluster is going to deploy kube-proxy, aws-node, and the eks-pod-identity-agent pods in addition to the sample application. So, when you're defining the NodePool constraints, consider that there are going to be extra pods and processes (i.e., kubelet) that will be scheduled into the nodes.

Let's confirm that Karpenter created the NodeClaim object by running this command:

```
$ kubectl get nodeclaim
```

You should get an output similar to this one:

```
NAME    TYPE        CAPACITY    ZONE        NODE        READY   AGE
def...  c6a.large   on-demand   eu-west-1c  ip-10-...   True    5m
```

Notice that just with this output, we already have valuable information about the node that Karpenter launched. You now know that the node was launched by the default NodePool, and that it's an on-demand EC2 instance of type c6a.large in the eu-west-1c Availability Zone. Remember, because it's an on-demand instance, Karpenter used the lowest-price allocation strategy when calling the EC2 Fleet API. When I ran this lab, the c6a.large instance type was the one with the lowest price. You could describe the NodeClaim by running this command:

```
$ kubectl describe nodeclaim
```

You should be able to see the values Karpenter used to make the call to the EC2 Fleet API. For instance, you can see the full list of instance types that were considered:

```
...
  Requirements:
    Key:         node.kubernetes.io/instance-type
    Operator:    In
    Values:
      c3.large
      c4.large
      c5.large
      c5.xlarge
      c5a.large
      c5a.xlarge
      c5ad.large
...
```

Once the node is registered to the cluster and ready, it becomes a candidate to schedule pods. This means that the unschedulable pod that caused this node to be launched should have been scheduled by kube-scheduler into this node. Let's confirm that by listing the pods:

```
$ kubectl get pods -o wide
```

As expected, the pod that had a Pending status now has a Running status. Also, since we added the -o wide parameter to the preceding command, you should be able to confirm that the pod was indeed scheduled to the new node that Karpenter launched. You can do this by matching the IP address you get here with the one you got when listing NodeClaims.

Removing the sample application

To finish this lab, make sure you're still in the chapter08 directory in the terminal, and let's remove the sample application by running this command:

```
$ kubectl delete -f montecarlopi.yaml
```

You should see no pods running, and in a matter of 10 seconds, Karpenter will start removing the node as there are no pods running in it anymore. You can describe the NodeClaim again, and you should see an output like this in the Events section:

```
...
    ...  Node is deleting or marked for deletion
    ...  Disrupting NodeClaim: Empty/Delete
    ...  Instance is terminating
...
```

We've removed a lot of information just to focus on the messages I wanted you to see. We'll be covering this behavior in more detail in the next chapter. But for now, you can see that as soon as Karpenter noticed that the node was empty, it cordoned the node so that kube-scheduler can't schedule any other pods in this node, as it's about to be terminated. Then, the Karpenter finalizer was triggered to terminate the EC2 instance.

All of this happened because NodePool has the following configuration:

```
...
  disruption:
    consolidationPolicy: WhenEmpty
    consolidateAfter: 1m
...
```

This cleanup process takes a few minutes. So, three or four minutes after you removed the pod, the node should have been removed from the cluster. By doing so, Karpenter will help you to keep an efficient Kubernetes cluster as long as the constraints in your workloads permit. We'll continue exploring this in more detail in the following chapter.

For now, let's move on to the next section to learn how you can influence scheduling decisions by adding constraints to your pods.

Workload scheduling constraints

When you deploy workloads on Kubernetes with Karpenter, you can specify a variety of scheduling constraints in your pod specs to control *where* and *how* those pods will run. These constraints ensure that your pods are scheduled on nodes that meet certain requirements, such as specific hardware specs, specific zones, or co-location (or separation) from other pods. As you've learned in a previous section, Karpenter honors these constraints to decide what nodes to provision for these pending pods.

Scheduling happens through **layered constraints**: the cloud provider defines broad limits (the universe of all available instance types, zones, etc.), then you define NodePool constraints (nodes that Karpenter can create), and finally, you define your pod's scheduling constraints. Keep in mind that a pod's constraints must fall within the requirements set by the NodePool, else pods will remain unschedulable. The following sections describe the major workload scheduling constraints you can use, how they work, and how Karpenter takes them into account when scaling your cluster. Even if you're not new to many of these concepts, don't skip it, as we'll explore how Karpenter behaves under certain scenarios.

Node selector

Sometimes you need to pin a workload to a certain category of nodes—for example, to a specific Availability Zone or a machine type with special hardware. Kubernetes offers the nodeSelector field as a straightforward way to constrain pods to nodes with a particular label. nodeSelector is essentially a key-value filter: the pod will only schedule on a node that has a matching label. For instance, if you know you want a pod to run in the AWS eu-west-1a Availability Zone, you could add a nodeSelector in the pod spec:

```
spec:
  nodeSelector:
    topology.kubernetes.io/zone: "eu-west-1a"
```

You can use any node label here—either well-known labels provided by Kubernetes (such as the zone, Region, instance type, operating system, etc.) or custom labels that you set on certain nodes. Common examples include selecting by kubernetes.io/os: linux for operating system-specific workloads, or a custom label such as environment: prod to place pods on production-designated nodes.

When Karpenter is deciding how to schedule a pending pod with a nodeSelector, it will attempt to launch a node that carries the requested label. In practice, you set up a NodePool with certain labels on the nodes that Karpenter will create. You *must* define custom labels while well-known labels will automatically be configured for you. You can check the Karpenter docs (https://karpenter.sh/docs/concepts/scheduling/#well-known-labels) to see the complete list of well-known labels. For example, as per the previous example, you can configure a NodePool that assigns the environment: prod label to all nodes, matching the nodeSelector we used before. The following NodePool snippet includes this custom label:

```
apiVersion: karpenter.sh/v1
kind: NodePool
metadata:
...
spec:
  template:
    metadata:
      labels:
        environment: prod
    spec:
...
```

It's important that the label in your nodeSelector is actually configured on some NodePool or existing nodes; if it's an arbitrary label that no current or potential node has, the pod will remain unschedulable. Notice that nodeSelector is a hard requirement—the scheduler (and Karpenter) won't ignore it. So, use it when you absolutely know the node must have that label. If you need more flexibility, such as a preference rather than a strict requirement, or a set of possible values, Kubernetes provides node affinity, which we will discuss next.

Node affinity

Node affinity is an advanced form of specifying node constraints within a pod, allowing expressions and soft preferences. It lives under the affinity field in the pod spec, and there are two types of node affinity:

- requiredDuringSchedulingIgnoredDuringExecution: Acts like a mandatory rule (similar to nodeSelector, but supports operators such as In, NotIn, Exists, NotExists, etc., and multiple conditions)

- preferredDuringSchedulingIgnoredDuringExecution: Acts as a *preference*—the scheduler will try to put the pod on a node that meets the criteria, but if none is available, it can schedule the pod elsewhere (unlike a required rule, which would block scheduling if not met)

With node affinity, you define one or more nodeSelectorTerms, each with one or more match expressions. Each term is effectively a list of label conditions that a node must satisfy for the pod to schedule on it (it's worth mentioning that Karpenter borrowed the node selector API for the NodePool requirements, and it adheres to it strictly). For example, suppose you prefer running a batch job on spot instances in either the eu-west-1a or eu-west-1b Availability Zone, but you can tolerate running with on-demand instances if no spot capacity is available. You might express that in a pod as follows:

```
spec:
  affinity:
    nodeAffinity:
      requiredDuringSchedulingIgnoredDuringExecution:
        nodeSelectorTerms:
          - matchExpressions:
              - key: "topology.kubernetes.io/zone"
                operator: In
                values: ["eu-west-1a", "eu-west-1b"]
      preferredDuringSchedulingIgnoredDuringExecution:
      - weight: 100
        preference:
          matchExpressions:
            - key: "karpenter.sh/capacity-type"
              operator: In
              values: ["spot"]
```

In this snippet, the requiredDuringSchedulingIgnoredDuringExecution section ensures the node's zone is either eu-west-1a or eu-west-1b. The preferredDuringSchedulingIgnoreDuringExecution adds a preference for nodes that have the karpenter.sh/capacity-type=spot label (a label Karpenter uses to denote spot instances). Because it's a preference, the pod *could* still land on an on-demand node if no spot node in those zones is available—but the scheduler will score spot nodes higher. weight: 100 just indicates the importance of this preference relative to other preferences (if any).

Behind the scenes, Karpenter will treat the required affinity exactly like a nodeSelector constraint—it must find or create a node in one of the specified zones or else the pod can't schedule. The preferred affinity is a bit different: Karpenter is aware of these preferences and will try to satisfy them when launching new nodes. In fact, Karpenter initially treats preferred affinities as if they were required when determining how to provision capacity for pending pods. It will attempt to launch a node that meets the zone requirement and is of the spot capacity type. If for some reason that's impossible (say spot instances are at their limit or none of the allowed instance types are available as spot), then Karpenter will relax the preference and consider on-demand capacity to get the pod scheduled.

This approach means that soft constraints can still influence Karpenter to create new nodes to satisfy your intent. It's worth noting that this can sometimes lead to more nodes than you might expect if you use a lot of "preferred" rules—Karpenter will prefer to add nodes to meet the preference rather than consolidating into fewer nodes to save cost. If you find that pods aren't bin-packed as tightly as expected, check whether a preferred affinity (or topology spread, which is discussed later) is causing Karpenter to deliberately spread out the pods by adding nodes.

> **Note**
>
> It's important to call out again that Karpenter does not schedule pods, so there are sharp edges with preferred affinities since kube-scheduler gets the first chance at scheduling and may relax constraints before Karpenter has a chance to provision capacity for the pod.

Moreover, use required affinities for things your pod absolutely cannot run without (specific hardware, compliance-related placement, etc.). Or use preferred affinities to give the scheduler a nudge in a certain direction (such as favoring cheaper spot instances or a particular zone for latency) while still allowing flexibility. Always ensure that your affinities align with the NodePools Karpenter can provision. For example, if you require a node label (as we saw in the previous example) that implies a certain instance type or zone, make sure a NodePool exists that covers that criterion. If you accidentally require an instance type or label that Karpenter isn't configured to provide, the pod will remain pending indefinitely. It's worth mentioning that Karpenter will still inform the user through events on the pod why this pod isn't schedulable in Karpenter's eyes as well.

Pod affinity and pod anti-affinity

Node selectors and node affinity deal with node labels, but sometimes the scheduling logic needs to consider other pods. **Pod affinity** and **anti-affinity** let you express rules about placing pods relative to other pods. This is useful for workload clustering or separation strategies. For example, you might want certain pods to run on the same host or zone as a particular service for data locality and latency needs—that's pod affinity. Or you might need to ensure that two replicas of the same application never run on the same node to avoid a single point of failure—that's pod anti-affinity.

Pod affinity/anti-affinity rules live under spec.affinity as well, in the podAffinity and podAntiAffinity sections. Like node affinity, they have requiredDuringSchedulingIgnoredDu ringExecution and preferredDuringSchedulingIgnoredDuringExecution modes. A *required* pod affinity means "do not schedule this pod *unless* there is an existing pod(s) with certain character- istics in the specified topology domain." A *required* podAntiAffinity means "do not schedule this pod *if* there is another pod with certain characteristics in the specified domain." The "topology domain" could be a node (identified by hostname), a zone, a Region, or any label you choose to indicate a domain of failure or locality.

Let's see an example of pod anti-affinity. Imagine a deployment of a web service with three replicas, where we want to ensure that no two replicas end up on the same node. We can add a required pod anti-affinity on the hostname (node) to repel pods from each other, like this:

```
spec:
  affinity:
    podAntiAffinity:
      requiredDuringSchedulingIgnoredDuringExecution:
        - labelSelector:
            matchLabels:
              app: web
          topologyKey: "kubernetes.io/hostname"
```

Here, we assume that each pod in the deployment has the app: web label. The rule says: "when scheduling a pod with the app: web label, do not place it on a node (topologyKey: kubernetes. io/hostname) that already has any pod with app: web." This guarantees that all three replicas will be on separate nodes or not scheduled at all. If we had used preferredDuringScheduling IgnoredDuringExecution instead, kube-scheduler would *try* to separate them but would still allow placing multiple on one node if no alternative existed.

Now, let's see an example of podAffinity. Consider a scenario with a backend and a frontend pod, where the frontend strongly benefits from being on the same Availability Zone as the backend (perhaps to minimize network latency). We could use a required podAffinity to ensure the frontend only schedules in a zone that already has a backend pod, like this:

```
spec:
  affinity:
    podAffinity:
      requiredDuringSchedulingIgnoredDuringExecution:
        - labelSelector:
            matchExpressions:
              - key: "system"
                operator: In
                values: ["backend"]
          topologyKey: "topology.kubernetes.io/zone"
```

This rule (based on the example) says the pod will only schedule in a zone where there is at least one pod with the system=backend label. If no such pod is running anywhere, then this pod won't schedule. In practice, required pod affinities are common when you have a set of pods that should always co-locate (such as a caching sidecar that must be on the same node as the main app, though Kubernetes now has better ways to handle that via DaemonSets, StatefulSets, or actual container sidecars within a pod). Preferred pod affinity could be used as a gentle hint, for example, "try to put my analytics pods in the same zone as the database for performance, but it's okay if not."

From Karpenter's perspective, pod affinity and anti-affinity are additional constraints that influence scheduling. Moreover, pod anti-affinity rules do not scale well since scheduling simulations now need to understand all existing pods in the cluster and their anti-affinities. If a pod cannot schedule due to a required anti-affinity (for instance, all current nodes have a conflicting pod), Karpenter will provision a new node to satisfy that rule. In our three-replica web service example, once each existing node has one pod, if we add one more pod, the fourth pod would remain pending—Karpenter would then launch another node so it can run without violating the one-per-node anti-affinity.

Similarly, with required pod affinity, if the rule specifies that a certain pod must be present, Karpenter can't do much unless that other pod is already running somewhere. Moreover, with pod affinity, if there are no pods running somewhere, Kubernetes will allow that first pod to go *anywhere*. Then, following pods must abide by the affinity constraint based on that previous pod scheduling. If it is running but just in a different topology (e.g., backend is in the eu-west-1a Availability Zone and none in eu-west-1b, so the frontend can only schedule in eu-west-1a), Karpenter will ensure to only create nodes in the allowed zone. Pod affinity/anti-affinity can also be set to preferred; as with node affinity, Karpenter will attempt to fulfill preferred affinities by launching nodes in a way that satisfies the preference (treating them as required initially). This means if you have a soft rule to spread two services apart, Karpenter might still add nodes to keep them apart for you. Use these features to ensure high-availability and co-location policies for your apps. Just be mindful that overly strict rules might cause pods to stay pending if the conditions can't be met, and overly loose (preferred) rules might lead to extra nodes being launched to satisfy preferences.

Tolerations and taints

While affinities and node selectors help attract pods to certain nodes, **taints** do the opposite: they repel pods from nodes unless the pod explicitly declares it can tolerate the taint. Taints are set on nodes (for example, via Karpenter's NodePool configuration or manually on a node), and a pod can include a matching **toleration** to indicate that it's okay to schedule there. This mechanism is often used to dedicate nodes to specific workloads or to isolate certain tasks. For instance, you might taint a group of GPU nodes with nvidia.com/gpu=true:NoSchedule to ensure that no pods land on those GPU nodes unless they actually need a GPU. Only pods that add a toleration for nvidia.com/gpu:NoSchedule will be allowed onto those nodes.

A toleration in a pod spec looks like this:

```
spec:
  tolerations:
    - key: "nvidia.com/gpu"
      operator: "Exists"
      effect: "NoSchedule"
```

This toleration means: "I tolerate any taint with the nvidia.com/gpu key and the NoSchedule effect, regardless of value." If the GPU nodes are tainted as in our example (the nvidia.com/gpu key and the NoSchedule effect), then this pod will be allowed to schedule on them (assuming it meets other criteria, such as resource requests, etc.). Typically, you would pair this with a resource request for a GPU as well (and possibly a nodeSelector/affinity for instance types that have GPUs), to fully express that the pod needs a GPU node, but also to make sure that workloads that do not need a GPU don't get scheduled on an instance that is going to be way more expensive than it needs.

Additionally, some workloads apply taints to nodes very early in their life cycle to signal that the node is not yet ready to run regular workloads. For example, CNI plugins or other system agents might temporarily add taints while performing initialization tasks. These taints are meant to be cleared automatically once the setup is complete, ensuring that user pods are only scheduled onto nodes that are fully prepared.

If your environment adds these kind of taints automatically, make sure you add equivalent startupTaints in your NodePool. This alignment makes Karpenter aware that the taints are expected and temporary. Without startupTaints in the NodePool spec, Karpenter may misinterpret the additional taint as a permanent scheduling barrier, concluding that the node is unusable and launching excess capacity unnecessarily.

From Karpenter's perspective, taints are another type of node constraint. NodePools can be configured with certain taints on all nodes they create. If a pod doesn't tolerate those taints, Karpenter will not consider that NodePool for provisioning a new node for the pod. In other words, the pod's tolerations must cover NodePool's taints in order for Karpenter to use it. For example, if you have a "spot" NodePool that taints its nodes with spot-instance=true:NoSchedule, only pods that include a matching toleration will ever get scheduled onto those spot nodes. This is a common pattern to segregate workloads: critical pods might *not* have that toleration (so they stick to on-demand nodes), while cost-sensitive pods do tolerate it (allowing them to run on cheaper spot nodes).

It's worth noting that tolerations by themselves do not *schedule* a pod onto a tainted node; they simply *allow* it. If a pod has a toleration for a taint, it can land on a node with that taint, but it could just as easily run on an untainted node if one is available and fits other constraints. So, if you intend to *force* a pod onto a certain set of nodes, you might use a combination of taints/tolerations and another constraint, such as a node affinity or nodeSelector for a label that only those tainted nodes have. Taints and tolerations are best used to implement broad exclusion policies. For example, you might taint all "prod" nodes with environment=prod:NoSchedule and ensure only pods that are labeled as prod (and have a toleration) go there, while dev/test pods have no toleration and thus get scheduled on other nodes.

Note

A common mistake is to taint NodePool's nodes and forget to add the corresponding toleration to the workload's pod spec. This results in the pod remaining unschedulable (kube-scheduler will keep it pending because it doesn't tolerate the node's taint), and Karpenter will not launch nodes for it unless there are other compatible pending pods. The pod will only schedule once it tolerates the taint or if it finds an untainted node. Always double-check that for any taint applied via Karpenter, the workloads meant for those nodes have matching tolerations.

Topology spread constraints

As your application scales, you often want to ensure that its pods are spread out to minimize the risk of failures and optimize resource usage. TSCs allow you to declaratively specify how pods should be distributed across failure domains or other topology domains (such as zones, nodes, or even custom labels). This is a more generalized and powerful mechanism than anti-affinity. Instead of just saying "not on the same node," you can say "try to keep the difference in the number of pods between zones to no more than X."

A TSC is defined in the pod spec under topologySpreadConstraints. You specify a label selector to group the pods of interest, usually all pods of your application. Then, define topologyKey, which is the node label defining the domain to spread across. Next comes maxSkew, which is the allowed difference between the domain with the most pods and the one with the fewest. Finally, we have a whenUnsatisfiable policy, which can be either DoNotSchedule or ScheduleAnyway. If whenUnsatisfiable is DoNotSchedule, the kube-scheduler will refuse to schedule a pod that would violate the maxSkew value—essentially making the spreading rule a hard requirement. If it's ScheduleAnyway, the kube-scheduler will still try to spread the pods, but it won't hold the pod back if the condition can't be satisfied; the pod will be scheduled and the imbalance allowed (the constraint is treated as a preference).

Let's illustrate this with an example. Suppose you have a deployment of an application with the app: web label, and you want to ensure that the replicas are balanced across Availability Zones and also across spot/on-demand capacity types for resiliency and cost savings. You might use two TSCs, like this:

```
...
    spec:
      topologySpreadConstraints:
        - topologyKey: "topology.kubernetes.io/zone"
```

```
        maxSkew: 1
        whenUnsatisfiable: DoNotSchedule
        labelSelector:
          matchLabels:
            app: web
    - topologyKey: "karpenter.sh/capacity-type"
      maxSkew: 2
      whenUnsatisfiable: ScheduleAnyway
      labelSelector:
        matchLabels:
          app: web

...
```

The first constraint ensures that the difference in the number of pods between any two zones does not exceed 1. It's marked as DoNotSchedule, which means Kubernetes will strictly enforce it: a new pod will wait (remain pending) if scheduling it would cause a larger skew in zone distribution than allowed. The second constraint tries to balance pods across the three capacity types (reserved, spot, and on-demand) that Karpenter can use. Here we allow a slightly larger skew of 2 and use ScheduleAnyway, so it's a soft rule—the scheduler will attempt to distribute evenly between spot and on-demand nodes, but if the spot capacity type isn't available, it won't prevent pods from running (they'll just all go to the other type).

How does Karpenter handle these? Karpenter is topology-aware. If a pod is pending because a TSC can't be satisfied with the current nodes, Karpenter will try to fix that by provisioning a new node in the required domain. For example, if you have six pods to spread across three zones, but all current nodes (and thus all running pods) are in eu-west-1a, new pods will remain unschedulable due to the DoNotSchedule constraint until nodes exist in the other two zones. Karpenter will observe this and, assuming your NodePool allows it, launch nodes in eu-west-1b and eu-west-1c to meet the distribution goal.

Each topology domain that's required but currently missing can trigger Karpenter to launch nodes that satisfy the constraint.

Scheduling nuances and minDomains for topology spread

Be mindful of the DoNotSchedule constraint. If no nodes exist in a required topology domain and Karpenter isn't allowed to provision there (because NodePool excludes certain zones or capacity types), pods can remain indefinitely pending. Always make sure your NodePools cover the topology domains you're targeting. Node labels are only considered as options if they match the node affinity of the pods. That's important to call out since it ensures that if a pod can't schedule in a zone because of a node affinity, that zone won't be used for topology calculations.

For example, if your pod defines a topology spread across three zones, either the NodePool must span those three zones or you must configure one NodePool per zone. It's important to note that the Kubernetes scheduler only operates based on nodes currently available in the cluster and is unaware of all possible topology domains defined by the cloud provider. This means if there are only nodes in two zones at scheduling time, even though a third zone is possible, the scheduler may continue to place pods only across those two zones while satisfying max skew constraints. For example, if there are two nodes—one in eu-west-1a and one in eu-west-1b—and a zonal TSC is applied with a max skew of 1, the scheduler will evenly balance pods between these two nodes. Meanwhile, Karpenter might later provision a node in a third zone (eu-west-1c), but until that node exists, the scheduler cannot schedule pods there.

To guarantee that the scheduler actually spreads across all three, you should also set minDomains=3, which communicates the minimum number of distinct zones required. Without minDomains, the scheduler will simply use whatever zones are available, even if it is fewer than intended. Similarly, for capacity type spreading, if your NodePool supports only on-demand capacity, pods will not run on spot instances. In scenarios where ScheduleAnyway is used, Kubernetes may still schedule pods despite skew across domains.

Additionally, there are a few nuanced points to consider. If topology spread is combined with zonal volume claims (such as EBS), Karpenter may add extra zonal affinity constraints when provisioning. This can change how the scheduler interprets the spread and potentially lead to skewed distributions. In these cases, using the nodeAffinity policy setting can help. You can instruct the scheduler to ignore node affinity generated from volumes when calculating TSCs, allowing pods to continue spreading as intended.

Kubernetes itself may also place more pods on the first available node if others are still initializing, which can create a temporary imbalance even when spread constraints are technically satisfied. For smaller workloads, this is another case where minDomains helps, since it enforces distribution across the intended number of domains rather than relying solely on pod count (as explained before).

In general, TSCs help you to spread pods across zones to reduce the blast radius during outages, and to spread across capacity types to improve resilience and cost savings. Karpenter responds dynamically to these constraints and preferences, and if necessary, provisions additional nodes to optimize the distribution.

PersistentVolume topology and zonal placement

Not all scheduling constraints come directly from the pod spec. When your pod uses persistent storage (**PersistentVolumeClaims**, or **PVCs**), the storage itself can impose scheduling constraints, usually in the form of topology requirements. For example, on AWS, an EBS volume exists in a single Availability Zone. If a pod claims an EBS PersistentVolume that's in the eu-west-1b Availability Zone, Kubernetes will *force* that pod to run on a node in eu-west-1b (this happens via an automatic node affinity on the pod based on the volume's NodeAffinity or the StorageClass topology). This is crucial to understand for stateful workloads: even if you didn't explicitly put a zone constraint on the pod, the system will do so because the data is only accessible in that zone. Karpenter detects these implicit storage constraints and accounts for them when provisioning nodes.

For dynamically provisioned volumes using the WaitForFirstConsumer binding mode (a common setting in storage classes for EBS, etc.), the volume isn't created until the pod is scheduled. In such cases, kube-scheduler (and Karpenter) knows the set of possible zones (from allowedTopologies in the storage class), but the volume can be placed in any one of them. Karpenter helps break this chicken-and-egg situation. When a pod with an unbound PVC is pending, Karpenter will look at the storage class and PVC to determine the possible zones. It might choose one of the allowed zones (often at random or based on where other pods are to maybe balance) and provision a node in that zone to host the pod. Once that node comes up and the pod is bound to it, the CSI driver will create the volume in that same zone and attach it. Essentially, Karpenter proactively picks a zone for your storage by bringing up compute there. This leads to faster scheduling for stateful pods on fresh volumes.

If the volume already exists (for instance, a StatefulSet pod being rescheduled with an existing PVC bound to a PersistentVolume in a specific zone), Karpenter will read the PersistentVolume's node affinity and restrict itself to that zone when launching a replacement node. It recognizes that "this pod *must* run in zone X because its data resides there" and so it won't create a node in any other zone for it. This prevents scenarios where Karpenter might otherwise waste time launching an unsuitable node.

As a user, you don't need to manually set any node affinity for PersistentVolumes—Kubernetes and Karpenter handle it. But you should ensure that your Karpenter configuration covers the necessary zones for your storage. If you use volumes in every Availability Zone of a Region, it's best to allow Karpenter to launch nodes in all those Availability Zones (or use multiple NodePools accordingly). If you accidentally restrict Karpenter's NodePools to a subset of zones, and a volume is created in a different zone, Karpenter won't be able to launch a new node, leading to a stuck pod.

Storage topology is an often-invisible constraint that Karpenter does account for. By using WaitForFirstConsumer and broad zone coverage, you enable Karpenter to dynamically place stateful workloads in the right zone when scaling out.

Requesting specific hardware

There are times when your workloads require particular hardware characteristics—for example, GPUs for AI/ML workloads, ARM64-based processors, or local NVMe storage for high I/O operations in workloads such as caches or databases. To help you with this, Karpenter allows you to explicitly steer provisioning toward specific hardware by using constraints and well-known labels in your workloads and NodePools.

Let's first talk about AI/ML workloads that will require the use of **GPU nodes**. First, you will need to create a dedicated NodePool that restricts instance types to those with GPUs and add a taint to keep other pods off these expensive nodes. For example, you might limit a NodePool to P3 instances and taint them with nvidia.com/gpu: true with a NoSchedule configuration. This ensures that only pods that explicitly request GPU nodes and tolerate the taint will be scheduled by the kube-scheduler on those nodes.

For instance, you'd need to define a `NodePool` like this:

```
apiVersion: karpenter.sh/v1
kind: NodePool
metadata:
  name: gpus
spec:
  template:
    spec:
      requirements:
        - key: node.kubernetes.io/instance-type
          operator: In
          values: ["p3.8xlarge", "p3.16xlarge"]
      taints:
        - key: nvidia.com/gpu
          value: "true"
          effect: NoSchedule
```

In this example, any new node will be a P3 instance with GPUs, and it carries a taint. A pod that needs this type of compute capacity must explicitly request a GPU node (e.g., `resources.requests["nvidia.com/gpu"]`) and include a toleration for `nvidia.com/gpu` to be scheduled on these nodes. When such a pod is pending, Karpenter will automatically consider only instance types that provide GPUs, ensuring the chosen node has the required hardware.

> **Note: Avoid over-restricting instance types**
>
> While the preceding example demonstrates instance-type restriction, we recommend using such constraints *only when workloads have strict compatibility requirements or performance expectations.* For instance, an ML job requiring GPU acceleration, or a latency-sensitive service that must run on the latest generation of compute-optimized instances (e.g., C7g), is a good candidate for instance-type constraints. In most cases, allowing Karpenter a wider selection of compatible types results in better availability, cost-efficiency, and resilience. In general, leave the workloads to decide which granular restrictions they want and avoid putting as many restrictions as possible in the `NodePools`.

Another example is to request a specific node that includes local storage for workloads that requires a high speed I/O disk. Karpenter can work with well-known labels to request hardware capabilities that aren't standard Kubernetes resources.

For instance, you can require instances with local NVMe SSDs by using the `karpenter.k8s.aws/instance-local-nvme` label in a pod. You can do this by specifying a node affinity for this label (e.g., the `Exists` operator) to indicate that it needs an instance with ephemeral NVMe storage, as in this code snippet:

```
...
  affinity:
    nodeAffinity:
      requiredDuringSchedulingIgnoredDuringExecution:
        nodeSelectorTerms:
          - matchExpressions:
              - key: "karpenter.k8s.aws/instance-local-nvme"
                operator: "Exists"
...
```

Similarly, a `NodePool` could include a requirement on this label to force all its nodes to have local disks.

Additionally, if you need a minimum size for the disk, the `Gt` operator can be used. For example, you can use `karpenter.k8s.aws/instance-local-nvme > 99` to require at least 100 GB of local SSD. This way, Karpenter will only consider instance types that offer the required disk capacity. Keep in mind that you need to ensure that your `NodeClass` is configured to mount and use the instance store.

Similarly, you can leverage labels to request nodes with specialized hardware attributes beyond CPU, memory, or GPUs. Examples include enhanced network performance capabilities, custom accelerators such as FPGAs, or storage-optimized hardware. Specifying these labels in your `NodePool` requirements ensures that nodes with the desired traits are provisioned. Correspondingly, as we explored before, pod affinity or `nodeSelector` configurations allow workloads to be scheduled onto these specialized nodes, enabling efficient use of unique hardware resources tailored to specific application needs.

Note

Kubernetes allows pods to request ephemeral storage as a schedulable resource, which represents temporary disk space on a node. However, Karpenter cannot fully map these requests to the actual physical ephemeral storage capacity of nodes when that capacity depends on specialized local hardware—such as instance store or NVMe disks—unless specifically configured for it. This creates a gap: pods may request ephemeral storage, but Karpenter might provision nodes without sufficient underlying local storage to meet those requests, potentially causing scheduling failures or inefficient resource use.

Because of this limitation, relying solely on ephemeral storage requests for node provisioning decisions can be insufficient. Instead, users should express special hardware needs explicitly through `NodePool` labels and pod affinity or toleration rules to guide Karpenter's scheduling. Over-provisioning other resources, such as CPU or memory, can also act as a proxy to influence node selection when ephemeral storage is critical. Additionally, isolating `NodePools` with unique hardware by taints and matching pod tolerations helps prevent general workloads from consuming these specialized nodes unintentionally.

minValues

The `minValues` feature allows you to specify a *minimum diversity of options* for certain `NodePool` constraints. This is especially useful when working with EC2 spot instances where you want to ensure that Karpenter has multiple instance types or families to increase diversification.

When you include `minValues` in `NodePool's` `requirements`, you're telling Karpenter's scheduler that the `NodeClaim` must offer at least a specified number of unique values for that requirement key. For example, you might require at least 2 different instance categories, 5 different instance families, and 15 total instance types to choose from. You can encode these requirements as follows:

```
...
requirements:
  - key: karpenter.k8s.aws/instance-category
    operator: In
    values: ["c", "m", "r"]
    minValues: 2
  - key: karpenter.k8s.aws/instance-family
```

```
    operator: Exists
    minValues: 5
  - key: node.kubernetes.io/instance-type
    operator: Exists
    minValues: 15
...
```

In this snippet, Karpenter will only consider that NodePool for provisioning if it can find at least that many distinct options that satisfy the pod's constraints. This prevents the NodePool from launching nodes if it would be limited to too few instance choices (thereby promoting instance type diversity). In other words, minValues is a tool for increasing resilience in spot-based environments by avoiding overly narrow pools, not an all-or-nothing gatekeeper.

Additionally, Karpenter supports a configurable min-values-policy that can relax the strict enforcement of minValues. When set to BestEffort, Karpenter will gradually reduce the minValues constraints if the full diversity cannot be met, allowing scheduling to proceed as long as some permutation of the requirements is satisfied. This behavior helps prevent scheduling failures or excessive delays in clusters with limited instance options, while still encouraging diversity when possible. The default policy remains Strict, which enforces full minValues compliance or skips the NodePool.

If a pending pod meets NodePool's basic requirements (labels, taints, etc.) but the NodePool cannot satisfy the minValues diversity for a key under the Strict policy, Karpenter will skip that NodePool for the scheduling attempt and fall back to another NodePool that meets the pod's needs. With the BestEffort relaxation policy, Karpenter reduces strictness to allow scheduling with partial diversity, minimizing skips and helping prevent pods from remaining unschedulable. Thus, minValues primarily guides pod placement toward NodePools with greater resource diversity rather than blocking cluster scaling entirely.

> **Note**
>
> You can apply minValues to multiple requirements. If the same label key appears with multiple constraints, Karpenter uses the highest minValues value among them as the effective minimum. For instance, if you have two requirements on instance-family (one with minValues: 5 and another with minValues: 3), kube-scheduler will require at least five distinct families for that NodePool to be considered.

Be mindful that `minValues` is a relatively new (alpha at the time of writing this book) feature in Karpenter. While it can prevent suboptimal scheduling, setting the values too high could also prevent any nodes from launching if your environment doesn't actually have that many options. Always test with realistic values that reflect how many distinct instance types or zones you expect to be available for a given `NodePool`.

NodePool weights

When you have multiple `NodePools` in a cluster, it's possible that a given pod could match more than one `NodePool`. The `NodePool` weight is a priority mechanism that influences which `NodePool` Karpenter will choose to provision a new node from. In effect, you can rank `NodePools` so that Karpenter tries your preferred capacity first. This is useful for implementing cluster-wide default node preferences, **fallback pools**, or cost optimization strategies (e.g., prefer spot but fall back to on-demand). The weight is defined by an integer (`spec.weight` in the `NodePool`) between 0 and 100, where higher values mean higher priority. If a pod is compatible with multiple `NodePools`, Karpenter will select the `NodePool` with the greatest weight (ignoring the relative cost of instances).

A common pattern is to designate one `NodePool` as the "default" for generic workloads, and others as specialized or fallback pools. For example, you might have a broad on-demand `NodePool` and a separate spot `NodePool`. By giving the spot `NodePool` a higher weight, you tell Karpenter to attempt spot capacity first for any pod that could use either. If that `NodePool` cannot satisfy the scheduling for that pod (e.g., no spot availability or it hits a defined limit), Karpenter will then consider the lower-weight (on-demand) pool. Weights can also prioritize using reserved instances or particular hardware first. We'll see this in practice in *Chapter 11* and *Chapter 12*.

It's important to understand that weights override Karpenter's cost-based decisions. Normally, Karpenter chooses the cheapest instance type that meets the requirements (with a few edge cases, such as having capacity constraints). But if you use weights, you are explicitly telling it to favor one `NodePool` over others *regardless of cost*. For example, if a more expensive instance type has a higher weight than a cheap spot pool, Karpenter will pick the reserved instance pool every time for matching pods, even if the spot option could save money. Only use weights when you intend to prioritize certain capacity sources or configurations above pure price optimization.

Summary

This chapter explored how Karpenter redefines node autoscaling by shifting the focus from infrastructure-first to application-first provisioning. Rather than relying on predefined node groups, Karpenter provisions nodes on demand based on unschedulable pods, helping reduce excess capacity and simplify cluster operations.

You were introduced to the key building blocks of Karpenter: NodeClasses, which, in the context of AWS, defines infrastructure settings such as AMIs and subnets; NodePools, which shape provisioning behavior and constraints; and NodeClaims, which represent the life cycle of provisioned nodes. With these components in place, Karpenter helps you to have a highly flexible, responsive, autoscaled cluster for nodes that fits a wide variety of workload profiles—from general-purpose applications to resource-intensive batch jobs or GPU-bound processes.

Importantly, this chapter also clarified two common misconceptions about how Karpenter works. First, Karpenter does not schedule pods—that responsibility remains entirely with kube-scheduler. Karpenter simply ensures that appropriate nodes are available when pods cannot be scheduled due to insufficient capacity. Second, Karpenter does not scale based on CPU or memory utilization metrics. Instead, it reacts to unschedulable pods and simulates scheduling outcomes to provision just enough capacity to fit them efficiently. You'd use tools such as KEDA or HPA to scale pods, which would inevitably cause you to have unschedulable pods at some point.

In the next chapter, you'll learn about other important features in Karpenter, such as consolidation, disruption, and drift.

Get This Book's PDF Version and Exclusive Extras

UNLOCK NOW

Scan the QR code (or go to packtpub.com/unlock).
Search for this book by name, confirm the edition,
and then follow the steps on the page.

*Note: Keep your invoice handy. Purchases made
directly from Packt don't require one.*

9

Node Autoscaling with Karpenter — Part 2

In the previous chapter, you got to know how Karpenter works in much more detail, and the most important aspects when using Karpenter. One in particular is that Karpenter works in tandem with kube-scheduler. We also explored how to define flexible, well-scoped NodePools and how to configure your workloads so that Karpenter can provision the right capacity based on application needs. But launching the right nodes is only part of the story. You also need to adapt to changes over time, reduce inefficiencies, and maintain alignment with the evolving state of your cluster and infrastructure policies.

In this chapter, we'll shift our focus from provisioning toward disruption and termination controllers. We'll explore how Karpenter replaces nodes that are no longer needed, and the handling of spot interruptions or node expirations. You'll learn that Karpenter not only does an efficient job when launching nodes but also when removing or replacing them. You'll learn the differences between voluntary and involuntary disruptions, and how Karpenter uses simulation logic to make these decisions safe.

Finally, we'll introduce a very powerful feature to help you with day 2 operations: **NodePool disruption budgets (NDBs)**, a critical feature that lets you throttle node changes based on rate, scope, and schedule. The features and topics we'll explore in this chapter will give you the control needed to make Karpenter work safely in production environments while still delivering on cost and efficiency goals.

By the end of this chapter, you'll not only understand how Karpenter disruption works, but also how to apply best practices around NodePool and NodeClass configuration, workload constraint design, and integration with existing EKS setups. All of this with only one mission in mind: to help you prepare to build more elastic, cost-effective, and responsive Kubernetes clusters using Karpenter.

We will be covering the following main topics:

- Removing nodes
- Disruption
- NodePool disruption budgets
- Karpenter best practices

Technical requirements

For this chapter, you'll continue using an Amazon EKS cluster. To avoid any problems, it's recommended to turn down any previous cluster you created, and instead create a new one from the template you'll find in this chapter. This is going to be the cluster you'll use from now on. You don't need to install any additional tools, as most of the commands are going to be run with kubectl and helm. You can find the YAML manifests for all resources you're going to create in this chapter in the chapter08 folder from the book's GitHub repository, which you already cloned in *Chapter 1*.

Removing nodes

In *Chapter 8*, we explored how Karpenter launches nodes. However, it's important to highlight that Karpenter consolidates the entire node lifecycle—from identifying optimization opportunities to executing coordinated shutdowns—within a unified system that interacts directly with both Kubernetes and cloud provider APIs. This architectural approach enables sophisticated decision-making about *when* and *how* to reclaim capacity while maintaining strict guarantees around workload availability and infrastructure cleanliness.

This chapter explores Karpenter's lifecycle management through two interconnected systems: the disruption controller, which implements the strategic logic for node selection and budget enforcement, and the termination controller, which orchestrates the complex choreography of graceful shutdown, encompassing pod eviction, infrastructure cleanup, and cloud resource termination. These mechanisms provide the foundation for what we'll explore later in more depth regarding consolidation strategies, drift detection, and disruption budget implementations.

Let's explore in more detail how Karpenter controls flow when removing nodes.

Control flow architecture

Karpenter's lifecycle management operates through a well-defined control. At its core, Karpenter sets a Kubernetes finalizer on each node and NodeClaim it provisions—this finalizer acts as a synchronization primitive, blocking deletion of the node object at the API level while the termination controller completes its shutdown sequence.

Disruption can be triggered through three pathways: automatically by the disruption controller executing methods such as consolidation or drift, manually through user-initiated deletion (kubectl delete node), or by external systems that send delete requests to node objects. Regardless of origin, all disruption flows converge on the same graceful termination process.

Let's explore these two controllers in more detail.

Disruption controller

Karpenter's disruption controller continuously evaluates whether nodes in your cluster should be removed or replaced. It follows a sequential process, checking one disruption reason at a time. It first checks whether nodes need updates due to configuration changes, then looks for opportunities to reduce costs.

For each node it evaluates, the controller follows these steps:

1. **Identifies and prioritizes candidates** based on whether they qualify for removal. Some nodes might be completely empty, others might be running workloads that could fit elsewhere, and still others might have outdated configurations that no longer match what you've specified.

2. **Validates evictability** by checking whether pods on the candidate node have blocking conditions. Pods with karpenter.sh/do-not-disrupt annotations or blocking PDBs will cause the controller to skip that node and revisit it in future iterations.

3. **Enforces disruption budgets** by consulting the NodePool's configured NDB. If too many nodes in that pool are already being disrupted, the controller defers action to maintain cluster stability.

4. **Simulates scheduling** for all evictable pods on the candidate node to determine whether replacement capacity is needed. This simulation runs against the current cluster state, accounting for topology constraints, affinity rules, and resource requirements.

5. **Pre-spins replacement nodes** based on the simulation results, launching them in parallel with the disruption process to minimize workload downtime. If replacement nodes fail to initialize, the controller removes disruption taints and restarts the evaluation process.

6. **Initiates deletion** by setting the node's `DeletionTimestamp`, which triggers the termination controller while the disruption controller moves on to evaluate the next candidate.

Karpenter continuously works through disruption opportunities while respecting both cluster-wide and workload-specific constraints. Now, let's explore how the termination controller works.

Termination controller

Once the disruption controller decides that a node should be removed, the termination controller takes over to handle the actual shutdown. In *Figure 9.1*, you can see that the termination flow is divided into six phases. When a node is marked for deletion, Kubernetes sets a `DeletionTimestamp` on the node object. Normally, this would immediately remove the node from the API, but Karpenter's finalizer prevents that from happening.

This lock gives the termination controller time to safely move workloads off the node, disconnect infrastructure dependencies, and properly terminate the underlying cloud instance. Without this mechanism, running `kubectl delete node` would simply remove the node object from Kubernetes while leaving the EC2 instance running—creating an orphaned resource that continues to cost money.

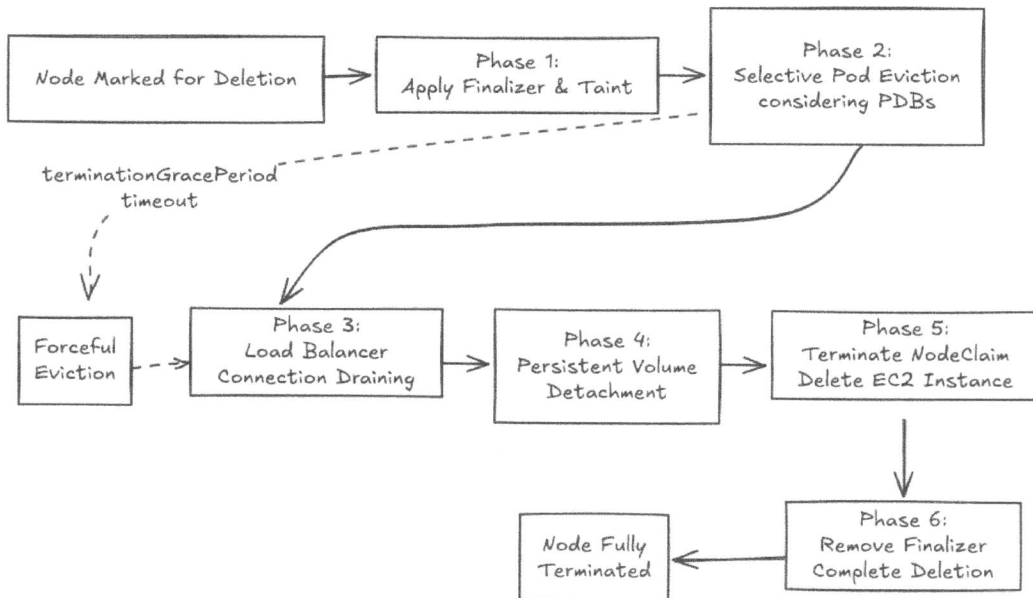

Figure 9.1 – Termination controller workflow

Let's walk through each of these phases to understand how Karpenter ensures nodes are removed safely and completely.

Phase 1: Taint application and scheduling prevention

Termination starts by adding the karpenter.sh/disrupted:NoSchedule taint to the node. This immediately prevents the Kubernetes scheduler from placing new pods on the terminating node, ensuring that the disruption surface doesn't expand during the drain process. This taint remains in place throughout the entire shutdown sequence.

Phase 2: Selective pod eviction considering PDBs

Rather than forcefully deleting pods, Karpenter uses the Kubernetes Eviction API to initiate graceful shutdown. This API-driven approach triggers the pod's terminationGracePeriodSeconds countdown and respects PDBs, ensuring that applications have adequate time to complete in-flight requests, flush buffers, and close connections cleanly. We'll explore in depth with a hands-on lab in *Chapter 12*.

Not all pods are evicted during this phase; the termination controller ignores these:

- DaemonSet pods are excluded from eviction because they represent cluster-level system services—log shippers, monitoring agents, network plugins, and security tools. By allowing these pods to continue running until the final moments of node termination, Karpenter ensures that observability and networking remain intact throughout the drain. This means that pod eviction events, drain progress, and any application-level errors during shutdown are properly captured and forwarded to your monitoring systems.

- Static pods managed directly by kubelet (not through the API server) are similarly ignored, as they follow their own lifecycle, independent of cluster control planes.

- Pods that tolerate the karpenter.sh/disrupted:NoSchedule disruption taint are allowed to remain, enabling workloads that explicitly opt into disruption tolerance to continue running during the transition.

- Succeeded or failed pods that have already completed their lifecycle don't require eviction and are skipped.

The controller monitors pod eviction progress continuously. If all workload pods successfully evict, the drain phase completes and the process advances. However, if PDBs block eviction indefinitely—or if pods have the karpenter.sh/do-not-disrupt annotation—the controller waits unless terminationGracePeriod has been configured on the owning NodeClaim.

Phase 3: Load balancer connection draining

When a pod backing a load balancer or Ingress service terminates, the Kubernetes service controller updates the load balancer's target group, removing the node's endpoints.

However, active connections to those endpoints may still be processing requests. Cloud provider load balancers implement connection draining, which keeps the target registered but stops routing new connections to it while existing connections complete. For AWS Application Load Balancers and Network Load Balancers, this delay is configurable (typically, 300 seconds by default), providing a buffer for long-lived HTTP requests or database connections to finish cleanly.

Karpenter's termination logic waits for the Kubernetes eviction process to complete before proceeding to infrastructure termination, which indirectly ensures that load balancer updates have propagated and connection draining windows have been respected. This coordination prevents connection resets that would manifest otherwise as 5XX errors or client timeouts. We'll also explore this in *Chapter 12*.

Phase 4: Persistent volume detachment

When a pod with mounted volumes is evicted, `kubelet` begins its termination sequence, which includes unmounting the volume from the filesystem and detaching it at the API level.

Karpenter's termination process waits for the node to be fully drained—meaning all evictable pods have been removed and their associated volumes have been safely unmounted and detached—before terminating the underlying instance. This prevents scenarios where an instance is terminated while volumes are still attached, which could result in volumes becoming stuck in the "detaching" state or, worse, data corruption if writes are in flight during forceful detachment.

Once volumes are cleanly detached, they become available for attachment to replacement pods running on other nodes, enabling stateful workloads to resume operation with their data intact.

Phase 5: NodeClaim termination and cloud resource cleanup

With all pods evicted and infrastructure dependencies cleanly disconnected, the termination controller proceeds to delete the underlying `NodeClaim`. For AWS environments, this triggers the termination of the EC2 instance through direct API calls.

During this phase, the controller monitors for an edge case: if the NodeClaim is deleted by an external process (perhaps manual cleanup or a cloud provider event), Karpenter detects the missing NodeClaim and immediately removes the finalizer from the node object, allowing Kubernetes to complete the deletion without waiting for termination steps that can no longer occur.

Phase 6: Finalizer removal and deletion completion

Once the cloud provider confirms that the instance has been terminated (or if the NodeClaim was already deleted), the termination controller removes the finalizer from the node object. This signals to the Kubernetes API server that all cleanup is complete, and the node object is finally deleted from etcd, concluding the termination sequence.

This termination workflow shows how Karpenter maintains complete control over node lifecycle execution. With this understanding of how nodes are safely removed, we can now examine why and when the disruption controller triggers these actions, exploring the specific scenarios that drive consolidation, the configuration changes that cause drift, and the budget mechanisms that control the pace of disruption across your cluster.

Disruption

After exploring how Karpenter gracefully terminates a node, we can now continue with what drives these node removals. Karpenter not only provisions nodes but also actively manages their lifecycle to maintain an efficient and up-to-date data plane. Any intentional termination of a node is known as a **disruption**. Disruptions can occur for various reasons: scaling down unused capacity, consolidating workloads onto fewer nodes, replacing nodes that have drifted from the desired configuration, handling voluntary node deletions, or responding to involuntary events such as spot interruptions.

As you will see in *Figure 9.2*, Karpenter categorizes these disruptions into two types:

- **Involuntary disruptions:** These are terminations that can't be avoided and require immediate action, such as EC2 spot interruptions, health events, or node expiration for compliance reasons. These disruptions have time constraints that force Karpenter to react quickly to replace nodes.

- **Voluntary disruptions**: These disruptions, in contrast, are actions that Karpenter proactively initiates to optimize the cluster, such as consolidation or drift, where there is no immediate urgency to terminate nodes. For voluntary disruptions, Karpenter respects PDBs and will not take action against critical applications that cannot be safely disrupted.

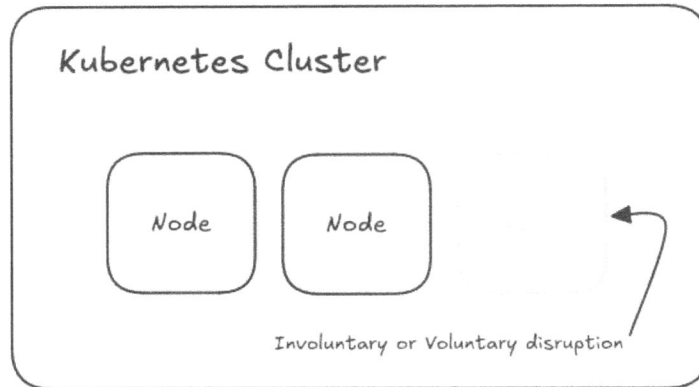

Figure 9.2 – Karpenter can disrupt nodes voluntarily or involuntarily

With voluntary disruptions, Karpenter simulates evictions, respects PDBs, and launches replacement nodes as needed. Involuntary disruptions, however, occur without warning, which means Karpenter cannot preemptively simulate evictions or coordinate replacements. Instead, it focuses on rapidly draining the affected node and rescheduling pods to maintain availability. EC2 spot interruptions falls into this category, as there's nothing you can do to stop a node from being terminated after receiving the interruption signal. You also have expireAfter, which is a mechanism Karpenter uses to maintain node freshness and manage risk in spot-heavy environments. We'll explore this feature later in this chapter.

Regardless of the disruption type, Karpenter adds a Kubernetes finalizer to each node it manages. This ensures that the node is properly drained before termination, even in cases of manual deletion. The finalizer blocks deletion of the node object while Karpenter's termination controller safely taints and drains the node before removing the underlying NodeClaim, ensuring a consistent termination flow in all scenarios

Having covered how Karpenter manages node termination across disruption scenarios, let's shift our focus to how consolidation helps to optimize resource usage within the cluster.

Consolidation

Before we dive into how consolidation works in Karpenter, let's take a step back and explore how Karpenter handles underutilization. As you know, Kubernetes schedules pods onto nodes based on scheduling constraints and resource availability at the moment of placement. However, once a pod is running, `kube-scheduler` doesn't go back later to see whether that pod could be packed more efficiently on a different node. Over time, as you scale workloads up and down and nodes come and go, the cluster's pod distribution can drift from optimal, often leaving nodes underutilized and driving up costs, as shown in *Figure 9.3*. Karpenter's **consolidation** feature tackles this by continuously re-evaluating how pods are spread across the cluster and *actively consolidating* them onto the fewest, most cost-efficient nodes needed.

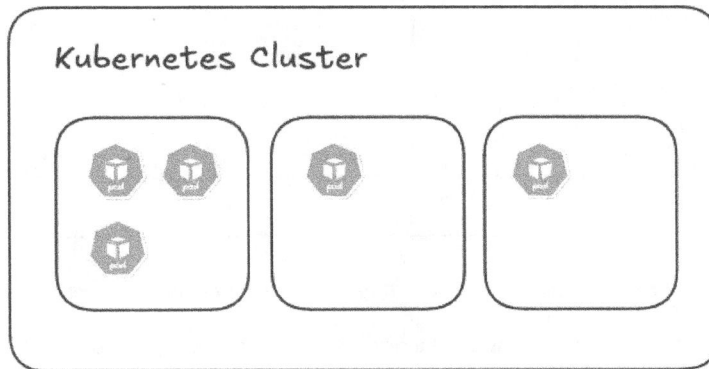

Figure 9.3 – After a scale-down event, nodes can be overprovisioned

Karpenter effectively simulates pod evictions on a regular cadence to find for consolidation opportunities, rather than relying on periodic polling intervals. When Karpenter determines that workloads can be shifted to fewer or more cost-effective nodes, it will launch replacements as needed before beginning node deprovisioning. The eligibility for deprovisioning is determined by evaluating factors such as PDBs, whether pods have been initialized, and readiness constraints. Once a node is selected for consolidation, Karpenter taints it with `karpenter.sh/disrupted:NoSchedule` to prevent new pods from being placed during the transition.

Before it evicts any pod, it verifies through simulation that the pod *can* be rescheduled onto another node. In other words, Karpenter makes sure that there's capacity elsewhere for every pod on a node before that node is disrupted. Furthermore, you can configure an NDB to define how many nodes in a `NodePool` can be disrupted at the same time (similar to a Deployment's `maxUnavailable`). We'll dive deep into this later on.

Let's go a bit deeper into how consolidation works by exploring which inefficiencies in a cluster Karpenter can remediate:

- **Remove empty nodes**: If a node isn't running any application pods (only DaemonSet pods or static pods), it's considered empty. These nodes contribute no useful work, so Karpenter will terminate them to eliminate waste, shown as the third node in *Figure 9.4*. It ignores DaemonSet pods when evaluating emptiness, since these run on every node by design. These nodes can be removed in parallel since they don't need replacements.

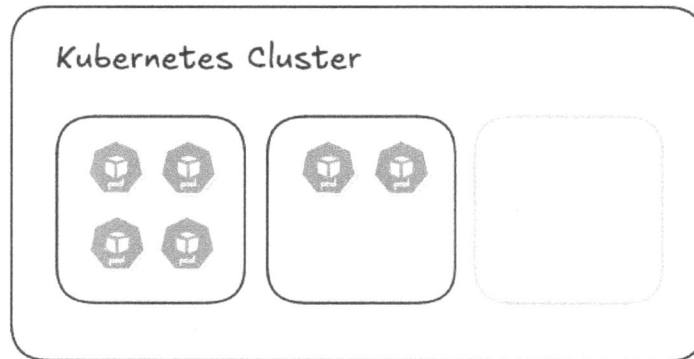

Figure 9.4 – Karpenter is removing the third node as it doesn't have pods running

- **Eliminate underutilized nodes**: If a node's running pods could all fit onto other existing nodes, Karpenter will consolidate the nodes by terminating them, as shown in *Figure 9.5*. This is similar to defragmenting the cluster; it frees up an entire node by packing its pods elsewhere. In practice, you might see scenarios where three half-used nodes can be consolidated into one fully-used node after Karpenter's consolidation, dramatically reducing the number of active nodes (and costs).

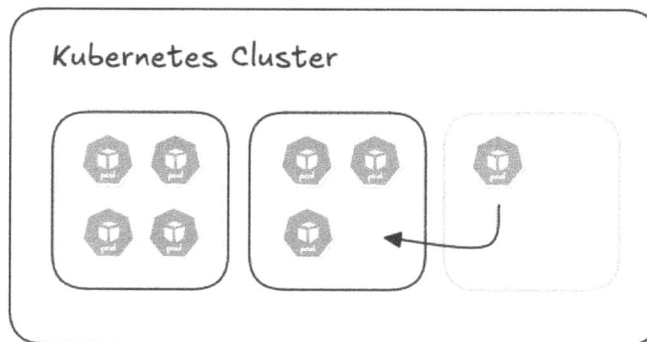

Figure 9.5 – Karpenter is forcing a node to be empty for optimization purposes

> **Note**
>
> Karpenter does multi-node consolidation by looking at two or more underutilized nodes that could be replaced by a single node. If Karpenter finds that the combined pods from Node A and Node B would fit on *one* new instance (and that instance would be cheaper than A+B), it will attempt to consolidate those together. This "many-to-one" consolidation uses a heuristic to choose likely node combinations without trying every possible mix.

- **Downsize to cheaper instances:** In cases where a node isn't completely empty but is oversized for its current load, Karpenter can replace it with a cheaper instance type. For example, if the workload is running on a 4xlarge instance type, Karpenter might provision a 2xlarge or Spot Instance type, and migrate the pods there. You can see this in *Figure 9.6*. This ensures that you're not paying for more capacity when unnecessary.

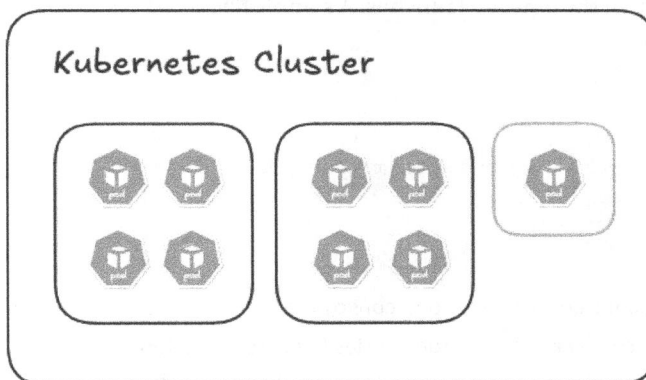

Figure 9.6 – Karpenter has forced the third node to be replaced with a smaller one

> **Note**
>
> If you're using Spot capacity, Karpenter also supports Spot-to-Spot consolidation through a feature gate that you need to enable. You can check how to do it in the Karpenter docs (https://karpenter.sh/docs/reference/settings/#feature-gates). However, it won't replace a Spot node with a cheaper Spot Instance unless it is able to submit an EC2 API Fleet request with at least 15 viable instance types. This safeguard helps ensure that replacement capacity is truly available and reduces the chance of running into capacity shortages during consolidation.

By default, consolidation is enabled and will consider both completely empty nodes and generally underutilized nodes for removal. You can control its behavior through the `spec.disruption` settings on your `NodePool`. For example, you could configure the `consolidationPolicy` field to `WhenEmpty` (only consolidate completely empty nodes) or `WhenEmptyOrUnderutilized` (the default, which also consolidates underutilized nodes). A corresponding `consolidateAfter` field defines how long Karpenter should wait after pods churn—pods are added or removed from a node—before treating that node as a consolidation candidate. This delay prevents thrashing—a situation where nodes are added and removed so frequently that the cluster becomes unstable or inefficient.

For instance, if a node's pods just terminated, Karpenter will wait the `consolidateAfter` duration to see whether new pods land there before deciding the node is truly idle. This prevents cases where, for example, you have a job orchestrator that needs time after old jobs finish to provision new jobs to the node. We can set `consolidateAfter` to a high enough value to allow this orchestrator to react, ensuring that Karpenter doesn't terminate a node and then immediately have to relaunch one when the new job launches. A sample `NodePool` configuration might look like this:

```
...
spec:
  disruption:
    consolidationPolicy: WhenEmptyOrUnderutilized
    consolidateAfter: 1m
...
```

In the preceding configuration snippet, `consolidationPolicy` is set to `WhenEmptyOrUnderutilized`, which means Karpenter will consider nodes for consolidation when they are underutilized. The `consolidateAfter` field is set to `1m`, indicating that Karpenter waits for one minute after pods schedule or leave a node before evaluating it for consolidation.

With this behavior configured, it is important to understand what happens when Karpenter skips consolidation, and the implications for cluster management and resource optimization.

What happens when Karpenter skips consolidation?

Although Karpenter seeks to optimize node usage, it won't just consolidate every node. There might be times when you'd expect Karpenter to run consolidation, but it won't happen. Several conditions can cause Karpenter to skip a node entirely during its consolidation evaluation. This behavior is intentional and helps avoid disrupting workloads that are difficult—or unsafe—to move. Let's see which conditions can make Karpenter skip consolidation.

Pod disruption budgets (PDBs)

Just in case you're not familiar, PDBs are Kubernetes policies that limit how many pods of an application can be voluntarily evicted at once, ensuring availability during disruptions. Karpenter honors PDBs when attempting to evict pods. If evicting a pod from a node would violate its PDB (for example, exceeding maxUnavailable or dropping below minAvailable), Karpenter skips that node entirely. No consolidation occurs unless all pods on the node can be evicted safely within their budgets. To help with visibility, Karpenter emits events on the node to explain this, often in the following form:

```
Unconsolidatable - pdb <namespace>/<name> prevents pod
evictions
```

Affinity constraints

Karpenter's consolidation respects both required and preferred inter-pod affinity and anti-affinity constraints; however, it handles them each differently. For *required* affinity/anti-affinity constraints, Karpenter won't consolidate a node if doing so would violate these hard requirements. In such cases, the node is considered unconsolidatable and skipped entirely from consolidation.

For the purposes of consolidation, Karpenter treats preferred affinity and anti-affinity constraints like required constraints. In the scheduling simulation, Karpenter evaluates pod placement options in this order:

1. Existing nodes honoring the preferred constraint

2. New nodes honoring the constraint

3. Existing and new nodes ignoring the constraint

This means Karpenter will often choose to launch new capacity with the *preferred* constraints before consolidating existing capacity without them. While Karpenter tries to honor these preferences to avoid node churn and prevent immediate consolidation after node launch, the prevention of immediate consolidation actually results from the scheduling and consolidation producing consistent decisions based on the same inputs. If both provisioning and consolidation ignored preferences, additional churn could occur. Preferred constraints can reduce consolidation effectiveness because Karpenter may avoid disrupting nodes to keep preferences intact, even when kube-scheduler could fit pods elsewhere, ignoring these preferences.

In other words, preferred constraints act as strong guidelines that Karpenter tries to respect during consolidation decisions, while required constraints are absolute blockers. If no existing or new node(s) can satisfy the required scheduling constraints, the pod is considered unmovable, and the entire node is excluded from consolidation.

Note

Since v1.6, Karpenter provides a configurable setting called PREFERENCE_POLICY that controls how preferred constraints are handled during both provisioning and consolidation decisions. By default, this is set to Respect, meaning Karpenter honors preferred affinity/anti-affinity rules and ScheduleAnyways topology spread constraints to avoid node churn and maintain workload distribution preferences.

However, you can set PREFERENCE_POLICY=Ignore to allow more aggressive consolidation that disregards these preferences. This setting affects both scheduling and consolidation phases. During consolidation, Karpenter will ignore preferred constraints when making optimization decisions, potentially allowing more cost-effective node arrangements. During provisioning, Karpenter's scheduler will also ignore preferences when creating new nodes for pending pods. It is important to note that this behavior can result in non-deterministic outcomes, regardless of the setting, because kube-scheduler only works with the nodes it sees at any given moment. For example, even with PreferencePolicy=Respect, a newly registered node might not yet be visible to kube-scheduler, leading it to place pods densely on fewer nodes. This can trigger immediate consolidation of empty nodes based on timing and scheduling loops rather than strict affinity rules.

karpenter.sh/do-not-disrupt annotation

Both pods and nodes can be marked with the karpenter.sh/do-not-disrupt: "true" annotation. When present, Karpenter will ignore the node for voluntary disruptions such as consolidation or drift. Starting in v1, expiration will still forcefully drain and terminate the node even if this annotation is set, though the annotation is respected during the drain process itself. This annotation is a useful override to temporarily pin critical workloads, and it can also serve as a valuable debugging tool when investigating node-related issues by preventing disruption during that time. Excessive use of this annotation, however, can reduce Karpenter's overall effectiveness in optimizing the cluster.

Insufficient available capacity

It's important to clarify what Karpenter considers "underutilized." Unlike CAS, which uses usage-based metrics, Karpenter evaluates underutilization purely by comparing the current cost of a node against the potential cost of a replacement node that could run the same workloads more efficiently.

Even if a node meets this cost-based underutilization criteria, consolidation will only occur if Karpenter finds viable placement for all of the node's pods. As of this writing, Karpenter will only consolidate one or more nodes into a single replacement node. If a consolidation action would result in two or more nodes—even if their combined cost would be lower—Karpenter won't perform it, since this could lead to unpredictable scheduling results that might actually make the cluster more expensive.

If the simulation fails to fit one or more pods due to hard constraints, taints, affinity rules, or resource limitations, Karpenter aborts the consolidation for that node. When consolidation is skipped, you can view the reasoning through events on the node:

```
Unconsolidatable - can't replace with a lower-priced node
```

These events help you debug why expected consolidations aren't occurring.

NodePool disruption budget limits

At the NodePool level, Karpenter supports NDBs to throttle how many nodes can be disrupted at once. Even if a node qualifies for consolidation, it will be skipped if acting on it would exceed the NodePool's configured disruption budget. We'll explore this in more detail later in the dedicated section for NDBs.

Generally, consolidation keeps your cluster lean by continuously right-sizing capacity to match current demand, working hand in hand with Karpenter's scaling-up logic.

Next, let's see consolidation in action through a hands-on lab.

Hands-on lab: Consolidating nodes after scaling events

We just looked at how consolidation works, but let's see how Karpenter either removes a node, replaces it with the cheaper one, or forces a restructure of pods in the cluster.

If you have your EKS cluster up and running, skip this step. Otherwise, if you turned down the EKS cluster to save costs, let's bring it up again by running the following commands:

```
$ cd /chapter08/terraform
$ sh bootstraph.sh
```

To get started with this lab, open your terminal and go to the /chapter09 folder:

```
$ cd chapter09
```

Confirm that you have the latest version of the default `NodePool` that you created in the previous chapter by running this command:

```
$ kubectl apply -f nodepool.yaml
```

Note the `disruption` block in the `NodePool`:

```
...
  disruption:
    consolidationPolicy: WhenEmptyOrUnderutilized
    consolidateAfter: 0s
...
```

With this configuration in place, the `NodePool` will consolidate nodes when Karpenter notices there's an opportunity to consolidate nodes into fewer or smaller ones. To see this quickly, we're asking Karpenter to react quickly with `consolidateAfter: 0s`.

In all labs in this chapter, you'll spend quite some time reading Karpenter logs. To make this task easier, let's create an alias in the terminal by running this command:

```
$ alias kl='kubectl -n karpenter logs -l app.kubernetes.io/name=karpenter
--all-containers=true -f --tail=20'
```

Next time you run kl in the terminal, you'll effectively be following the last 20 lines of the Karpenter controller pods in real time.

To see consolidation in action, we first need to launch a few pods. Let's deploy the Monte Carlo PI app, which, for now, is only requesting three replicas. For this lab, we'll be increasing the CPU and memory for the pods to make it easier to predict the size of each node launched. Run this command:

```
$ kubectl apply -f montecarlopi.yaml
```

Wait around three or four minutes until you see that the pods are running. Keep running this command until you see the pods with a `Running` status:

```
$ kubectl get pods,nodeclaims
```

Now, let's scale the application up to 10 replicas and wait for Karpenter to create an additional node for the new pods. Having two nodes will allow us to see consolidation in action. Run this command:

```
$ kubectl scale deployment montecarlo-pi --replicas 10
```

Wait again for about three to four minutes until you see all the pods with a Running status.

> **Note**
>
> To simplify this lab, we're doing a manual scaling operation of the workloads. But in a production environment, we would use KEDA to scale the workload.

At this point, you should have two nodes launched by Karpenter to host the 10 replicas of your application. We got two nodes, one with a c6a.xlarge instance type and another one with a c6a.2xlarge instance type. You can confirm this by running this command:

```
$ kubectl get nodeclaims
```

So far, we've seen that Karpenter does a good job launching only the nodes it needs. It first launched an xlarge node, and when you scaled the deployment to add more replicas, it launched 2xlarge to fulfill the demand. But Karpenter doesn't stop at just provisioning. It does a very good job when you scale down your replicas too. To see this in action, let's scale down the deployment to six replicas. Run these commands:

```
$ kubectl scale deployment montecarlo-pi --replicas 6
$ kl
```

Pay close attention to the log messages; the interesting ones are these:

- disrupting node(s), meaning that Karpenter identified an opportunity to make the cluster more efficient, and in the same log line, you'll see this: "reason":"underutili zed","decision":"delete","disrupted-node-count":0,"pod-count":3. Notice that Karpenter decided to delete a node impacting only three pods. Why delete a node? Because you removed four pods, Karpenter decided that the best option was to evict three pods from the xlarge node, so that kube-scheduler will schedule them in the 2xlarge node. This leaves the xlarge node empty, giving a valid reason to be deleted.

- tainted node, meaning that as soon as Karpenter marked this node to be deleted, it put a taint so no other pods could be scheduled in this node, since it's about to be removed.

- deleted node and deleted nodeclaim, meaning that once the node is empty, Karpenter deleted the node along with its respective NodeClaim.

As you can see, Karpenter was easily able to determine how to make the cluster more efficient and took only a single action to do it, reducing application disruption. We'll dive deeper into how you can control and reduce the downtime of your application in *Chapter 12*. For now, let's continue with the next experiment.

Press *Ctrl + C* to exit the command you had running to read the Karpenter logs. Now, let's scale down the number of replicas to 3. Run these commands:

```
$ kubectl scale deployment montecarlo-pi --replicas 3
$ kl
```

Let's understand what Karpenter did by reading the logs. The important bits are these:

- Same as before, the first log you see is that Karpenter is disrupting a node. But this time, notice that the decision is different since it's replacing the node: `"reason":"underut ilized","decision":"replace","disrupted-node-count":1,"replacement-node- count":1,"pod-count":3`. You only had one node, so Karpenter couldn't force evictions of pods to move them around. Therefore, the best available option was to launch a smaller node, an `xlarge` node, as the `2xlarge` node was now too big. You can see that right after this log line, Karpenter started to launch the replacement node. Only after this new node was ready did Karpenter start the removal process of the `2xlarge` node.

- `tainted` node, meaning that as soon as the new node was ready, Karpenter put a taint in the disrupted node so no other pods could be scheduled in this node as it is about to be removed.

- `deleted` node and `deleted` `nodeclaim`, meaning that once the disrupted node is empty, Karpenter deleted the node along with its respective `NodeClaim`.

This is awesome! But remember that Karpenter can also replace a node with a cheaper purchase option, such as an EC2 Spot Instance. So, let's see that in action.

Press *Ctrl + C* to exit the command you had running to read the Karpenter logs. Then, scale the deployment to 10 replicas again:

```
$ kubectl scale deployment montecarlo-pi --replicas 10
```

Wait around three or four minutes, and now you should have two nodes again. Note that these two nodes are on-demand instances. This is because the default `NodePool` only supports on-demand as the `karpenter.sh/capacity-type` requirement.

Modify the `nodepool.yaml` file so that it also supports Spot Instances, like this:

```
...
        - key: karpenter.sh/capacity-type
          operator: In
          values: ["on-demand","spot"]
...
```

Apply this change by running the following commands:

```
$ kubectl apply -f nodepool.yaml
$ kl
```

This time, we're not going to get into the details of these log lines; note that Karpenter took the two existing on-demand instances that you had and replaced them with spot instances. Based on the logs you read, notice that Karpenter takes the same approach as before when replacing a node. First, Karpenter launches the new node, and only when the new node is ready does the removal of the disrupted node start.

Press *Ctrl + C* to exit the command you had running to read the Karpenter logs. Now, check again the nodes you have; you'll see that all nodes are Spot Instances. Run this command:

```
$ kubectl get nodeclaims
```

To finish with this lab, run this command to delete all pods:

```
$ kubectl delete -f montecarlopi.yaml
```

If you wait about two minutes, you'll see that Karpenter has removed the nodes it launched as they were empty. Again, this is consolidation in action.

As you can see, Karpenter does a very good job working in tandem with kube-scheduler to launch only the nodes needed for your applications. When you have consolidation enabled, it does a very good job at removing empty nodes, replacing them with cheaper nodes, and even forcing pod evictions to make a better use of the existing nodes in the cluster. All these actions are taken to ensure that you have an efficient data plane while reducing application pod disruption. Now, let's continue exploring other disruption features in Karpenter, such as drift.

Drift

Kubernetes follows a reconciliation paradigm where controllers continuously work to align the actual state of resources with their desired state as defined in configuration manifests. This ensures that systems remain consistent and self-healing even when changes occur.

Karpenter applies this same reconciliation approach to node management through **drift** detection. While consolidation is about removing excess capacity, drift is about maintaining desired state. Drift detection in Karpenter will replace nodes that no longer match the current specifications defined in your Karpenter configs (NodePools and any associated NodeClasses or AWS settings). Think of it as Karpenter's way of doing rolling upgrades or reconciling configuration changes to ensure that your cluster converges to the new desired state.

For example, if you update EC2NodeClass to use a new AMI, as shown in *Figure 9.7*, or a different instance type, the already-running nodes are now "drifted" from what you desire. Karpenter can detect that and gradually recycle those nodes so that your cluster converges to the new state.

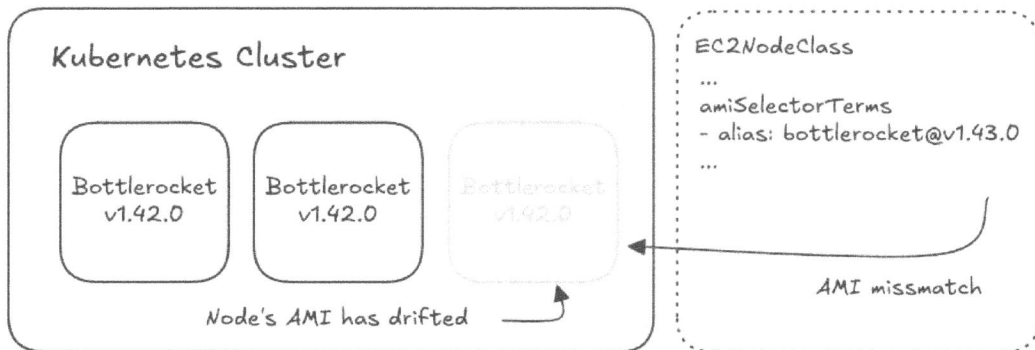

Figure 9.7 – After updating EC2NodeClass, the existing node configurations have drifted

What causes drift?

Drift can be triggered not only by user changes to your node specifications but also by external factors that cause the actual state of resources to diverge from what your Karpenter configurations point to, let's explore a few scenarios that cause drift:

- **New AMIs:** If a new version of an AMI is released, your existing nodes will drift. Let's say you've configured your EC2NodeClass object(s) to select an AMI version by tag. When a new AMI becomes available, all existing nodes on the old AMI will be considered drifted. Karpenter will detect that the node's image ID doesn't match the newly desired image and mark the node as drifted. In other words, AMI drift is an automated node upgrade mechanism. From the application's perspective, drift-based replacement is a rolling upgrade of the nodes.

  For example, say you upgraded your EKS cluster from 1.31 to 1.32 and updated your NodeClass to use the 1.32 AMI. Karpenter will start replacing the old 1.31 nodes with new 1.32 nodes, respecting any PDB and/or NDB limits. This can greatly simplify node management in EKS. You don't have to manually cordon and drain nodes or use a separate upgrade tool. Karpenter effectively does it for you, driven by the declarative changes you make to its specs.

- **Instance families or hardware changes:** If you modify the allowed instance types or other capacity constraints in your NodePool, some nodes might fall out of spec. For instance, if you previously allowed the m7 family and now switch to only allow c7, any running m7 nodes are no longer compliant. Karpenter will treat those nodes as drifted and replace them with the new instance type. Conversely, expanding the set of instance families usually does not drift existing nodes as long as they still satisfy the new requirements. For example, going from *only m7* to *m7 or c7* does not immediately replace the m7 nodes, since they're still valid in the broader set.

- **Networking or security changes:** On your NodeClass, you might update which subnets or security groups Karpenter should use for new nodes. For subnets, since instances belong to only one subnet, a node won't be considered drifted as long as its current subnet is still included in subnetSelectorTerms. In other words, simply changing the set of allowed subnets won't immediately cause drift if the node's subnet remains valid. However, security groups work differently. Because multiple security groups can be attached to a node and they enforce security constraints, any change to the security group selectors causes Karpenter to consider all nodes with the old security group configuration as drifted. Karpenter will then roll these nodes to ensure they have the updated security groups.

- **Kubernetes version:** If you upgrade your clusters to a new Kubernetes version, you'll likely want nodes on the new version as well. Karpenter doesn't explicitly check the kubelet version on nodes, but if you use the "alias" field in EC2NodeClass to select AMIs, drift detection will catch when the alias points to a new AMI version and trigger node replacement. Similarly, if you adjust static fields in the NodePool or NodeClass such as labels or taints, those changes propagate only to new nodes. One thing Karpenter doesn't consider for drift are changes to purely "behavioral" settings that don't reflect in the node itself. For example, tweaking a NodePool's disruption budget or weight won't mark nodes as drifted because those settings aren't going to affect the configuration of the node.

Now that we explored what changes can cause nodes to drift from their desired state, let's explore how Karpenter detects this drift and initiates node replacement accordingly.

How drift is detected

Let's dive a bit deeper into how drift works. Karpenter employs a mechanism analogous to Kubernetes Deployments' pod-template hash. Each NodePool (and NodeClass) gets an annotation that is a hash of the node template spec. Whenever the NodePool's relevant fields change, the hash will change. Karpenter compares this to a similar hash stored on each NodeClaim to see whether a node's configuration is out of date. If there's a mismatch, meaning the node's spec no longer matches the NodePool's desired spec, Karpenter marks that node (NodeClaim) with a drifted condition.

You can observe this in the NodeClaim object description or in Karpenter's logs. Karpenter's drift detection is continuous. So, as soon as you push a new AMI into the config, nodes will get flagged as drifted almost immediately. There are some special-case rules to avoid false positives. As noted, if a new spec broadens an option (such as adding an instance family), Karpenter won't count existing nodes as drifted if they still fit within the new parameters. But any change that truly renders the node's attributes non-compliant will trigger drift.

Managing drift carefully

While drift automation is powerful, it needs to be managed. A naive configuration might unintentionally cause all your nodes to drift at once. A classic example is using an AMI selector that always grabs the "latest" image. The moment a new AMI is released (which could be in the middle of a business day), every node suddenly becomes outdated. Karpenter would then proceed to replace nodes as allowed by budgets. In a large cluster, even a controlled rollout could mean many pods restarting.

To avoid uncontrolled AMI drift, I recommend that you pin a specific AMI ID, use a version alias (non-latest), or use a manually updated tag, so that you decide when to initiate the drift replacement. In other words, you might test a new AMI, then update the NodePool's AMI selector during a maintenance window so that drift happens on your schedule. If you do rely on an automated latest AMI, be sure that your NDB only allows a few nodes to be updated at once so you don't replace too many nodes at the same time. The goal is to reap the benefits of drift (automatic node updates) without surprising downstream effects.

Another tip is that you can disable or defer drift if needed. In earlier versions of Karpenter, drift was behind a feature gate. In Karpenter v1.x, it's on by default; however, you can still effectively pause drift actions by adjusting the NodePool drift budget to zero or using the do-not-disrupt controls mentioned.

Some teams, for instance, relax drift's budget or remove do-not-disrupt annotations to let Karpenter roll the nodes. This approach gives a mix of automation and control.

In summary, drift handling ensures that nodes don't live indefinitely with old configurations. Whether it's applying critical security patches via new AMIs, migrating to different instance families, or just keeping nodes in sync with your latest provisioning rules, Karpenter will ensure that you are always converging on your desired state.

Combined with consolidation, drift means Karpenter not only scales your cluster on demand but also continuously improves and refreshes it in line with your infrastructure changes. Overall, Karpenter's disruption features (scale-down, consolidation, and drift) make it a full lifecycle manager for nodes in Kubernetes. It not only launches the right nodes for new pods, but also manages and optimizes those nodes continuously.

Now, let's see drift in action with a hands-on lab.

Hands-on lab: Drifted nodes after updating AMI

To see how Karpenter reacts when a node drifts from its desired configuration, we'll do an update to the default EC2NodeClass. In *Chapter 12*, you'll practice upgrading a cluster to see how drift helps you with major updates. For this chapter, the idea is that you can see its value in a simple lab. So, let's go back to your terminal.

Similar to the consolidation hands-on lab, if you already have your EKS cluster up and running, continue with this lab. Otherwise, go back to the consolidation lab and follow the initial steps to create the EKS cluster and deploy a default NodePool and EC2NodeClass, and then come back to this lab.

Before we see nodes drift, we need to have nodes running, and to have nodes running, we need to have pods running. So, let's deploy the Monte Carlo app by running this command:

```
$ kubectl apply -f montecarlopi.yaml
```

Wait around three or four minutes until you see three pods and one node running:

```
$ kubectl get pods,nodeclaims
```

Pay close attention to the EC2NodeClass definition in the nodepool.yaml file:

```
...
  amiSelectorTerms:
    - alias: "bottlerocket@1.34.0"
...
```

Bottlerocket v1.34.0 is not the latest version. So, let's make sure the nodes we're running have a more recent version. Change the version in the default EC2NodeClass by updating the nodepool. yaml file to this:

```
...
   amiSelectorTerms:
     - alias: "bottlerocket@1.38.0"
...
```

Apply this change by running the following commands:

```
$ kubectl apply -f nodepool.yaml
$ k1
```

> **Note**
>
> If the k1 command didn't work, go back to the consolidation lab to recreate the alias.

Pay close attention to the log messages; the interesting ones are these:

- disrupting node(s), meaning that Karpenter identified that the node has drifted from its desired configuration. In the same log line, you'll see this: "reason":"drifted","dec ision":"replace","disrupted-node-count":1,"replacement-node-count":1,"pod-count":3. As you expect, it's a very similar behavior from when Karpenter is running consolidation to disrupt a node, but this time, the reason is different.

- Karpenter immediately started to launch a new node that matches the desired configuration from EC2NodeClass. You can see that the log lines reflect these actions by reading the log messages: "created nodeclaim", "launched nodeclaim", "registered nodeclaim", and "initialized nodeclaim".

- Finally, the disrupted node is tainted ("tainted node"). So, no new pods are scheduled here. And when the node is empty, Karpenter deletes the node ("deleted node") and its respective NodeClaim ("deleted nodeclaim").

As you can see, Karpenter was able to notice very quickly that the running nodes drifted from their desired configuration.

Press *Ctrl* + *C* to exit the command you had running to read the Karpenter logs. To confirm that the new node is actually running with the desired Bottlerocket version, run this command to see only the OS-IMAGE column from Karpenter nodes:

```
$ kubectl get nodes -l karpenter.sh/nodepool -o custom-columns=OS-IMAGE:.
status.nodeInfo.osImage
```

You should see an output similar to this one:

```
OS-IMAGE
Bottlerocket OS 1.38.0 (aws-k8s-1.32)
```

To finish with this lab, let's remove the Monte Carlo app with this command:

```
$ kubectl delete -f montecarlopi.yaml
```

In this lab, you were able to see drift in action by updating the AMI to a more up-to-date version. Karpenter was able to identify this change, and immediately started to roll-out a new node with the new desired configuration.

Great! So that covers our need for upgrading our nodes, but what about nodes that have no configuration change and would live on the node for months otherwise? How do we make sure that these nodes stay healthy, in compliance with our security requirements, and avoid data fragmentation problems. For that, we have node expiration. Let's explore that feature.

Expiring nodes

The expireAfter setting in a NodePool defines the maximum lifetime for any node provisioned by that pool. Once a node's uptime exceeds this configured duration, Karpenter will initiate its deprovisioning process, even if the node is healthy and in use. It's worth mentioning that this is an involuntary disruption because it cannot be deferred or throttled with NDBs. The primary use cases for expireAfter include avoiding long-lived Spot instances that may be more susceptible to interruption.

A common example would be setting expireAfter: 720h (30 days) to ensure nodes don't persist indefinitely in the cluster. You can specify durations in a Go duration format (e.g., 30m, 6h, 7d, or 720h). When the configured expiry time is reached, Karpenter initiates the deprovisioning flow, honoring PDBs and performing a drain unless blocked. By default, the expiration will just initiate the drain, but the drain can occur effectively indefinitely. To enforce an absolute maximum node lifetime, pair expireAfter with terminationGracePeriod in NodePool. This sets a hard limit for graceful shutdown before the node is forcefully removed. For example, if nodes must never exceed 30 days, you can set expireAfter to 28 days and terminationGracePeriod to 2 days, ensuring that no node exceeds 30 days in the cluster. Karpenter will begin draining when expiration is hit, and after the grace period elapses, any remaining pods are forcibly terminated, and the node is deleted.

Note that, unlike the other disruption fields, expireAfter is part of the node template spec. Also, you need to be aware that changing the expireAfter value in a NodePool does not update existing nodes. Instead, it marks them as *drifted*, triggering Karpenter to gradually replace them with nodes that conform to the new policy. Also note that workloads protected by strict PDBs or that use the karpenter.sh/do-not-disrupt: "true" annotation may block or delay expiration-based terminations. This is why setting terminationGracePeriod may be useful. As such, you need to carefully coordinate these constraints in environments that rely on regular node turnover to manage cost, performance, or compliance.

While expireAfter makes sure that nodes are eventually replaced based on age, it doesn't control how that termination impacts a workload. The terminationGracePeriod setting was introduced to allow users to enforce a hard timeout on this draining process—mainly to prevent nodes from getting stuck indefinitely, which can be common in development environments or with misconfigured PDBs. Once the specified termination grace period elapses, remaining pods are forcibly deleted and the node is removed, regardless of PDBs or annotations. While this provides a safety valve for stuck workloads, in production environments, it's generally recommended to monitor and manually remediate drains instead of relying heavily on this automated cap.

I've mentioned terminationGracePeriod a couple of times, but let's explore it in more detail next.

Graceful node termination

By default, Karpenter always performs graceful draining when a node is deprovisioned for voluntary reasons (expiration, consolidation, or drift), it waits for workloads to terminate cleanly before proceeding with forceful removal. No pods are aggressively killed unless configured otherwise—graceful shutdown is the baseline.

Kubernetes itself includes a pod-level field, terminationGracePeriodSeconds (defaulting to 30 seconds), which controls how long kubelet will wait for a pod to exit cleanly after receiving a termination signal. Karpenter's terminationGracePeriod on the NodePool works at the node level, setting the maximum amount of time allowed for all draining to complete before force-terminating the node (and any remaining pods).

Picture a workload that needs to flush metrics, close connections, or write final logs before exiting. Without any buffer, those shutdown routines may be cut short, leading to data loss, failed user requests, or noisy alerts. Karpenter solves this by allowing you to configure terminationGracePeriod on your NodePool: a window of time that Karpenter will wait after initiating the shutdown process, before forcefully terminating the node. During this period, Karpenter drains the node, honoring PDBs, letting kubelet gracefully stop the running pods.

For example, you might configure a NodePool with `terminationGracePeriod: 300s`, giving workloads up to 5 minutes to exit cleanly. That might sound like a lot, but for some stateful, latency-sensitive apps, or long-running jobs that you don't want to be constantly interrupted; it's what could make the difference between a graceful shutdown and an outage. As said before, this setting becomes especially important when combined with involuntary mechanisms such as `expireAfter`, where termination isn't driven by workload optimization but by enforced policy. It's your last line of defense in giving pods a chance to shut down on their own terms.

While `terminationGracePeriod` controls *how* a node is terminated, it doesn't really allow you to say *when* a node is terminated, including describing how many nodes can be disrupted at once. That's where NDBs come in: providing a broader policy to limit the scope of voluntary disruptions across the cluster.

NodePool disruption budgets

In the previous section, we introduced NDBs, which help you control how aggressively Karpenter can disrupt nodes in your cluster. Not all applications can tolerate frequent node terminations. NDBs, configured in the `disruption` section of a NodePool, allow you to throttle voluntary disruptions—including consolidation of empty or underutilized nodes and drift-based reprovisioning. You can configure these budgets to completely block terminations, control the rate at which nodes are disrupted (both as percentages and absolute numbers), and even establish maintenance windows that restrict when disruptions can occur. NDBs help you maintain the stability and availability of a cluster by ensuring that cost optimization activities don't overwhelm your workloads with excessive node churn.

By default, if you do not configure any budgets, Karpenter will apply a built-in budget that limits disruptions to 10% of the NodePool at any time, like this:

```
apiVersion: karpenter.sh/v1
kind: NodePool
metadata:
  name: default
spec:
...
  disruption:
    budgets:
      - nodes: "10%"
```

In other words, Karpenter will only disrupt up to 10% of the nodes concurrently for voluntary disruptions, as shown in *Figure 9.8*. For example, in a NodePool of 20 nodes where a drift operation is going to cause a disruption, this budget permits Karpenter to disrupt 2 nodes at a time.

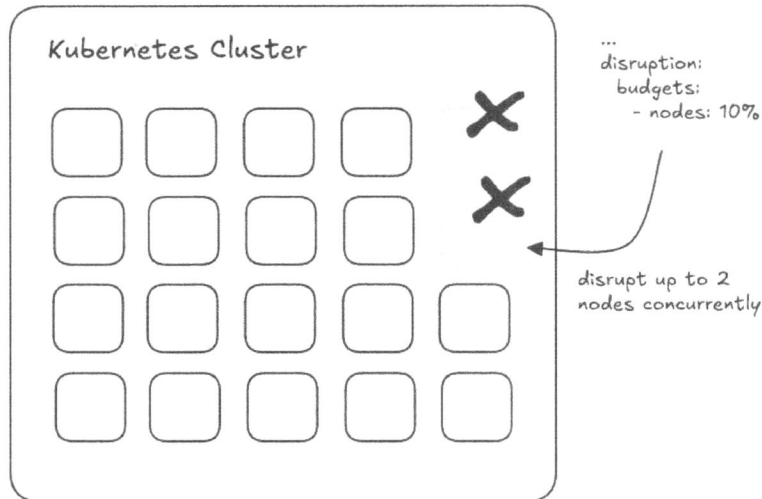

Figure 9.8 – An NDB to allow disruption up to 10% at a time

It's important to emphasize that NDBs only control voluntary disruptions; they do not block involuntary or forceful disruptions such as node expiration, AWS interruption signals (such as spot interruptions), or manual node deletion. Those will proceed regardless of any configured budgets. You should think of NDBs as a mechanism to limit the rate and impact of voluntary optimizations on your workloads while maintaining cluster efficiency.

Moreover, when you configure an NDB, Karpenter determines how many nodes it may disrupt at once by first counting all nodes owned by the NodePool, then subtracting any nodes already being deleted or marked NotReady. This is a key safety feature—by including nodes in a bad or NotReady state, NDBs help prevent the roll-out of further disruptions when issues are detected. For example, if a problematic AMI causes node instability, the NDB will restrict further node replacements until you can investigate and remediate. This mechanism works in tandem with PDBs, which will also halt disruption of nodes if application readiness or stability is impacted by a change ensuring both node and pod level safeguards.

If you specify a percentage, such as nodes: "20%", Karpenter computes the allowed disruptions as roundup(total_nodes * 0.2) - total_deleting - total_notready. For example, on a 10-node pool, up to 2 nodes may be disrupted concurrently. If, instead, you specify a fixed number, such as nodes: "5", Karpenter uses 5 - total_deleting - total_notready, regardless of pool size. Whether you choose a percentage or an absolute count depends on whether you want your disruption limit to scale with cluster size or remain a constant ceiling.

But you can do more with NDBs, including setting time windows and increasing their granularity. Let's explore how to configure time windows to allow disruptions in a NodePool.

Disruptions by schedule

In addition to controlling how many nodes can be disrupted, you can also configure when these nodes can be disrupted. NDBs support scheduling rules so that budgets can be time-bound. To do so, you need to configure a schedule along with a duration, allowing you to define time windows during which a particular budget is in effect. Say, for example, that you want to configure a budget that completely blocks disruptions during business hours (say from 9 AM to 5 PM) or you want to only allow node upgrades to occur on a certain day of the week (such as Monday).

In order to properly configure Karpenter to handle these requirements, you need to describe your requirements in terms of blocking operations, when Karpenter *can't* perform certain actions. You describe the starting point for the budget with the schedule field and then describe how long from that point that the budget should last with the duration field. Effectively, Karpenter will treat the budget as active starting at the scheduled time and lasting for the specified duration. Outside that window, that budget does not apply, though other budgets could. To make the schedule configuration easier, you can use standard cron syntax (like you did with KEDA cron scaling rules in *Chapter 5*) or macros such as @daily. Just keep in mind that time zones are not supported. Karpenter evaluates the cron times in **Coordinated Universal Time (UTC)**.

To understand this configuration better, let's use a practical example. Following the previous example, where we want to pause disruption during weekdays from 9 AM to 5 PM (in UTC), the configuration will look like this:

```
apiVersion: karpenter.sh/v1
kind: NodePool
metadata:
  name: default
spec:
  ...
```

```
disruption:
  budgets:
    - nodes: "0"
      schedule: "0 9 * * 1-5"
      duration: 8h
```

As you can see from this configuration, it's using nodes: "0", meaning no nodes can be disrupted during the scheduled window. The cron expression 0 9 * * 1-5 translates to "at minute 0 of hour 9, every Monday through Friday." Combined with duration: 8h, this covers the 09:00 to 17:00 UTC time on weekdays, as shown *Figure 9.9*.

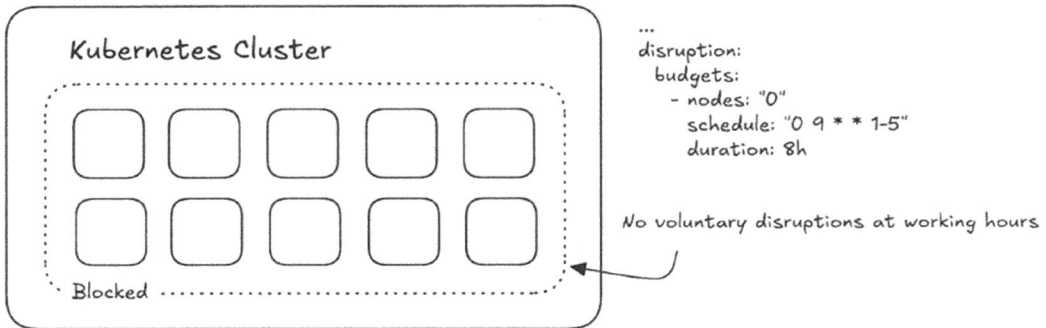

Figure 9.9 – A budget rule blocking voluntary disruptions during working hours

During that period, if Karpenter needs to voluntarily disrupt a node, it will be paused because the allowed disruptions for nodes is 0. After 17:00 (UTC) on weekdays and on weekends, this particular budget no longer applies. This kind of schedule ensures that scale-downs due to consolidation won't happen when you expect high user traffic, but can catch up after hours.

Note

Keep in mind that if you apply nodes: "0" without a schedule, Karpenter will never voluntarily terminate nodes. Make sure this is really what you want; often, it's better to use 0 in a time-limited window, rather than blocking all disruptions indefinitely.

Disruption by reasons

Besides being able to configure how many nodes and at what times those nodes can be disrupted, you can be more granular by configuring *which* reasons nodes can be disrupted. NDB rules can target specific **disruption reasons**. Karpenter categorizes voluntary disruptions by the following reasons: "Empty" (a node has no schedulable pods), "Underutilized" (a node is underutilized per consolidation logic), or "Drifted" (a node configuration is out-of-sync with the NodePool specification). You can limit budgets to only apply to certain reasons via the reasons field.

This simple configuration is very powerful. For instance, reasons become useful when you might allow a higher disruption *X* reason, but a very low-rate disruption for a different *Y* reason or when you want to completely block consolidation of underutilized nodes during the day, but always want to allow empty nodes to be deleted. If a budget's reasons list is omitted, it applies to all disruption reasons by default, and this is the configuration we've been using in all the previous examples.

Let's see what this configuration will look on a NodePool. Suppose we want to allow a higher disruption rate for drifted nodes (since we care a lot about applying security patches). To do this, we can define a budget as follows:

```
apiVersion: karpenter.sh/v1
kind: NodePool
metadata:
  name: default
spec:
  ...
  disruption:
    budgets:
      - nodes: "25%"
        reasons:
          - "Drifted"
  ...
```

In this NodePool, the first budget says that up to 25% of the NodePool can be disrupted only if the nodes are Drifted. It's worth saying that you can specify more than one reason for a budget. But because we're only using one reason, and Underutilized is being left out here, that means there is never any budget constraining it and it's still wide open. It's important to recognize that if there is no budget with a matching reason for a disruption method, then that disruption method can disrupt as many nodes as it wants at one time.

Suppose the NodePool has launched 40 nodes; 25% means that it will allow Karpenter to disrupt 10 nodes at a time. If the NodePool is small (e.g., 8 nodes, where 25% is 2), then 2 empty/drifted nodes can be disrupted.

Multiple disruptions budgets

Let's take NDBs to the next level. Within NDBs, you can combine multiple budgets on the same NodePool to create layered controls. If multiple budgets are defined, the most restrictive budget wins, since Karpenter takes the minimum allowed disruptions across all applicable budgets.

A common pattern is to use a percentage budget to scale with cluster size and an absolute budget as a hard ceiling. For example, you can combine nodes: "20%" with nodes: "5". In a small cluster, the 20% might be under 5 nodes, but in a large cluster, it might be higher. "5" ensures you never disrupt more than 5 at once.

Layered budgets can also mix always-on and scheduled rules. For instance, you might have an always-on budget of 10% for general use, and an additional budget of "0" during a nightly backup window to prevent disruption at that specific time. Again, Karpenter will always enforce the most conservative budget applicable, so layering gives you fine-grained control.

What about adding reasons to the mix? When Karpenter is about to disrupt a node for a specific reason, it will evaluate all budgets that either apply to that reason or apply to all reasons, and then enforce the lowest allowed disruption count among those applicable budgets. This means you can define overlapping budgets (some global, some reason-specific), and Karpenter will always respect the tightest constraint for the given scenario.

Let's add an extra budget to the example we used in the previous section. In addition to the 25% budget for Empty or Drifted nodes, you also want to keep tighter control on underutilized nodes. We can define separate budgets as follows:

```
apiVersion: karpenter.sh/v1
kind: NodePool
metadata:
  name: default
spec:
  ...
  disruption:
    budgets:
      - nodes: "25%"
        reasons:
```

```
        - "Empty"
        - "Drifted"
    - nodes: "5"
```

Same as before, the first budget says that up to 25% of the NodePool can be disrupted if the nodes are either Empty or Drifted. The second budget (with no reasons specified) acts as a global cap of five nodes for *any* disruption.

For an Empty or Drifted node, Karpenter considers both budgets: the 25% budget (specific to that reason) and the global "5 nodes" budget. It will allow disruptions up to the most restrictive of the two. So, if the NodePool has 40 nodes, 25% would allow 10 nodes; the second budget allows 5. Thus, Karpenter will only disrupt 5 empty/drifted nodes at a time (the minimum of 10 and 5). If the NodePool is small (e.g., 8 nodes, where 25% is 2), then at most 2 empty/drifted nodes can be disrupted (minimum of 2 and 5).

For an underutilized node, only the second budget applies (since we didn't list "Underutilized" in the first budget's reasons). That means underutilized nodes are limited to five at a time in this example. If we hadn't provided the second budget at all, underutilized nodes would fall back to the default 10% budget (unless you specifically removed it). So, always ensure that each reason you care about is covered by at least one budget, or include a catch-all budget.

NDBs help manage node disruptions at the cost of slowing down automated consolidation and drift actions. Make sure to tailor your NDBs to balance this trade-off. Critical workloads and time periods could benefit from strict budgets, whereas non-critical workloads could benefit from the increased consolidation and drift agility that loose budgets enable.

Let's now see NDBs in action.

Hands-on lab: Disruption budgets

Suppose you're introducing Karpenter to your cluster. Even though consolidation and drift are features that you'd like to use, you first need to gain some confidence with Karpenter; thus you want to start by controlling *when* Karpenter can voluntarily disrupt your nodes. As you progress in your journey of efficiency, you'll start to be more flexible with consolidation, but want to block any drift operation. You plan to perform upgrades manually and on demand in the short-term. How would you implement this approach? By using NDBs! Let's see how.

Similar to the consolidation and drift hands-on labs, if you already have your EKS cluster up and running, continue with this lab. Otherwise, go back to the consolidation lab and follow the initial steps to create the EKS cluster and deploy a default `NodePool` and `EC2NodeClass`. Then, come back to this lab.

Let's start by exploring the `NodePool`'s `disruption` section in the `nodepool.yaml` file. Notice that you won't find any budget configuration. This means that it's going to use the default configuration of disrupting 10% of nodes at once. But you're new to Karpenter, so you want to start by blocking *any* disruption operation. How do you block these disruptions? By defining a 0 budget.

To simplify these changes, there's another file: `nodepool.disruption.yaml`. The main change we'd like to focus on is the budget section. It looks like this:

```
...
  disruption:
    consolidationPolicy: WhenEmptyOrUnderutilized
    consolidateAfter: 0s
    budgets:
      - nodes: "0"
...
```

Apply this change by running the following command:

```
$ kubectl apply -f nodepool.disruption.yaml
```

Next, deploy the Monte Carlo app by running this command so we can have some nodes to play around with:

```
$ kubectl apply -f montecarlopi.yaml
```

Wait around three or four minutes until you see three pods and one node running:

```
$ kubectl get pods,nodeclaims
```

Now, let's scale the application to 10 replicas to get a second node:

```
$ kubectl scale deployment montecarlo-pi --replicas 10
```

Wait around three to four minutes for this new node and pods to be ready. At this point, you should have two nodes launched by Karpenter to host the 10 replicas of your application. In my case, I got two nodes, one with a `c6a.xlarge` instance type and another one with a `c6a.2xlarge` instance type.

Now that we have the setup we wanted, let's scale the app down to three replicas:

```
$ kubectl scale deployment montecarlo-pi --replicas 3
```

If you remember what happened in the consolidation lab at this point, Karpenter should move all pods to the 2xlarge node and remove the xlarge node. However, check the events from the default NodePool by running this command:

```
$ kubectl describe nodepool default
```

You'll see that the last event has the following message: No allowed disruptions for disruption reason Underutilized due to blocking budget. And if you check the number of nodes and NodeClaims again, you'll still see the 2xlarge and xlarge nodes. So, the disruption budget we configured worked. It blocked all voluntary disruptions, such as consolidation, from happening.

Now, we'd like to allow some consolidation actions to occur, but don't want Karpenter to go crazy and start consolidating all of our nodes at once. Let's open up the budget a bit to allow *some* disruptions to occur. Change the budget section of the nodepool.disruption.yaml file to look like this:

```
...
  disruption:
    consolidationPolicy: WhenEmptyOrUnderutilized
    consolidateAfter: 0s
    budgets:
      - nodes: "25%"
...
```

This will give some budget to Karpenter to continue with consolidation. So, let's apply this change by running these commands:

```
$ kubectl apply -f nodepool.disruption.yaml
$ kl
```

You should see the "message":"disrupting node(s)" log message. Karpenter will continue removing the xlarge node, forcing all pods to now be scheduled in the 2xlarge node. Let's assume that by doing this experiment, you are now more confident in your application being disrupted by consolidation. So, you're going to leave that budget the way that it is, at 25%. But, you still don't want Karpenter performing drift operations for you; you want to conduct those manually. Right now, we haven't specified a reason for our budget, meaning the budget applies to all voluntary disruptions. So, we need to apply a second budget to block drift operations.

To achieve this, your nodepool.disruption.yaml file should look like this:

```
...
  disruption:
    consolidationPolicy: WhenEmptyOrUnderutilized
    consolidateAfter: 0s
    budgets:
      - nodes: "25%"
      - nodes: "0"
        reasons:
          - "Drifted"
...
```

With these budgets configured, you're blocking drift disruptions, but allowing any other disruption by removing 25% (rounded up) of the nodes at once. Let's apply this change by running this command:

```
$ kubectl apply -f nodepool.disruption.yaml
```

Now, let's reduce the number of replicas to 3 to force Karpenter to replace the existing 2xlarge node with a smaller one:

```
$ kubectl scale deployment montecarlo-pi --replicas 3
```

You can go and monitor the Karpenter logs by running the k1 command, but you don't need to. Wait around three to four minutes, and you'll see that Karpenter ran consolidation by replacing the existing node with a smaller one.

Let's see whether the budget for drift is working. Notice that the default NodePool reverted the change you made before by upgrading the Bottlerocket version to v1.38.0:

```
...
  amiSelectorTerms:
    - alias: "bottlerocket@1.34.0"
...
```

Change the node.disruption.yaml file to use the v1.38.0 version by replacing the 34 number with 38. Then, apply the change by running this command:

```
$ kubectl apply -f nodepool.disruption.yaml
```

Describe the default Nodepool by running this command:

```
$ kubectl describe nodepool default
```

You should see that the last event is showing the message: No allowed disruptions for disruption reason Drifted due to blocking budget. As you can see, the multiple budget configuration worked as expected. If you wanted to resume the drift operation, you would simply need to give enough budget to the drift rule.

To finish with this lab, let's remove the Monte Carlo app with this command:

```
$ kubectl delete -f montecarlopi.yaml
```

In this lab, you were able to see multiple NDBs in action by progressively adding one by one after you understood the impact of each budget. You also tested each rule, even when you had multiple budgets. So, make sure you follow this approach when adding more budgets in your production clusters. Test each budget independently, but also make sure you test the interactions between the budgets when you combine them. NDBs can be very powerful, but they can also inherently inhibit Karpenter from achieving the goal of making the cluster as efficient as possible.

NDBs are the tool that Karpenter provides you to control disruption of nodes, but Kubernetes already has PDBs to control disruption of applications, so a natural question arises: How are these two budget concepts intended to work together? Well, let's explore what combining these two concepts actually looks like in practice.

Working with PDBs

When you combine PDBs and NDBs, it becomes crucial to understand their complementary roles. PDBs operate at the application level, and they are Kubernetes policies that guarantee that a minimum number, or percentage, of pods should remain available during voluntary evictions, preventing an entire deployment or replica set from losing too many replicas at once. Conversely, NDBs are platform-level controls within Karpenter that regulate how many nodes may be drained concurrently for reasons such as emptiness, underutilization, or drift.

In practice, Karpenter always respects PDBs when draining nodes, which means that it won't evict pods if doing so would violate a PDB. Therefore, those pods block further termination of that node until the PDB's conditions are met. However, PDBs by themselves do not prevent Karpenter from starting to drain several nodes at the same time, as long as the pods on each node can be safely evicted individually. NDBs fill this gap by enforcing a global cap on concurrent node disruptions, ensuring that Karpenter never floods the cluster with too many parallel drains, even when each node passes its PDB check.

To integrate both controls effectively, align your NDB settings with your applications' PDBs and redundancy requirements. In practice, NDBs are most valuable as a platform-level safety net to limit simultaneous node disruptions across the fleet, regardless of whether every application has a properly configured PDB. For example, if multiple applications lack PDBs, setting an NDB such as nodes: "10%" or a fixed ceiling ensures that too many nodes are not drained or replaced at once, protecting platform-wide stability even in the absence of granular application safeguards.

Conversely, highly scalable stateless workloads might comfortably sustain a 20% disruption budget. Always define PDBs for critical applications. Where pods or nodes must never be voluntarily disrupted, add the karpenter.sh/do-not-disrupt: "true" annotation. This layered strategy—using NDBs to limit overall node churn, PDBs to safeguard application pods, and do-not-disrupt annotations for immovable components—ensures both cluster stability and efficient resource optimization.

But there's another edge case. When you use Spot instances, keep in-mind that spot interruptions are involuntary and impose a short time limit (usually two minutes in AWS) on pod evictions. While Kubernetes and Karpenter respect PDBs during the drain, AWS will forcefully terminate the instance after the notification period, meaning that pods will be killed even if budgets would otherwise block disruption indefinitely. There's nothing you can do to stop that disruption. Involuntary disruptions can affect a node at any time, triggering immediate pod evictions regardless of your budgets. So, configure PDBs narrowly for critical workloads, and set NDBs conservatively (for example, nodes: "1") so that Karpenter never voluntarily drains more than one node at once.

However, even with a one-node NDB in place, there remains a risk that you could get several interruptions that could breach your PDB's minimum availability threshold. Since PDBs don't block involuntary disruptions, losing more than two nodes would drop your running pods below the required count, violating the PDB and potentially causing application downtime. To mitigate this risk, consider increasing your replica count so that your PDB can tolerate multiple simultaneous failures. But this needs to be based on your risk tolerance.

Let's move on to the next section to explore best practices for Karpenter.

Karpenter best practices

To maximize both efficiency and reliability when using Karpenter, let's explore a layered approach you could take across your NodePools, EC2NodeClasses, and your workloads. This is based on many customer interactions, and frequently asked questions on either GitHub or other public channels such as Slack.

NodePools

At the NodePool level, and at the workload (or pod) level to some extent, these are the practices I'd recommend you consider when using Karpenter to scale your data plane. Keep in mind that even though Karpenter is focused only on scaling nodes, you can influence how Karpenter launches nodes from the pod constraints:

- **Keep NodePool count manageable**: Aim to have a small number of NodePools whenever possible. Don't overcomplicate the setup if not needed. Over-dividing by team, environment, or use case can make management harder and reduce Karpenter's flexibility. If you're transitioning from CAS, it's fine to start with multiple NodePools to mimic old node group behavior. But in the long term, refactor your setup into fewer, more generic NodePools. I've seen other companies follow a simple and scalable pattern like this:

    - One flexible default NodePool for general workloads, with broad instance type and capacity settings. The last thing you want is to have a pending pod waiting for the cluster to provide capacity.

    - One dedicated system NodePool for infrastructure-critical workloads (e.g., CNI, CoreDNS). You might want to have special needs in terms of disruptions or be less aggressive with upgrades of the nodes.

    - For workload-specific NodePools, divide by workload type, such as batch jobs versus web applications, or those with unique hardware/software needs like GPUs or performance sensitive.

- **Limit scheduling constraints**: Only define scheduling constraints (e.g., zone, instance type, and capacity type) when all your workloads explicitly require it. Karpenter works best when it has maximum flexibility to select optimal instance types. The more restrictive your NodePool, the more likely Karpenter will struggle to find matching capacity.

- **Avoid over-specifying instance types**: While it's tempting to specify a single preferred instance type, this limits Karpenter's ability to balance cost and availability. Let it choose from a broad list of compatible instances by setting requirements such as instance categories (c, m, r, etc.) rather than exact types.

- **Minimize NodePool requirements for cost optimization**: If your goal is to allow Karpenter to consolidate aggressively and maintain lean infrastructure, avoid unnecessary affinities or topologies with, or soft preferences in your workload specs. Over-constrained requirements force Karpenter to keep underutilized nodes active longer than necessary.

- **Enforce NodePool resource limits**: To control spending, cap the total CPU and memory per NodePool using limits in a NodePool. You can also steer Karpenter to use reserved capacity first by defining capacity type priorities. This protects your bill by preventing overscaling or excessive use of nodes.

Let's explore the recommendations for NodeClass.

NodeClass

Even though we covered NodeClass for an AWS ecosystem, the following practices still apply regardless of the cloud provider you use, so make sure you do the following:

- **Use a shared NodeClass**: A NodeClass should reflect the baseline infrastructure config: AMIs, IAM roles, tags, subnets, and security groups. Share the same NodeClass across multiple NodePools when workloads have similar infrastructure needs.

- **Use a tag-based discovery for subnets and security groups**: Prefer selectors using tags over static IDs. Tag your subnets and security groups (e.g., karpenter.sh/discovery: my-cluster) and use selectors to match them. This allows portability between clusters or environments.

- **Configure secure and minimal permissions**: Always define the role in your NodeClass with least-privilege permissions. Use IMDSv2 with restricted hop limits to isolate instance metadata from workloads.

- **Avoid uncontrolled AMI drift**: Avoid using latest AMI versions in production. Pin to a specific AMI version to control rollouts and avoid unplanned disruptions. We'll dive deeper into the drift operation in the next chapter.

Lastly, let's explore the recommendations for your workloads.

Workloads

There are also some recommendations regarding the pods for your workloads:

- **Consider defining PDBs**: Even less critical workloads will benefit from some level of protection, but you should adjust the aggressiveness of each PDB based on the application's criticality. For highly available or tolerant applications, a more permissive PDB may be appropriate, while stateful or mission-critical services should use stricter budgets. Karpenter's eviction logic will always honor these constraints before draining any node. If you're running Spot instances, consider the additional impact of involuntary disruptions when choosing your PDB settings.

- **Annotate immovable pods or nodes with karpenter.sh/do-not-disrupt: "true"**: For stateful workloads or licensed-software nodes that cannot survive eviction, this annotation ensures Karpenter never targets them for voluntary disruptions.

- **Use taints/tolerations together with nodeSelector**: If you need to tie workloads with a NodePool, combine nodeSelector with taints/tolerations for a deterministic scheduling. This combination ensures workloads land only on intended nodes and avoids unintended matches that can trigger new node provisioning.

- **Always set resource requests to your pods**: At this point, this should be crystal clear. But keep in mind that for Karpenter to scale nodes efficiently, pods must declare resources.requests for CPU and memory. Without them, you won't have a deterministic result, and it will be hard to find out why your workloads are having problems or your nodes are not the ones you really need.

And that's it for now. You've explored the foundations of Karpenter. We spent quite some time covering how Karpenter works under the hood with the mission of helping you get the most out of it, and to understand why Karpenter ends up launching (or removing) certain nodes at a certain point in time.

Summary

This chapter was all about going from just launching nodes to running a production-grade Karpenter setup that can optimize and maintain itself without surprises. Specifically, you learned about how Karpenter handles node disruptions. We explained how Karpenter continuously simulates pod movement to consolidate capacity, and how it performs rolling node replacements to handle drift from the desired configuration. Finally, we covered how NDBs help you limit how many nodes can be voluntarily disrupted at once, letting you scale down, upgrade, or rebalance without losing control.

You also reviewed a series of best practices to get the most out of Karpenter. These include using fewer, more flexible NodePools; avoiding unnecessary constraints in both NodePools and workloads (or pods); combining taints, tolerations, and node selectors for more deterministic scheduling (but only when strictly needed); and leveraging instance diversity to optimize for both cost and reliability.

The most important things to remember are as follows:

- Karpenter doesn't schedule pods or scale on resource utilization; it reacts to unscheduled pods.

- Consolidation and drift are powerful, but they can cause churn if left unchecked. If your workloads can't handle this, it's better to take a conservative approach.

- PDBs and NDBs are your primary safeguard for controlling that churn.

You now have the tools to shape how Karpenter behaves, not just at the moment of need, but over time, ensuring your clusters stay lean, aligned, and predictable. Let's continue on to the next chapter to discover how to operate and manage your Karpenter setup with monitoring and troubleshooting.

10

Karpenter Management Operations

The time has come to explore how to operate your Kubernetes clusters now that you have Karpenter managing the compute nodes for the data plane. To operate Karpenter successfully, you need to do more than just keep it running to have an efficient cluster. As your workloads evolve or grow, so do the challenges: sudden cost spikes, nodes that don't register, pods stuck pending despite capacity being added, or consolidation loops that churn instances unexpectedly. Without observability and diagnostic practices in place, these issues can quickly erode the benefits Karpenter is meant to provide.

In this chapter, we move from the "what" and "how" of Karpenter's features to the "why": why it behaves a certain way, and what to do when it doesn't behave as expected. You'll learn how to troubleshoot common problems, including misbehaving consolidation policies, zone imbalance from topology constraints, and cost surprises from subtle scheduling dynamics. We'll introduce essential commands, log analysis techniques, and a purpose-built tool to parse Karpenter's controller logs.

But, *understanding* Karpenter's internals is only one part of the equation; observability and metrics are the other. Karpenter exposes Prometheus metrics to allow you to observe how it operates. We'll explore which ones to monitor, why they matter, and what they reveal about cluster health, node efficiency, and cloud provider interactions. You'll also learn how to deploy Grafana dashboards to turn raw metrics into visual signals you can track over time or alert on.

By the end of this chapter, you'll be able to operate Karpenter with confidence.

We will be covering the following main topics:

- Advanced operations and troubleshooting
- Common operational challenges
- Node Auto Repair for unhealthy node handling
- Upgrading Karpenter
- Observability and metrics

Technical requirements

For this chapter, you'll continue using an AWS EKS cluster. To avoid any problems, it's recommended to turn down any previous cluster you created, and instead create a new one from the template you'll find in this chapter. This is going to be the cluster you'll use from now on. You don't need to install any additional tools, as most of the commands are going to be run using kubectl and helm. You can find the YAML manifests for all resources you're going to create in this chapter in the chapter10 folder from the Book's GitHub repository, which you already cloned in *Chapter 1*.

Advanced operations and troubleshooting

So far, we've explored all Karpenter features that will help you run efficient Kubernetes clusters. Still, we can't deny that at some point you might have problems with autoscaling your nodes. Even though you now have an idea of how Karpenter works, it's critical that you also understand how to properly run it in a production environment. To get started with this chapter, let's dive into the very first task you need to go deeper into: troubleshooting Karpenter.

Troubleshooting Karpenter

Before we actually dive into the specific situations that you can run into with Karpenter, let's look at the ways that Karpenter surfaces troubleshooting information to its users: logs, metrics, and events.

So, let's explore the commands you'll be using while troubleshooting.

Getting Karpenter events

Karpenter also provides object-related information as a complement to logs in the form of Kubernetes events. **Events are directly tied to a Kubernetes object and contain a reason, message, and timestamp.** This is a common paradigm, and this same mechanism is used elsewhere in Kubernetes to expose object information, such as for pods and nodes.

To read events from an object, you need to describe them, like this:

```
$ kubectl describe OBJECT <name>
```

Where OBJECT could be NodeClaim, NodePool, node, pod, and so on, and <name> is the name of the object. For instance, say you describe a NodeClaim by running this command:

```
$ kubectl describe nodeclaim <name>
```

You'll see something similar to this at the end of the output:

```
Events:
    Type      Reason                Age   From         Message
    ----      ------                ----  ----         -------
    Normal    Unconsolidatable      57s   karpenter    ...
    Warning   InstanceTerminating   9s    karpenter    ...
    Normal    DisruptionBlocked     2s    karpenter    ...
```

During the following sections, we'll refer to this approach of describing Kubernetes objects as "describing the events." Before we continue with other troubleshooting methods, let me list the events Karpenter will emit to help you spot problems easily.

Events reference table

The following table contains most of the events that Karpenter emits. The aim of this table is that you have it as a reference point when looking for relevant information while debugging.

Event Reason	Object Type	Description	Message
DisruptionBlocked	Node, NodeClaim, NodePool	Indicates that disruption is blocked due to budget constraints or other conditions	"No allowed disruptions due to blocking budget"
DisruptionLaunching	NodeClaim	Emitted when launching a replacement NodeClaim during disruption	"Launching NodeClaim: Drift"

Event Reason	Object Type	Description	Message
DisruptionTerminating	Node, NodeClaim	Emitted when terminating nodes/NodeClaims during disruption	"Disrupting Node: Drift"
DisruptionWaitingReadiness	NodeClaim	Emitted when waiting for readiness before continuing disruption	"Waiting on readiness to continue disruption"
Unconsolidatable	Node, NodeClaim	Indicates a node cannot be consolidated due to constraints	Various messages about why consolidation is blocked
FailedScheduling	Pod	Emitted when a pod fails to schedule	"Failed to schedule pod, {error details}"
NoCompatibleInstanceTypes	NodePool	Emitted when no instance types match NodePool requirements	"NodePool requirements filtered out all compatible available instance types"
Nominated	Pod	Emitted when a pod is nominated to a node/NodeClaim	"Pod should schedule on: nodeclaim/{name}"
NodeRepairBlocked	Node, NodeClaim, NodePool	Emitted when node repair is blocked	Various reasons why repair is blocked
Disrupted	Pod	Emitted when a pod is deleted to accommodate node termination	"Deleting the pod to accommodate the terminationTime..."

Event Reason	Object Type	Description	Message
Evicted	Pod	Emitted when a pod is evicted during node termination	"Evicted pod: {reason}"
FailedDraining	Node	Emitted when node draining fails	"Failed to drain node, {error}"
TerminationGracePeriodExpiring	Node, NodeClaim	Emitted when termination grace period is about to expire	"All pods will be deleted by {time}"
AwaitingVolumeDetachment	Node	Emitted when waiting for volume attachments to be deleted	"Awaiting deletion of bound volumeattachments ({names})"
FailedConsistencyCheck	NodeClaim	Emitted when NodeClaim consistency checks fail	Various consistency check failure messages
InsufficientCapacityError	NodeClaim	Emitted when there's insufficient capacity to launch a NodeClaim	"NodeClaim {name} event: {error details}"
UnregisteredTaintMissing	NodeClaim	Emitted when the unregistered taint is missing from a NodeClaim	"Missing karpenter.sh/unregistered taint which prevents registration related race conditions"
NodeClassNotReady	NodeClaim	Emitted when the NodeClass is not ready	"NodeClaim {name} event: {error details}"
SpotInterrupted	Node, NodeClaim	When AWS sends a spot interruption warning for an instance	"Spot interruption warning was triggered"

Event Reason	Object Type	Description	Message
SpotRebalanceRecommendation	Node, NodeClaim	When AWS recommends rebalancing spot instances	"Spot rebalance recommendation was triggered"
InstanceStopping	Node, NodeClaim	When an EC2 instance receives a stopping signal	"Instance is stopping"
InstanceTerminating	Node, NodeClaim	When an EC2 instance is being terminated	"Instance is terminating"
InstanceUnhealthy	Node, NodeClaim	When AWS reports an instance as unhealthy	"An unhealthy warning was triggered for the instance"
TerminatingOnInterruption	Node, NodeClaim	When Karpenter initiates termination due to interruption	"Interruption triggered termination for the NodeClaim/Node"
WaitingOnNodeClaimTermination	EC2NodeClass	When EC2NodeClass deletion is waiting for NodeClaims to terminate	"Waiting on NodeClaim termination for [names]"
(No Reason)	NodePool	When Karpenter cannot resolve the NodeClass for a NodePool	"Failed resolving NodeClass"
(No Reason)	NodeClaim	When Karpenter cannot resolve the NodeClass for a NodeClaim	"Failed resolving NodeClass"

Event Reason	Object Type	Description	Message
(No Reason)	NodeClaim	When spot instance launch fails due to missing service-linked role permissions	"Attempted to launch a spot instance but failed due to \"AuthFailure. ServiceLinkedRole CreationNotPermitted\""

Table 10.1 – Karpenter Controller events reference table

I'd recommend you check the book's GitHub repository to get the latest version of this table, as Karpenter might have changed some of the preceding events by the time you're reading this book. The events reference table is at /chapter10/events.md.

Next, let's explore how you can check Karpenter logs, including commands I've found useful.

Getting Karpenter logs

We can get Karpenter logs by running the same command that we ran during the exercises in previous chapters. In general, it's good to store this alias, since you're probably going to be getting Karpenter logs *a lot*. To create an alias in your terminal, run the following command:

```
$ alias kl='kubectl -n karpenter logs -l app.kubernetes.io/name=karpenter
--all-containers=true -f --tail=20'
```

With this, next time you run kl in your terminal, you'll see the latest 20 log lines in real time from all the Karpenter pods.

> **Note**
>
> To help you explore Karpenter logs, you can use LogParserForKarpenter (lp4k), an AWS Labs project for parsing Karpenter's controller logs. In a production environment, you'll have days or weeks of logs. Sifting through them manually is tedious. lp4k can ingest Karpenter logs (from STDIN, files, or a running pod) and output a CSV with a structured summary of Karpenter's actions. You can decide later how to use that CSV file. For example, you could build a report with tools such as Amazon QuickSight or Microsoft Power BI.

I suggest you add the preceding command to your terminal profile, which, depending on your setup (or OS), means that you'll add the preceding exact line to the end of a file such as ~/.profile, ~/.bashrc, ~/.zshrc, and so on.

For instance, I'm using ~/.zshrc, and this command makes the kl alias available every time I open a new terminal:

```
$ echo "alias kl='kubectl -n karpenter logs -l app.kubernetes.io/
name=karpenter --all-containers=true -f --tail=20'" >> ~/.zshrc
```

To avoid re-opening a terminal, run this command:

```
$ source ~/.zshrc
```

If you're not using ~/.zshrc, then adjust the previous commands accordingly.

> **Note**
>
> We recommend you read Karpenter logs with kubectl only when you're getting started or want to review something very quickly. In a production environment, the recommended way to explore logs is to use a centralized logging strategy and review logs there instead, since logs can be lost with kubectl if the pod terminates.
>
> A centralized logging strategy means collecting logs from all your Kubernetes pods and nodes into a single, persistent storage location where you can search, analyze, and retain them long-term—even after pods are deleted or restarted. For instance, a common approach is the EFK Stack (Elasticsearch, Fluentd, Kibana). In EFK, you deploy Fluentd as a DaemonSet to collect logs from all nodes, send them to Elasticsearch for storage and indexing, and visualize them in Kibana.

Exploring status conditions

Karpenter includes critical debugging information directly in the status conditions of its CRDs, making it easier to understand why nodes aren't being provisioned, why disruption isn't occurring, or what's blocking initialization. Rather than solely relying on logs or events, you can inspect the state of NodePools, NodeClaims, and EC2NodeClasses to get immediate visibility from Karpenter actions.

Kubernetes uses status conditions as a standard way to communicate the state and health of resources. Karpenter follows this pattern, adding detailed conditions to its custom resources that explain what's happening, or what's preventing actions from happening. These conditions include a type, status (True/False/Unknown), reason, and a human-readable message that provides context.

Similar to events, to read status conditions from an object, you need to describe them, like this:

```
$ kubectl describe OBJECT <name>
```

Where `OBJECT` could be `NodeClaim`, `NodePool`, node, pod, and so on, and `<name>` is the name of the object. For example, after running the preceding command, you might see that a `NodeClaim` shows `Initialized: False` with a message such as "gpu resource not registered." You know that a GPU instance type was launched, but the NVIDIA device plugin or GPU operator isn't running, preventing the `nvidia.com/gpu` resource from appearing in the node's allocatable capacity.

These conditions are particularly valuable during initial setup or after configuration changes. For example, rather than waiting for provisioning to fail and digging through logs, you can immediately see validation errors in the `EC2NodeClass` status.

Now that you're equipped with a set of very useful commands, let's proceed to explore the most common issues you might encounter while using Karpenter.

Common operational challenges

So far, with the hands-on labs you've been practicing, you've been able to explore and understand how Karpenter works in a prepared setup where we know how Karpenter is going to behave. However, it's likely that, at some point, you are going to encounter problems in your cluster. It's important to understand the common operational challenges that users run into when they run Karpenter, so you can quickly solve them when you see them in production yourself.

In this section, we'll cover how to troubleshoot common issues in Karpenter around cost, node provisioning, consolidation, drift, and scheduling, as well as specific cases where PDBs are blocking scale-down operations. You'll learn what signals to look for (logs, events, metrics) and the recommended resolutions to these issues. Let's get into it.

Cost spikes

Karpenter is great at helping you lower compute costs by actively removing or replacing under-utilized nodes and packing workloads onto more efficient instance types. However, misconfigurations can still lead to increased costs. These spikes often result from rapid scaling events or churn in node provisioning. Let's analyze a few common scenarios where you might see this happening.

Consolidation churn

Consolidation is a feature that helps reduce costs by removing under-utilized nodes. It's enabled by default on each NodePool. However, there's inherent tension: consolidation that's too aggressive can cause excessive node churn and pod disruptions, impacting reliability, while consolidation that's too conservative leaves idle capacity running longer, increasing costs.

If consolidation is causing too many disruptions, causing application latency spikes or PDB violations, you can use NDBs to limit how many nodes can be consolidated simultaneously, spreading disruption over time while still allowing optimization to occur. Alternatively, increase consolidateAfter to reduce consolidation frequency.

The consolidateAfter setting controls how long Karpenter waits after a node becomes eligible (either empty or under-utilized) before considering it for consolidation. This operates on a per-node basis. Each node has its own timer that starts when it meets the consolidation criteria.

```
spec:
  disruption:
    consolidationPolicy: WhenEmptyOrUnderutilized
    consolidateAfter: 30s
```

Setting consolidateAfter too long has a hidden cost of nodes remaining idle longer, increasing costs proportionally. Ideally, during that window, the scheduler may place new pods on them. But if that's not the case, you'll be paying for idle resources.

The preceding shows a default configuration, but the appropriate consolidateAfter value depends on your workload patterns. Let's explore a few examples:

- **Short-lived batch jobs (30s - 1m):** For frequent batch processing or CI/CD workloads that complete quickly, a short interval such as 30 seconds to 1 minute allows Karpenter to reclaim capacity promptly as jobs finish. This minimizes waste while giving enough time for the next job to potentially reuse the node.

- **Microservices with frequent scaling (1m - 5m):** For applications that scale up and down throughout the day (e.g., API services responding to traffic patterns), a 1-5 minute window balances responsiveness with stability. This prevents consolidation from triggering during brief traffic dips that might reverse within minutes.

- **Long-running applications with occasional scaling (5m - 15m):** For workloads that scale infrequently but run for hours or days, a longer interval such as 5-15 minutes reduces churn. This gives the scheduler more time to place new pods on existing capacity before consolidation removes nodes, reducing the frequency of pod migrations.

What you need to keep in mind is to tune the consolidation timing so that Karpenter removes spare capacity promptly to reduce costs, but not so fast that it interferes with normal pod scheduling or causes excessive pod evictions.

Having extra capacity due to scheduling preferences

Another common source of cost spikes comes from how Karpenter provisions capacity in response to pod scheduling constraints. When pods specify preferences or requirements for distribution across topology domains (zones, nodes, etc.), Karpenter may launch multiple nodes in parallel to satisfy those constraints. But as soon as the first node becomes Ready, the kube-scheduler immediately assigns all pending pods to it, even if other nodes are still initializing. If one node happens to register slightly faster and has enough capacity, it may get all the pods, leaving the other nodes completely unused. Karpenter then detects the empty nodes and consolidates them, but not before they've incurred brief but real costs (EC2 instance charges, EBS volumes, etc.).

This over-provisioning most commonly occurs with the following:

- **Topology Spread Constraints (TSCs) with minDomains**: When pods require spreading across a minimum number of zones or nodes, Karpenter provisions capacity in multiple domains.

- **Preferred pod affinity/anti-affinity**: When using preferredDuringSchedulingIgnored DuringExecution, the scheduler attempts to honor preferences but isn't strictly required to. This can result in Karpenter provisioning nodes based on the assumption that preferences will be followed, only to have the scheduler make different placement decisions.

- **Preferred topology spread with ScheduleAnyway**: When using whenUnsatisfiable: ScheduleAnyway, the scheduler does its best to spread pods but allows it to violate the constraint if necessary. Karpenter may provision nodes expecting spread, but the scheduler might concentrate pods differently.

To minimize unnecessary node provisioning, make your scheduling constraints as explicit and mandatory as possible:

- **For TSCs:** Use whenUnsatisfiable: DoNotSchedule combined with appropriate minDomains and maxSkew values to force the scheduler to wait for proper distribution. With minDomains: 3 and maxSkew: 1, the scheduler will place one pod in each of the first three zones that come online. Once all three zones have at least one pod (satisfying minDomains), subsequent pods can be placed with no more than 1 pod difference (maxSkew: 1) between any two zones. This prevents all pods from concentrating on the first ready node while ensuring proper zone distribution.

- **For pod affinity/anti-affinity and node affinity**: Use requiredDuringSchedulingIgnored
  DuringExecution instead of preferredDuringSchedulingIgnoredDuringExecution when
  distribution is critical. This ensures pods must be placed on different nodes, preventing
  the scheduler from placing multiple pods on the same node even if it becomes ready first.

The key principle across all these scenarios is to use hard constraints (required, DoNotSchedule)
rather than soft preferences (preferred, ScheduleAnyway) when you need guaranteed distribution
or placement. This gives both Karpenter and the scheduler clear, unambiguous rules to follow,
reducing the chance of provisioning capacity that won't be used.

DaemonSet taints cause the launch of extra nodes

A trickier cause of node churn and cost spikes involves DaemonSets that apply taints during
initialization. For example, CNIs like Cilium often apply a taint such as node.cilium.io/agent-
not-ready=NoSchedule to block workloads until networking is fully initialized. If Karpenter isn't
told to expect this behavior, it can overreact.

What happens is that a new node launches, the DaemonSet applies a taint, and the kube-scheduler
will temporarily avoid scheduling pending pods to this node. Karpenter sees that pods are still
unschedulable and incorrectly assumes more capacity is needed, causing it to launch another
node. By the time the taint is removed and pods start running on the original node, the second
one is no longer needed and gets consolidated. If the taint removal is slow, this cycle can repeat,
leading to wasted resources and unnecessary scaling events.

To prevent this, you can explicitly declare these expected startup taints using the startupTaints
field in your NodePool, like this:

```
spec:
  startupTaints:
    - key: node.cilium.io/agent-not-ready
      effect: NoSchedule
```

This tells Karpenter: "Don't treat this taint as a blocker; it's expected." As a result, Karpenter will
wait for the node to become fully schedulable rather than preemptively launching another one.

This pattern doesn't just apply to the CNI; it applies to other DaemonSets too, including security
agents or service meshes.

Let's now explore some challenges regarding node management.

Node provisioning challenges

At times, you might find that Karpenter doesn't launch nodes as expected, or you might find nodes are created but fail to register in the cluster. A common symptom is having pods stuck in a Pending state even though Karpenter has taken action to add capacity. These situations often trace back to NodeClass and NodePool configuration issues, AWS limits, or environmental constraints. Let's explore them in more detail.

Subnet and security group selection

One frequent issue is an incorrect or missing subnet or security group selector in the EC2NodeClass. For example, if you are selecting subnets on karpenter.sh/discovery: CLUSTER_NAME and your subnets aren't tagged with this tag, or subnetSelectorTerms doesn't match *any* tags, Karpenter won't know where to place the nodes. The logs or status conditions on the NodeClass will typically show an error such as this:

```
launching node: no subnets matched selector terms
```

Similarly, if security group selectors don't match any groups, provisioning fails with security group-related errors. To fix this, ensure your subnets and security groups are properly tagged and that your selectors match them. Here's a working example:

```
spec:
  subnetSelectorTerms:
    - tags:
        karpenter.sh/discovery: kubernetes-autoscaling
  securityGroupSelectorTerms:
    - tags:
        karpenter.sh/discovery: kubernetes-autoscaling
```

Check the EC2NodeClass status conditions (as described in the previous section) to confirm that SubnetsReady and SecurityGroupsReady are both True.

Invalid launch templates or block device mappings

Another common failure is caused by invalid launch templates or AMI/user data settings. For instance, referencing a non-existent block device might result in the following:

```
InvalidBlockDeviceMapping: Invalid device name /dev/xvda
```

This typically means your EC2NodeClass includes an incorrect root volume device name. For most EKS-optimized AMIs, the correct device is /dev/xvda or /dev/sda1, depending on the AMI. Review your blockDeviceMappings configuration and ensure it matches the AMI's expected device names.

IP address exhaustion in subnets

A frequently overlooked failure mode is subnet IP exhaustion, which manifests differently than other provisioning issues. EC2 may successfully launch the instance, and the node may even register with Kubernetes, but pods remain stuck in the ContainerCreating state with FailedCreatePodSandBox errors. This occurs for the following reasons:

- The subnet doesn't have enough available IP addresses to assign to new EC2 instances. Karpenter can't launch nodes at all, and you'll see capacity errors in the logs.

- The instance launches and gets a primary IP, but when the VPC CNI tries to assign secondary IPs to pods (for pod networking), none are available. Pods get stuck waiting for IPs even though the node appears healthy.

To diagnose IP exhaustion, check your subnet's available IP count in the AWS console or via the following:

```
$ aws ec2 describe-subnets --subnet-ids <subnet-id> --query 'Subnets[*].
AvailableIpAddressCount'
```

To address the IP exhaustion problem, you need to consider the following recommendations, ordered from most preferred to least preferred:

- **Spreading pods across more subnets/zones**: Use topologySpreadConstraints on topology.kubernetes.io/zone to distribute nodes more evenly, preventing a single subnet from being saturated

- **Expanding IP address space**: Increase the CIDR block size for your subnets or add additional subnets to your VPC and tag them for Karpenter to discover

- **Using custom networking**: Configure the VPC CNI to use separate subnets for pod networking, isolating pod IPs from node IPs

- **Considering IPv6**: EKS supports IPv6 clusters, which eliminate IP exhaustion concerns (though IPv6 has other limitations to evaluate)

But you might also have capacity problems due to other reasons; let's explore them.

Insufficient Instance Capacity error (ICE)

The InsufficientInstanceCapacity error, or ICE, is very specific to AWS, and it means that they do not have available hardware to fulfill your instance request in the selected availability zone and instance type combination. Even though the error is specific to AWS, the solution applies to any Karpenter implementation: broaden instance type diversification.

If your NodePool requirements specify a very narrow set of instance types (e.g., only c6i.32xlarge) or constrain provisioning to a single availability zone, you're more likely to encounter capacity constraints because Karpenter has fewer options. To minimize ICE impact, you can do the following:

- **Broaden instance type selection**: Allow multiple instance categories and sizes in your NodePool requirements. For instance, use c, m, r categories
- **Enable multiple availability zones**: Ensure your subnetSelectorTerms includes subnets in at least 2-3 availability zones.

ICE errors are logged by Karpenter and typically resolve automatically through retries. If they persist, expanding instance type and zone options is the only solution.

Quota limits

Distinct from insufficient capacity, InstanceLimitExceeded errors indicate you've hit your cloud account's service quota for a specific instance type or vCPU count. In AWS, these are account-level limits that they enforce to prevent runaway resource consumption.

To resolve quota issues, you need to request a quota increase. Request higher limits for the specific instance families or vCPU types you need. Approvals typically occur within 24-48 hours. Unlike ICE errors, quota issues won't resolve automatically, so you must either increase quotas or reduce your instance usage to stay within limits.

Let's move on to another common operational challenge around consolidation.

Consolidation failures

You may notice that some nodes remain in the cluster even though they appear underutilized or idle. Naturally, you'd expect Karpenter to remove or replace them. This is a common source of confusion (and cost complaints) we've seen often, as discussed earlier in this chapter.

Karpenter will only consolidate a node if doing so won't violate scheduling constraints and if all pods can be safely rescheduled elsewhere. If it detects a blocker, it skips the node and emits an informative event.

To see what's happening, inspect the node's events:

```
$ kubectl describe node <NODENAME>
```

You might see something like this:

```
...   pdb default/backend prevents pod evictions
```

This typically means one or more pods are protected, either by a PDB or the `karpenter.sh/do-not-disrupt` annotation. For example, if a deployment has a PDB that requires at least 1 pod always available and you're only running 1 replica, Karpenter can't evict it without violating the PDB. That node becomes unconsolidatable by design.

Another common event is this:

```
...   can't replace with a cheaper node
```

This means Karpenter evaluated the pods on the node and determined that no cheaper instance could replace the current one, even if some pods could be packed elsewhere.

Beyond PDBs and cost checks, pod constraints often prevent consolidation. These include the following:

- Node affinity or anti-affinity rules
- Topology spread constraints (especially strict ones)
- Resource limits that make it impossible to co-locate pods elsewhere

Karpenter logs often reveal exactly *why* consolidation didn't proceed, and that Karpenter is behaving correctly, even if it seems like it's ignoring idle capacity.

Pods remain pending

If a pod is pending but not marked unschedulable, Karpenter might ignore it. This can happen if the scheduler hasn't had a chance to attempt scheduling yet or if the delay is elsewhere. To understand when Karpenter will react, you need to look at the pod's status conditions, specifically the `PodScheduled` condition.

If the `PodScheduled` condition shows a different reason, such as `SchedulerError`, or if the pod is pending due to waiting on `PersistentVolumeClaim` binding, `init` container failures, or image pull issues, in such cases, Karpenter won't provision capacity because the pod isn't blocked on node availability.

Assuming the pods are unschedulable solely due to a lack of resources, Karpenter should pick them up and launch nodes for them. If it doesn't, check if the pods have requirements that none of your NodePools can satisfy. For example, if a pod specifies a node selector for a GPU instance (e.g., nvidia.com/gpu) but none of your NodePools allow GPU instance types, Karpenter won't be able to launch a node. The Karpenter controller logs will usually print a message such as Unable to schedule pod ... with details.

So far, I've focused on scenarios where pods can't start due to provisioning problems. But even after nodes successfully launch and pods are scheduled, issues can still arise. Nodes themselves can become unhealthy due to hardware failures, kernel panics, network problems, or corrupted container runtimes. When this happens, pods may get stuck in ContainerCreating, CrashLoopBackOff, or other error states even though the node appears to exist. Karpenter can continuously monitor node health conditions and automatically replace nodes that have entered unhealthy states. Let's explore this Karpenter feature next.

Node Auto Repair for unhealthy node handling

Karpenter has a **Node Auto Repair** (**NAR**) feature that detects when a node is unhealthy. When an unhealthy node is found, Karpenter replaces it automatically. When NAR is enabled, Karpenter monitors the condition of each node. If a node's status shows certain unhealthy conditions for an extended time (i.e., for 10 or 30 minutes, depending on the failure type), Karpenter will forcibly terminate and replace that node, as shown in *Figure 10.2*.

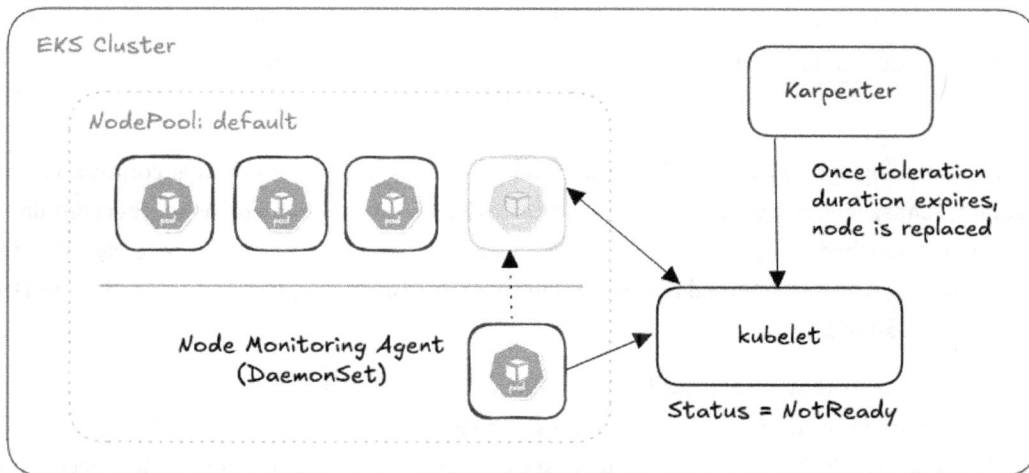

Figure 10.1 – NAR in action, replacing a node that has been NotReady for too long

NAR relies on signals of node health from either the built-in kubelet conditions or additional ones reported by a monitoring agent such as **AWS Node Monitoring Agent** or **Node Problem Detector**. Karpenter has toleration thresholds for unhealthy node conditions. When these tolerations are exceeded, Karpenter considers the node unhealthy and triggers the repair.

The following tables show exactly which conditions trigger automatic repair and their corresponding toleration durations:

Type	Status	Toleration Duration
Ready	False	30 minutes
Ready	Unknown	30 minutes

Table 10. 2 – Kubelet node conditions

The kubelet's Ready condition is the most fundamental health check. When a node reports Ready: False or Ready: Unknown for 30 consecutive minutes, it indicates that the kubelet can't communicate properly with the API server or has encountered critical internal errors that prevent it from accepting new workloads.

Type	Status	Toleration Duration
AcceleratedHardwareReady	False	10 minutes
StorageReady	False	30 minutes
NetworkingReady	False	30 minutes
KernelReady	False	30 minutes
ContainerRuntimeReady	False	30 minutes

Table 10.3 – Node monitoring agent conditions

Node monitoring agents extend this health checking by reporting more granular conditions. For instance, ContainerRuntimeReady: False indicates that Docker, containerd, or another container runtime has crashed or become unresponsive. Similarly, AcceleratedHardwareReady: False detects GPU or other accelerated hardware failures that typically require faster remediation (10 minutes instead of 30).

When NAR detects that a node has breached one of these toleration durations, it forcefully terminates the node by setting the NodeClaim's terminationGracePeriod to 0s, bypassing the standard graceful drain procedures we discussed earlier. This aggressive approach is necessary because unhealthy nodes often can't complete normal drain operations.

For example, a node with a crashed container runtime can't cleanly stop pods. NAR performs a hard deletion without coordinating replacement capacity first, triggering the same forceful termination flow that applies to any node deletion without a grace period.

Preventing cascading failures

But what happens in scenarios where there's a network partition? If a single **Availability Zone (AZ)** experiences a partition, a significant portion of your cluster may start reporting unhealthy Ready: Unknown conditions. Should Karpenter forcefully tear down this entire AZ during the outage?

To prevent this scenario, Karpenter includes a critical safety mechanism: **it will not perform repairs if more than 20% of nodes in a NodePool are unhealthy simultaneously.** This threshold prevents cascading failures where widespread infrastructure issues trigger mass node termination that could destabilize the entire cluster. When the 20% threshold is exceeded, Karpenter assumes something broader is wrong and stops automated repair, allowing operators to investigate and resolve the underlying cause.

Enabling NAR

To enable NAR in your cluster, you need to do the following:

- Deploy a node monitoring agent to surface extended health conditions beyond the kubelet's basic Ready check
- Enable the NodeRepair=true feature gate in your Karpenter deployment

Once enabled, NAR operates automatically without additional configuration, monitoring nodes and replacing unhealthy ones based on the toleration thresholds shown in the preceding table.

Let's see how this Karpenter feature works with the next hands-on lab.

Hands-on lab: NAR in action

During this hands-on lab, you're going to deploy an application to the cluster, wait for Karpenter to launch a node, and then cause that node to go NotReady for a long period of time. When this happens, Karpenter should react and launch a replacement node to make the application ready again. To begin, let's enable the NodeRepair feature so we can see Karpenter in action.

1. Enable the NodeRepair feature

The NAR feature is not enabled by default; therefore, you need to change the `NodeRepair` feature gate to `true` to enable it. To do so, open a new terminal and run the following command:

```
$ kubectl -n karpenter get deployment karpenter -o yaml | sed
's|NodeRepair=false|NodeRepair=true|' | kubectl apply -f -
```

This command will change the `FEATURE_GATES` environment variable and will roll out the Karpenter controller pods with the new setting. To check that Karpenter is up and running, run the following command:

```
$ watch kubectl get pods -n karpenter
```

Once the new pods are running, make sure you're in the `chapter10/noderepair` folder from the GitHub repository, and run the following command to deploy the sample application:

```
$ kubectl apply -f .
```

After waiting around three to four minutes for the new node to be ready, check that the application is up and running with this command:

```
$ watch kubectl get pods
```

Let's do one more check before we test the NRA feature.

2. Check that the Node Monitoring Agent is running

Now that we have the application up and running, let's first confirm that we have the **Node Monitoring Agent (NMA)** running in the new node.

> **Note**
>
> AWS uses the Node Monitoring Agent to detect failure conditions on the node. Other cloud providers may use other agents, including the **Node Problem Detector (NPD)**.

In our setup, the NMA has been installed through Terraform when creating the EKS cluster. To be more specific, you can find the following snippet in the `main.tf` file, where we added it as an add-on to the cluster:

```
module "eks" {
  ...
  cluster_addons = {
```

```
...
eks-node-monitoring-agent = {
  most_recent = true
}
```

You should have three instances of the agent running in the cluster. To confirm it, run this command:

```
$ kubectl get pods -l app.kubernetes.io/name=eks-node-monitoring-agent -n
kube-system
```

You should see something like this—one pod for the Karpenter node and two for the managed node group nodes:

```
eks-node-monitoring-agent-6lzxr 1/1 Running 0 15m31s
eks-node-monitoring-agent-wsv4x 1/1 Running 0 15m31s
eks-node-monitoring-agent-x5nr2 1/1 Running 0 3m46s
```

Now it's time to inject a failure into the node to see how Karpenter handles it.

3. Inject a failure into the node

To inject a failure into a node, we are going to use a script that will stop the containerd service on the node, preventing any containers from running properly. This will force the node to go to NotReady.

So, to force the node to be malfunctioning, run the following command:

```
$ ./fail.sh
```

Wait around three minutes to see the node change its status to NotReady. You can run the following command to monitor it:

```
$ watch kubectl get nodes
```

To avoid the replacement node failing, let's remove the pod we created using the preceding script so that we make sure that our replacement node doesn't fail:

```
$ kubectl delete pod debug-kill-containerd --force
```

After a few seconds, the pod should be removed.

4. Wait for Karpenter to replace the node

This will require you to have a bit of patience. As mentioned before, NRA needs to wait for 30 minutes to consider that the node won't recover from a NotReady status. So, I recommend you avoid deploying any other workload to the cluster, and open a new terminal with the following command running to watch the Karpenter logs:

```
$ kubectl -n karpenter logs -l app.kubernetes.io/name=karpenter --all-
containers=true -f --tail=20
```

After the 30-minute threshold has passed, you should see that Karpenter will start to react with log messages like this:

```
..."annotated nodeclaim",...,"controller":"node.health"...
..."tainted node",...,"controller":"node.termination"...
..."found provisionable pod(s)",...
```

Notice that Karpenter starts to remove the node, and immediately after, launches a replacement node so that kube-scheduler has a place to schedule the pods that were running on the failed node.

> **Note**
>
> As mentioned before, at the time of writing this book, NRA is in alpha, and you need to enable it. In the future, the implementation details might change, so always check the Karpenter docs (https://karpenter.sh/docs/concepts/disruption/#node-auto-repair) to see if you'll need to do something else to use this feature.

Alright, it's time to continue with the next section to explore how to upgrade Karpenter.

Upgrading Karpenter

Upgrading Karpenter in a Kubernetes cluster must be done with planning and caution. Karpenter is a critical component. It actively controls node lifecycles, so an improper upgrade could potentially disrupt workloads or cause cost surprises. In this section, we'll outline a few considerations that you should evaluate during an upgrade.

1. Pre-upgrade checks

First and foremost, start by reading the release notes of the version you plan to upgrade to, as well as the upgrade guide (https://karpenter.sh/docs/upgrading/upgrade-guide/) for any special steps. The official upgrade guide compiles known breaking changes and required actions for specific version jumps.

Pay close attention to changes in CRD versions. If you are making a CRD upgrade, follow the dedicated migration guide associated with that version. In general, you should not skip multiple minor versions during an upgrade. For example, do not jump from 0.32 straight to 0.36 without reading intermediate changes; it's recommended to go through each minor version sequentially to reduce the blast radius of changes.

Validate IAM permissions for the new version before upgrading. New releases sometimes require additional permissions (for AWS new EC2 APIs, etc.). The upgrade guide or release notes will mention this. Also, check if there are new CRDs or changes to existing ones.

It's wise to back up your Karpenter configuration in Git; that is, export all your NodePool and NodeClass objects. Having these as YAML manifests in Git is a good practice anyway. This way, if something goes wrong, you can easily restore or reapply settings.

2. Stage the upgrade

Test the upgrade in a staging environment that mirrors production. In staging, you might simulate workloads and see how Karpenter behaves after upgrading. Running a few tests, such as scaling up a deployment or forcing a drift by changing a NodePool field, can give confidence. It's also worth noting that metrics and alarms should be configured in staging so that it's clear whether there are any regressions between versions.

3. Upgrade process

The actual upgrade is typically done via Helm. Karpenter is stateless, so it can be safely interrupted without data loss. As a result, upgrading the controller usually just involves replacing the deployment with the newest image.

It's important to consider the time you are performing the upgrade. During the brief period Karpenter is restarting, no new scale-ups will happen. Generally, the hand-off period between versions should be nearly instant (around 10s for the lease hand-off to occur); however, if there is an issue with the latest version, you may block all scale-ups until you roll back. For this reason, I recommend that you upgrade Karpenter during a **maintenance window** if you have one, or at a low-traffic time. Leverage the Kubernetes deployment upgrade strategy to roll out the new pods.

After deploying the new version, monitor the Karpenter controller logs and metrics closely. Look for any errors on startup (e.g., an inability to start webhooks or CRD schema issues). If you see errors about webhooks failing, perhaps the new image couldn't start the webhook server. For more specific and up-to-date advice, always consider checking Karpenter's troubleshooting guide at `https://karpenter.sh/docs/troubleshooting/`.

4. Post-upgrade verification

After the upgrade completes, verify that Karpenter is functioning correctly. Check the controller logs (using the alias we created before) for any errors or warnings:

```
$ kl
```

Deploy a small test workload that requires new node provisioning to confirm Karpenter can successfully launch nodes. Additionally, check that existing `NodePools` and `NodeClaims` report healthy status conditions, as described earlier in this chapter.

It's helpful to keep the previous version's manifest handy for a rollback. If you encounter a severe issue (e.g., the new Karpenter version starts deleting nodes erroneously or crashes repeatedly), you should roll back quickly. **However, rollbacks when CRDs have changed carry significant risk and deserve careful consideration.**

When you upgrade Karpenter, the CRDs often receive updates that add new fields, modify validation rules, or change behaviors. If you configure these new fields and then roll back to an older version that doesn't recognize them, that configuration data is lost. The older controller simply ignores fields it doesn't understand.

Some CRD changes involve structural modifications or field migrations where data gets transformed during upgrade. Rolling back after these transformations can result in permanent data loss if the older version can't interpret the new structure. Usually, minor version rollbacks (e.g., v1.1 → v1.0) work because Kubernetes controllers ignore unknown fields, but major version rollbacks may be impossible without manual CRD manipulation or complete object recreation.

Frequent upgrades, ideally tracking within 1-2 minor versions of the latest release, reduce the surface area of changes in any single upgrade. **Don't wait too long between upgrades.** The more frequently you upgrade, the less painful it becomes. Each upgrade involves smaller incremental changes, reducing the risk of compatibility issues and making problems easier to diagnose when they do occur. This principle applies broadly to software maintenance. Incremental updates are safer and more manageable than large version jumps.

In conclusion, treat Karpenter upgrades as a mini-project: plan, test, execute, and verify. Use a CI/CD pipeline to automate applying the Helm chart and running post-deployment validations. To enrich these validations, let's explore which Karpenter metrics are key to monitoring in a production environment, and how you can access them using Grafana.

Observability and metrics

Operating Karpenter at scale requires you to have a good level of observability. You need to know what it's doing under the hood. Fortunately, Karpenter exposes a wealth of Prometheus metrics to give you the insight you need to operate it in production.

In this section, we'll cover the important metrics that Karpenter emits, alongside the use cases where you need them. I won't cover every metric that the controller emits, but the key ones will get mentioned. Most of the metrics that I'll cover are going to be aligned with the topics we explored earlier in this chapter.

> **Note**
>
> If you want to check the latest version of the metrics list that the Karpenter controller emits, please visit the official docs at `https://karpenter.sh/docs/reference/metrics/`.

Cluster resource efficiency metrics

Karpenter exposes several metrics that help you understand how efficiently your cluster uses resources, identify cost optimization opportunities, and monitor overall cluster health. The following metrics will help you track resource utilization and capacity management:

- **Cluster resource utilization**: To get the percentage of the cluster's allocatable (reserved) CPU/memory currently requested by pods, you can refer to the metric called `karpenter_cluster_utilization_percent`. It essentially measures overall cluster resource reservation.

  A lower value (e.g., consistently <50%) indicates under-utilization. The cluster has unreserved capacity that could potentially be eliminated to save costs. This should indicate to you that Karpenter's consolidation algorithm isn't acting on the nodes. This could be for a number of reasons, including: 1) A misconfiguration of consolidation settings, 2) Too few instance types specified in the `NodePool`, or 3) A bug in Karpenter. In practice, you'd want to see this metric not so low that you're wasting resources, and as high as possible (i.e., >90% utilization is great) as long as Karpenter is able to spin up nodes fast enough. For example, if cluster reservation hovers around 30% for long periods, it might signal an opportunity for consolidation (removing underutilized nodes), whereas if it regularly peaks near 100%, you may need to allow Karpenter to add more nodes or increase NodePool limits to handle the load.

Keep in mind that this metric reflects resource request utilization, not actual resource consumption. If your applications have poorly configured resource requests—either over-provisioned or under-provisioned—this metric becomes misleading. A cluster showing 90% utilization based on requests might actually have nodes running at 40% actual CPU usage if requests are inflated. Karpenter can only optimize node provisioning based on what pods request, not what they actually need.

- **Scaling activity**: To track how many nodes Karpenter has created and terminated in total (labeled by NodePool), you can use the metrics karpenter_nodes_created_total and karpenter_nodes_terminated_total. These metrics include a reason label that provides insight into why nodes were created or terminated. For example, provisioned for nodes created to satisfy pending pods, or expired, drifted, empty, or underutilized for terminated nodes based on the specific disruption trigger. This reason label is valuable for understanding scaling patterns and diagnosing whether node churn is due to consolidation, drift detection, expiration policies, or other factors.

Steadily increasing the metric for ..._created_total alongside matching increases in ..._terminated_total indicates node churn. Occasional node creations/terminations are expected as workloads fluctuate, but a high rate of churn might signal overly aggressive consolidation.

You can watch these metrics to ensure Karpenter isn't "thrashing" nodes unnecessarily. For instance, if you notice Karpenter creating and terminating dozens of nodes daily, you might investigate your consolidation settings or workload scheduling to find a more stable balance. On the other hand, a lack of any node terminations, despite low utilization, could mean consolidation is disabled or being blocked (e.g., by PDBs), leaving savings on the table.

- **Consolidation decisions:** When Karpenter performs consolidation decisions, it fires a metric called karpenter_voluntary_disruption_decisions_total. This metric tracks any time Karpenter makes a voluntary disruption decision and is labeled by reason (like the ones we explored before), which can be drifted, underutilized, or empty too. To specifically monitor consolidation activity, you can filter for reason="underutilized" or reason="empty", or use drifted as a reason to monitor drifted nodes.

  Essentially, it increments when Karpenter decides to terminate a node voluntarily (e.g., to eliminate idle capacity). A higher value here (especially a steady increase over time) indicates Karpenter is actively consolidating the cluster by terminating unnecessary nodes, a positive sign for cost optimization. A low or zero value, in contrast, might indicate that consolidation isn't happening even if the cluster has idle resources.

  As an example, you might observe this metric jump whenever a daily batch job completes: Karpenter could decide to remove several now-empty nodes (reflected by increments in the "deletion" decision count), which confirms that it's proactively reducing waste. If this metric remains flat while your cluster utilization is low, it may alert you to investigate why Karpenter isn't consolidating (ensuring consolidationPolicy is set appropriately and no policies are blocking node termination).

- **NodePool capacity usage:** Karpenter exposes metrics that show you the resource usage of a NodePool (karpenter_nodepools_usage) and the limit set on the NodePool (karpenter_nodepools_limit). By taking the ratio of these two values, you can **determine how "utilized"** a NodePool is. Particularly, you can tell if a NodePool's utilization is near 100%, where it can't provision any more resources.

  The one ending with ..._usage reports the total resources currently provisioned (i.e., CPU, memory, ephemeral storage, etc.), labeled per NodePool, while ..._limit is the maximum allowed resources for that NodePool. The ratio of usage to limit is crucial for cost control. When a NodePool's reservation approaches 100% of its limit, Karpenter will stop launching new nodes for that NodePool. It's wise to keep usage well below the limit under normal conditions. For example, one could alert if a NodePool exceeds ~80% of its capacity for a sustained period. This will warn you that you're nearing the cap and should consider raising the limit or adding capacity.

  For example, imagine you set a NodePool limit of 100 CPU cores and, over time, nodepools_usage creeps up to ~95 cores. At that point, any new workload requiring more than 5 cores would remain unscheduled.

- **Hourly node cost and instance availability**: Karpenter provides pricing insight metrics such as `karpenter_cloudprovider_instance_type_offering_price_estimate`, which estimates the hourly cost of each instance type by capacity type and zone. This metric is called an "estimate" not because the value is uncertain, but because it may not reflect actual costs for several reasons: Spot prices fluctuate in real time and the metric uses a point-in-time value, and it doesn't account for any account-level discounts (such as Reserved Instances, Savings Plans, or enterprise agreements) that would reduce your actual billing costs.

  While this metric can be useful for rough cost calculations, such as multiplying running nodes by their hourly price, it's primarily used internally by Karpenter for scheduling decisions when selecting the most cost-effective instance types.

  For operational monitoring, the `karpenter_cloudprovider_instance_type_offering_available` metric is often more valuable. This metric tracks instance type pool availability over time for each instance type, capacity type (On-Demand/Spot), and AZ combination. When you encounter ICE errors, this metric helps you identify which specific instance type/zone/capacity combinations are experiencing availability issues. Over time, patterns in this data can inform adjustments to your `NodePool`'s instance type requirements. For example, if certain instance types consistently show low availability in particular zones, you can deprioritize them or exclude those zones from selection.

While resource utilization metrics help you understand how efficiently your cluster uses capacity, the next set of metrics focuses on your workload and Karpenter's operational performance and reliability.

Provisioning reliability and performance metrics

It's important to monitor how quickly a node becomes available to workloads and how the entire provisioning pipeline performs end to end. The following metrics will help you gain better visibility about reliability and performance:

- **Pod startup time**: To measure how long it takes for a pod to go from creation to actually running on a node, you can refer to the metric called `karpenter_pods_startup_duration_seconds`.

  Shorter durations are better. This means Karpenter was able to spin up a node and get the pod scheduled quickly. If this metric's values start creeping up, it indicates pods are waiting longer for capacity. For example, if you normally see pods scheduled in ~60–90 seconds but now many are taking 5+ minutes, something has slowed down the provisioning flow. Possible causes include cloud infrastructure delays (instance spin-up times can vary), larger container images pulling on the new nodes, running out of IP addresses, or insufficient capacity requiring retries.

In practice, you can use this metric to set SLOs for scaling (e.g., "90% of pods start within 2 minutes"). Any significant deviation might signal the need for intervention. If your pod startup time metric is consistently high (several minutes), it's a sign to investigate. Check if Karpenter is struggling to find a fitting instance type, if there are networking issues delaying node readiness, or if perhaps the cluster is at capacity and hitting limits.

- **Pending pods queue:** The `karpenter_scheduler_queue_depth` metric tracks the number of pods that are currently waiting to be scheduled by Karpenter's internal scheduler. This represents pods that Karpenter has determined are eligible for scheduling but are awaiting node capacity.

This metric only includes pods that Karpenter considers eligible for scheduling. If Karpenter determines a pod isn't eligible, that pod won't appear in this queue depth metric—for example, if no NodePool can satisfy pod requirements, or because it has scheduling constraints that no configuration can meet. The total number of pending pods on the cluster may be higher than this metric indicates. **This metric is specifically designed to monitor the performance of Karpenter's scheduler, not to count all pending pods in the cluster.**

Ideally, this value stays at 0, or spikes only briefly as Karpenter recognizes pending pods and launches new nodes. However, sustained high queue depth requires investigation. Rather than alarming on any non-zero value, which could fire spuriously during brief provisioning windows, monitor the rate of change over time. If the queue depth is consistently growing or decreasing too slowly (indicating Karpenter isn't keeping up with demand), that's the signal to investigate.

For example, if `queue_depth` is growing and at the same time you see that the `NodePool` usage has hit its limit or `cloudprovider_errors` is firing, it's likely Karpenter is unable to add capacity. For instance, Karpenter may be unable to add capacity if you hit your service quota for vCPUs or volumes; Karpenter node launches will fail. Or, Karpenter might be unable to add capacity if you hit a large number of ICE errors due to a lack of capacity in the pools.

- **Node launch versus registration**: Karpenter provides metrics that indicate counts of NodeClaims that have hit different lifecycle stages: launched, registered, and initialized. These are tracked under karpenter_nodeclaims_created_total, karpenter_nodes_created_total, and status condition transition metrics, respectively.

  As discussed in *Chapter 8*, when Karpenter provisions capacity, it first creates a NodeClaim and launches the cloud instance (the "launched" stage). Once that instance boots up and the node object registers with the Kubernetes API server, it reaches the "registered" stage. Finally, when all initialization steps complete, the node reaches the "initialized" stage. Monitor this by comparing rate(karpenter_nodeclaims_created_total[5m]) minus rate(karpenter_nodes_created_total[5m]). If this difference remains positive and significant, something is wrong—for example, networking issues, IAM permission problems preventing kubelet registration, boot script failures, or image errors.

  Rather than alerting on the absolute difference between cumulative counters, monitor the karpenter_nodeclaims_terminated_total metric with reason="registration_timeout". This reason label specifically indicates that a NodeClaim failed its liveness check, meaning it didn't reach registration within Karpenter's expected timeout window.

  When you see registration timeouts, check the Karpenter controller logs and describe the affected NodeClaims to diagnose the root cause. Often, this reveals IAM role issues, subnet connectivity problems, or user data script failures that prevent the kubelet from successfully starting and registering with the API server.

- **Status condition state:** Karpenter exposes detailed metrics about the current state of its custom resources through status condition metrics. These are extremely useful for understanding the health of your cluster and diagnosing issues in real time. Let's explore some of the key metrics.

  The operator_nodeclaim_status_condition_count reports the current number of NodeClaims in specific condition states, labeled by name, namespace, type (e.g., Launched, Registered, Initialized, Ready), status (True/False/Unknown), and reason. This metric provides an instant snapshot of your cluster's health. For example, you can monitor how many NodeClaims are currently in the Ready=False state, which directly indicates unhealthy nodes.

  The operator_nodeclaim_status_condition_current_status_seconds tracks how long each NodeClaim has been in its current condition state. This is critical for detecting stuck nodes. For instance, if a NodeClaim remains as Registered=Unknown for more than 5 minutes, it likely indicates a node initialization problem.

The `operator_nodeclaim_status_condition_transition_seconds` measures how long `NodeClaims` spent in a given state before transitioning to the next state. This helps you understand performance characteristics of your provisioning pipeline—for example, how long it typically takes nodes to go from `Launched=True` **to** `Registered=True`, which reveals network and kubelet startup performance.

The `operator_nodeclaim_status_condition_transitions_total` counts the total number of transitions for each condition type and status. This helps identify churn. If you see frequent transitions between `Ready=True` and `Ready=False`, it indicates nodes are flapping between healthy and unhealthy states.

Similar metrics exist for `NodePools` (`operator_nodepool_status_condition_*`) and `EC2NodeClasses` (`operator_ec2nodeclass_status_condition_*`), allowing you to monitor the health and state transitions of your entire Karpenter configuration hierarchy.

These status condition metrics complement the earlier troubleshooting section on debugging with status conditions. While `kubectl describe` shows you the current state of individual resources, these metrics aggregate that information across your entire cluster, making it easy to spot patterns and detect issues at scale.

- **Cloud provider API errors:** Karpenter exposes a metric to see the total number of errors returned from cloud provider calls: `karpenter_cloudprovider_errors_total`. In Karpenter's architecture, "cloud provider" refers to the abstraction layer that implements core operations for instances. For AWS, this includes operations such as launching EC2 instances, terminating them, or querying instance details.

  Under normal operation, this should stay at 0 or near zero. Any spike in `cloudprovider_errors_total` means Karpenter encountered a failure when interacting with the cloud. Common reasons are hitting resource limits, permission issues, or transient API outages.

  When this metric increments, Karpenter typically emits events or logs describing the error. However, there are cases where errors are silently ignored if they represent no-ops. For example, if Karpenter attempts to delete an instance that's already been terminated, this won't generate a log or event since the desired state is already achieved. The error doesn't add operational value; it's simply confirming the instance is gone.

  If you notice this climbing, it's often a sign that manual intervention is needed. For instance, a burst of errors with reason `VolumeLimitExceeded` or `CPUQuotaExceeded` indicates your AWS account limits have been reached. You'd need to request a quota increase or adjust `NodePool` zones/instance types.

It's important to distinguish between degradation and total failures. For example, if one `NodePool` or instance type fails but others succeed, it's a partial degradation. Conversely, persistent errors with no capacity provisioned mean a total block. Imagine Karpenter is trying to launch spot instances, but AWS has none available. You would see the error count rise labeled with `InsufficientInstanceCapacity` while no capacity would be provisioned. In summary, `cloudprovider_errors_total` is an early warning for when Karpenter's requests to the cloud are failing.

Some of the metrics discussed are featured in Karpenter's recommended monitoring dashboards. In fact, the Karpenter project provides pre-built Grafana dashboards that visualize these key metrics for you. These dashboards include panels for cluster utilization, `NodePool` capacity, provisioning latency, and more. In the next section, we'll walk through deploying a default Prometheus and Grafana stack and loading these Karpenter dashboards.

Hands-on lab: Deploy the Karpenter Grafana dashboard

In this hands-on lab, we will deploy Prometheus and Grafana on an Amazon EKS cluster. You will then configure Prometheus to scrape Karpenter's metrics and set up Grafana dashboards to visualize those metrics.

First, add the necessary Helm chart repositories:

```
$ helm repo add prometheus-community https://prometheus-community.github.io/helm-charts
$ helm repo add grafana https://grafana.github.io/helm-charts
```

You've added the official Helm charts for Prometheus (which includes `kube-prometheus-stack`) and Grafana.

Now deploy the Prometheus and Grafana stack via the `kube-prometheus-stack` Helm chart. This chart will create the namespace, install the Prometheus Operator, Prometheus server, Alertmanager, and Grafana:

```
$ helm install prometheus prometheus-community/kube-prometheus-stack
--namespace monitoring --create-namespace
```

By default, the chart also comes with a collection of Kubernetes monitoring dashboards and alerting rules for your cluster.

Karpenter exposes its metrics in Prometheus format at a metrics endpoint (default :8080/metrics on the Karpenter service). We need to instruct Prometheus to scrape this endpoint. The kube-prometheus-stack uses ServiceMonitor CRDs for discovering targets. So, we'll create or enable a ServiceMonitor for Karpenter. Make sure you're in the /chapter10 folder from the GitHub repository for the book, and run the following command:

```
$ kubectl apply -f servicemonitor.yaml
```

After enabling the ServiceMonitor, Prometheus will begin scraping Karpenter's metrics. You should eventually see metrics such as karpenter_build_info (build/version info) being collected.

Let's confirm that the Prometheus server is successfully scraping Karpenter. The Prometheus UI is not exposed externally by default, so we'll expose it to use it locally. Open a new terminal and run the following:

```
$ kubectl -n monitoring port-forward svc/prometheus-kube-prometheus-
prometheus 9090:9090
```

In a web browser, go to http://localhost:9090. Navigate to **Status > Target health** in the UI (or /targets). You should see a target for Karpenter's metrics (it may appear as the Karpenter service in the list of scrape targets). Ensure its state is **UP**, indicating Prometheus is successfully scraping it.

With the Prometheus server collecting data, we can now visualize Karpenter metrics in Grafana. The kube-prometheus-stack already installed Grafana for us. We'll use kubectl port-forward to access it and then import dashboards. Open a new terminal and run the following:

```
$ kubectl -n monitoring port-forward svc/prometheus-grafana 3000:80
```

This forwards your local port, 3000, to the Grafana service (which by default listens on port 80 inside the cluster). Now you can reach Grafana at http://localhost:3000 in a new browser window. To log in, specify the Grafana admin credentials. The username is admin. The password was generated and stored in a Kubernetes Secret when we installed the chart. Fetch it with the following:

```
$ kubectl get secret -n monitoring prometheus-grafana -o jsonpath="{.data.
admin-password}" | base64 --decode ; echo
```

Use this password to log in to Grafana.

Karpenter's community has created ready-to-use Grafana dashboards for visualizing Karpenter metrics. We can load these dashboards into Grafana by running the following commands (you can get the commands at /chapter10/dashboards.md in the GitHub repository to make it easier to copy/paste).

First, create the capacity dashboard:

```
$ curl -s https://karpenter.sh/preview/getting-started/getting-started-
with-karpenter/karpenter-capacity-dashboard.json -o karpenter-capacity-
dashboard.json
$ kubectl create configmap karpenter-capacity-dashboard \
  --from-file=karpenter-capacity-dashboard.json \
  --namespace monitoring
$ kubectl label configmap karpenter-capacity-dashboard \
  grafana_dashboard=1 \
  -n monitoring
```

Then, create the performance dashboard:

```
$ curl -s https://karpenter.sh/preview/getting-started/getting-started-
with-karpenter/karpenter-performance-dashboard.json -o karpenter-
performance-dashboard.json
$ kubectl create configmap karpenter-performance-dashboard \
  --from-file=karpenter-performance-dashboard.json \
  --namespace monitoring\
$ kubectl label configmap karpenter-performance-dashboard \
  grafana_dashboard=1 \
  -n monitoring
```

Make sure you have the terminal open with the Grafana service port-forwarded and open the following URL in a new browser window: `http://localhost:3000/dashboards`. You should see new dashboards under Grafana's dashboard list (for example, "Karpenter Capacity" and "Karpenter Performance").

Open one of these dashboards. You should see panels displaying Karpenter metrics—for instance, charts for Node Launches vs. Registrations, Node Pool Utilization vs. Limits, Pending Pod Counts, Provisioning Latency, and so on. Data should be present, populating the graphs.

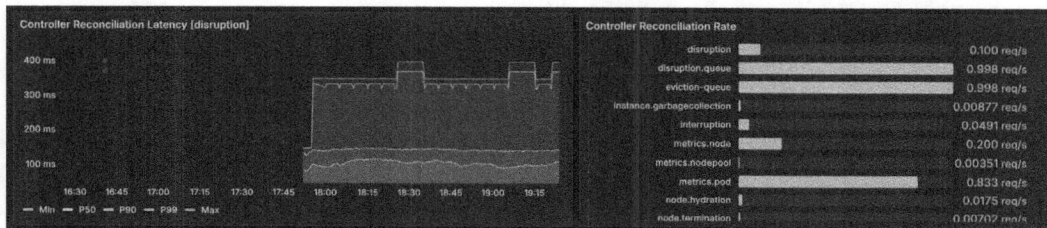

Figure 10.2 – Example of a Grafana dashboard monitoring Karpenter metrics

Each dashboard should reflect real-time data from your cluster. For example, the **Karpenter Capacity dashboard** will show the number of nodes Karpenter has provisioned, their CPU/Mem usage, and distribution across zones/instance types. The **Karpenter Performance dashboard** might show Karpenter controller metrics and any errors.

In this lab, you deployed a monitoring stack using Prometheus/Grafana and integrated it with Karpenter. You had to create a `ServiceMonitor` to scrape metrics from the Karpenter controller. You uploaded two community-maintained Karpenter dashboards and used them to explore how Karpenter responds to unschedulable pods, how many nodes it provisions or terminates, and whether it's operating as expected.

Summary

Managing a Kubernetes cluster with Karpenter is not just about enabling autoscaling but knowing how to monitor and operationalize autoscaling. It's about understanding how Karpenter's decisions are made, where things can go wrong, and how to detect and correct them before they disrupt your workloads or impact cluster costs.

Throughout this chapter, we explored common operational challenges: what causes sudden bursts in spending, why nodes might not consolidate when idle, how scheduling constraints or startup taints can lead to unnecessary overprovisioning, and what to look for when pods don't schedule. We showed how to use built-in Kubernetes commands, event inspection, and the AWS Labs log parsing tool (`1p4k`) to uncover hidden patterns in controller behavior.

We also explored the value of Prometheus metrics in tracking Karpenter's decisions. We grouped metrics by use case to help you understand what each metric tells you and when you should alarm and react to irregular behavior. Then, we deployed a complete observability stack (Prometheus, ServiceMonitor, and Grafana) with pre-built dashboards to visualize that telemetry in action.

These dashboards are more than just pretty charts. They give you the ability to diagnose cluster inefficiencies, ensure consolidation is active, validate that your NodePool limits aren't being hit prematurely, and spot provisioning failures before they escalate. These are just scratching the surface. You can extend and tailor these dashboards to meet your specific needs. Moreover, together with structured logging, you now have a full toolkit for observability and troubleshooting.

In the next chapter, we shift from monitoring and troubleshooting to an only hands-on chapter. You'll apply everything you've learned so far by combining KEDA and Karpenter with very common use cases.

Part 4

Use Cases, Patterns, and Recommendations

At this point, you've learned about the mechanics of KEDA and Karpenter – how they work, how to configure them, and how to troubleshoot them. But knowing how the tools work is different from knowing how and when you can actually use them in your environment. This final part is about connecting all of that to common use cases and practical patterns.

We'll start by looking at common use cases where KEDA and Karpenter are a great fit: web applications that need to handle variable traffic, batch jobs that run based on events, GPU workloads where compute costs can get out of hand quickly, and how to cost-optimize your cluster further with proper rightsizing and compute flexibility. For each one, you'll learn about the specific considerations and best practices that make autoscaling work reliably.

Then we'll cover two patterns that come up constantly in production. The first is about shutting down non-production environments when nobody's using them, which sounds simple but has a lot of gotchas when you actually try to implement it. The second focuses on fault-tolerant workloads and why autoscaling works so much better when your applications can handle disruptions gracefully. If your workloads aren't there yet, you'll understand what needs to change and why it matters.

Finally, we'll wrap up with some broader thoughts on how to approach autoscaling – what to prioritize when you're setting up rules, how to balance complexity with effectiveness, and where the ecosystem is heading. By the end of this part, you'll have a clearer picture of how to apply everything you've learned to your specific situation.

This part has the following chapters:

11

Practical Use Cases for Autoscaling in Kubernetes

At this point, you've spent quite some time in the previous chapters exploring a lot of details about autoscaling in Kubernetes. You've learned the basics, you've explored how tools such as KEDA and Karpenter work, and I've shared several tips and tricks to help you get the most out of them. Now, it's time to bring all those lessons together with practical, hands-on examples. In this chapter, we'll spend time with the terminal, and you'll see how KEDA and Karpenter can help you build efficient and cost-optimized clusters automatically, growing and shrinking as demand shifts.

The focus here isn't just on completing the labs and copying/pasting the commands I've included. The focus is on understanding the impact these tools can have on different types of workloads and realizing the concrete benefits of autoscaling in real-world scenarios. For example, we'll explore distinct use cases that represent the most common scenarios where autoscaling delivers significant value:

- **Web applications:** We'll revisit the Monte Carlo PI simulation app—this time, scaling based on requests per second rather than CPU usage or latency, so that you can see how proactive scaling can prevent performance degradation before it impacts users
- **Batch jobs:** Using RabbitMQ-driven message processing, you'll learn how to protect long-running jobs from voluntary disruptions while still benefiting from efficient resource management
- **Compute cost optimization:** Through a systematic approach involving ARM-based instances, proper rightsizing, and spot instances, you'll learn how to achieve cost reductions without sacrificing performance

- **GPU-based workloads**: Finally, you'll deploy a PyTorch image classification model and explore the unique challenges of scaling GPU workloads, including bootstrap time optimization and custom scaling metrics

Throughout these labs, you'll see how different metrics drive scaling behavior, or how cluster resources can be optimized in real time. Each use case builds upon the previous one, with the aim of helping you understand how to apply autoscaling strategies to your own cluster(s). Bring your terminal back, as autoscaling labs are resuming next.

We will be covering the following topics in this chapter:

- Common workloads for autoscaling
- Use case 1: Web applications
- Use case 2: Batch jobs
- Use case 3: Compute cost optimization
- Use case 4: GPU-based workloads

Technical requirements

For this chapter, you'll continue using an Amazon EKS cluster. To avoid any problem, it's recommended to turn down any previous cluster you created, and instead create a new one from the template you'll find in this chapter. This is going to be the cluster you'll use from now on. You don't need to install any additional tools, as most of the commands are going to be run using kubectl and helm. You can find the YAML manifests for all resources you're going to create in this chapter in the chapter11 folder from the book's GitHub repository, which you already cloned in *Chapter 1*.

Common workloads for autoscaling

After spending quite some time exploring what autoscaling really means in a Kubernetes environment, let's put all the pieces of the puzzle together and start exploring how KEDA and Karpenter can work together to help you maintain an efficient Kubernetes cluster that grows and shrinks based on demand.

Although you can perfectly apply all the principles and practices you've learned so far from a variety of workloads, in this chapter, we're going to cover only the most common ones where we've seen these tools have a big impact on cluster efficiency.

But before we jump into those, let's make sure we have an EKS cluster up and running.

Hands-on lab: Create an EKS cluster with batteries included

Before we do any of the following labs in this chapter, we need to make sure we have a proper EKS cluster up and running with all the tools we'll need. We're going to continue using the same Terraform template we've been using in previous chapters, but with the addition of Karpenter, KEDA, k6, and Prometheus/Grafana add-ons deployed into the cluster.

I recommend that if you already have an Amazon EKS cluster running, destroy it using the cleanup. sh script, and create it again with the additional add-ons that you'll use for this chapter. We're going to keep it simple. Head back to the GitHub repository and change the directory to /chapter08:

```
$ cd chapter08/terraform
```

We've added specific files to deploy Karpenter, KEDA, k6, and Prometheus/Grafana add-ons in Terraform, but with a .txt extension file. So, let's remove that first with this command:

```
$ for f in *.tf.txt; do mv "$f" "${f%.txt}"; done
```

Now, you're ready to launch the cluster by running this command:

```
$ sh bootstrap.sh
```

Wait around 15 or 20 minutes, then update your .kubeconfig file to connect to the cluster by running the following command (change the eu-west-1 region if you're using a different one):

```
$ aws eks --region eu-west-1 update-kubeconfig --name kubernetes-
autoscaling
```

Confirm that you have access and that all the pods are running with this command:

```
$ kubectl get pods --all-namespaces
```

You finish this lab when you see all pods with a Running status.

Next, let's explore in detail the first common use case from the list.

Use case 1: Web applications

Let's start with the first example we used a few chapters ago to see autoscaling in action with a Monte Carlo PI simulation app. This time, to see Karpenter in action, we'll send more traffic than before to the application, and we'll scale based on the throughput (the number of requests per second). Moreover, as said before, we're going to use tools such as k6 to automate the load tests. **k6** is a tool designed to help you simulate how applications perform under heavy usage by generating load and tracking responses.

The information you get back will be more relevant in subsequent labs, but we want to start using it now to make the load test consistent.

The purpose of this first use case is to see KEDA adding more pods as the requests per second go up (I'll dive deeper into this topic in this lab). Karpenter then launches only the nodes needed at that precise moment, and that will continue to happen until the load test is complete. Then, when the pods are not needed, KEDA will scale down, making the nodes empty, so then Karpenter will remove them, making the cluster efficient. See *Figure 11.1* with all the components involved in this use case:

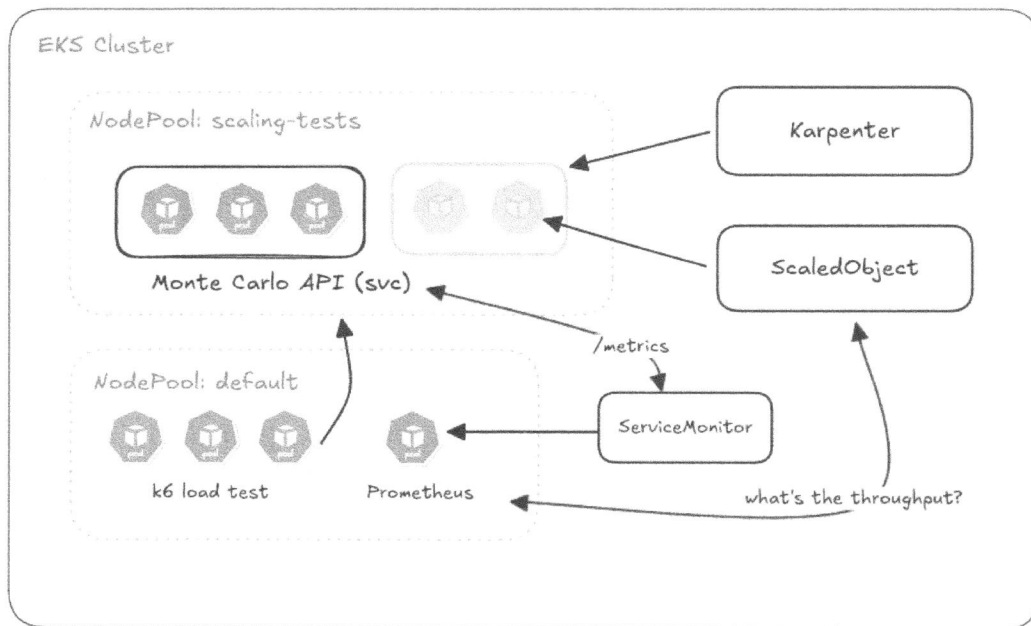

Figure 11.1 – Autoscaling a web app with KEDA and Karpenter

As you can see, there are quite a few components. Don't worry about them for now; we'll explore each of them in the next lab. For now, just notice that in addition to the Monte Carlo deployment, ScaledObject, and ServiceMonitor we used in *Chapter 4*, we're adding Karpenter with a dedicated NodePool for pods we'll test. We want to use a dedicated NodePool to avoid having pods not related to this application running in these nodes. This will avoid consolidation, removing pods that could impact the test results, such as removing k6 pods.

Let's see all of this in action in the next hands-on lab.

Hands-on lab: Autoscaling a web application

Go back to your terminal; it's time to see end-to-end autoscaling in action in Kubernetes with KEDA and Karpenter. By now, you should already have an EKS cluster with all the tools and components we'll use. We did that first so that we could focus on the relevant components to see this use case in action.

1. Deploy Karpenter NodePool

As we mentioned before, we're going to use a dedicated NodePool for the application we'll use in this chapter. You don't need to create a NodePool per workload. We're doing it this way for simplicity in these labs. So, for this lab, the NodePool has the following label:

```
metadata:
  labels:
    intent: scaling-tests
```

We'll then need to configure the pods accordingly to use this NodePool.

Go back to your terminal, and open the /chapter11/webapp folder:

```
$ cd chapter11/webapp
```

Create the dedicated NodePool with taints by running this command:

```
$ kubectl apply -f nodepool.yaml
```

To confirm that the NodePool is going to work, check its status by running this:

```
$ kubectl get nodepools,ec2nodeclass
```

You should see the default and scaling-tests NodePools, and the default EC2NodeClass with a value of True in the READY status column.

2. Deploy the application

With Karpenter ready to launch nodes, let's deploy the Monte Carlo application. In the same way as what we did in *Chapter 4*, the Deployment object does not define a replicas number because we want to avoid rewriting the number of replicas KEDA would set if we need to reapply the manifest. However, by default, Kubernetes will deploy one pod anyway. If ScaledObject is configured to have minReplicaCount: 0, then KEDA will remove this pod. For an HTTP-based workload, this might not be applicable or even real in a live environment.

To make sure the pod constraints match the dedicated NodePool, we configured nodeSelector, like this:

```
nodeSelector:
  intent: scaling-tests
```

Deploy the sample application by running this command:

```
$ kubectl apply -f montecarlopi.yaml
```

You should see one pod with a Pending status because the pod constraints don't match with any existing node, but they match with the scale tests NodePool. So Karpenter is already launching the new node for this application. You should see, in a matter of 30 seconds or less, a new NodeClaim being created. Check that's happening with this command:

```
$ kubectl get nodeclaim
```

Wait for two to three minutes, and you should see the new node and the pod running.

3. Deploy the KEDA scaling object

Before we dive into scaling the application, let's prepare the KEDA autoscaling rule. First, we need to create a ServiceMonitor to scrape all the metrics available from the application and send them to Prometheus. To do so, just run this command:

```
$ kubectl apply -f servicemonitor.yaml
```

Give it two to three minutes to become stable. If you'd like to confirm that it's working, you can do a port forward to expose the Prometheus service and explore the /targets endpoint. All the specific details about how to do it can be found in *Chapter 4*.

Next, create the KEDA ScaledObject with this command:

```
$ kubectl apply -f scaledobject.yaml
```

However, let's pause for a moment and explore what's different this time. Notice that the rule now looks like this:

```
...
metricName: http_requests_total
threshold: "25"
query: |
sum(rate(http_requests_total{namespace="default",pod=~"montecarlo-pi-.*"}
[2m]))
...
```

The query, the metric, and the threshold are different. Let's explore each of them individually:

- metricName: We're using the http_requests_total metric that the application is emitting. The Monte Carlo PI application was written in Go, and by using the Prometheus library, every time the application receives a request, it tracks the number of invocations it has received. If you go and explore the source code at chapter02/src/main.go in the GitHub repository, you'll see this:

```
httpRequestsTotal = prometheus.NewCounterVec(
    prometheus.CounterOpts{
        Name: "http_requests_total",
        Help: "Count of all HTTP requests",
    },
    []string{"code", "method"},
)
```

  Then, the ServiceMonitor collects all these data points and stores them in Prometheus so that we can use this data to scale.

- threshold: This is the number we're aiming for the application to handle across all its replicas, which, in this case, is 25 **requests per second** (**RPS**). We'll dive deeper into the rationale behind why I chose this number after exploring the query we're using in this scaling rule.

- query: It's using the metric exposed by the application, and it's using the rate() function to get the RPS per pod. Then, the query aggregates these values across all pods from the Monte Carlo deployment to use the total incoming load, and not just the load per pod.

To confirm that the KEDA autoscaling rule will work, wait around 30 seconds, then run this command:

```
$ kubectl describe hpa keda-hpa-montecarlo-pi-latency
```

You should see an event with a condition message like this:

```
the HPA was able to successfully calculate a replica count from external
metric ...
```

Before we continue with the lab, let's pause for a moment and think about why we're using a different metric to scale. First, I wanted you to see that KEDA can work with a variety of metrics, not just CPU, memory, or latency, which are very common. Second, scaling based on requests per second means that you can scale proactively before individual pods become overwhelmed. When you receive a spike of traffic, latency might not increase at the same rate, and when the metric crosses the desired threshold, it might already be too late to add more capacity.

But how do you decide which number to use as a threshold for RPS? Well, what's key here is that you know how much load a single pod can have. If you set a threshold of 25 RPS per pod, and with 2 pods, the application can collectively handle 60 RPS, KEDA will scale to 3 pods (60/25 = 2.4, rounded up to 3) to maintain optimal performance if the load increases. That's why it's important to run load tests constantly to tune in this number, which is what you're going to do next.

4. Run load test

As mentioned before, we're going to use k6 to script the load test and will run it in the Kubernetes cluster. Typically, the testing component should live outside of where the application is running. But for this lab, we're going to run it in the same cluster. Just please keep in mind that for a production setup, you need to run your load test components outside.

We've created a k6-script.js file with all the code that k6 will use to run the test. Please explore this file to see how the test is configured. So, let's upload this script to a ConfigMap by running this command:

```
$ kubectl create configmap k6-load-test-script --from-file=k6-script.js
```

Next, create the k6 load test job in Kubernetes with this command:

```
$ kubectl apply -f k6-load-test.yaml
```

This will create a CRD object that the k6 controller can manage and will launch a few pods to prepare the load test. Then, it will create a load test pod that will run the script we uploaded to the ConfigMap. You can explore what's happening by using this command:

```
$ kubectl logs -l k6_cr=montecarlo-load-test -f
```

What you're looking at here is the k6 logs showing the progress from the load test that will run for a few minutes. For now, you need to move to the next step. But the test is done. You'll see a report of the success and error rate, along with the latency numbers you got while the test was running, like this:

```
http_req_duration.......................................................:
avg=773.74ms min=7.79ms med=26.34ms max=3.95s p(90)=2.37s p(95)=2.84s
```

Now, let's monitor how HPA is adding more replicas, and Karpenter is adding more nodes.

5. See autoscaling in action

To see what's happening, open a new terminal and run this command:

```
$ watch kubectl get hpa,pod,nodeclaims
```

For instance, you'll see something like this for the HPA rule:

```
...  TARGETS          MINPODS MAXPODS REPLICAS
...  24521m/25 (avg) 1       10      6
```

Notice how the RPS starts to increase, going beyond the threshold of 25 RPS. The value shows as 24521m because Kubernetes reports metrics in milli-units (so 24,521m = 24.521). Next, additional replicas will be launched besides the ones that are already running. You're seeing KEDA and HPA in action. Also, because there's no capacity in the cluster, Karpenter will launch the capacity needed to scale the application. You can see how many nodes end up launching by looking at the NodeClaims created.

Once the test is finished, wait a moment to see what happens. Pods will be removed as the RPS is going to zero. This will cause some nodes to be empty, and then Karpenter will remove the nodes, and you'll be back to having the initial infrastructure you had when you started. This will take a while because of the advanced autoscaling configuration in HPA, scaling out as soon as possible, and being more conservative when scaling down.

You only launched the pods and nodes you needed, nothing else. Then, KEDA and Karpenter removed the resources created as there's no other workload running now.

6. Cleanup

That was it. Now, to make sure you have a full cleanup, run this command to force Karpenter to remove any node that's currently running:

```
$ kubectl delete -f montecarlopi.yaml
```

Wait for a few minutes, and you'll see how Karpenter's consolidation process will remove the empty nodes, scaling the data plane down to zero. Don't delete the NodePool as we're going to continue using it in the next lab.

Let's proceed now with the next use case to explore scaling to and from zero nodes.

Use case 2: Batch jobs

During this second use case, we're going to continue using the same hands-on lab used when showing how KEDA can scale jobs driven by messages from a RabbitMQ queue. During this lab, you'll also see Karpenter scaling down to zero nodes again. But this time, we'll add a protection mechanism for voluntary disruptions (i.e., consolidation or drift) to let jobs finish. See *Figure 11.2* with all the components involved in this use case.

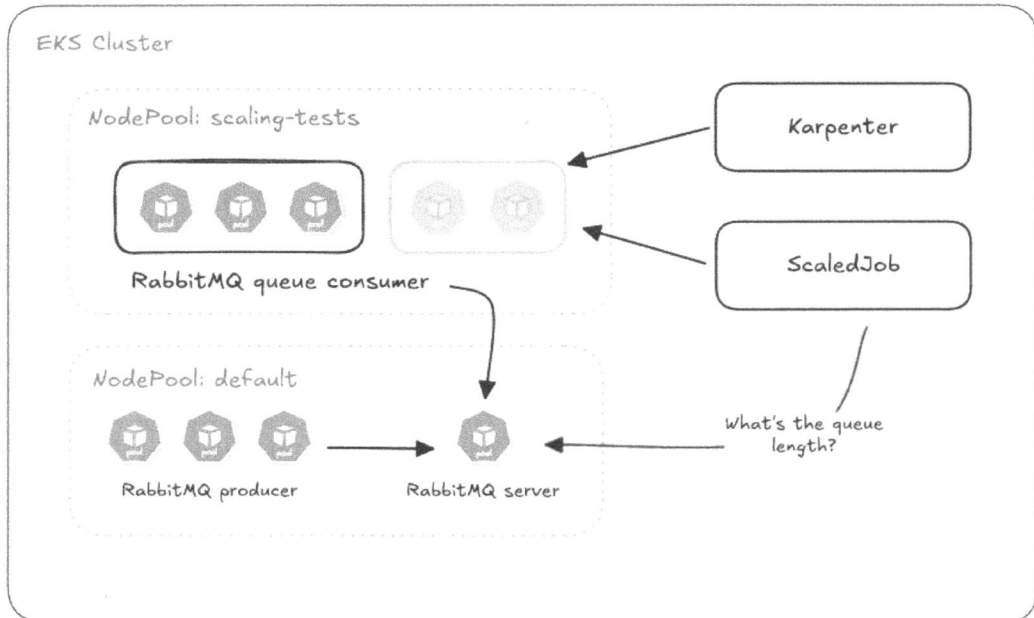

Figure 11.2 – Autoscaling a job workload with KEDA and Karpenter

As before, we'll explore each component from the diagram during the hands-on lab. But notice that in addition to a ScaledJob object from the *Chapter 4* lab, we're going to reuse the same NodePool as before because the protection mechanism is going to come from the pods, and not from a Karpenter NodePool.

Although during this lab we're focusing on data processing jobs, the same pattern could apply to machine learning training, continuous integration/delivery agents (i.e., GitLab, Jenkins, or GitHub action runners), and any other type of workload where you need to scale from/to zero.

Let's get back to the console; it's time for your next hands-on lab.

Hands-on lab: Autoscaling jobs

For this lab, we're going to use the same application we used in *Chapter 4* when we were exploring how to autoscale jobs with KEDA. However, in the current setup, there are no nodes available to run these jobs, so Karpenter must launch these nodes. But the added complexity here is that now we know that Karpenter can remove or relaunch nodes when these are being underutilized, which is fine, but at the same time, you would want the jobs running to finish what they're doing and not get interrupted (even if it's for the sake of optimizing the cluster resources).

So, let's go back to the terminal and explore how to autoscale jobs. If you don't have a cluster up and running, go back to the beginning of this chapter and create one with all the batteries included, as this lab assumes you have KEDA and Karpenter already installed.

1. Deploy the RabbitMQ server

Let's start by deploying a RabbitMQ server to your cluster by running these commands:

```
$ /common/rabbitmq.sh install
```

Wait around two minutes, and the RabbitMQ pod should be running. Notice that we're using nodeSelector.intent=apps to intentionally deploy RabbitMQ in nodes launched by the default Karpenter Nodepool, which has the intent: apps label.

When the RabbitMQ pods are running, proceed with the next step.

2. Deploy the message producer application

As mentioned before, we're going to use the same producer application we used in *Chapter 4*, but with a few changes, considering that Karpenter is in place now. Not that they're necessarily needed, but these changes are basically to make sure the application uses only nodes launched by Karpenter.

All the files we're going to use are in the /chapter11/job/ folder. Change the directory to that location and continue. So, for starters, we added nodeSelector and tolerations to use the scaling-tests NodePool, like this:

```
nodeSelector:
  intent: scaling-tests
tolerations:
- key: scaling-tests
  operator: Exists
```

Then, we changed the parameter of the messages to produce the following:

```
- name: MESSAGE_COUNT
  value: "1200"
```

Deploy the producer application, a Kubernetes job, that will run for a few seconds:

```
$ kubectl apply -f producer.yaml
```

Wait for Karpenter to launch a new node. Then, after around two minutes, you'll see the job with a Completed status. If you want to confirm that the messages have arrived at RabbitMQ, expose the service locally with this command:

```
$ kubectl port-forward svc/rabbitmq 15672:15672
```

Go to http://localhost:15672/#/queues/%2F/autoscaling in a browser. On the login screen, just enter user as the username and autoscaling for the password. You should see some queued messages as shown in *Figure 11.3*:

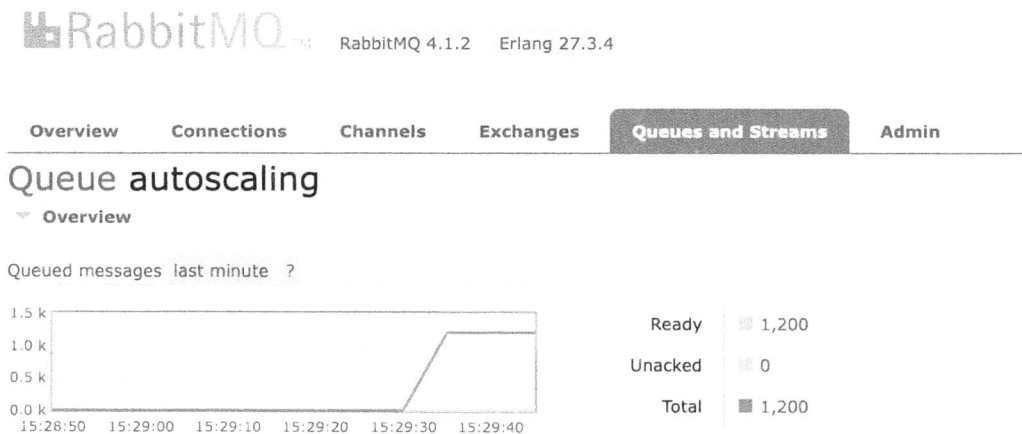

Figure 11.3 – Producer application was able to send messages to RabbitMQ

Keep in mind that this producer application can be run as many times as you want. We're simply generating messages for the consumer application to consume. So, if you want to see autoscaling in action a few times, you might want to deploy the producer application a few times, too.

Go to the next step to deploy the application responsible for consuming these messages.

3. Deploy the message consumer application

The consumer application is really a ScaledJob rule that, when there are messages in the queue to consume, will create the necessary Kubernetes jobs to consume those messages. For ScaledJob to connect to RabbitMQ, you need to first deploy a couple of auth resources:

- The Secret object to store the RabbitMQ password
- The TriggerAuthentication object to connect to RabbitMQ using the Secret object for the password

To create these objects, run the following command:

```
$ kubectl apply -f auth.yaml
```

The following resources we're going to create are the ScaledJob resource we mentioned before (named queue-job-consumer) and an additional Kubernetes job (named very-important-job) to showcase how you can protect these pods from any voluntary disruptions, such as Karpenter consolidation or drift. These two objects are defined in the consumer.yaml file.

Let's start with the queue-job-consumer object. We're not going to explore this resource in detail, as we already did in *Chapter 4*. So, we'll focus only on the additions for this lab.

First, the most important section is metadata. Here, we're defining the app: queue-job-consumer label that we will use to spread pods within availability zones. Additionally, the most important configuration is the annotations section. Here, the annotation we're adding is to tell Karpenter that these pods can't be evicted for voluntary disruptions. For instance, if Karpenter decides that the underlying node can't be replaced by a smaller one, it won't do it until these pods are no longer running. The following is the snippet I'm referring to:

```
metadata:
  labels:
    app: queue-job-consumer
  annotations:
    karpenter.sh/do-not-disrupt: "true"
```

The next important change we had to add to use the dedicated NodePool was to add the following nodeSelector and tolerations sections to both jobs:

```
nodeSelector:
  intent: scaling-tests
  karpenter.sh/capacity-type: on-demand
tolerations:
- key: scaling-tests
  operator: Exists
```

Then, for the consumer application only, we added a topology spread constraint to segregate the pods within different availability zones to avoid having to run all the needed pods in the same zone. The configuration looks like this:

```
topologySpreadConstraints:
- labelSelector:
    matchLabels:
      app: queue-job-consumer
  maxSkew: 1
  topologyKey: topology.kubernetes.io/zone
  whenUnsatisfiable: ScheduleAnyway
```

Notice that we're configuring a preferred affinity with ScheduleAnyway. In the case that one zone is down, Kubernetes can schedule the affected replicas into the other active zones.

The second job, called very-important-job, is launching a pod that will run for a certain period of time shorter than the producer application pods. The idea here is to force a consolidation event and see how the consumer application pods are not evicted because of the do-not-disrupt annotation. So, the important configuration for this job is the command we're running inside the container:

```
command: ['sh', '-c', 'echo A very important Job is
  running; sleep 60']
```

Now that you've explored the resources, we'll deploy both workloads to consume all the queued messages from RabbitMQ (if there are no messages, you won't see the same set of actions described in this lab). Let's do it by running this command:

```
$ kubectl apply -f consumer.yaml
```

You should see several pods with the `Pending` status and a few `NodeClaims` being created. Run the following command:

```
$ kubectl get nodeclaims
```

You should see that nodes are going to be spread within availability zones, and at least one of those nodes is much bigger than the others. For instance, you could have two `xlarge` nodes and one `4xlarge` node where the `very-important-job` pod should be running.

4. See autoscaling in action

Something similar to before is going to happen. New pods are going to be created by KEDA as there are still messages in the queue pending to be processed, and Karpenter will create the necessary nodes to run all these pods. Even though that's very interesting to observe, we want to focus our attention this time on how the `do-not-disrupt` annotation is protecting the consumer application pods when the `very-important-job` job is complete.

> **Note**
>
> In this hands-on lab, we're using the default `NodePool` that has `consolidationPolicy` set to `WhenEmptyOrUnderutilized`. This allowed us to force a voluntary disruption when we removed some pods. However, when you're working with batch jobs, you might want to consider using `WhenEmpty` instead, especially for long-running jobs or jobs that don't implement checkpointing. This will help you to keep disruption to a minimum.

So, wait for the pod from this job to run, then run the following command to see the events from all the `NodeClaims`:

```
$ sh explorenodeclaim.sh
```

You can explore the script we used, but basically, we're watching all events filtered by the `NodeClaim` objects. Look at them closely. Once `very-important-job` is complete, Karpenter is going to notice that there's an opportunity to optimize the existing nodes by replacing them with smaller ones. So, you'll see events such as the following:

```
... .. DisruptionBlocked ... Pod has "karpenter.sh/do-not-disrupt"
annotation ...
```

This is the proof that the annotation worked, and Karpenter respects any voluntary disruption. Therefore, it is a recommended practice to annotate your jobs this way to prevent their pods from being evicted. Once the consumer application has finished processing all the messages from the queue, Karpenter can proceed to optimize your nodes, so you'll see events like these:

```
... Node is deleting or marked for deletion
... Disrupting NodeClaim: Empty/Delete
... Instance is terminating
```

If you want to run only the scaling part again, you only need to run these commands:

```
$ kubectl delete -f consumer.yaml
$ kubectl apply -f producer.yaml
```

Wait around two minutes for all the messages to land, then run this:

```
$ kubectl apply -f consumer.yaml
```

You can repeat this as many times as you want. Play with the number of messages you send, the number of replicas you can create, and so on.

5. Cleanup

To clean all the resources you created from this lab, just run the following command:

```
$ kubectl delete -f .
```

Then, delete the RabbitMQ server with this command:

```
$ helm uninstall rabbitmq
```

Notice we're not deleting the `scaling-tests` NodePool as we'll keep using it.

Now, let's move to the next section to explore how to cost-optimize your cluster using Spot instances, ARM-based instances, and proper rightsizing.

Use case 3: Compute cost optimization

Now that we've explored how KEDA and Karpenter can help you autoscale web-based applications and job-based workloads, let's take a closer look at another common use case where Karpenter helps you to cost-optimize your compute costs in a cluster. We'll focus on what you can do with Karpenter, and how, by only making a few changes to the NodePool (and sometimes to your application), you can reduce the compute costs dramatically.

During the following lab, you'll start with a non-optimized workload so that you can see the cost reduction while you make the changes. You're going to use a visualization tool called eks-node-viewer, which shows you the efficiency of a cluster in terms of the allocated resources, the estimated monthly compute cost, and the hourly price, among other things. Then, we'll introduce optimizations such as using ARM-based instances, right-sizing overprovisioned pods, and using spot instances. You'll see how Karpenter's consolidation process will implement all these optimizations in real time.

This optimization path you're about to explore is the one we've seen many companies implement. Some follow the exact same path, others change the order due to many different reasons, but the result remains the same: cost-optimize the compute costs of their Kubernetes clusters.

Hands-on lab: Optimizing compute costs

Go back to your terminal and make sure you have your EKS cluster up and running. If not, you can go back to the first lab in this chapter and create it. Once you're ready, let's start by installing the eks-node-viewer tool.

1. Install eks-node-viewer

If you're using a Mac, you can install eks-node-viewer by simply running these two commands:

```
$ brew tap aws/tap
$ brew install eks-node-viewer
```

Then, skip the next paragraph and confirm that the tool is working.

If you're not using a Mac, then you need to install the tool manually. But before you can do that, you need to install the latest version of Go (the programming language). To do so, just head over to https://go.dev/doc/install and follow the instructions for your **operating system (OS)**. Once Go is installed, simply run the following command:

```
$ go install github.com/awslabs/eks-node-viewer/cmd/eks-node-viewer@latest
```

To confirm that the tool is working, run this command:

```
$ eks-node-viewer
```

You should see something like what is shown in *Figure 11.4*:

```
2 nodes (    1680m/3860m) 43.5% cpu ▇▇▇▇▇▇▇▇               $0.222/hour | $162.060/month
30 pods (0 pending 30 running 30 bound)

ip-10-0-31-122.eu-west-1.compute.internal cpu ▇▇▇▇▇      41% (15 pods) m4.large/$0.1110 On-Demand - Ready -
ip-10-0-6-22.eu-west-1.compute.internal   cpu ▇▇▇▇▇      46% (15 pods) m4.large/$0.1110 On-Demand - Ready -
●
←/→ page ● q: quit
```

Figure 11.4 – The eks-node-viewer tool showing nodes in an EKS cluster

As you can see, in the top-right corner, there's an hourly and monthly estimated cost of all the nodes from the EKS cluster. Leave this command running in a separate terminal, as you'll be monitoring it while completing this lab.

2. Deploy the sample application

Open a new terminal and change the directory to the /chapter11/cost-optimized folder. Then, explore the montecarlopi.yaml file. As you can see, it's the same application we've been using, but the only remarkable section is the requests one:

```
resources:
  requests:
    cpu: 1
    memory: 512Mi
```

Notice that all the pods will be requesting one whole CPU and 512 Mi of memory, which, for now, is fine. So, deploy the application by running this command:

```
$ kubectl apply -f montecarlopi.yaml
```

Nothing new should happen here; Karpenter will notice that there are 10 unscheduled pods, and will proceed to launch the node that kube-scheduler will use to schedule these pods. Rerun the eks-node-viewer tool in the terminal where you had it. But, this time, filter the nodes launched by the scaling-tests NodePool, like this:

```
$ eks-node-viewer -node-selector intent=scaling-tests
```

Take note of the estimated monthly cost. In our case, it is $479.347 because it launched one On-Demand node of the c6a.4xlarge type. Your result might differ, but either way, just take note of this cost, as we'll see how this will be reduced.

3. Change the NodePool to use ARM-based instances

The first change we're going to do to bring costs down is to allow our NodePool to launch ARM-based instances, which, in AWS, are Graviton-based instances. The reason is that, as we learned in previous chapters, when Karpenter launches On-Demand instances, the call it makes to the EC2 API is using the lowest-price allocation strategy. This means that from the list of instance types Karpenter sent in the call, EC2 will launch a new node of the type with the lowest price, and ARM-based instances tend to be cheaper than x86-based instances (i.e., c6a.4xlarge).

Additionally, we won't change anything in the application we deployed. Although you can add a constraint with nodeSelector or affinities asking specifically for ARM-based instances, the NodePool we're using doesn't support it yet.

So, open the file in /chapter11/webapp/nodepool.yaml and add arm64 to the list of kubernetes.io/arch requirements in the NodePool; it should look like this:

```
- key: kubernetes.io/arch
  operator: In
  values: ["amd64","arm64"]
```

Apply the changes by running this command (assuming your terminal is in the cost-optimized folder; otherwise, adapt it accordingly):

```
$ kubectl apply -f ../webapp/nodepool.yaml
```

Run the following command to read the Karpenter controller logs:

```
$ kubectl -n karpenter logs -l app.kubernetes.io/name=karpenter --all-containers=true -f --tail=20
```

Wait a few minutes for Karpenter to notice that you have added the arm64 architecture to the NodePool. You should see something like this in the logs:

```
… "message":"disrupting node(s)", …
reason":"underutilized","decision":"replace" …
```

We've stripped down the logs because we just wanted to confirm that the node was replaced by a Graviton instance because of Karpenter's consolidation loop, and to prove that, in some cases, it's better to give flexibility to Karpenter to launch from a variety of instance types.

To confirm that the price went down, check the eks-node-viewer terminal. When we ran this lab, Karpenter decided to launch a c6g.4xlarge instance, making the estimated monthly cost $426.101, giving us an 11.11% cost reduction.

4. Change the workload requests after proper rightsizing

As you can imagine, optimization is a journey. You need to constantly keep an eye open for the number of requests your workloads have, as they might be under-provisioned, which will impact your application performance. But they can also over-provision, which will impact your bill.

In *Chapter 2*, you learned the importance of rightsizing your workload properly. So, in this lab, we'll skip that part and assume that after a few days of monitoring your workload, you noticed that you need to adjust the number of resources the workload is requesting. Therefore, you won't request 1 CPU and 512 Mi of memory, like this:

```
resources:
  requests:
    cpu: 1
    memory: 512Mi
```

Instead, you'll now request 256 milli-cores and 256 Mi of memory. To do so, you need to change the /chapter11/cost-optimized/montecarlopi.yaml file to this:

```
resources:
  requests:
    cpu: 256m
    memory: 256Mi
```

Apply the changes by running this command (assuming your terminal is in the cost-optimized folder; otherwise, adapt it accordingly):

```
$ kubectl apply -f montecarlopi.yaml
```

Kubernetes will roll out the new pods. Check the eks-node-viewer terminal. You should see that the node has approximately 17% of its resources allocated. Similar to what you did before, run the command to read Karpenter logs. You should see that the consolidation process started again, and you can confirm it with log messages like this:

```
... "message":"disrupting node(s)", ...
,"reason":"underutilized","decision":"replace ...
```

The replacement node is now c6g.xlarge as your workload needs fewer resources. In terms of costs, check the eks-node-viewer terminal. In our case, when we ran the lab, the monthly cost was $106.507, giving us a 75.01% cost reduction. 75% is a very high number, and most likely, you'll need to go through different rounds of changes to adjust the requests your workload needs.

However, what I wanted to show here is how big the impact is when you do proper rightsizing, and how Karpenter will always try to optimize as much as possible (depending on workload and NodePool constraints) to get the best efficiency of a Kubernetes cluster.

The next step in our journey is to allow the NodePool to launch spot instances.

5. Change the NodePool to Spot instances

Before you change the NodePool, let's have a quick overview of what spot instances are. Spot is a purchase option with stepper discounts from the On-Demand price, it's spare capacity from EC2. To launch Spot instances, Karpenter is using the price-capacity-optimized (**PCO**) allocation strategy when making the call to the EC2 Fleet API. As we discussed in *Chapter 8*, when Karpenter finishes the bin-packing process, it sends a list of instance types to the EC2 Fleet API. With PCO, AWS picks the types that have more spare capacity available and then chooses the one with the lowest price. In other words, prioritize capacity then price.

It's important that you remember the previous information because it's going to help you understand what's about to happen. For now, let's add the spot option to the karpenter.sh/capacity-type requirement in the scaling-tests NodePool. It will look like this:

```
- key: karpenter.sh/capacity-type
  operator: In
  values: ["spot", "on-demand"]
```

Run the following command to apply the changes:

```
$ kubectl apply -f nodepol.yaml
```

Immediately check the Karpenter logs again, and around 10 seconds later, you should see some logs like this:

```
... "message":"disrupting node(s)", ...
"reason":"underutilized","decision":"replace", ... "replacement-
nodes":[{"capacity-type":"spot","instance-types":"c6g.xlarge, m6g.xlarge,
c7g.xlarge, c6gd.xlarge, c8g.xlarge and 41 other(s)"}]}
```

Notice that Karpenter's consolidation process started because it noticed that even though the existing c6g.xlarge instance was the cheapest type before, it's on-demand. And because we added spot, Karpenter replaced the on-demand instance with a spot instance. Moreover, Karpenter not only asked for a different purchase option, but it also added more than 41 instance types to the EC2 Fleet API call to get the best node in terms of capacity and price.

Check the eks-node-viewer terminal again. When the replacement is done, you should now see that the estimated monthly cost is reduced again. In our case, we got m6g.xlarge (a different family from before; we had one from the c family) with an estimated monthly spot price of $49.056, giving us a 53.96% cost reduction. Just by letting the NodePool use spot instances, we got a 50% cost reduction.

> **Note**
>
> It's important that you keep in mind that Karpenter currently supports three capacity types through the karpenter.sh/capacity-type requirement: spot, on-demand, and reserved. When your NodePool allows all these options, Karpenter (starting from v1.3) will always attempt to launch nodes using reserved capacity first—specifically in AWS, leveraging **On-Demand Capacity Reservations (ODCRs)** if available. Since v1.6, Karpenter also supports Amazon EC2 Capacity Blocks for ML, which is an option to reserve accelerated compute instances. If reserved capacity isn't an option, it will then consider spot instances, and only if neither reserved nor spot is available will it look to provision on-demand nodes.
>
> Additionally, when Karpenter is told that capacity is not available for a specific instance type and zone, it records this unavailability and caches the result for three minutes. During this cache period, Karpenter avoids making repeated attempts to provision the same instance type in that zone. After the cache expires, if there is still a need to provision nodes, Karpenter will retry starting again with the highest priority capacity type (such as spot again).

6. Cleanup

To clean all the resources you created from this lab, just run the following command:

```
$ kubectl delete -f .
```

As you can see, using Karpenter with Graviton and Spot instances is a must-have combo to optimize for cost in your EKS clusters. Keep in mind that whichever path you follow in this journey (whether you want to start with rightsizing or Spot, then Graviton), the order of factors does not affect the final product.

Now, let's explore the final use case, where you'll deploy GPU instances.

Use case 4: GPU-based workloads

The final use case, but no less important, in this book is about scaling **Graphics Processing Unit (GPU)** workloads such as deep learning model inference, training, or high-performance compute tasks. Although we could dedicate a few chapters to this topic, let's briefly explore why these types of workloads require some attention. For starters, unlike CPUs, which can be easily virtualized and shared across multiple processes, GPUs are designed for massive parallel processing and typically require exclusive access by individual containers.

At the time of writing, in Kubernetes, GPUs can't be easily fractioned like CPU resources. They are more expensive and scarcer than CPUs. Moreover, you often need specialized drivers, runtime environments, and vendor-specific device plugins to function properly in containerized environments.

> **Note**
>
> It's worth mentioning that the Kubernetes community is actively addressing GPU-specific limitations through several key initiatives. First, there's **Dynamic Resource Allocation (DRA)**, which graduated to beta in Kubernetes 1.32 and is expected to reach GA in v1.34, and it represents the most significant advancement. DRA replaces the current device plugin model with fine-grained, dynamic resource allocation supporting GPU sharing, partitionable devices, and sophisticated filtering. Second, enhanced GPU virtualization through NVIDIA with **Multi-Instance GPU (MIG)** support, which allows a single GPU to be partitioned into multiple. And, for older GPUs, **time-slicing** techniques and the CUDA **Multi-Process Service (MPS)** are being integrated as well, allowing Kubernetes to share GPU access between multiple pods and improve overall utilization. Lastly, there's a topology-aware scheduling feature, so workloads are placed on nodes based on GPU hardware layout and bandwidth. So, keep an eye on how this ecosystem evolves.

Additionally, for GPU-based workloads such as **Large Language Models (LLMs)**, its performance is typically impacted by metrics such as **Time to First Roken (TTFT)**, tokens, inference throughput, latency, and so on. You can't get these from the node. You can't really use the same approach to scale a CPU-based workload. You'll also need tools such as the NVIDIA **Data Center GPU Manager (DCGM)** to collect GPU telemetry to find out whether you're making efficient use of provisioned GPUs, as GPU nodes can be extremely expensive.

Note

While this book focuses on Karpenter and KEDA for GPU workload autoscaling, there are several specialized schedulers and frameworks offering advanced GPU optimization capabilities that are worth considering. For instance, the NVIDIA KAI Scheduler (open sourced from **Run:ai**) provides capabilities such as GPU sharing, gang scheduling, and batch job prioritization, and enables fractional GPU allocation and DRA. Additionally, some teams may choose to even replace kube-scheduler entirely with alternatives such as Volcano or Apache YuniKorn, which offer more sophisticated batch scheduling capabilities, or gang scheduling for distributed workloads, and advanced resource management policies. While these tools can enhance GPU resource utilization and provide advanced scheduling capabilities, they introduce additional complexity and are beyond the scope of this chapter's focus.

So, efficient autoscaling is going to be very helpful, and this hands-on lab will help you have a first approximation to scaling these types of workloads. The diagram in *Figure 11.5* shows the components you'll be deploying during this lab.

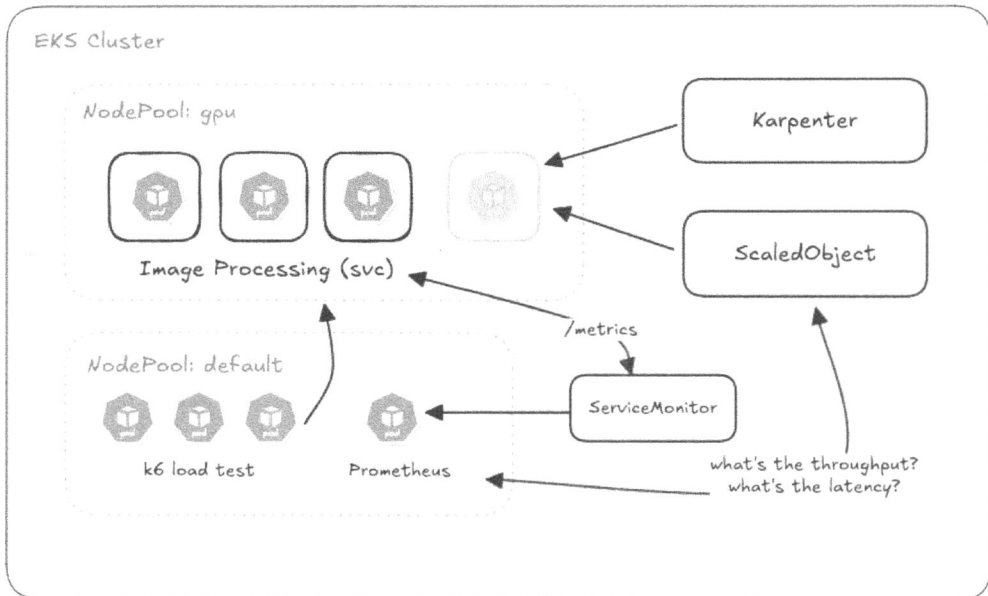

Figure 11.5 – Image processing application using GPU-based nodes

As you can see, the components aren't that different from the first use case we explored in this chapter. However, you'll notice that as we start deploying the solution, we'll need to deploy certain tools unique to GPU-based workloads and implement mechanisms to improve the startup time of containers in new nodes. So, let's go back to the terminal and get started with the last lab of this chapter.

Hands-on lab: Autoscaling GPU-based workloads

To explore how autoscaling works in GPU-based workloads in more depth, we're going to deploy a PyTorch-based image classification model, designed to accept image URLs and return classification results based on what the model understands the image to be. Also, the application is exposing a /metrics endpoint to expose the number of requests and latency metrics to let KEDA configure scaling rules using these metrics. It's the same approach we've used before to scale based on latency or requests per second.

1. Deploy the EC2NodeClass resource

Before you start, make sure you're in the right folder by opening a new terminal. Then, run this command:

```
$ cd chapter11/gpu/
```

The first step is to deploy EC2NodeClass. You can find the details of this resource in the chapter11/gpu/nodeclass.yaml file. Let's explore some of the most important sections. First, we're going to use Bottlerocket as the OS:

```
amiFamily: Bottlerocket
amiSelectorTerms:
  - alias: bottlerocket@v1.42.0
```

As the workload and NodePool constraints request a GPU instance, Karpenter will pick the corresponding EKS-accelerated AMI version from Bottlerocket. And it's worth highlighting that we're going to use Bottlerocket for two reasons. First, because it's going to use the AMI that comes with the NVIDIA GPU device plugin to allow kube-scheduler to schedule GPU-based workloads that can offer GPUs. If we'd decided to use a different AMI, we'd have to install the device plugin manually. The device plugin runs as a DaemonSet on GPU-enabled nodes to do things such as exposing GPU information for Kubernetes (i.e., number of GPUs), tracking the health of GPUs, setting up the NVIDIA driver and container toolkit, and so on. Without these device plugins, Karpenter could launch a GPU node, but kube-scheduler wouldn't be able to schedule pods there, as by default, nodes in Kubernetes don't expose GPU information.

The second reason why we're using Bottlerocket is that it comes with two volumes: one for the OS and another for data. The data volume is going to be used to store data such as metadata from containers and container images. Essentially, it would look like this:

```
blockDeviceMappings:
  - deviceName: /dev/xvdb
    ebs:
      volumeSize: 100Gi
      volumeType: gp3
      deleteOnTermination: true
      throughput: 1000
      iops: 4000
```

This data volume is important because container images for GPU-based workloads tend to be big, and this would impact startup time. So, when you have a data volume, you can attach storage snapshots that already come with the data you need. We're going to make use of this feature later in this lab.

> **Note**
>
> If you're not using snapshots for storing container images, I recommend configuring Karpenter to use the RAID0 instance store policy. RAID0 is a storage configuration that stripes data across multiple disks to improve performance by allowing simultaneous read/write operations, with the downside of no redundancy (if any single disk fails, all data is lost). In AWS, certain instance types come with multiple local disks (ephemeral storage). A RAID0 configuration allows containerd, kubelet logs, and other crucial components to run on **Non-Volatile Memory Express** (**NVMe**) storage for significantly improved I/O performance. To enable this configuration, include the following in the EC2NodeClass spec: instanceStorePolicy: RAID0.

For now, let's create the EC2NodeClass resource by running this command:

```
$ kubectl apply -f nodeclass.yaml
```

Let's continue with the next step to deploy the NodePool.

2. Deploy the NodePool

You can find the details of this resource in the chapter11/gpu/nodepool.yaml file. Let's explore some of the most important sections. In the requirements section, you have the following configuration:

```
    ...
  - key: karpenter.k8s.aws/instance-category
    operator: In
    values: ["g"]
  - key: karpenter.k8s.aws/instance-gpu-manufacturer
    operator: In
    values: ["nvidia"]
  - key: kubernetes.io/arch
    operator: In
    values: ["amd64"]
```

Here's where you're constraining the NodePool to only launch instances from the g family, where the manufacturer is nvidia and the architecture is amd64 (or x86). For instance, Karpenter could launch a g5.2xlarge instance.

To avoid having workloads that won't benefit from using GPU nodes, we're adding a taint. This means that we're going to be intentional about the workloads that require a GPU node by adding its corresponding toleration. This section in the NodePool looks like this:

```
  taints:
    - key: nvidia.com/gpu
      value: "true"
      effect: NoSchedule
```

Additionally, we're adding a limit to constrain the maximum number of GPUs that the NodePool can launch. The configuration is the following:

```
  limits:
    nvidia.com/gpu: "10"
```

Lastly, once a GPU node has been provisioned, we'd like to keep it as long as it's empty. So, the consolidation policy is using WhenEmpty, like this:

```
  disruption:
    consolidationPolicy: WhenEmpty
    consolidateAfter: 5m
```

Let's create the NodePool by running this command:

```
$ kubectl apply -f nodepool.yaml
```

Let's deploy the application to confirm that Karpenter can provision GPU nodes.

3. Deploy the sample application

You can find the details of the application in the chapter11/gpu/ image-processing-app.yaml file. Let's explore some of the most important sections. For starters, we're including the necessary constraints to match the pods with the NodePool by using nodeSelector and tolerations. The configuration looks like this:

```
nodeSelector:
  nvidia.com/gpu.present: "true"
  karpenter.k8s.aws/instance-gpu-name: "t4"
tolerations:
- key: nvidia.com/gpu
  effect: NoSchedule
  operator: Exists
```

The label matches the NodePool label, and the toleration matches the taint we configured before. Moreover, since GPU-based workloads are typically sensitive to specific GPU capabilities, this workload requests nodes with NVIDIA T4 GPUs by specifying t4 as the instance-gpu-name constraint.

The other important section is where we defined how many GPUs each pod is going to request. For this constraint, we have the following:

```
resources:
  limits:
    nvidia.com/gpu: 1
```

Something is odd, right? We're not following the recommendation we've been talking about across the whole book. There are no requests, and in fact, we're instead using limits to say what the maximum number of GPUs this pod can use. Let's understand why this configuration is like this.

To begin with, this isn't a Karpenter-specific requirement, but rather a Kubernetes-wide constraint for extended resources such as GPUs. Unlike CPU and memory resources that can be fractionally allocated and overcommitted, GPUs are discrete hardware units managed by device plugins that cannot be shared between containers by default. When you specify `nvidia.com/gpu: 1` in the `limits` section, Kubernetes automatically sets `requests` to the same value, ensuring that your container receives exclusive access to exactly one GPU.

Karpenter reads these `requests` values to make node provisioning decisions, selecting proper GPU instance types based on the aggregate GPU requirements of pending pods. You can't omit `limits` while specifying only `requests`, and if you specify different values for GPU `requests` and `limits`, you'll get a validation error.

With this clear, let's deploy the application by using this command:

```
$ kubectl apply -f image-processing-app.yaml
```

Now, run the following command, and wait around three minutes to see the application with a Running status:

```
$ watch kubectl get pods,nodeclaims
```

Once the application is up and running, close that command (press *Ctrl + C*), and let's make sure that the application is working. First, let's run the following command to access the application locally:

```
$ kubectl port-forward svc/gpu-inference-service 8080:80
```

Then, run this command in a new terminal to confirm that it works (replace IMAGE_URL with any public image URL from the internet):

```
$ curl -X POST http://localhost:8080/predict \
    -H 'Content-Type: application/json' \
    -d '{"image_url": "https://IMAGE_URL"}'
```

You should get an output like this one:

```
{"confidence":0.7931427955627441,"device_used":"cuda:0","predicted_
class":980,"source_url":"https://IMAGE_URL"}
```

For now, the output doesn't matter much; we're interested mostly in whether it doesn't return an error and whether it seems to be working.

4. Speed up bootstrap time

Before we jump into the scaling section, let's work on improving the bootstrap time of the application. You might have noticed that this type of application took several minutes to be in a Running state. The GPU node launched by Karpenter didn't take too much time to be ready. If you monitored the status of the pod, most of the time, its status was ContainerCreating. Let's inspect the events from the pod; while we wait, run this command, making sure you use the proper name of the pod:

```
$ kubectl describe pod image-processing-app-ID
```

You should see that the pod is spending its time pulling the container image. Once this is completed, you should see an event stating how much time it took to pull the image—something like this:

```
  Normal  Pulled    24s    kubelet          Successfully pulled image
"christianhxc/image-processing-app:latest" in 1m16.821s (1m16.821s
including waiting). Image size: 5673570611 bytes.
```

In this case, it took 1 minute and 16 seconds. You might think that's not too long. But when you need to add more replicas because the demand is growing, this might be too much.

To speed up this process, you need to make sure that all (or at least the biggest) container image layers are already present in the node. This is the moment when the data volume from Bottlerocket becomes handy. You can use a snapshot of a volume to mount it to the node and start the instance with preloaded data. So, we're going to make use of that volume to pre-download the container image of our application.

To do so, you need to launch a new EC2 instance using Bottlerocket, pull the container image you want to have preloaded, take a snapshot of the volume, and then use that snapshot in EC2NodeClass. Even though this process sounds too complex, AWS has a project called bottlerocket-images-cache on GitHub, and we're going to use it to generate a snapshot we could reference later.

Open a new terminal, and clone the GitHub repository using these commands:

```
$ git clone https://github.com/aws-samples/bottlerocket-images-cache.git
$ cd bottlerocket-images-cache
```

Then, you simply run the snapshot.sh script to generate the snapshot. The script has a few parameters you can use, depending on your needs. First, you need to specify the region using the -r parameter; this is where the snapshot will be created. We're going to keep it simple by only passing the size of the volume size using the -s parameter. As the final argument, you need to pass the full name of the container image.

For this lab, just run the following command (you might want to change the region if using a different one):

```
$ ./snapshot.sh -r eu-west-1 -s 100 docker.io/christianhxc/image-
processing-app:latest
```

This will start doing the process I described before, automatically. You only need to wait around 10 minutes for the process to finish. The more container images you add to this script, and the bigger they are, the more time it will take to finish. You should be getting an output like the following:

```
... I - [1/8] Deploying EC2 CFN stack Bottlerocket-ebs ...
...
... I - [8/8] Cleanup.
... I - Stack deleted.
... I - ----------------------------------------------------
... I - All done! Created snapshot in eu-west-1: snap-0123456789abcdef0
```

Once the script has finished, you should see a snapshot ID, which we'll be using later.

> **Note**
>
> If you had problems running the preceding script, make sure you review the README file from the GitHub repository of the tool to better understand how it works and which permissions you need to run the script.

5. Update EC2NodeClass

Now that you have a snapshot ID, let's change the EC2NodeClass configuration. We already have the configuration we need to change, but it's commented. Go back to the GitHub repository folder, open the chapter11/gpu/nodeclass.yaml file, and find the following line:

```
# snapshotID: snap-0123456789abcdef0
```

Then, uncomment that line by removing the # character, and replace snap-0123456789abcdef0 with the exact snapshot ID you got after using the snapshot.sh script before.

Make sure your terminal is in the chapter11/gpu folder and apply the new configuration by running the following command:

```
$ kubectl apply -f nodeclass.yaml
```

As soon as you change EC2NodeClass, Karpenter will notice that the existing node has drifted from its configuration. Therefore, a new NodeClaim will be created, and a new node will be launched using the snapshot ID you provided as the data volume. Wait for the new pod to be in a Running state and inspect the events from the pod again by describing the pod. Run this command, making sure you use the proper name of the pod:

```
$ kubectl describe pod image-processing-app-ID
```

You should see an output like this:

```
   Normal     Pulled              35s     kubelet              Successfully pulled
image "christianhxc/image-processing-app:latest" in 654ms (654ms including
waiting). Image size: 5673570611 bytes.
```

Notice how the pull time decreased significantly to only 654ms. This will be a similar setup to the one we had in the first lab from this chapter. When you need to scale the application, you'll have new replicas up and running in a fraction of the time. Let's see that in action.

6. Deploy the autoscaling rules

The first step is to deploy ServiceMonitor to scrape the metrics from the application and store them in Prometheus, as this will be the source of the metrics we'll use to scale the application. In your terminal, run the following command:

```
$ kubectl apply -f servicemonitor.yaml
```

Give it two to three minutes to become stable. If you'd like to confirm that it's working, you can do a port forward to expose the Prometheus service and explore the /targets endpoint. All the specific details about how to do it can be found in *Chapter 4*.

Next, create the KEDA ScaledObject with this command:

```
$ kubectl apply -f scaledobject.yaml
```

To confirm that the autoscaling rule will work, wait around 30 seconds, then run this command:

```
$ kubectl describe hpa keda-hpa-image-processing-app
```

You should see an event with a condition message like this:

```
the HPA was able to successfully calculate a replica count from external
metric ...
```

This means that the HPA was able to query Prometheus successfully. Before you start sending any load to the application to test this autoscaling rule, let's pause for a moment and review what we've done with the `ScaledObject` object we just deployed.

For starters, we're using the following rules to speed up scaling out and slow down scaling in:

```
advanced:
  horizontalPodAutoscalerConfig:
    behavior:
      scaleUp:
        stabilizationWindowSeconds: 0
        policies:
        - type: Percent
          value: 100
          periodSeconds: 5
      scaleDown:
        stabilizationWindowSeconds: 120
        policies:
        - type: Percent
          value: 100
          periodSeconds: 30
```

From this, the `scaleUp` setting immediately allows doubling the replica count within just five seconds whenever scaling out, with no delay. With this, you ensure a rapid response to spikes in load. Conversely, the `scaleDown` setting enforces a 120-second stabilization period before pods are reduced, only permitting scaling in by up to 100% every 30 seconds. You might not want to remove a GPU node as fast, as you might need to schedule more pods soon. It's a trade-off you need to consider; maybe for a fraction of the time, you'll have an underutilized capacity, but you won't risk getting the capacity again when you need it.

The other important setting relies on the `triggers` section; it looks like this:

```
triggers:
- type: prometheus
  metadata:
    serverAddress: ...
    metricName: gpu_inference_request_rate
    threshold: '40'
    query: ...
```

```
  - type: prometheus
    metadata:
      serverAddress: ...
      metricName: gpu_inference_latency_p95
      threshold: '2'
      query: ...
```

From this, you can see that we have two triggers for this rule: one for the request rate and another for latency. With the application we're using here, what matters really is the inference requests it can handle, and that its response (latency) stays under the threshold. When multiple triggers are defined in ScaledObject, scaling decisions are based on whichever trigger reaches its threshold first. Essentially, the most urgent need dictates the scaling action.

This means that if either the request rate surpasses its limit or the latency rises beyond the defined value, the HPA will react by scaling up the deployment. The reason we've added both triggers is to create a more adaptive scaling strategy: if demand increases, scaling can happen due to request volume; if response times begin creeping up (even if traffic is steady), it can also trigger scaling. As you can see, it's not really about scaling using one metric only. You need to understand what dictates that your application is working as expected, and you only get this by understanding the scaling patterns of your application.

Alright, enough for now, let's run a load test to see autoscaling in action.

7. Run load test

As we're going to follow a similar approach to the one in the first hands-on lab in this chapter, let's just deploy the k6 load test resources with the following command:

```
$ kubectl apply -f k6.yaml
```

The main difference with the previous script is that, this time, we're sending much more traffic than before, simply because the application is very different and it can process more requests. You can explore what's happening by using this command:

```
$ kubectl logs -l k6_cr=gpu-inference-load-test -f
```

What you're looking at here is the k6 logs showing the progress from the load test that will run for a few minutes. For now, you need to move to the next step, but once the test is done, you'll see a report of the success and error rate, along with the latency numbers you got while the test was running, like this:

```
http_req_duration..............................................:
  avg=2.64s min=0s med=2.06s max=15.1s p(90)=6.94s p(95)=7.5s
```

Now, let's monitor how HPA is adding more replicas and how Karpenter is adding more nodes.

8. See autoscaling in action

Open a new terminal, and run the following command:

```
$ watch kubectl get hpa,scaledobject,pods,nodeclaims
```

Notice how rapidly the RPS and latency are starting to go up. Like before, when you see a number such as 20813m/40, it means that the RPS is 20 because Kubernetes reports metrics in milli-units. In this case, the requests are under the threshold. However, the latency went above the threshold with 2576m/2 or 2.5 seconds. Therefore, the HPA started to add more replicas, but because there's not enough capacity in the cluster, Karpenter started to launch new nodes. Notice as well how the new nodes are not taking too much time to be ready because of the improvements we made to preload the container image.

> **Note**
>
> If new nodes are not being launched, it is most likely due to a problem with service quotas in your AWS account. Check the Karpenter logs to see whether that's the case. If you don't remember how to check the logs, go back to *Chapter 10*. To request a quota increase, check the AWS docs (https://docs.aws.amazon.com/servicequotas/latest/userguide/request-quota-increase.html).

Once the test is finished, the metrics for requests and latency will go down to zero. I'd recommend you wait for HPA to remove the replicas and Karpenter to remove the nodes automatically. The idea is that you see the scaleDown policy working, emptying the node, and Karpenter's consolidation process removing the node as it's empty. This whole automated cleanup will take at least 10 minutes to complete. However, if you don't want to wait, proceed with the next step to clean up all resources.

Note

If, for some reason, you couldn't run all the previous commands in time to see all the components interacting with each other, run the test again by running the commands from the previous step. However, before you run it again, make sure you're in the same state as before, meaning that you need to wait for the extra pods and nodes to be removed. You can remove them manually, but make sure you also remove `ScaledObject`.

9. Cleanup

Finally, to make sure you have a full cleanup, run this command to remove the application:

```
$ kubectl delete -f image-processing-app.yaml
```

Wait for a few minutes, and you'll see how Karpenter's consolidation process will remove the empty nodes, scaling the data plane down to zero. Then, run the following command to remove the rest of the resources left:

```
$ kubectl delete -f .
```

Ignore the `NotFound` errors as you've removed some of those resources already.

Congratulations! With this one, you've completed all the labs from this chapter. You experienced first-hand how autoscaling works in Kubernetes with the most common use cases using KEDA, Karpenter, and even other open source tools such as k6.

Summary

In this chapter, you've learned how KEDA and Karpenter work together to create efficient and cost-optimized Kubernetes clusters. Each scenario highlighted critical patterns that apply across different workload types. I hope that at this point, you see that metric selection matters. Which metrics? Well, that will depend on your understanding of what influences the performance of your application. For instance, in the case of web applications, they typically benefit from scaling on requests per second rather than reactive metrics such as CPU usage. GPU workloads could benefit from multiple triggers to handle different load patterns effectively. Choose metrics that reflect your application's actual health indicators. It's a continuous improvement process, really.

We also explored how immediate scale-up with conservative scale-down prevents performance issues while avoiding resource waste. Moreover, you learned techniques and practices to run workloads and clusters as efficiently as possible. For instance, ARM-based instances deliver 10–15% savings immediately. Proper rightsizing can reduce costs by 50–75%, depending on how good or bad the work you did when configuring requests for your workloads. Also, Spot instances add another 50%+ reduction. More importantly, you were able to see again how Karpenter's consolidation handles these optimizations automatically as you make these changes. For large containers, pre-loading container images is crucial, and you can do it by using volume snapshots or `RAID0` instance store policies.

To close this chapter, it's important to note the importance of testing and monitoring continuously. Load testing with tools such as k6 helps you define proper thresholds. Tools such as `eks-node-viewer` provide real-time estimated cost and efficiency feedback. Even though you explored here with very specific use cases, make sure you apply these patterns systematically and refine based on your specific workload characteristics and usage patterns. Every application, even in the same company, is different.

Let's move on to the final chapter, where you'll explore some patterns that will continue diving deeper into KEDA and Karpenter integration. I'll also give you a final set of recommendations, projects, and future trends within the autoscaling ecosystem in Kubernetes.

12

Patterns and Recommendations

Congratulations! You've reached the final chapter of this book. Here, you'll explore some patterns and recommendations for efficient Kubernetes autoscaling using KEDA and Karpenter. As I want you to continue practicing in this chapter, there will be some hands-on labs so you can see for yourself how to implement patterns such as scaling down to zero nodes and working with fault-tolerant workloads in Karpenter. These labs will help you maximize the cost optimization aspect of Karpenter.

As part of the hands-on labs, we'll revisit Kubernetes constructs to improve your workload's resiliency with settings such as `terminationGracePeriodSeconds`, leveraging `preStop` hooks, and using readiness probes, showing how these patterns plug into your autoscaling workflows to minimize downtime. You'll also find guidance on topics such as integrating Spot capacity safely and increase your confidence to even use it in a production environment.

In the previous chapters, we've been exploring how to use different metrics to scale our workloads, but in this chapter, we'll spend some time reflecting on which metrics or triggers we can use to scale. The aim is to help you think about what influences the performance of your application, then decide how and when you need to scale.

Lastly, we'll wrap things up by looking at the future trends of both KEDA and Karpenter based on what the contributors have shared at conferences such as KubeCon, discussions on GitHub issues, and even meeting nodes from working group meetings.

We will be covering the following main topics:

- Scaling down to zero
- Fault-tolerant workloads

- Ending notes
- Future trends

Join me in this final chapter—it's time to bring up your cluster and terminal again.

Technical requirements

For this chapter, you'll continue using an Amazon EKS cluster. You'll continue using the cluster you've been working with since *Chapter 8*. You don't need to install any additional tools as most of the commands are going to be run with kubectl. You can find the YAML manifests for all of the resources you're going to create in this chapter in the chapter12 folder in the book's GitHub repository, which you cloned in *Chapter 1*.

Scaling down to zero

One of the main benefits of autoscaling in Kubernetes is that you can pay only for what you use. With KEDA, you learned that depending on the application type, you can scale down to zero replicas and KEDA can activate autoscaling when needed. Moreover, we also explored KEDA's ability to schedule when replicas from an application are needed. In Karpenter, you can also scale down to zero nodes when there are no pods running in those nodes. In other words, Karpenter can remove nodes when they're empty. Additionally, Karpenter can remove a node after a consolidation process when there are underutilized nodes.

However, even though KEDA and Karpenter can technically help you to scale down to zero, there are times when simply configuring minReplica: 0 in a deployment with Karpenter consolidation enabled might not be enough. Most clusters have a mix of workloads, constraints, and configurations that make it difficult or complex to scale down to zero. For instance, you might think about creating a CronJob to set all replicas to zero, but what if you have ScaledObjects overriding that configuration? Or what if you have NodePools that don't have consolidation enabled? You might need to consider other constraints specific to your environment.

One simple approach to scale to zero nodes on non-production clusters consists of using Karpenter and two CronJobs without considering too many constraints, as discussed previously. One CronJob will be responsible for removing nodes launched by Karpenter NodePools during designated off-hours, such as 5 P.M. to 9 A.M. on weekdays. These CronJobs run scripts that set the NodePool resource limits to zero and delete any existing NodeClaims, effectively shutting down all nodes that were launched by Karpenter, as seen in *Figure 12.1*:

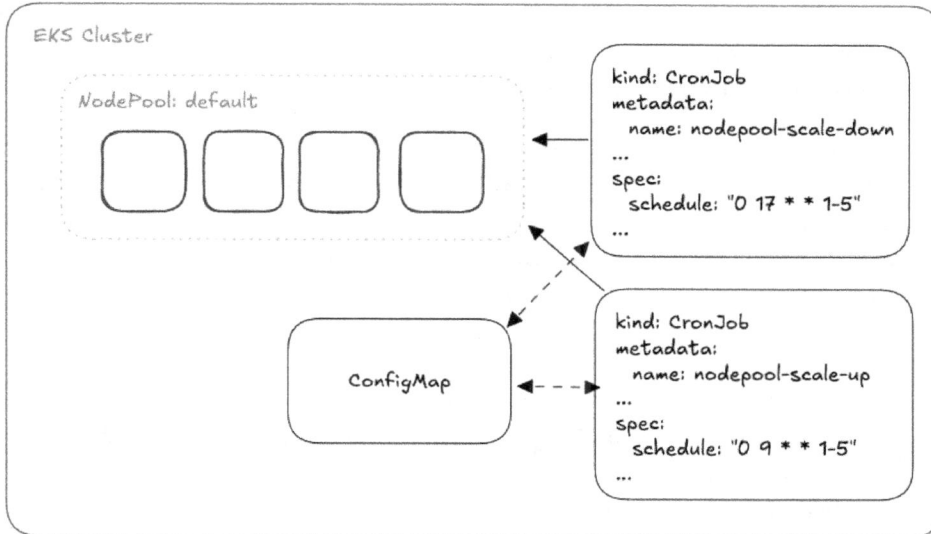

Figure 12.1 – Two CronJobs to keep nodes running from 9 A.M. to 5 P.M. on weekdays

We're going to assume that we want to have nodes running during working hours. So, effectively, this is what is going to happen:

- We might not want to scale down to zero all nodes in the cluster; so, we're going to use a ConfigMap to list the NodePools that will be affected.

- From Monday to Friday at 5 P.M., the first CronJob will run. This job will set the limits of each NodePool to zero (limits: 0) and will add an annotation to the NodePool with its previous limits configuration to revert this to its original value when reactivating the NodePool. Setting a limit to zero will pause the NodePool as even if there are unschedulable pods, Karpenter won't be able to launch nodes. But that alone won't remove existing nodes. Therefore, the next step will be removing NodeClaims from each affected NodePool. This will trigger a finalizer from the NodeClaim to remove the node from the cloud provider, effectively scaling the nodes down to zero.

- From Monday to Friday at 9 A.M., the second CronJob will restore the limits configuration from each NodePool. With this, Karpenter will be able to again launch the nodes that are needed based on the unschedulable pods in the cluster due to the NodeClaims that the first job removed.

- We might need to pause or activate NodePools manually, or outside the mentioned schedule. To do so, we can simply copy the CronJob definition without a schedule. You'll see this in action in the next hands-on section.

This approach is configurable as we might want to change the schedule and include only certain NodePools from the cluster. Also, it doesn't change any other existing resource we might have, such as ScaledObjects or workload constraints. And in case of an emergency, we can always activate (or pause) the NodePools. Let's see this in action in the following hands-on lab.

> **Note**
>
> If you plan to use this solution with GitOps tools such as Argo CD or Flux CD, you'll need to configure your GitOps controller to ignore or exclude NodePool resources from automatic reconciliation. This prevents reverting the temporary `limits` changes and annotations that the CronJobs apply to NodePools during scale-down/scale-up operations. Moreover, keep in mind that the rest of the components (RBAC, ConfigMap, CronJobs, etc.) need to be under the version control tool you're using (i.e., Git).

Hands-on lab: Scaling to zero nodes

In this hands-on lab, we're going to deploy the resources we explored before, and we're going to see the CronJobs in action without having to wait for the hours defined in the schedule. Open a new terminal and make sure you have the cluster up and running.

1. Deploying a sample application

First, let's deploy a simple application to see the scale-down job in action. In your terminal, make sure you're in the book's GitHub repository and run this command:

```
$ cd chapter12/scaletozero/
```

Then, deploy the application with a few replicas by running this command:

```
$ kubectl apply -f montecarlopi.yaml
```

This will create the necessary nodes, and when they're up and running, the pods should be running too. You can monitor this by running this command:

```
$ watch kubectl get pods,nodeclaims
```

You're only doing this to have nodes running that will be removed at the scheduled time. In this lab, you'll manually use the script from the CronJob to remove the nodes.

2. Deploying the service account

For these jobs, we won't use the default service account as we'd like to limit the actions that these pods can perform. Therefore, we're going to create a Kubernetes service account, a cluster role, and a cluster role binding to limit the actions to all NodePools and NodeClaims, along with read permissions for the ConfigMap to get the list of NodePools to scale.

Run the following command:

```
$ kubectl apply -f nodepool-scheduler/rbac.yaml
```

In the CronJobs, we're going to reference the service account we just created.

3. Deploying the ConfigMap

The ConfigMap we're going to use is very simple. We're using this approach as we'd like to make it easy to change if you decide to add or remove NodePools that will be affected by the CronJobs. The content looks like this:

```
...
data:
  managed-nodepools: "default"
  timezone: "UTC"
```

As you can see, we're now only going to remove nodes from the `default` NodePool. You can add others by using a comma separator, like this: `"default, gpu"`.

Let's create the ConfigMap by running the following command:

```
$ kubectl apply -f nodepool-scheduler/config.yaml
```

When you decide to add a new NodePool to the list, you need to update the data of this ConfigMap.

4. Deploying the scale-down CronJob

The YAML manifest for the scale-down job is in the `nodepool-scale-down.yaml` file. Please open and review it. I'm not including the code here as it might change in the future, but essentially, the CronJob is running a script that does what we explored before:

- Jobs will run from Monday to Friday at 5 P.M. (UTC)
- Gets the list of NodePools affected from the ConfigMap

- For each NodePool, does the following:

    - Annotates it with the existing `limits` configuration. This is to restore its configuration when recreating the nodes.

    - Sets `limits` to 0 to ensure no new nodes are created temporarily.

    - Removes all the NodeClaims from the NodePool to remove the nodes created manually. This is needed as Karpenter won't remove nodes after you change `limits` to 0.

To deploy this CronJob, simply run the following command:

```
$ kubectl apply -f nodepool-scheduler/nodepool-scale-down.yaml
```

You're now covered with the scaling down to zero operation. But you also need to have a way to resume Karpenter launching nodes the next working day. Let's do that.

5. Deploying the scale-up CronJob

Similar to before, the YAML manifest for the scale-up job is in the `nodepool-scale-up.yaml` file. Open it and review it. This CronJob is simpler:

- Jobs will run from Monday to Friday at 9 A.M. (UTC)
- Gets the list of NodePools affected from the ConfigMap
- For each NodePool, does the following:

    - Restores the `limits` configuration from the annotation. This will enable the NodePool to launch capacity from now on.

    - Removes the annotation to keep it clean in case the `limits` configuration changes before the other job runs again.

As you can see, it's simply enabling the NodePool to launch capacity again. When we set `limits` to 0 before, we blocked the NodePool and removed the nodes manually. Therefore, we left all the pods that match these NodePools unschedulable. So, by restoring the previous `limits` configuration, Karpenter can launch the nodes again.

So, run the following command to create the job:

```
$ kubectl apply -f nodepool-scheduler/nodepool-scale-up.yaml
```

You're now covered when you need to have the capacity back again.

6. Scaling down manually

Let's not wait for the jobs to run at the scheduled time; we'll run them manually. There are going to be times when you might need to bring the capacity down/up again outside of the schedule. So, let's explore the alternative of running these jobs manually and test that they work right now.

As you already have some nodes running, let's start testing the scale-down job. To do so, let's create a temporary job based on the existing one. Use this command:

```
$ kubectl create job test-scale-down-$(date +%s) --from=cronjob/nodepool-
scale-down -n kube-system
```

Monitor the NodeClaims by running this command:

```
$ watch kubectl get nodeclaims
```

You should see how nodes are being removed. Stop the command when there are no more NodeClaims.

7. Scaling up manually

Let's revert this process by resuming the NodePools when removing the limits: 0 setting. You can confirm that there are unschedulable pods waiting for nodes to be available in the cluster. Run this command:

```
$ kubectl get pods
```

You should see the list of pods in a Pending status. Let's say you need to bring the capacity back right now. Similar to before, run the following command to create a temporary job based on the scale-up CronJob we created before with a schedule:

```
$ kubectl create job incident-scale-up-$(date +%s) --from=cronjob/
nodepool-scale-up -n kube-system
```

Monitor the NodeClaims in the cluster once more by running this command:

```
$ kubectl get nodeclaims
```

You should see how the NodeClaims are being recreated.

Even though you've tested this manually, you can feel more confident about it working when the CronJobs with the schedule run. They will either bring the nodes down to zero or restore the nodes when you need to resume the NodePools from creating capacity when it's needed.

8. Cleaning up

To remove the sample application created in this lab, run this command:

```
$ kubectl delete -f .
```

To remove the CronJobs to scale down to zero and scale up from zero, simply run the following command:

```
$ kubectl delete -f nodepool-scheduler/.
```

And that's it! That's how you create a solution to remove nodes and bring them back during certain times of operation or perform the same action manually. Let's switch gears a little bit and explore the recommendations when working with fault-tolerant workloads in Kubernetes.

Fault-tolerant workloads

Fault-tolerant workloads refer to applications designed to continue operating correctly even when individual components fail or are disrupted. In Kubernetes, these workloads leverage redundancy, health checks, and graceful degradation strategies to maintain service availability despite pod evictions, node failures, or resource constraints. While pod disruptions can occur due to various reasons, including scaling down applications when demand decreases, Karpenter's node consolidation process optimizing cluster resources, or routine maintenance operations, this section will primarily focus on one of the most common and time-sensitive scenarios: *Spot instance interruption notices.*

Spot interruptions provide a perfect case study for fault tolerance because they give you a brief warning window (typically two minutes) before the underlying compute capacity disappears, making them an ideal scenario to demonstrate how proper implementation of Kubernetes primitives and monitoring can minimize service impact during involuntary disruptions.

This topic is very close to me as I've been working with several companies helping them run fault-tolerant workloads in Kubernetes to take advantage of the Spot discounts. As a quick reminder, Spot offers larger discounts on compute nodes but the peculiarity is that these nodes are interruptible. However, to take advantage of this, your workloads need to be fault-tolerant. As my good friend Boyd McGeachie once said, "Spot is the reward for a good architecture." You can access these significant discounts without a major impact when your workloads are well architected.

Spot interruptions shouldn't be a problem as containers are used to being treated as cattle and not pets, meaning that containers are expected to be terminated constantly due to different reasons, such as containers running **out of memory** (**OMM**) or rolling updates.

However, the application isn't fault-tolerant just because you're using containers. And if they are, you might want to make the most of the nodes you have before they're terminated.

For instance, in AWS, when you receive a Spot interruption, you have two minutes to try to gracefully shut down your application. As soon as you receive this notification, you might want to delay the node termination as much as possible (i.e., 90 seconds) so that you can close connections, process in-flight requests, establish checkpoints, persist logs, and so on. I've very often heard teams say that they use Spot because they don't want to run out of capacity. However, Spot interruptions are just one of the many reasons why a node can be terminated. Other reasons might include host maintenance, unhealthy hosts, voluntary disruptions (i.e., Karpenter consolidation), or even manual deletions (by mistake). So, you should just better prepare to handle these disruptions.

Kubernetes and Karpenter already come with built-in features to help you gracefully shut down your pods and nodes. For instance, Kubernetes features such as preStop life cycle hooks, readiness probes, and termination grace periods can help you manage pod disruptions. Moreover, in AWS, Karpenter can monitor an Amazon SQS queue populated by EC2 interruption events, delivered via EventBridge rules for Spot termination notices or scheduled retirements, and as soon as a warning arrives, Karpenter cordons and drains the at-risk node and immediately launches replacement nodes with the same resource footprint. This end-to-end flow ensures that workloads on interrupted Spot (or other) nodes are rescheduled without waiting for Kubernetes' default eviction timeout, minimizing both downtime and capacity gaps.

So, let's explore in more depth how you can reduce the impact from the Kubernetes side first, and then from the application code side as well.

Using Kubernetes primitives

I'm starting with the Kubernetes primitives because this is where teams can rapidly implement mechanisms to reduce the impact of termination notices. Before I start giving you the recommendations, let's have a quick recap of the Kubernetes primitives we're going to explore:

- **preStop hook:** A life cycle handler that runs a user-defined command or HTTP call before the container receives termination signals, letting your application execute any cleanup logic.
- **Readiness probe:** A health check (HTTP, TCP, or command) that determines whether a pod should receive new traffic. When the probe fails, Kubernetes removes the pod from service endpoints, preventing any new requests.

- **Termination grace period**: A configurable delay (in seconds) between sending a SIGTERM and a forced SIGKILL to containers, allowing in-flight requests to complete or clean up routines to finish. By default, this period is 30 seconds. If these are new words for you, let me quickly brief you: **SIGTERM** is a gentle termination signal sent by the kubelet to give processes time to shut down gracefully, and **SIGKILL** is an immediate, uncatchable kill signal sent after the grace period expires, forcibly stopping any remaining processes.

When a pod is evicted, Kubernetes follows the sequence shown in *Figure 12.2*. The pod is immediately removed from Service endpoints to stop receiving new traffic; the kubelet issues a SIGTERM and invokes any preStop hooks; and the termination grace period timer starts. While the pod is already deregistered from internal Kubernetes Service endpoints, readiness probes continue to play a critical role during this period—especially when external load balancers such as AWS ALB are involved. A properly implemented readiness probe should immediately fail upon receiving SIGTERM, signaling to external systems that the pod is no longer ready to serve traffic, ensuring graceful deregistration from all routing layers. If the container hasn't exited by the end of the grace period, SIGKILL ensures it's cleaned up.

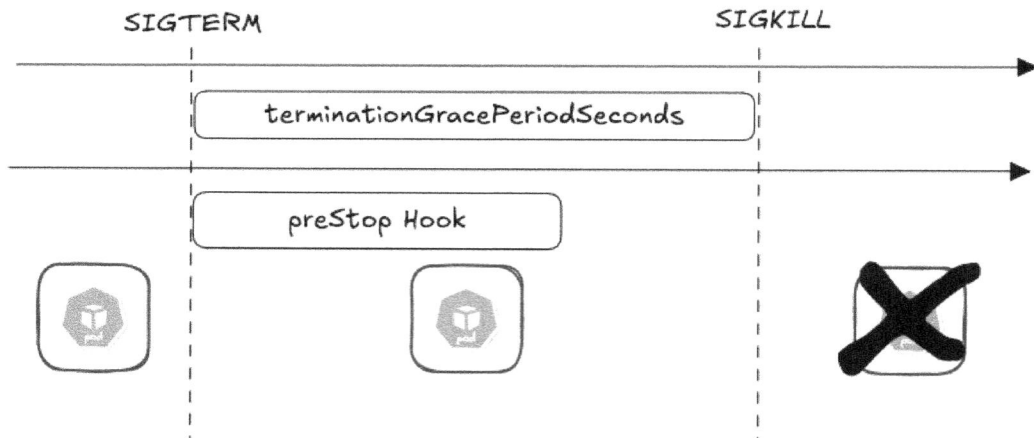

Figure 12.2 – Graceful shutdown using a preStop life cycle hook

When you combine preStop hooks, readiness probes, and an appropriate termination grace period, you minimize both traffic disruption and data loss during pod eviction. So, all of this sounds good, but let's see it in action in the next hands-on lab.

Hands-on lab: Handling node disruptions using Kubernetes primitives

In this lab, we're assuming that we don't want to or can't make any changes to the application code, so we'll focus only on how to use some of the Kubernetes primitives we explored before. The application we're going to use doesn't have a health check endpoint that we can use for a readiness probe. So, we'll skip that primitive for now and explore it in more detail in the next hands-on lab.

Bring back your cluster and open a new terminal.

1. Using only Spot instances

Before we start, the NodePool you deployed using Terraform only supports on-demand instances. You need to update it to use only Spot instances. You can change that manually but I'm going to use a command to change the NodePool.

In your terminal, run the following command:

```
$ kubectl patch nodepool default --type='json' -p='[{"op": "replace",
"path": "/spec/template/spec/requirements/2/values", "value":["spot"]}]'
```

Essentially, the preceding command will update your NodePool to this:

```
...
    - key: karpenter.sh/capacity-type
      operator: In
       values: ["spot"]
...
```

We're making this change because we want to make sure that the nodes Karpenter launches are only Spot nodes. The aim is to simulate an interruption and see how Karpenter handles it too.

Now, make sure you're in the book's GitHub repository and run this command:

```
$ cd chapter12/fault-tolerant/prestop/
```

From now on, all commands will use files from the psrestop folder.

2. Deploying a sample application

We're going to continue using the same application we've been using before, but with two additional settings. You can find the YAML manifest in the `montecarlopi.yaml` file. Open it, and notice that first we have the `preStop` hook within the `container` spec, like this:

```
...
lifecycle:
  preStop:
    exec:
      command:
      - /bin/sh
      - -c
      - |
        echo "$(date): preStop hook started" > /proc/1/fd/1
        echo "Performing cleanup operations..." > /proc/1/fd/1
        sleep 75
        echo "$(date): preStop hook cleanup completed" > /proc/1/fd/1
...
```

We're running a series of commands when the hook is invoked. Notice that we're redirecting the output to /proc/1/fd/1 because only the main container process (PID 1) has its `stdout`/`stderr` captured by Kubernetes logging. Right now, we're only interested in reading logs with `kubectl logs`, so writing to /proc/1/fd/1 ensures the `preStop` hook logs appear when inspecting logs live. Moreover, we have a `sleep` command of 75 seconds to simulate cleanup operations.

The other important configuration is the termination grace period. By default, it's 30 seconds. With the `preStop` hook, we're delaying the termination process to 75 seconds. But because the default `terminationGracePeriodSeconds` value is 30, the pod will be removed before it can print the final log line saying that the cleanup hook completed. We're changing the default value by adding this line within the pod spec:

```
...
    terminationGracePeriodSeconds: 90
...
```

Notice that we're extending the grace period to 90 seconds. Why 90? Because it's higher than 75 (`preStop`) and lower than 120 (the Spot interruption notice). The idea here is to take advantage of the two-minute notification from Spot and use it to process in-flight requests, close connections, persist logs, and so on.

So, deploy the application using this command:

```
$ kubectl apply -f montecarlopi.yaml
```

We're keeping it simple by deploying only one replica. Wait for the pod to be in a running state, then proceed with the next step.

3. Monitoring application logs live

We're going to keep it simple for now and monitor logs from the pods using `kubectl logs`. In the next hands-on lab, we'll be sending logs to an external tool as the recommendation is to use that approach in a production environment.

Open a new terminal and run the following command:

```
$ kubectl logs -f -l app=montecarlo-pi
```

With this command, you'll see the logs from the `preStop` commands.

4. Sending a Spot interruption

Go back to the other terminal (or open a new one) to send a Spot interruption. I'm going to use a tool called `ec2-spot-interrupter` (*https://github.com/aws/amazon-ec2-spot-interrupter*). To install it on a Mac, you simply run the following commands:

```
$ brew tap aws/tap
$ brew install ec2-spot-interrupter
```

If you're not using a Mac, you can install it manually using `make`, but if you can't install the tool (or don't want to), you can find a Bash script in the GitHub repository within the folder of this hands-on lab. The file is called `spot_interrupt.sh`, and you can simply run it with `$ ./ spot_interrupt.sh`. For now, I'm assuming you're using the tool I mentioned before, so run the following command:

```
$ ec2-spot-interrupter --interactive
```

This will list all the Spot instances you have. You should only have one, so pick it by pressing the spacebar on your keyboard. Then, press *Enter* and *Enter* again, leaving the default value for how long to wait to send the interruption notice. As soon as this happens, through EventBridge and AWS SQS, Karpenter will notice that the instance is about to be terminated and will cordon the node (no more pods are allowed to be scheduled), then it will initiate the drain operation by evicting the pods in that node.

Here's where the preStop hook will start running. Keep an eye open to the terminal where you're monitoring the application logs and you should see the following output:

```
... 08:12:32 UTC 2025: preStop hook started
Performing cleanup operations...
... 08:13:47 UTC 2025: preStop hook cleanup completed
```

If you see the "clean up completed" log message, it means that the preStop hook worked and the pod was terminated gracefully. Run the following command:

```
$ watch kubectl get pods,nodeclaims
```

You will see how the pod is up and running again in a matter of seconds because Karpenter initiated the node replacement as soon as it received the Spot interruption. You can inspect the Karpenter logs, and you should see these logs confirming that those actions were performed:

```
... initiating delete from interruption message
... tainted node
... found provisionable pod(s)
... computed new nodeclaim(s) to fit pod(s)
... created nodeclaim
... launched nodeclaim
... registered nodeclaim
... initialized nodeclaim
... deleted node
... deleted nodeclaim
```

I removed most of the logs to keep it readable, but notice how Karpenter executed the steps I mentioned in the expected order. Pay close attention to the date and times in the logs. You'll notice that you were able to run the cleanup process before the node was deleted.

It's worth mentioning that even though we've extended the time to keep the node running as much as possible, when we receive a Spot interruption, the two-minute warning can't be extended. That's why we used a grace time of up to 90 seconds.

5. Cleaning up

Let's clean up the resources we created for this lab by running the following command:

```
$ kubectl delete -f .
```

We're removing the application as we'll deploy a new version in the following lab.

Handling termination signals within the application

What you did in the previous section, using Kubernetes primitives to gracefully shut down your application, is absolutely recommended. However, to take fault tolerance to the next level, you should also prepare your applications themselves to handle termination events. What I mean by this is that while Kubernetes sends SIGTERM to your containers and invokes life cycle hooks, embedding signal handling logic in your code ensures that each service can perform domain-specific cleanup, persist in-flight work, and shut down in the safest way possible, as shown in *Figure 12.3*.

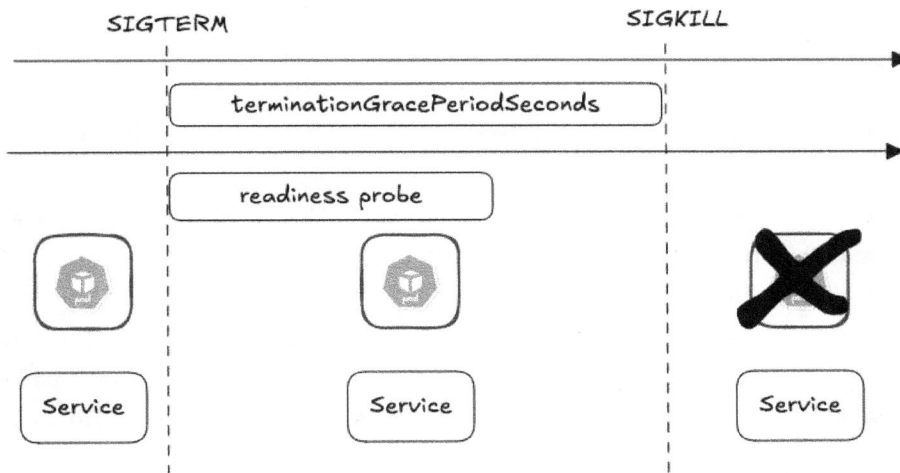

Figure 12.3 – Graceful shutdown handling the SIGTERM signal and readiness probes

To complement your SIGTERM, implement a /healthz endpoint that actively responds to your application's shutdown state. This endpoint should immediately return HTTP 503 when the SIGTERM handler is triggered, ensuring that external systems—particularly cloud load balancers—can detect the shutdown and stop routing traffic promptly. For instance, you should add something like this within your pod spec:

```
readinessProbe:
  httpGet:
    path: /healthz
    port: 8080
  initialDelaySeconds: 5
  periodSeconds: 10
  timeoutSeconds: 2
  failureThreshold: 3
```

However, many applications lack a dedicated health check endpoint. It's very common to hear from teams that they're having too many 500-type errors when receiving an interruption, simply because pods continue receiving requests even as they're torn down. A properly wired readiness probe prevents that scenario by removing the pod from load balancer pools before it exits.

To configure readiness probes effectively for graceful shutdown, I recommend starting by defining sensible defaults that match your application's startup and load characteristics. A common approach is the following:

- `initialDelaySeconds`: Set this to the time your application needs to finish bootstrapping before it can serve requests. For example, if your service initializes caches or external connections for five seconds, use `initialDelaySeconds: 5`.

- `periodSeconds`: Choose a check interval that balances quick failure detection with minimal overhead. A 10-second interval (`periodSeconds: 10`) is often a good starting point.

- `timeoutSeconds`: Specify how long Kubernetes should wait for your endpoint to respond. If your health endpoint typically responds in under one second, `timeoutSeconds: 2` gives you a margin for brief hiccups.

- `failureThreshold`: Control how many consecutive failures you will tolerate before marking the pod unready. For instance, a threshold of three failures means the pod will be removed from service after approximately 30 seconds of unsuccessful probes, helping ensure in-flight requests have time to complete.

I highly recommend that you wire your SIGTERM handler to your application's shutdown routine so that it first performs any necessary cleanup. When your SIGTERM handler marks / `healthz` as unhealthy, Kubernetes will remove the pod after approximately `periodSeconds` × `failureThreshold`, ensuring no new traffic hits it while it finishes existing work.

This combination of application-level shutdown logic and readiness probes keeps your pods draining cleanly and avoids errors when they go offline. Let's see this in action.

Hands-on lab: Handling node disruptions in code and using probes

In this hands-on lab, you'll deploy an improved version of the application we've been using so far. You can find the source code in the `chapter12/fault-tolerant/src/` folder in the GitHub repository of this book. Even though the application is written in Go, the principles and techniques used here apply to other programming languages too. The difference relies on exactly how to do it, but that's out of the scope of this book.

Let's explore some important parts of the relevant code that is making this application fault-tolerant and ready for a graceful shutdown.

0. Using only Spot instances

If you had to recreate the Amazon EKS cluster, make sure that the default NodePool is going to launch only Spot instances. In your terminal, run the following command:

```
$ kubectl patch nodepool default --type='json' -p='[{"op": "replace",
"path": "/spec/template/spec/requirements/2/values", "value":["spot"]}]'
```

You should see that the NodePool was updated.

1. Deploying the sample application

We're not going to explore this line by line. We're going to focus only on the lines of code that do most of the job when handling the graceful shutdown. In the main.go file, you'll find the handleGracefulShutdown function. This is where the SIGTERM signal is being captured and starts the graceful shutdown, and you'll be able to see a log of when this happened. The following is the initial code of the function:

```
func handleGracefulShutdown(server *http.Server) {
    sigChan := make(chan os.Signal, 1)
    signal.Notify(sigChan, syscall.SIGINT, syscall.SIGTERM)

    sig := <-sigChan
    log.Printf("Received shutdown signal: %v", sig)
    gracefulShutdownCounter.Inc()
    ...
```

Then, the function marks the application as not ready by changing the isReady variable to false, like this:

```
    // Mark application as not ready (stops new traffic)
    atomic.StoreInt64(&isReady, 0)
    applicationReadiness.Set(0)
    log.Println("Application marked as not ready ...")
    ...
```

This causes the /ready endpoint from the application to fail, signaling to internal and (especially) external load balancers (such as AWS ALB) that the pod is shutting down. You can find readinessProbe in the chapter12/fault-tolerant/probes/montecarlopi.yaml file, like this:

```
readinessProbe:
  httpGet:
    path: /ready
    port: 8080
```

Then, in the handleGracefulShutdown function, you'll find that it simulates a cleanup operation by simply waiting for a few seconds. This time can't be greater than two minutes as we want to be done before the node is gone. As this application is used for learning purposes, we just wait, but this could be actions such as closing database connections or persisting data from memory.

Finally, you can see that it's logging the final message of completion, like this:

```
log.Println("Application shutdown complete")
```

We're adding this log simply to confirm that when the node terminates, the application was able to process a graceful shutdown.

Proceed to deploy the sample application by running these commands:

```
$ cd chapter12/fault-tolerant/probes/
$ kubectl apply -f montecarlopi.yaml
```

For simplicity, we'll deploy only one pod so it's easier to read the logs when the instance is terminated. Wait for the NodeClaim and pod to be up and running. You can check that with this command:

```
$ kubectl get pods,nodeclaims
```

Once the pod is in a Running status, proceed with the next step to learn how to read the application logs.

2. Monitoring application logs using Loki

We've been using Prometheus to store application metrics that we've been using to configure autoscaling rules with KEDA. Also, we've been using Grafana to explore metrics from KEDA and Karpenter. In this lab, we'll be using Loki, a log aggregation tool from Grafana Labs, to store application logs. We'll continue using Grafana as the interface to query these logs. I'm assuming you created the Amazon EKS cluster using the Terraform template from *Chapter 8*. This cluster already comes with Loki installed, and Grafana configured to use Loki as a data source as well.

To confirm that Loki is installed, run the following command:

```
$ kubectl get daemonset -n monitoring
```

You should see the `loki-promtail` DaemonSet.

To read the application logs from Loki, you need to open the Grafana interface. To do so, run the following command:

```
$ kubectl port-forward svc/prometheus-grafana 3000:80 -n monitoring
```

Then open `http://localhost:3000/` in a browser window and use `admin` as the username and `prom-operator` as the password. Next, head over directly to `http://localhost:3000/explore` to explore the logs. You should see a text box saying **Enter a Loki query (run with Shift+Enter)**. Click on that text box and paste the following query:

```
{namespace="default", app="montecarlo-pi"}
```

This query is filtering logs from pods with the `app="montecarlo-pi"` label/value from the `default` namespace. Click on the **Live** button in the top-right corner. You should see a screen like the following:

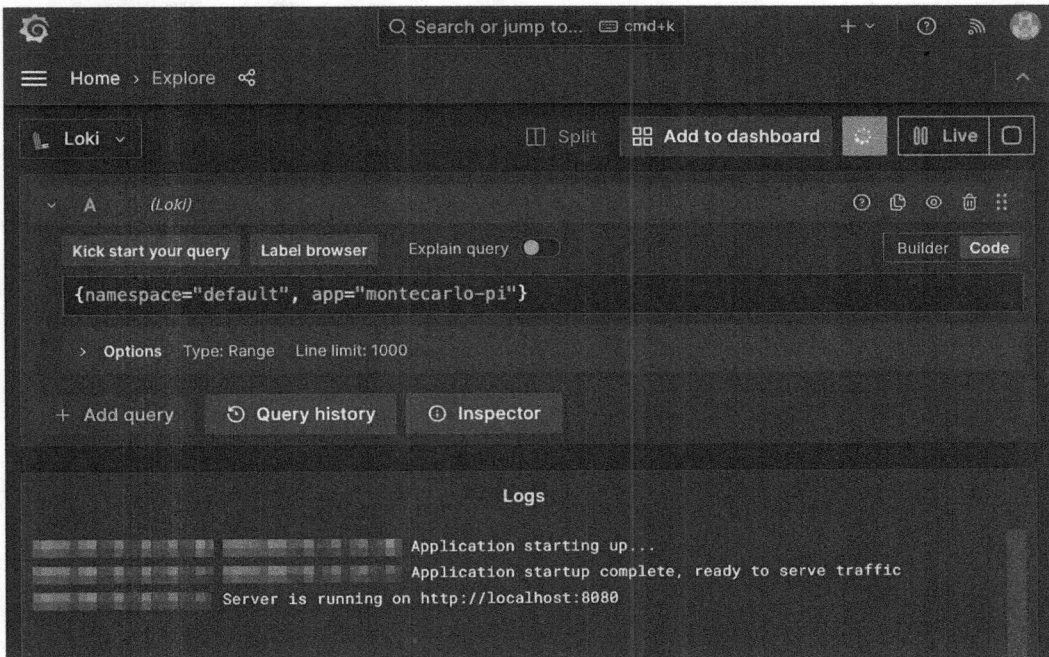

Figure 12.4 – Grafana UI showing the Loki integration to read application logs

You should see the application startup logs. Because you clicked on the **Live** button, all new logs that the application emits will appear here automatically. This will be useful when we send the Spot interruption next.

Don't close the terminal where you're doing the port forward to access Grafana.

3. Sending a Spot interruption

Instead of simply deleting a Spot instance, we're going to simulate a Spot termination. This simulation consists of sending the Spot termination notice, waiting for the two-minute warning to complete, and then removing the node. This is very useful as we'd like to test how the application will react when a real Spot interruption comes. You'll be able to test how Karpenter reacts to that interruption notice and how all the constructs we've been building will interact with each other.

To send a Spot interruption, you could simply go to the EC2 console, pick an instance, and interrupt it. Instead, we're going to use a command-line tool to keep all our actions in the terminal. The tool we're going to use is the **Amazon EC2 Spot Interrupter**. To install it on a Mac, you need to run the following commands:

```
$ brew tap aws/tap
$ brew install ec2-spot-interrupter
```

This will take about five minutes to finish.

> **Note**
>
> If you're not using a Mac, I've created a Bash script that you can find in the GitHub repository (`chapter12/fault-tolerant/spot_interrupt.sh`). This script will do something similar to the preceding command line, but with the difference that you can't choose an instance. If you want to change its behavior of which instances to interrupt, open the file and modify variables such as `INSTANCE_NAME_TAG`.

Then, to run it, you simply run the following command:

```
$ ec2-spot-interrupter --interactive
```

Notice that the preceding command has the `--interactive` flag, which means that in the same terminal, you'll see the list of Spot instances and can choose the ones you'd like to interrupt. You should see an output like this:

```
Which Spot instances would you like to interrupt?
> [x] i-0123456ab78cde901 (karpenter-default)
```

If you're not running anything else in this cluster, only one instance should show up. Select it by pressing the spacebar on your keyboard, and then press *Enter*. The tool will ask you for a delay time to send the interruption notice, which by default is 15 seconds. Accept that and press *Enter* again. You should see an output like this:

```
✅ Rebalance Recommendation sent
⏳ Interruption will be sent in 15 seconds
✅ Spot 2-minute Interruption Notification sent
...
```

Go back to the browser window where you were exploring the application logs in Grafana. You should start seeing the application logs saying that it was able to capture the SIGTERM signal, and that the graceful shutdown has started:

```
... 22:04:07 Received shutdown signal: terminated
... 22:04:07 Starting graceful shutdown...
... 22:04:07 Application marked as not ready, stopped accepting new
traffic
... 22:04:07 Performing application cleanup operations...
```

Notice the time of the log lines from before. As soon as Karpenter received the Spot interruption notice, it not only cordoned and started to drain the node, but it also launched a new Spot instance. You can confirm that by exploring the Karpenter logs and watching for any new NodeClaim as you've done before. However, this time we're going to continue focusing on the application logs.

In my test, around 40 seconds later, the replacement instance was up and running, and the new pod was started as the logs say so:

```
... 22:04:46 Application starting up...
... 22:04:51 Application startup complete, ready to serve traffic
... Server is running on http://localhost:8080
```

Keep monitoring the logs, and you'll see that a few seconds later (less than two minutes), the application finished its cleanup, and it's shutting down gracefully, like this:

```
... 22:05:22 Application cleanup operations completed
... 22:05:22 Shutting down HTTP server...
... 22:05:22 Server shutdown completed successfully
... 22:05:22 Application shutdown complete
```

You can continue testing sending Spot interruption by increasing the number of replicas and nodes. Send interruptions to more than one node and see how Karpenter is launching replacement nodes as soon as it sees the interruption. Even though you technically have 120 seconds to do some extra work, I'd recommend you complete the graceful shutdown in less time.

As you saw, if your application is fault-tolerant and stateless, it can take advantage of the steeper discounts from Spot as Karpenter will always launch replacement capacity as soon as possible.

4. Cleaning up

To finish with this lab, simply run the following command to delete the application:

```
$ kubectl delete -f montecarlopi.yaml
```

And that's it, this is how you take autoscaling to the next level by making your applications meet your performance needs by launching extra capacity. Karpenter isn't just going to launch the minimum capacity you need; it is also going to launch the cheapest type possible, such as Spot. And when a Spot interruption comes, it will help you to keep your system reliable by launching a new node. This is why it becomes crucial that your bootstrap time is short as well, so the disruption impact is reduced to its minimum.

This was the last hands-on lab of the chapter. Let's start wrapping up this chapter.

Ending notes

We'll start by exploring a project I started a while ago to help you configure Karpenter for common use cases such as spreading pods within zones, splitting on-demand and Spot nodes, and more.

Karpenter Blueprints

After delivering many sessions about Karpenter, I started to notice that there were some frequent questions about how to use Karpenter. Even though the answers could be found in Karpenter's documentation, it was spread out in different places, and most of the time, people wanted to test things quickly. I had built a lot of demos that I used at conferences and workshops. So, I decided to make those publicly available on GitHub under the name of **Karpenter Blueprints** (`https://github.com/aws-samples/karpenter-blueprints`).

In this repository, you'll find an **Infrastructure-as-Code** (**IaC**) template to create an Amazon EKS cluster with Karpenter installed, pretty much what is available in the repository for this book. Then, you'll find a list of common scenarios that includes which problem is being addressed, the key configuration sections, and how to test each blueprint independently.

At the time of writing, there are 14 blueprints available. The most common ones are the following:

- High availability: Spread pods across AZs and nodes
- Split between on-demand and Spot instances
- Prioritize savings plans and/or Reserved Instances
- Work with Graviton instances
- Overprovision capacity in advance to increase responsiveness
- Work with stateful workloads using EBS
- Update nodes using Drift
- Protect batch jobs during the consolidation process
- NodePool disruption budgets
- Deploy an NVIDIA GPU workload

Even though I'm the one who started the project, it has been kept live thanks to the amazing 11 (as of now) contributors. Some of them have created their own blueprints, while others have helped to review issues and even do massive upgrades with every new version of Kubernetes and Karpenter.

If you want to keep up to date with common scenarios and recommendations about Karpenter, make sure you keep this repository on your radar as we try to keep it up to date with every new feature that Karpenter adds. Also, if you find a problem or want to contribute, create an issue and a pull request.

Let's continue with the next section, where we'll revisit the topic of how to properly configure autoscaling rules now that we know how KEDA and Karpenter contribute in this space.

So, what's the best autoscaling rule?

There's no silver bullet here, and honestly, that's probably not the answer you were hoping for. But the reality is that which metrics you use will determine how fast or slow you can scale and, more importantly, whether you're scaling at the right time or when it's already too late.

Let's walk through what actually happens when your application needs to scale. Say you have a ScaledObject with KEDA running a query to Prometheus every 30 seconds to get your requests per second metric:

```
apiVersion: keda.sh/v1alpha1
kind: ScaledObject
metadata:
  name: montecarlo-pi-latency
spec:
  scaleTargetRef:
    name: montecarlo-pi
  triggers:
  - type: prometheus
    metadata:
      serverAddress: http://prometheus:9090
      metricName: http_requests_per_second
      threshold: '10'
      query: sum(rate(http_requests_total[1m]))
```

Prometheus itself is scraping your application metrics every 15 seconds by default. Already, we're looking at potential delays of 45 seconds just to detect that scaling is needed. Then, HPA takes this information and makes a scaling decision, which by default happens every 15 seconds. Once new pods are created, they might become unschedulable, triggering Karpenter to add new nodes, which takes around 40 seconds if starting from scratch.

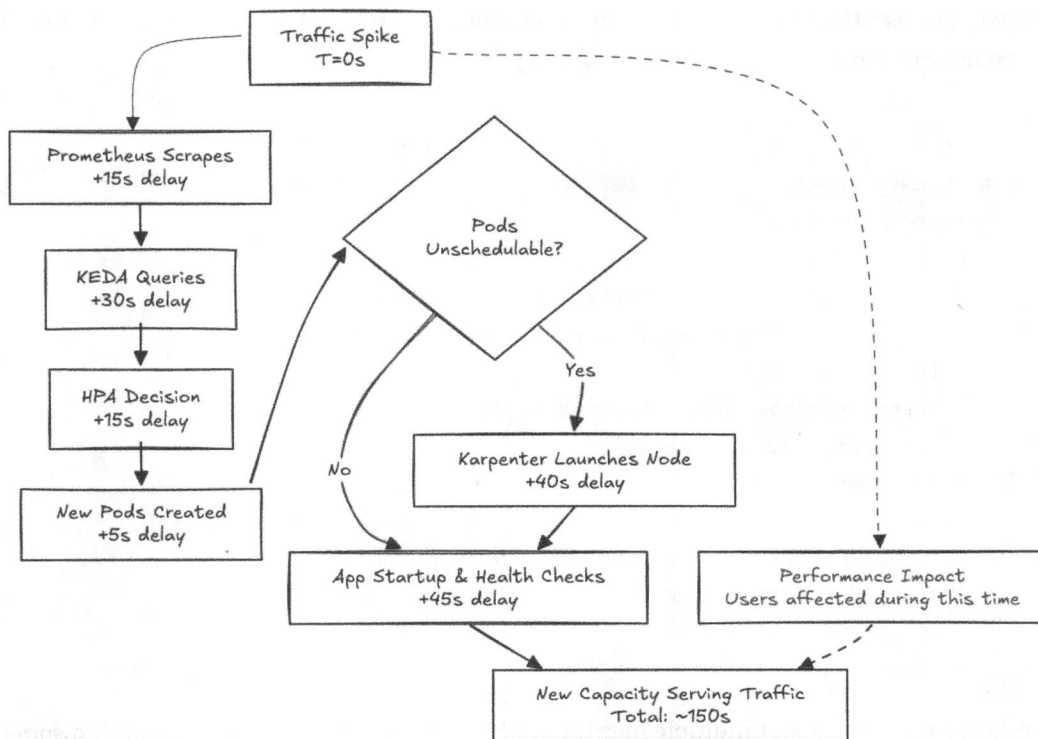

Figure 12.5 – Scaling timeline from end to end with KEDA and Karpenter

You're looking at roughly 90–120 seconds from the moment your application starts experiencing increased load until new capacity is actually serving traffic. This assumes everything works perfectly with no delays. In practice, add another 30–60 seconds for application startup time, health checks, and load balancer registration.

Now, a few years ago, I came across some fascinating insights from Brendan Gregg, Netflix's performance architect, who literally wrote the book on systems performance. His work on *"why CPU utilization can be misleading"* is incredibly relevant here. By the time CPU spikes enough to trigger scaling, your users are already experiencing degraded performance. It's like trying to add more lanes to a highway after the traffic jam has already formed. Gregg's research shows that traditional CPU percentage metrics include memory stall cycles, so what looks like 90% CPU utilization might actually be only 30% real computation work.

The way I've seen this work in practice is by using multiple metrics with different purposes. Here's an example of a more sophisticated scaling setup:

```
...
  triggers:
  # Primary metric: requests per second
  - type: prometheus
    metadata:
      serverAddress: http://prometheus:9090
      metricName: requests_per_second
      threshold: '10'
      query: sum(rate(http_requests_total[1m]))
  # Safety net: CPU utilization
  - type: prometheus
    metadata:
      serverAddress: http://prometheus:9090
      metricName: latency_p95
      threshold: '70'
      query: sum(histogram_quantile(0.95, rate(http_request_duration)))
```

But here's the thing about multiple metrics in HPA: it doesn't average them out or find some middle ground. It takes the highest scaling recommendation from all your metrics. So, if your RPS metric says you need three replicas, but your latency metric says you need eight, you're getting eight. This can work in your favor as a safety mechanism, but it can also lead to overscaling if you're not careful with your thresholds.

What I've found works better than chasing the perfect single metric is understanding what actually impacts your application's performance and then building scaling rules around those signals. For a web API, that might be request latency combined with active connections. For a data processing pipeline, it could be queue depth and processing time. For ML inference workloads, you're probably looking at tokens per second or time-to-first-token. The key is accepting that you're making trade-offs. Scale too early and you're paying for resources you don't need. Scale too late and your users notice. Scale too aggressively and you might trigger cascading effects in downstream services.

This is why I keep coming back to the idea that efficient autoscaling isn't about finding the one perfect metric. It's about understanding your application's behavior, knowing your SLAs, and designing scaling policies that balance performance, cost, and reliability.

At the end of the day, the best autoscaling rule is the one that helps you sleep better at night knowing your applications will handle traffic spikes without breaking the bank or your SLAs. And more often than not, that's going to be a combination of metrics rather than relying on any single golden signal.

Let's move on to the next section to explore the future trends in autoscaling for Kubernetes using KEDA and Karpenter as a reference.

Future trends

It's an exciting time for autoscaling in Kubernetes. As you can tell by now, it's not only about configuring HPA rules and making sure your cluster has the capacity you need. If you want to make the most of it, projects such as KEDA and Karpenter exist to help many teams implement efficient autoscaling in their Kubernetes clusters.

Both of these projects are very active and keep adding new features. Therefore, my aim with this section is to highlight the future trend I see based on the discussions on GitHub issues, community working group notes, and even what some users report on the internet. Let's start with KEDA.

KEDA

At KubeCon London 2025, KEDA contributors shared an update about where the project is headed next. They focused on realistic, practical improvements that the community is actively working on, as well as some aspirational goals still on the horizon. If you want to keep up with ongoing developments, the best way is to follow their talks or join the discussions on GitHub.

So, the first trend is **predictive scaling**, which remains the long-term horizon that everyone wants, but it's still more aspiration than delivery. In the KubeCon session, the maintainers admitted that building models to anticipate traffic, rather than merely reacting to it, "has been on our wish list for a while" (KubeCon London session, 2025). You'll also find community work in the PredictKube project (`https://keda.sh/blog/2022-02-09-predictkube-scaler/`), which experiments with AI-driven forecasts up to six hours ahead. Keep an eye on that GitHub repo if you're curious about early prototypes.

Second, **HTTP-based scaling** is moving toward production readiness, but with caveats. As Jorge reminded attendees, "HTTP scaling is still in alpha beta version" because features such as WebSocket support aren't there yet (KubeCon London session, 2025). The HTTP add-on repository (`https://github.com/kedacore/http-add-on`) itself warns of "rough edges" and invites contributors to harden it before declaring it stable. If your use case depends on synchronous request patterns, this is one to test in sandbox environments now, but don't bet your SLAs on it just yet.

Third, **OpenTelemetry (OTel) integration** is arguably the most concrete roadmap item. This builds directly on the challenges I outlined earlier about latency in metric collection: the back-and-forth between Prometheus, KEDA, and the application itself. The KubeCon London session highlighted how moving metric collection into a lightweight OTel sidecar avoids the round-trip through Prometheus and slashes latency (KubeCon London session, 2025). On KEDA's GitHub repository, issue #3078 tracks the discussion around embedding the OTel collector per namespace to prevent metric collisions, though contributors caution about resource overhead and await better multi-instance support from the OTel project.

KEDA's future depends on merging proactive insights, smoother HTTP experiences, and zero-latency metrics into a cohesive whole. Track the KubeCon session recording and those GitHub issues to stay in the loop.

Let's now explore the future trends in Karpenter.

Karpenter

Even though we have focused in this book on AWS to deeply explore Karpenter, the project has been expanding to other providers as well. There's a lot happening under the hood that's worth paying attention to. Most of the trends I'm capturing here are based on what I see on GitHub issue discussions and the Karpenter working group meetings.

First, Karpenter is expanding its **multi-cloud support**. Karpenter has moved quickly beyond AWS. After the CNCF donation, the AWS provider became the example for how to implement Karpenter integrations against `karpenter-core`. From this point onward, you can now see the production-ready implementations for Azure Kubernetes Service (`Azure/karpenter-provider-azure`) and the active development for GCP (`cloudpilot-ai/karpenter-provider-gcp`). Beyond these providers, you can find in the core repository a list of contributions from Alibaba Cloud, Bizfly Cloud, IBM Cloud, Proxmox, and Oracle Cloud Infrastructure, reflecting how the trend is to have a multi-cloud ecosystem such as Cluster Autoscaler.

A very recent feature is **NodeOverlays**, which is in alpha at the time of writing. Let me give you some context first. Karpenter's scheduling simulation doesn't know about your savings plans, Reserved Instances, or custom hardware configurations. So, it makes provisioning decisions based on list prices and standard instance specs, which often don't match reality. NodeOverlays lets you override pricing information or inject custom resources into the scheduling simulation. For example, if you have savings plans that make certain instances cheaper than Spot pricing, you can adjust those rates so Karpenter provisions accordingly. Or if you're running custom GPU slices, you can add those as extended resources. If your systems have any kind of custom pricing or hardware configuration, this feature is worth tracking.

Moreover, **Dynamic Resource Allocation (DRA) integration** is becoming a game-changer for specialized workloads. DRA, introduced in Kubernetes v1.26 as an alpha API, lets pods request resources beyond the traditional CPU and memory. Think GPUs, FPGAs, NVMe volumes, or any custom device managed by a device plugin. This API fills a longstanding gap where complex applications couldn't express the exact hardware slices they needed, forcing workarounds or over-provisioning. With DRA, workloads declare precise resource claims, and Karpenter can schedule and provision nodes that satisfy those claims natively, reducing waste and startup latency. Karpenter maintainers have noted that the original DRA design proved hard to integrate into autoscalers, but a collaboration between the autoscaling SIGs has produced a revised DRA spec slated for Kubernetes v1.30. Once upstream stabilizes the API, Karpenter will be able to honor DRA requests directly, unlocking optimized scheduling for ML inference, hardware-accelerated computing, and new device types without custom provisioning logic.

On the disruption front, **workload-aware disruption handling** is gaining traction. Users want the ability to annotate pods with a time-to-completion, instructing Karpenter not to evict critical jobs before they finish. Use cases for this include ML training and long-running batch jobs where a simple PDB isn't sufficient. Contributors are exploring annotations that carry both a grace period and priority, allowing Karpenter to defer drains until jobs reach their safe completion window.

In terms of capacity management, **CapacityBuffer** and **WarmPool support** are moving from ideas to prototypes. The concept is to pre-warm a small pool of ready-to-use nodes, either via Kubernetes' buffer for StatefulSets or a built-in warm pool, to eliminate cold-start delays for predictable workload surges.

This field evolves quickly, especially as the demand to run AI/ML workloads on Kubernetes increases. So, keep an eye open for the discussions happening on GitHub issues, the working group meetings, and alpha features that come from time to time.

With that in mind, we've reached the end of this chapter and the book itself. Let's finish with a summary of this chapter.

Summary

This final chapter brought together the hands-on labs, architectural insights, and forward-looking guidance that define efficient autoscaling in Kubernetes. You began with a lab for a zero-scale scenario: a CronJob that controlled NodePool limits and cleaned up NodeClaims, ensuring clusters have nodes only for a specific period, such as working hours. From there, you explored what considerations you need to have to deploy fault-tolerant workloads with Karpenter, learning that *"Spot is the reward for a good architecture."* Moreover, you mastered Kubernetes primitives such as extending the default termination grace period of a pod to retain nodes as much as possible, and writing preStop hooks so applications can shut down cleanly even when code changes aren't an option. Then, you learned how an application can handle the SIGTERM signal from code. You also saw the importance of exposing a readiness endpoint, so pods are gracefully unregistered from the internal and external load balancers, minimizing disruption during node termination.

I also introduced the Karpenter Blueprints project, where you saw how curated examples can accelerate the adoption of best practices. Then, in the *So, what's the best autoscaling rule?* section, you saw why no single metric suffices and how combining signals such as requests per second, queue depth, and latency percentiles lets you tailor scaling to your service's true needs.

Finally, we explored the future trends of KEDA and Karpenter, including new or improved feature integrations such as DRA and control plane offloading to workload-aware disruption controls, warm pools, and NodeOverlay to influence Karpenter's scheduler simulation.

Efficient Kubernetes autoscaling isn't a destination; it's a practice of continuous refinement using KEDA and Karpenter to ensure your applications scale with precision, resilience, and cost in mind. Feel free to connect with me on LinkedIn and let me know how this book and all the hands-on labs have helped you to run your workloads in Kubernetes efficiently. If you can, I'd be interested in knowing how many pods and nodes you've been able to remove, contributing to saving the planet, one pod at a time.

Till next time! Happy autoscaling! Thanks for reading :)

Get This Book's PDF Version and Exclusive Extras

UNLOCK NOW

Scan the QR code (or go to packtpub.com/unlock).
Search for this book by name, confirm the edition,
and then follow the steps on the page.

*Note: Keep your invoice handy. Purchases made
directly from Packt don't require one.*

13

Unlock Your Exclusive Benefits

Your copy of this book includes the following exclusive benefits:

- ⟲ Next-gen Packt Reader
- 🖥 DRM-free PDF/ePub downloads

Follow the guide below to unlock them. The process takes only a few minutes and needs to be completed once.

Unlock this Book's Free Benefits in 3 Easy Steps

Step 1

Keep your purchase invoice ready for *Step 3*. If you have a physical copy, scan it using your phone and save it as a PDF, JPG, or PNG.

For more help on finding your invoice, visit https://www.packtpub.com/unlock-benefits/help.

> **Note:** If you bought this book directly from Packt, no invoice is required. After *Step 2*, you can access your exclusive content right away.

Step 2

Scan the QR code or go to `packtpub.com/unlock`.

On the page that opens (similar to *Figure 13.1* on desktop), search for this book by name and select the correct edition.

Figure 13.1: Packt unlock landing page on desktop

Step 3

After selecting your book, sign in to your Packt account or create one for free. Then upload your invoice (PDF, PNG, or JPG, up to 10 MB). Follow the on-screen instructions to finish the process.

Need help?

If you get stuck and need help, visit `https://www.packtpub.com/unlock-benefits/help` for a detailed FAQ on how to find your invoices and more. This QR code will take you to the help page.

Note: If you are still facing issues, reach out to `customercare@packt.com`.

‹packt›

packtpub.com

Subscribe to our online digital library for full access to over 7,000 books and videos, as well as industry leading tools to help you plan your personal development and advance your career. For more information, please visit our website.

Why subscribe?

- Spend less time learning and more time coding with practical eBooks and Videos from over 4,000 industry professionals
- Improve your learning with Skill Plans built especially for you
- Get a free eBook or video every month
- Fully searchable for easy access to vital information
- Copy and paste, print, and bookmark content

At www.packtpub.com, you can also read a collection of free technical articles, sign up for a range of free newsletters, and receive exclusive discounts and offers on Packt books and eBooks.

Other Books You May Enjoy

If you enjoyed this book, you may be interested in these other books by Packt:

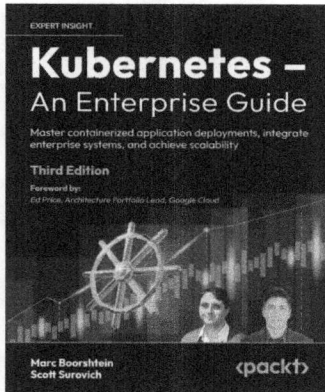

Kubernetes – An Enterprise Guide - Third Edition

Marc Boorshtein, Scott Surovich

ISBN: 978-1-83508-6-957

- Manage secrets securely using Vault and External Secret Operator
- Create multitenant clusters with vCluster for isolated environments
- Monitor Kubernetes clusters with Prometheus and visualize metrics using Grafana
- Aggregate and analyze logs centrally with OpenSearch for deeper insights
- Build a CI/CD developer platform by integrating GitLab and ArgoCD
- Deploy applications in an Istio service mesh and enforce security with OPA and GateKeeper
- Secure container runtimes and prevent attacks using KubeArmor

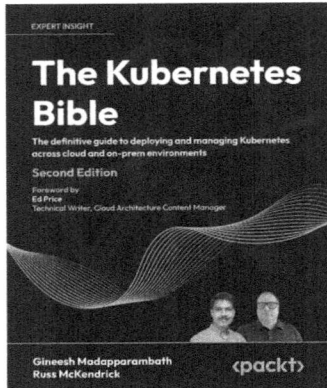

The Kubernetes Bible - Second Edition

Gineesh Madapparambath, Russ McKendrick

ISBN: 978-1-83546-4-717

- Secure your Kubernetes clusters with advanced techniques
- Implement scalable deployments and autoscaling strategies
- Design and learn to build production-grade containerized applications
- Manage Kubernetes effectively on major cloud platforms (GKE, EKS, AKS)
- Utilize advanced networking and service management practices
- Use Helm charts and Kubernetes Operators for robust security measures
- Optimize in-cluster traffic routing with advanced configurations
- Enhance security with techniques like Immutable ConfigMaps and RBAC

Packt is searching for authors like you

If you're interested in becoming an author for Packt, please visit authors.packt.com and apply today. We have worked with thousands of developers and tech professionals, just like you, to help them share their insight with the global tech community. You can make a general application, apply for a specific hot topic that we are recruiting an author for, or submit your own idea.

Share your thoughts

Now you've finished *Kubernetes Autoscaling*, we'd love to hear your thoughts! Scan the QR code below to go straight to the Amazon review page for this book and share your feedback or leave a review on the site that you purchased it from.

https://packt.link/r/1836643837

Your review is important to us and the tech community and will help us make sure we're delivering excellent quality content.

Index

www.ingramcontent.com/pod-product-compliance
Lightning Source LLC
Chambersburg PA
CBHW081039220326
41598CB00038B/6925

*9 7 8 1 8 3 6 6 4 3 8 3 8 *